The Devil in History

The publisher gratefully acknowledges the generous support of the Ahmanson Foundation Humanities Endowment Fund of the University of California Press Foundation.

The Devil in History

Communism, Fascism, and Some Lessons of the Twentieth Century

Vladimir Tismaneanu

UNIVERSITY OF CALIFORNIA PRESS
Berkeley · Los Angeles · London

University of California Press, one of the most
distinguished university presses in the United States,
enriches lives around the world by advancing
scholarship in the humanities, social sciences, and
natural sciences. Its activities are supported by the UC
Press Foundation and by philanthropic contributions
from individuals and institutions. For more information,
visit www.ucpress.edu.

University of California Press
Berkeley and Los Angeles, California

University of California Press, Ltd.
London, England

Library of Congress Cataloging-in-Publication Data

Tismaneanu, Vladimir.
    The devil in history : communism, fascism, and
some lessons of the twentieth century / Vladimir
Tismaneanu.
        p.   cm.
    Includes bibliographical references and index.
    ISBN 978-0-520-23972-2 (cloth : alk. paper)
    1. Communist state—History.   2. Communism—
History—20th century.   3. Fascism—History—
20th century.   4. Totalitarianism—History—20th
century.   I. Title.
    JC474.T497   2012
    335.43—dc23
                                    2012012796

20   19   18   17   16   15   14   13   12
10   9   8   7   6   5   4   3   2   1

*In memory of Tony Judt, Leszek Kołakowski,
and Robert C. Tucker, great scholars and noble
intellectuals, whose writings inspired many
reflections in this book.*

Contents

Foreword

This is a book about political passions, radicalism, utopian ideals, and their catastrophic consequences in the twentieth century's experiments in massive social engineering. More precisely, it is an attempt to map and explain what Hannah Arendt called "the ideological storms" of a century second to none in violence, hubris, ruthlessness, and human sacrifices. I began thinking about these issues as a teenager in Communist Romania, when I had the chance to read a clandestinely circulated copy of Arthur Koestler's novel *Darkness at Noon*. I was born after World War II to revolutionary parents who had embraced anti-Fascist Communist values before the war. They had fought with the International Brigades in the Spanish Civil War, where my father lost his right arm at the age of twenty-four at the battle of river Ebro; my mother—a medical school student—worked as a nurse. I grew up listening to countless conversations about major figures of world Communism, as well as the Stalinist atrocities. Names like Palmiro Togliatti, Rudolf Slánský, Maurice Thorez, Josip Broz Tito, Ana Pauker, or Dolores Ibarruri were frequently whispered during dinner table conversations.

Later, as a sociology student at the University of Bucharest, I ignored the official calls to distrust "bourgeois ideology" and did my utmost to get hold of forbidden books by Milovan Djilas, Karl Jaspers, Hannah Arendt, Raymond Aron, Isaiah Berlin, Karl Popper, Leszek Kołakowski, and other antitotalitarian thinkers. Confronted with the grotesque follies of Nicolae Ceaușescu's dynastic Communism, I realized that I was living in a totalitarian regime run by a delusional leader who exerted absolute control over the population via the Communist Party and the secret police. It was for this reason that I became intensely interested in the occulted traditions of Western Marxism and the Frankfurt School theorists' attempt to rehabilitate subjectivity. My PhD dissertation, defended in 1980, was entitled *Revolution and Critical Reason: The Political Theory of the Frankfurt School and Contemporary Left-Wing Radicalism.* From the writings of Theodore W. Adorno, Walter Benjamin, Erich Fromm, Max Horkheimer, and Herbert Marcuse, I learned about the tribulations of negativity in the age of total administration and inescapable alienation. I read Georg Lukács, Karl Korsch, and Antonio Gramsci, and I found in their ideas (especially their early writings) an antidote to the mindless optimism of Marxism-Leninism.

Although Romania was a socialist state committed to Marxist tenets and thus ostensibly left-wing, especially after 1960, the ruling party started to embrace themes, motifs, and obsessions of the interwar Far Right. When Nicolae Ceauşescu came to power in 1965, he exacerbated this trend, and the ideology came to blend residual Leninism with an unavowed yet unmistakable Fascism. This was only an apparent paradox. Years later, when I read Robert C. Tucker's masterful biography of Stalin, I was struck by his brilliant analysis of "Bolshevism of the Extreme Right." As in the case of the Soviet Union after 1945, or of Poland during the last years of Władisław Gomułka's rule with the rise to power of the ultranationalist faction of the Partisans, headed by minister of the interior, General Mieczysław Moczar, the Romanian Communist regime was becoming increasingly idiosyncratic, xenophobic, and anti-Semitic. When I published my history of Romanian Communism in 2003, I coined a term for this hybridization: national-Stalinism. During all these years I thought about the deep affinities between apparently irreconcilable movements and ideologies. I reached the conclusion that, in times of moral and cultural disarray, Communism and Fascism can merge into a baroque synthesis. Communism is *not* Fascism, and Fascism is *not* Communism. Each totalitarian experiment had its own irreducible attributes, but they shared a number of phobias, obsessions, and resentments that could generate toxic alliances, like the Nazi-Soviet Pact of August 1939. Furthermore, their geographical proximity allowed the unfolding of genocidal practices between 1930 and 1945 in what Timothy Snyder called the "Bloodlands," which took a toll of approximately 14 million people. This disaster started with Stalin's war on peasants, especially in Ukraine, and culminated in the absolute horror of the Holocaust.

This is a book about the incarnation of diabolically nihilistic principles of human subjugation and conditioning in the name of presumably pure and purifying goals. It is not a historical treatise (although history is present on every page), but rather a political-philosophical interpretation of how maximalist utopian aspirations can lead to the nightmares of Soviet and Nazi camps epitomized by Kolyma and Auschwitz. I discuss the major similarities, the saliently irreducible distinctions, and the contemporary reverberations of these totalitarian tyrannies. I also examine the deradicalization of Soviet-style regimes, the exhaustion of ideological fervor, and the rise of alternative, civic-oriented expressions of democratic sensibilities. The purpose of this book is to provide readers (students, journalists, historians, political scientists, philosophers, and a general audience) with some conclusions about a cataclysmic time that no words could capture as accurately and as disturbingly as the paintings of the German artist Anselm Kiefer. Like those canvases, the twentieth century has left behind a devastated landscape full of corpses, dashed illusions, failed myths, betrayed promises, and unprocessed memories.

Many of this book's ideas were discussed with my late friend, the great historian Tony Judt. I also had the privilege to engage in many conversations with one of the wisest analysts of Marxism and Soviet Communism, Robert C. Tucker. Both Judt and Tucker emphasized the immense role of ideas in history and warned against any kind of positivistic determinism. They taught about the frailty of liberal values, and about the obligation to not give up but rather to continue fighting for them against all odds. The Polish thinker Leszek Kołakowski, often and accurately described as the philosopher of Solidarity, also had a major influence in shaping my ideas. I was the first to translate an essay by Kołakowski into Romanian in the late 1980s, in the alternative cultural journal *Agora,* which was published in the United States, edited by dissident poet Dorin Tudoran, and distributed illegally in Romania. I sent a copy to Leszek Kołakowski, who responded with a wonderful letter saying that, although he did not read Romanian, he could make sense, using his Latin and French, of my short introduction. One of the major projects I undertook in post-Communist Romania was to coordinate the publication of a translation of his masterful trilogy on the main currents of Marxism. Nobody grasped better than Kołakowski the appalling presence of the devil in the totalitarian experiments of the twentieth century. All three hoped that mankind would internalize a few lessons from these catastrophes. I dedicate this book to the memory of these three major scholars.

Such a synthesis cannot be achieved in a few years. Overly optimistic, I signed a contract with the University of California Press in 2004, convinced that I would finish the book by the end of 2005. Then I realized that there were still too many issues I needed to think about. In the following years, I got involved in the institutional effort to analyze the Communist dictatorship in Romania. I learned terrifying details about the Stalinist technologies of destructiveness employed by Romanian communists. The work for this book started in 2001, when Tony Judt offered me the possibility to spend a month at the Remarque Institute at the New York University, where I presented a lecture on topics directly related to this volume, focusing on the French polemics around the *Livre Noir du communisme*. I continued my research in June 2002 as a one-month fellow at the Institute for the Sciences of Man (IWM) in Vienna. In January 2003, I was a fellow at Indiana University's Institute for the Humanities, where I gave a lecture on the totalitarian temptation and benefited from Jeffrey C. Isaac's insightful comments. In 2008–2009, as a fellow at the Woodrow Wilson International Center for Scholars, I conducted research on twentieth-century utopian radicalism as well as moral justice in post-Communist Romania. I benefited from the exceptional research skills of my two assistants, Eliza Gheorghe and Mark Moll. Books continued to come out that inspired me to rethink some of the early hypotheses, including Robert Gellately's path-breaking work *Lenin, Stalin, Hitler: The Age of Social Catastrophe* (2007), which I reviewed in the outstanding journal *Kritika*. Another important volume was *Beyond Totalitarianism* (2009), edited by Sheila Fitzpatrick and Michael Geyer. In April 2009, Timothy Snyder invited me to participate in the seminar "Hitler and Stalin: Comparisons Renewed" at Yale University, where I exchanged views with several distinguished scholars, including Saul Friedländer, Norman Naimark, Lynne Viola, and Amir Weiner. Throughout these years, in his gently encouraging way, Stanley Holwitz, who had superbly edited my *Stalinism for All Seasons* at the University of California Press (2003), continued to inquire about the status of the manuscript. I kept reassuring him that I had not forgotten it. In fact, I had continued to think only about this, and in March 2010 I gave a lecture at the University of California at Berkeley titled "The Devil in History," which presented the ideas published here in the prologue. Following that presentation, I had long discussions with historians

John Connelly and Yuri Slezkine, who provided me with provocative suggestions.

Finally, in February 2011, the manuscript was completed. I sent it to Niels Hooper at the University of California Press, who expressed interest in the project. I received two immensely insightful peer reviews and followed many of the reviewers' suggestions, especially in emphasizing the peculiar nature of the Bolshevik worshipping of the party, the connections between Marx and Lenin, and the still amazing infatuation of important intellectuals with the Communist utopia. I have developed many ideas included in this book in articles published since 2005 in the pages of *Times Literary Supplement* as well as essays for the excellent Romanian monthly *Idei in dialog,* edited by the brilliant philosopher Horia-Roman Patapievici.

This achievement would not have been possible without the enthusiastic commitment and creative research offered by Bogdan Cristian Iacob, a graduate student at the Central European University (he defended his dissertation in June 2011) who became my closest collaborator in 2007. I wish to express cordial thanks to all those who, throughout these years, have generously been my engaging partners in this endeavor. First and foremost, I express my gratitude to my wife, Mary Sladek, and my son, Adam Volo Tismaneanu, with whom I had endless discussions about the totalitarian monsters and their legacies. Mary read various drafts of this book and offered insightful suggestions. On various occasions, Adam asked me to explain the similarities and differences between Hitler and Stalin. Like so many of us, he still wonders who was worse. Intellectual friends and colleagues whose ideas and suggestions have helped me shape my own interpretations and who undoubtedly deserve mention, including some who have passed away, include Bradley Abrams, Dragoş Paul Aligică, Cătălin Avramescu, Matei Călinescu, Daniel Chirot, Aurelian Craiutu, John Connelly, Michael David-Fox, Karen Dawisha, Ferenc Fehér, Dan Gallin, Pierre Hassner, Agnes Heller, Jeffrey Herf, Paul Hollander, Dick Howard, Charles Gati, Irena Grudzinska-Gross, Jan T. Gross, Jeffrey C. Isaac, Constantin Iordachi, Ken Jowitt, Tony Judt, Bart Kaminski, Gail Kligman, Mark Kramer, Claude Lefort, Gabriel Liiceanu, Mark Lichbach, Monica Lovinescu, Steven Lukes, Daniel Mahoney, Adam Michnik, Mircea Mihăieş, Iulia Motoc, Vlad Mureşan, Mihail Neamţu, Virgil Nemoianu, Martin Palouš, Horia-Roman Patapievici, Marta Petreu, Andrei Pleşu, Cristian Preda, Ilya Prizel, Saskia Sassen, Marci Shore, Timothy Snyder, Vladimir Solonari,

Ioan Stanomir, Radu Stern, Valeriu Stoica, Mihai Şora, Gale Stokes, Robert C. Tucker, Cristian Vasile, Christina Zarifopol-Illias, Viktor Zaslavsky, Vladislav Zubok, Annette Wieworka. Special thanks to my graduate students at the University of Maryland, who have been remarkable partners of dialogue during the seminars on Marxism, Bolshevism, Fascism, Nazism, and the meanings of political radicalism.

October 10, 2011

Prologue

Totalitarian Dictators and Ideological Hubris

When I used the image of Hell, I did not mean this allegori-
cally, but literally: it seems rather obvious that men who have
lost their faith in Paradise will not be able to establish it on
earth; but it is not so certain that those who have lost their
belief in Hell as a place of the hereafter may not be willing
and able to establish on earth exact imitations of what people
used to believe about Hell. In this sense I think that a
description of the camps as Hell on earth is more "objective,"
that is, more adequate to their essence than statements of
a purely sociological or psychological nature.

—Hannah Arendt, *Essays on Understanding*

No century witnessed and documented so much atrocious suffering,
organized hatred, and devastating violence as the twentieth. The concentration camps represented the ultimate humiliation of human beings, the
destruction of their identity, their inescapable dehumanization, and
their mass annihilation. Neither Communism nor Nazism can be understood without taking into account the centrality of what Albert Camus
once called *l'univers concentrationnaire*. In his book *If This Is a Man*, the
Italian writer and Auschwitz survivor, Primo Levi, wrote:

> Perhaps it is not possible to comprehend, indeed perhaps one should not
> even try, since to comprehend is almost to excuse. Let me explain: to "com-
> prehend" a human intention and action means (even etymologically) to con-
> tain it, to contain its perpetrator, by putting oneself in his place, identifying
> with him. Now, no normal person could ever identify with Hitler, Himmler,
> Goebbels, Eichmann, and countless others. While this appalls us it is also relief
> since it is probably just as well that their words (and also, alas their deeds)

should remain beyond our comprehension. Those words and deeds are inhuman, indeed anti-human, without historical precedent and barely comparable
to the cruelest manifestations of the biological struggle for existence.[1]

In Stalinized Romania between 1949 and 1951, a diabolical experiment took place, meant to transform the six hundred inmates of the
Pitești penitentiary (all students arrested for real or imagined antiregime
activities) into "new men." The method, apparently inspired by Soviet
pedagogue Anton Makarenko's teachings as adopted by the secret police
in the Soviet Union and its satellites, was supposed to make the victims
their own tormentors and thereby "educators." A phalanx of regime collaborators, headed by a former Fascist arrested in 1948 on charges of
having lied about his past, engaged in unspeakable, barbaric brutalities
against their fellow prisoners, who experienced two levels of transformation: the external re-education and the inner one, when the victim turned
into a tormentor. There were only two possibilities for the inmates: to
become accomplices or to die under horrifying conditions. In fact, as one
of the very few survivors of this lurid experiment said, there was a third
possibility: to go insane.

What happened in Nazi and Communist camps (Pitești was for all
practical purposes such an institution) was bound to destroy basic features of humanity such as compassion, reason, and solidarity.[2] Historian
Timothy Snyder superbly concluded his essential work *Bloodlands* by
stating that "the Nazi and Soviet regimes turned people into numbers. . . .
It is for us as humanists to turn the numbers back into people."[3] The
basis for these horrors was the conviction that human beings can become subjects for radical social engineering conducted by self-appointed
custodians of universal happiness. To paraphrase a historian, the twentieth century became destructive once "the historically self-conscious
presumption that contingency abounds and has to be managed, that
chaos is about to take over and has to be negotiated, that society can be
designed and revolution made"[4] became the justification for sacralizing
the *political* and converting it into a substitute for traditional religions.
This book is a comprehensive, comparative essay on the intellectual origins, the crimes, and the failure of the radical totalitarian movements that
ravaged the last century: Communism and Fascism. It therefore starts
from the premise that in this "age of extremes" (Hobsbawm) the question
of evil is the basic question.[5]

For Polish philosopher Leszek Kołakowski, Bolshevism and Fascism
represented two incarnations of the disastrous presence of the devil in

history: "The devil . . . invented ideological states, that is to say, states whose legitimacy is grounded in the fact that their owners are owners of truth. If you oppose such a state or its system, you are an enemy of truth."[6] Both movements pretended to purify humanity of agents of corruption, decadence, and dissolution and to restore a presumably lost unity of humanity (excluding, of course, those regarded as subhuman, social and racial enemies). For the Communists, the fiend was represented by private property, the bourgeoisie, the priests, the kulaks. The Nazis identified the Jewish "vermin," "Judeo-Bolshevism," "Judeo-plutocracy," and Marxism as the sources of all calamities. Fascism (and its radical version, Nazism) was adamantly anti-Communist. In the 1930s, Stalinism made anti-Fascism a pillar of its propaganda, seducing intellectuals and galvanizing resistance movements worldwide. Indeed, in the absence of anti-Fascist rhetoric, it is hard to imagine Stalinism becoming such an extraordinary magnet for so many otherwise intelligent and reasonable individuals. These people were convinced that by supporting the Popular Fronts, especially during the Spanish Civil War, they were opposing Nazi barbarism. The Communist International's propaganda machine defended human rights against the abominable atrocities perpetrated by the Nazis, obscuring the fact that, until 1939, most mass crimes in Europe were in fact committed by Stalinists in the USSR.[7]

Both revolutionary party-movements execrated and denounced liberalism, democracy, and parliamentarianism as degradations of true politics, which would transcend all divisions through the establishment of perfect communities (defined as classless or racially unified). Fundamentally atheistic, both Communism and Fascism organized their political objectives in discourses of alleged emancipation, operating as political religions meant to deliver the individual from the impositions of traditional morality and legality.[8] To employ Italian political thinker Emilio Gentile's terminology, both were forms of a sacralization of politics of an exclusive and integralist character that rejected "coexistence with other political ideologies and movements," denied "the autonomy of the individual with respect to the collective," prescribed "the obligatory observance of [their] commandments and participation in [their] political cult," and sanctified "violence as a legitimate arm of the struggle against enemies, and as an instrument of regeneration."[9] In the universe of these political movements, evil carried the name of those who refused, rejected, or did not qualify for the illumination delivered by the infallible party gospels. In the case of left-wing totalitarianism, historian Igal Halfin provides an excellent formulation: "The apotheosis of Communist history—humanity holding hands and marching toward a classless paradise—cannot thus be disassociated from Stalin's systematic attempt to eliminate those who reached the Marxist well but refused to drink from it."[10] Or, to turn to Nazism, for Hitler, Jews incarnated evil simply because for him they fell below the pale of humanity. They were simultaneously cowardly and omnipotent, capitalist and Communist, ostentatious and insidious, and so on. After seeing with Goebbels the so-called documentary *The Eternal Jew,* a piece of heinously crude propaganda, the German dictator concluded that "these are no longer human beings. They are animals. So it's not humanitarian but a surgical task. Otherwise Europe will perish through the Jewish disease."[11]

Psychological and psychopathological explanations for these uniquely murderous regimes are not sufficient. Whereas Stalin and Hitler were incontrovertibly driven by paranoid exclusionary and exterminist impulses, it would be hard to consider Lenin a mentally unbalanced individual. As a matter of fact, even a staunch critic of Bolshevism like Christian existentialist philosopher Nikolai Berdyaev saw Lenin as a paradoxical personality, an antidemocratic, neo-Jacobin revolutionary, yet a humane individual, animated by a thirst for equality and even a passion for freedom. Moreover, an additional dilemma that haunts any attempt at understanding the horrors of the twentieth century lies in the difficulty of fathoming "the level of the pathological debauchery accepted, approved of, and sustained by masses of people—including highly intelligent ones—and coming to be regarded as normal and justifiable practice."[12] Here is where the understanding of Fascism and Communism's revolutionary passion becomes vital. It is this spirit of radical transformation and renewal that mobilized the masses who pushed forward both movements throughout their existence. Fascism and Communism were incarnations or materializations of "a revolutionary experience of standing on the edge of history and proactively changing its course, freed from the constraints of 'normal' time and 'conventional' morality."[13] Both were born in the wreckage of the First World War in a Europe that seemed to have entered a new era where politics had to be radically redefined toward the glorious dawn of new left or right civilizations.

In fact, the catastrophe started earlier, in the Bolshevik apocalyptic vision of an unprecedented break with all liberal values and traditions, including the pluralist ethos of international social democracy. Going beyond the established comparisons between Hitler and Stalin, historian Robert Gellately brought Lenin back into the story of totalitarian political movements as the true architect of the Bolshevik dictatorship, the real founder of the gulag system, a fervent ideologue convinced that his vanguard party (a revolutionary political invention that shattered the praxis of international social democracy) was entrusted by an almost mystically defined history to achieve its goals and make humanity content forever, no matter the human costs. And the costs were indeed appalling, defying our capacity for representation. Ideological fanaticism mixed with all-consuming resentment explain Lenin's destructive ambitions. Lenin was not only the founder of political propaganda, the supreme priest of a new ecclesiology of the omniscient, infallible party, but also the demiurge of the concentration camp system and the apostle of universal terror. A true Bolshevik, Martin Latsis, one of the Cheka's leaders, said in 1918, "We are not waging war on individual persons. We are exterminating the bourgeoisie as a class. During the investigation, we do not look for evidence that the accused acted in deed or word against the Soviet power. The first questions you ought to put are: to what class does he belong? What is his origin? What is his education and profession? And it is these questions that ought to determine the fate of the accused."[14]

In the same vein, Hitler saw the war with the Soviet Union and Western democracies as an ideological crusade meant to totally destroy the ideologically dehumanized enemy.[15] Gellately quotes the recollections of one of Hitler's secretaries: "We will win this war, because we fight for an idea, and not for Jewish capitalism, which drives the soldiers of our enemies. Only Russia is dangerous, because Russia fights with the same fanaticism as we do for its worldview. But the good will be the victor, there is nothing else for it."[16]

Bolshevism cannot be understood without admitting Lenin's paramount role. Without Lenin, there would have been no Bolshevism. Stalin was indeed the beneficiary of a system that Lenin had imagined and developed. In the absence of the ideology developed by Lenin, these regimes would have remained traditional tyrannies.[17] Indeed, as sociologist Daniel Chirot emphasized, we deal with two types of despotic regimes: tyrannies of corruption (the traditional ones) and tyrannies of certitude, based on ideological hubris.[18] It was the ideological pretense, the conviction that he was fulfilling a grandiose historical mission, that made Lenin engage in his reckless attempt to radically transform society. In his footsteps, Stalin pursued the same all-transforming agenda: nature, science, and language all had to be subordinated to the sacrosanct goal. The same ideological ardor, impervious to doubt or self-questioning, motivated Hitler's delusional visions of global race warfare.[19] As Arthur Koestler demonstrated long ago, totalitarian movements disregard ethics and despise moral absolutes: "Since about the second half of the nineteenth century our ethical brakes have been more and more neglected until totalitarian dynamism made the engine run amok. We must apply the brake or we shall crash."[20]

In spite of its claim to transcend alienation and rehabilitate human dignity, Communism was morally sterilized, or, in the words of Steven Lukes, it suffered from moral blindness.[21] Once it subordinated the notion of the good to the interests of the proletariat, Communism annulled the universality of moral norms. The same can be said about Fascism, with its exaltation of the primeval tribal virtues and total disregard for the common humanity of all human beings. Both assigned to the state its own morality, granting *only* to it the right to define the meaning and ultimate aim of human existence. The *ideological state* became the supreme and absolute value within the framework of an eschatological doctrine of revolution. The horrors that defined the past century were thus possible because of a "moral inversion": "The state's crimes [were] explicable not as crimes but as necessary precautions to prevent greater injustice."[22] Through the cult of absolute unity along the path to salvation by knowledge of history, both Communism and Fascism produced new and total social and political projects centered on purifying the body of the communities that fell prey to these ideological spells. The new men or women brought about by these movements left behind their "little ego, twitching with fear and rickets," for they had surrendered what the proletarian writer Maxim Gorky called despairingly the "farce of individuality."[23] Or, as a former member of the German Communist Party once declared: "A man who fought alone could never win; men must stand together and fight together and make life better for all engaged in useful work. They must struggle with every means at their disposal, shying at no lawless deed as it would further the cause, giving no quarter until the revolution triumphed."[24] A strikingly similar statement can be found in Nazi chef propagandist Joseph Goebbels's early novel, *Michael: A German Destiny:* "What makes up the modern German is not so much cleverness and intellect as the new spirit, the willingness to become one with the people, to devote oneself and sacrifice oneself to it unstintingly."[25] Indeed, the times called for the dissolution of the individual into a heroic collective built on the rubble of a modernity that was declared defunct. Either from the left or from the right, the horrors of the twentieth century came about once "modernist revitalization movements" (in the words of Roger Griffin) became full-fledged state programs of social engineering.

Stalin's former henchman and close associate Vyacheslav Molotov's unrepentant evaluation of the Great Terror exemplifies the new dynamic between power and morality: "Of course there were excesses, but all was permissible, to my mind, for the sake of the main objective— keeping state power! ... Our mistakes, including the crude mistakes, were justified."[26] Once these political movements constructed their vision of modernity on the principle of a chosen, purified community crossing the desert of history from darkness into light, there could be only one solution for those who failed to meet their inclusionary criteria: excision.[27] Unsurprisingly, the same Molotov explained the oppression of the families of those purged, executed, deported, or assassinated as prophylactic action: "They had to be isolated. Otherwise, they would have spread all kinds of complaints, and society would have been infected by a certain amount of demoralization."[28] Similarly, in 1926, Yemelyan Yaroslavsky, an official Bolshevik historian and Joseph Stalin's confidant, justified the purges decided at the sixteenth party conference (April 1929) as a method of protecting "the cells of the party and soviet organism from 'degeneration.' "[29]

Such affliction-weary rhetoric about the body politic was hardly different from that employed by Himmler in his speech to SS leaders at Posen in October 1943. The Reichsführer-SS described Nazi policies as extermination of "a bacterium because we do not want in the end to be infected by the bacterium and die of it. I will not see so much as a small area of sepsis appear here or gain a hold. Wherever it may form, we will cauterize it."[30] To paraphrase Italian historian Gaetano Salvemini, both Fascism and Communism decided they had found the key to happiness, virtue, and infallibility, and were prepared to kill in applying it to specific societies.

THE ENIGMA OF TOTALITARIANISM

Herein lies the essence and mystery of the totalitarian experiences of the twentieth century: "The complete rejection of all barriers and all restraints that politics, civilization, morality, religion, natural feelings of compassion, and universal ideas of fraternity have constructed in order to moderate, repress, or sublimate the human potential for individual and collective violence."[31] The real similarities between the Communist and Fascist experiments (the crucial role of the party, the preeminence of ideology, the ubiquitous secret police, the fascination with technology, the frenzied cult of the "New Man," the quasi-religious celebration of the charismatic leader) should not blur significant distinctions (one being the absence of Nazi show trials or intraparty permanent purges). Nevertheless, historian Eugen Weber judiciously remarked that "the distinction between fascism and communism is relative rather than absolute, dynamic rather than fundamental." Under the circumstances, one cannot help but ask the same question as Weber: "Isn't this fundamental similarity between totalitarian creeds and systems at least as important as their differences of view?"[32] This book engages in a dialogue with the most influential contributions to these morally and politically urgent questions. The twentieth century was plagued by agonizing ideological polarizations whose effects continue to haunt our times.

I agree with political scientist Pierre Hassner that despite the differences between Stalinism and Nazism, their fundamental and defining common characteristic was their genocidal frenzy. Or, to use Sheila Fitzpatrick and Michael Geyer's formulation, "The phenomenon of the gulag as a manifestation of Soviet state violence and the Holocaust as the central site of Nazi terror conveys the unmistakable message that the two regimes were *bent on genocide* [my italics]."[33] On the one hand, both Stalinism and Nazism looked for "objective enemies" and operated with notions of collective, even genetic guilt. Obviously, the Bolshevik vision stigmatized political "sins," whereas the Nazi *Weltanschauung* reified biological distinctions. In his enormously significant toast of November 7, 1937, on the occasion of the twentieth anniversary of the Bolshevik coup, as recorded by the Comintern leader Georgi Dimitrov and in his diary, a speech meant to be known only by the top party and People's Commissariat for Internal Affairs (NKVD) elite, Stalin said, "Whoever attempts to destroy the unity of the socialist state, whoever seeks the separation of any of its parts or nationalities—that man is an enemy, a sworn enemy of the peoples of the USSR. And we will destroy each and every such enemy, even if he was an old Bolshevik; we will destroy all his kin, his family. We will mercilessly destroy anyone who, by his deeds or his thoughts,—yes, his thoughts—threatens the unity of the socialist state. To the complete destruction of all enemies, themselves and their kin! (Approving exclamations: To the great Stalin!)"[34]

At the same, the party apparatus never played as powerful a role in Nazi Germany as it did in Stalin's Russia. In fact, Hitler envied Stalin for having been able to place political officers as ideological watchdogs in the army. Historian Ian Kershaw stresses the fact that even when Martin Bormann took over the party leadership in May 1941, thus bringing "the Nazi Party's interference and scope for intervention in shaping the direction of policy to a new plane," the internal contradictions and incoherencies of the National Socialist state remained.[35] The Nazi Party (NSDAP) never enjoyed the same charismatic status that the Bolshevik vanguard had acquired. In Hitler's Germany, loyalty belonged to the Führer as the embodiment of the pristine *völkisch* community. In Stalin's Russia, the zealots' allegiances went to the leader to the extent that they saw him as the incarnation of the party's wisdom.

When he maintained that the cadres decided everything, Stalin really meant it (with him being the ultimate arbiter of promotions and emotions): "A great deal is said about great leaders. But a cause is never won unless the right conditions exist. And the main thing here is the middle cadres. . . . They are the ones who choose the leader, explain our positions to the masses, and ensure the success of our cause. They don't try to climb above their station; you don't even notice them. . . . Generals can do nothing without an officer corps."[36]

STALIN, HITLER, AND THE APOTHEOSIS OF TERROR

This indeed is a crucial distinction between Stalin and Hitler. Stalin for most of his rule was successful in finding a synthesis between government and ideology, system-building and ideological expansion. His politics of mobilization, however destructive for the Soviet population, did not obliterate the formal mechanisms of state administration. In Germany by contrast, "Hitler was at one and the same time the absolutely indispensable fulcrum of the entire regime, and yet largely detached from any formal machinery of government." In this context, the institutions of the Nazi state were transformed into "a panoply of overlapping and competing agencies dependent in differing ways upon the 'will of the Führer.'"[37] In the Soviet Union, Stalin successfully managed to etatize the Leninist utopia—what he called "building socialism in one country." In Germany, governmental disorder became an inescapable facet of the Nazi polity's cumulative radicalization. This difference between Stalinism and Nazism lies at the basis of Timothy Snyder's explanation for Stalin's inability to instrumentalize a new wave of terror against the Jews in the aftermath of the Second World War. The Soviet leader "found himself threatening security chiefs, rather than instructing them. . . . They [his subordinates] were constantly hindered by a certain attention to bureaucratic property and even, in some measure, to law."[38] According to political scientist Kenneth Jowitt, Leninism, understood as an organizational mode, was constructed upon the core idea of the "impersonally charismatic" party. Stalin, despite his development of the original model and his absolutism, simply could not bring another Great Terror upon a party that had just vindicated its historical messianism in what came to be called the Great Patriotic War for the Defense of the Motherland. Either the party, with its extraordinary organizational skills, was the main hero of the victory over the Nazi aggressors or it was a shelter of vicious enemies that needed to be exposed. Initiating a new onslaught against the Communist elite would have subverted the Great Patriotic War myth.

True, Lenin was not the embodiment of the party bureaucracy. In this respect, Robert Gellately draws fine and necessary distinctions: during the Great Terror, Bolshevism created universal fear among all strata of the population. The Leninist project, as developed by Stalin, meant a continuous aggression of the party-state against all social groups, including the much-acclaimed proletariat and its party. Mass mobilization and fear were not mutually exclusive, and millions of ordinary citizens became involved in the bloody dramaturgy of hysteria and persecution.[39] David Priestland correctly emphasizes that the specific dynamics of the Bolshevik regime under Stalin were the result of an ideological context similar to that of Lenin's years at the helm of the Russian Communist Party. Stalin continually agonized over finding the right combination of "proletarian consciousness as a vital force in history and politics," science-driven progress, and the vision of a society or world structured according to class origin.[40]

Communism and Fascism shared a similar obsession with continually moving forward to avoid the damning specter of stagnation. Mao once stated that "our revolutions are like battles. After a victory, we must at once put forward a new task. In this way, cadres and the masses will forever be filled with revolutionary fervor instead of conceit."[41] Eugen Weber proposed a similar diagnosis for Fascism: "The fascist must move forward all the time; but just because precise objectives are lacking he can never stop, and every goal attained is but a stage on the continuous treadmill of the future he claims to construct, of the national destiny he claims to fulfill."[42] On the path to permanent transformation, both Communism and Fascism engineered (or, rather, aimed at) the extinction of the individual by inventing equally binding criteria of faith, loyalty, and status crystallized into a master political myth. And, indeed, this defines the religiousness of a collective existence—"Quand on met toutes les ressources de l'esprit, toutes les soumissions de la volonté, toutes les ardeurs du fanatisme au service d'une cause ou d'un être qui devient le but et le guide des pensées et des actions [When one subjects all resources of the spirit, all the will's submissions, all the ardors of fanaticism to a cause or a being that becomes the goal and the guide of all thoughts and actions]."[43]

Both Stalinism and Nazism emphasized the need for social integration and communal belonging through the exclusion of specific others. Historian Richard Overy describes the two regimes as "all holistic dictatorships." They relied on "creating complicity, just as they operate[d] by isolating and destroying a chosen minority, whose terrorized status confirm[ed] the rational desire of the rest to be included and protected."[44] Their legitimacy was based upon a synthesis between coercion and consent. In this sense, totalitarianism was embodied by the masses, who "gave life and direction to it."[45] Both the Soviet Union and Germany went through massive social and political tumults in the aftermath of the First World War. By the time Stalin and Hitler came into power there was indeed "a wide popular consensus for a politics without conflict and a society without divisions."[46] In reestablishing and re-creating social order, these states proved to be both repressive and paternalistic. Society was structured according to categories such as class, race, nationality, and gender, each with specific consequences on the inclusion-exclusion axis. Both the Soviet Union (and later, the East European countries) and Germany were realigned demographically, geographically, and biologically according to imagined projects of the perfect citizenry. The developmental and exterminist metaphors adopted and implemented by the two dictators and their power apparatuses became the life framework for the subject population, the groundwork for the reinvention of both individual and collective identities. The macrostrategies of the state suffered a process of translation and adaptation into microstrategies of the individual. Socialization turned into political practice, into an effort to align "what one does with what s/he thinks and says about what s/he does."[47]

Political practice was the area where the citizen came to terms with the deliberately ideological lived environment. Under the circumstances, terror could be used to refer to "a complex sensibility of existential dislocation that affects the population broadly under totalitarian rule."[48] Stalinism and Nazism were "states of terror" (as Overy puts it) because they tried to achieve homogenization by creating "battle communities" (in the words of Fritzsche) within which already existent differences were the subject of grotesque public dramatization and the object of elimination through "capillary organization" (Gentile's term) and constant mobilization. Collective and individual dislocation under conditions of state mobilization and state violence generated new social realities that sustained both genocide and a sense of belonging and unity in "fractured (German) and quicksand (Soviet) societies" (Geyer). Both of them were "extreme consequences of secular humanism" (Gentile) echoing the disillusionment and despair brought on by the traumatic experience of the Great War.[49]

Fascism and Communism, as political movements, were resolutions to a painfully and universally felt "sense-making crisis" throughout Europe.[50] Born out of the cataclysmic barbarism and unprecedented violence of World War I, these apocalyptical movements proclaimed the advent of the millennium in this world or, to use political philosopher Eric Voegelin's formulation, they tried to immanentize the eschaton, to build Heaven on Earth, to eliminate the distinction between the City of Man and the City of God.[51] Between 1914 and 1918, "in four years the belief in evolution, progress and history itself was wiped out" as the war "ripped up the historical fabric and cut everyone off from the past suddenly and irretrievably."[52] Communism and Fascism were reactions to this perceived anomy. They were attempts to give birth to a new sense of transcendence and belonging. From this point of view, they were, as Roger Griffin insightfully remarked, radical political modernisms.

IDEOLOGY AND INTENTIONALITY

The official Communist creed was rationalistic and lionized the legacies of the Enlightenment, while the Nazi ideologues (Alfred Rosenberg, Joseph Goebbels, Alfred Baumler, Otto Strasser) insisted on the power of irrational, vital energies and scorned the allegedly sterilizing effects of reason. The reality was that, underneath the ostensible philosophical incompatibilities between the two rival ideologies, Nazism contained a number of tactical affinities with the much-decried Marxism. Hitler himself admitted that he found inspiration in Marxist patterns of political struggle: "I have learned a great deal from Marxism, as I do not hesitate to admit. I don't mean their tiresome social doctrine or the materialist conception of history, . . . and so on. But I have learned from their methods. The difference between them and myself is that I have really put into practice what these peddlers and pen-pushers have timidly begun.

The whole National Socialism is based on it . . . National Socialism is what Marxism might have been if it could have broken its absurd and artificial ties with the democratic order."[53]

It is well known that there are scholars who resist the very idea of a comparison between Communism and Fascism. Comparison can (but not always does) diminish the uniqueness of the absolute horror symbolized by the Holocaust and can overlook the fact that the ideological intentions were significantly different between the Communist and Fascist, or rather, Nazi, projects. Still, both were revolutionary ideologies that aimed to destroy the status quo (that is, the bourgeois order) and its enshrined values. Both movements proclaimed the leading role of a community of chosen individuals grouped within the party. Both detested bourgeois values and liberal democracy. One carried to an extreme a certain Enlightenment universalism, the other made an absolute of racial particularism. Lenin did not nourish xenophobic propensities, but Stalin did. At the end of his life, Stalin behaved like a rabid anti-Semite and prepared horrific pogroms. Both Hitler and Stalin used propaganda to dehumanize their enemies, the Judeo-Bolsheviks, the Trotskyites, and the Zionists. Fascism and Communism equally put themselves in position to "blast a specific era out of the homogeneous course of history."[54] They both aimed to demolish the past in the name of the future. Both totalitarianisms cultivated the myth of youth, rebirth, and the future.

Lenin, Stalin, and Hitler would not have been able to achieve their goals had they not known how to regiment, mobilize, and include large social strata in their efforts. Whereas Bolshevism was primarily a repressive ideocratic dictatorship, Nazism was, at least for its first years in power, a consensus dictatorship. Both represented the triumph of ideological constructs rooted in scientism, organicism, historicism, and voluntarism. For Lenin, class struggle was the ultimate justification for the ruthless persecution of aristocrats, priests, and wealthy peasants. The dehumanization of the enemy started basically with Lenin. This does not mean that Nazism was simply a response to Bolshevism, a panic-ridden reaction to an external cause (as suggested by German historian Ernst Nolte).[55] The ideological roots of Hitler's politics were endogenous. There was a proto-Fascist tradition in Germany as well as in France.[56] Still, at a certain moment, Stalinism incorporated the motifs and symbols of the ultranationalist Right and became, as Alexander Yakovlev and Robert C. Tucker have argued, "Bolshevism of the extreme right."[57] Timothy Snyder judiciously underlined that "the special quality of Nazi racism is not diluted by the historical observation that Stalin's motivations were sometimes national or ethnic. *The pool of evil simply grows deeper* [my emphasis]."[58]

Indeed, both Hitler and Stalin spoke of ethnic cleansing. For example, between 1937 and 1938, most of the victims of the Great Terror were either class or national enemies. However, a nuance emphasized by Snyder offers a caveat to the comparison between these two extremisms. In fact, Stalinism did not transform mass murder into political history, as happened in Nazi Germany. For Stalin, "mass murder could never be anything more than a successful defense of socialism, or an element in a story of progress toward socialism."[59] But, to take Snyder's point further, Communism, like Fascism, undoubtedly founded its alternative, illiberal modernity upon extermination. The Communist project, in such countries as the USSR, China, Cuba, Romania, or Albania, was based precisely on the conviction that certain social groups were irretrievably alien and deservedly murdered.

Communism's appetite for ethnic cleansing, on top of "sociocide" (to use Dan Diner's term), was not rooted simply within Stalin's phobias and idiosyncrasies. Zhdanovism (the anticosmopolitan campaigns after 1946), the secret pogrom of the early 1950s, and the Slánský affair were part and parcel of the (il)logic of mature Stalinism.[60] Ironically, they represented a victory of sorts by Nazism over its main ideological rival. As Martin Amis points out, the anti-Jewish terror planned by Stalin "would have modeled itself on the older Bolshevik idea or tactic of inciting one class to destroy another. It would have resembled the Red Terror of 1918 with the Jews very approximately in the role of the bourgeoisie."[61] Erik van Ree correctly emphasized that the real ideological originality of mature Stalinism was the synthesis between nation and class and between *two* main goals, national development and world Communism.[62] The process of state-building in the Soviet Union produced very un-Marxist results. Instead of withering away, the bureaucratic Leviathan, abysmally corrupt and incurably inefficient, reached astronomic dimensions. Or, following the analyses of Ken Jowitt and Terry Martin, Stalinism talked about modernization but practiced neotraditionalism.

In short, it is no longer possible to maintain and defend the image of a relatively benign Lenin whose ideas were viciously distorted by the sociopath Stalin. Ideological obsession was the crucial element that determined the decisions of totalitarian leaders. They lived off ideology, in ideology, for ideology. The Bolshevik and Nazi messianic sects were tightly knit ideological constructions. The closest analogy, which I owe to

Ken Jowitt, would be the fortress, the hermetically isolated castle whose inhabitants think and act alike. In spite of other questionable statements, Ernst Nolte is right when he underlines that, whereas Lenin was a Russian politician and Hitler a German one, the story was much more complicated. They were ideological prophets, and only ideology could explain the course of their historical interventions: "The fundamental question remains the *exacerbation (Überschiessen)* of *novelty,* of the *hiatus* which constituted the properly ideological. It is the ideological which begets the most meaningful actions. There may exist deep differences between the ideologies, but each one is defined by this simultaneous overcoming and by a kernel of legitimate and convenient elements and only ideological extremism that can equally generate and destroy."[63]

Robert Gellately bluntly and unequivocally portrayed Lenin as "a heartless and ambitious individual who was self-righteous in claiming to know what was good for 'humanity,' brutal in his attempt to subject his own people to radical social transformation, and convinced he held the key to the eventual overthrow of global capitalism and the establishment of world Communism."[64] It is hard not to agree with him when he writes: "Lenin introduced Soviet Communism, complete with new secret police and concentration camps. . . . Once in power, Lenin enthusiastically hunted down anyone who did not fit in or who opposed the new regime, and he introduced the Communist Party purges that periodically called forth nationwide witch hunts. . . . Lenin did not become dictator simply by taking on the mantle of chairman of Sovnarkom (in effect its premier). Rather, he made his will prevail by his control of the great Marxist texts and perhaps above all by his ferocity."[65]

Again, Ernst Nolte and Richard Pipes are not mistaken in examining the conflict between the two totalitarian states as one between similar constructions rooted in ideological frenzy and utopian hubris. After Hitler's coming to power in January 1933, "two great *ideological states* faced each other in Europe, two states whose attitude, in last analysis, was determined by conceptions, which considered themselves interpretations of both past and future world history, and who used these interpretations to make sense of human life."[66]

Lenin created the praxis of voluntarism and Manichaeism necessary for the success of revolutionary action. In Lenin's political cosmology there was no way to reconcile the proletariat and the bourgeoisie; the triumph of the former was predicated on the destruction of the latter. In the same vein, as World War II confronted the Nazis with possible defeat, Hitler and his acolytes resorted to a radical acceleration of their genocidal policies against the Jews. The idea was that no peace with the Jews could be reached, under any circumstances.

Lenin's impact on Marxism and his responsibility for the ethical abyss and the immense human sacrifice generated by Communism in the twentieth century is, I think, superbly expressed in the following formulation from Denis Holier and Betsy Wing: "Marxism brought history out of its infant stages, out of its speechless moments, and gave it a soundtrack. . . . Lenin discovered that history spoke the language of dialectical materialism. But one needs an announcer to broadcast the script." And that radio was Radio-Moscow with the single voice of the Communist Party of the Soviet Union. To continue this argument, only when the irradiating ideological center "ceased to be decipherable for the Marxist decoders" was it possible for "the contract of silence" regarding the criminality of Bolshevism to hold sway and the emancipation from *Diamat* to gain traction in the intellectual and political history of Marxism in Europe.[67] Ironically, it was precisely the disenchanted return to "the great Marxist texts," a forgotten and betrayed tradition, that allowed successive waves of revisionist de-Stalinization to rock the boat of the utopian party-state. There was no such tradition in the Nazi experience and no original, presumably humanist Holy Writ for disillusioned National Socialists to dream of resurrecting. Ian Kershaw, commenting on the failed attempt by Goebbels and Albert Speer to approach Hitler in 1943 on what they perceived as the endemic problems of the Nazi state (among which, at least for Goebbels, was the absence of radicalization of the home front), concluded unambiguously: "They were holding to the illusion that the regime was reformable, but that Hitler was unwilling to reform it. What they did not fully grasp was that the shapeless 'system' of governance that had emerged was both the inexorable product of Hitler's personalized rule and the guarantee of his power."[68]

In conclusion, the key distinction between these two horrendous projects of the twentieth century lies in revisionism or similar developments that simply could not be imagined or implemented under the Nazi regime. The Nazis had no humanist original project to invoke—no enlightened reservoir of betrayed libertarian hopes to be resurrected against the abominations of Hitlerism. A Khrushchev-style blow to Hitler's mystical cult is just not imaginable. The impact of Marxist revisionism and critical intellectuals can hardly be overestimated. The adventure of revisionism led Communist intellectuals beyond the system denounced as the cult of personality. Critical Marxism turned into post-Marxism, and even to liberal anti-Marxism. From within, true believers found Leninism wanting in its most powerful ambition, that of responding in a positively engaging way to the challenges of democratic modernity. As historian Vladimir Zubok argued, "The ethos of educated civic participation, resistance to the immorality of the communist regime, and belief in humane socialism was a feature common to the efforts of Russian, Polish, and Czech reformers and liberal-minded people of culture."[69] This growing common ground of civic empowerment and emancipation became most obvious in 1968 and later in the echoes of the dissident movement in Western Europe. Apostasy appeared once the ideological fanaticism of Communist regimes was denounced from within. Leninism, in contrast to Fascism, ultimately collapsed in Europe because it lost its quasi-religious, hierocratic credentials.

CHAPTER I

Utopian Radicalism
and Dehumanization

We must carry along with us 90 million out of the 100
million of Soviet Russia's inhabitants. As for the rest, we have
nothing to say to them. They must be annihilated.

—Grigory Zinoviev, *Severnaya kommuna,* September 19, 1918

For man, therefore, who despite a corrupted heart yet
possesses a good will, there remains hope of a return to the
good from which he has strayed.

—Immanuel Kant, "Concerning the Indwelling of the Evil Principle
    with the Good, or, on the Radical Evil in Human Nature."

In order to massacre them, it was necessary to proclaim that
kulaks are not human beings. Just as the Germans proclaimed
that Jews are not human beings. Thus did Lenin and Stalin:
kulaks are not human beings. But that is a lie. They are
people! They are human beings!

—Vassily Grossman, *Forever Flowing*

La relation dialectique entre communisme et fascisme est
au centre des tragédies du siècle.

—François Furet, "Sur l'illusion communiste"

Understanding the meanings of the twentieth century is impossible if
we do not acknowledge the uniqueness of the revolutionary left and
right experiments in reshaping the human condition in the name of presumably inexorable historical laws. It was during that century that, using
Leszek Kołakowski's inspired term, "the Devil incarnated himself in His-

tory." The ongoing debate on the nature and the legitimacy (or even acceptability) of comparisons (analogies) between the ideologically driven revolutionary tyrannies of the twentieth century (radical Communism, or rather, Leninism, or, as some prefer, Stalinism) on one hand and radical Fascism (or, more precisely, Nazism) on the other bear on the interpretation of ultimate political evil and its impact on the human condition.[1] In brief, can one compare two ideologies (and practices) inspired by essentially different visions of human nature, progress, and democracy, without losing their *differentia specifica,* blurring important doctrinary but also axiological distinctions? Was the essential centrality of the concentration camp, the only "perfect society," as Adam Michnik once put it, the horrifying common denominator between the two systems in their "highly effective" stage? (Zygmunt Bauman writes about our age as a "century of camps."[2]) Was François Furet right in assuming that Communism's heredity was to be detected in the post-Enlightenment search for mass democracy, whereas Fascism symbolized the very opposite?[3] Was Fascism, as Eugen Weber asserted, "a rival revolution" that saw Communism *only* as a "competitor for the foundation for power" (in the words of Jules Monnerot)?[4]

Comparisons between Communism and Fascism and between Stalinism and Nazism are both useful and necessary. My comparative endeavor focuses on the common ground of these political movements, while also recognizing their crucial differences.[5] Moreover, I agree with Timothy Snyder that "the Nazi and Stalinist systems must be compared, not so much to understand the one or the other but to understand our times and ourselves."[6] Communism and Fascism forged their own versions of modernity based on programs of radical change that advocated homogenization as well as social, economic, and cultural transformation presupposing "the wholesale renovation of the body of the people."[7] They were both founded upon immanent utopias rooted in eschatological fervor. To put it differently, the ideological storms of the twentieth century were the expression of a contagious hubris of modernity. Therefore, the lessons we learn by comparing and contrasting them have a universal, almost timeless meaning for any society that wants to avoid a disastrous descent into barbarity and genocidal forms of extermination. Contemporary dilemmas of a globalized world can only benefit from examination of the disastrous fallacies of the past.

THE LENINIST MUTATION

Here it is important to highlight the point made by Claude Lefort and Richard Pipes: Leninism was a mutation in the praxis of social democracy, not just a continuation of the "illuminist"-democratic legacies of socialism. Equally significant, precisely because he insisted so much on the "causal nexus" and counterrevolutionary anguish and fears, German historian Ernst Nolte did not fully grasp the nature of Fascist anti-Bolshevism as a new type of revolutionary movement and ideology, a rebellion against the very foundations of European modern civilization. Indeed, as Furet (and, earlier, Eugen Weber and George Lichtheim) insisted, Fascism, in its radicalized, Nazi form, was not simply a reincarnation of counterrevolutionary thinking and action.[8] Nazism was more than just a reaction to Bolshevism, or to the cult of progress and the sentimental exaltation of abstract humanity symbolized by the proletariat. It was in fact something brand new, an attempt to renovate the world by getting rid of the bourgeoisie, the gold, the money, the parliaments, the parties, and all the other "decadent," "Judeo-plutocratic" elements. So Fascism was not a counterrevolution, as the Comintern ideologues maintained; rather it is itself a revolution. Or, to use Roger Griffin's more figurative phrasing, "The arrow of time points not backwards but forwards, even when the archer looks over his shoulder for guidance where to aim." According to the same author, Fascism was "a revolutionary form of nationalism. . . . [T]he core myth that inspires this project is that only a populist, trans-class movement of purifying, cathartic national rebirth (palingenesis) can stem the tide of decadence."[9] At stake is the reaction to the "system," that is, to bourgeois-individualistic values, rights, and institutions. When Lenin disbanded the Constituent Assembly in January 1918, he was sanctioning a long-held scorn for representative democracy and popular sovereignty. The one-party system, emulated by Mussolini and Hitler, was thus invented as a new form of sovereignty that was contemptuous of individuals, fragmentation, deliberation, and dialogue. On January 6, 1918, celebrating the dissolution of pluralism, *Pravda* published the following:

> The hirelings of bankers, capitalists, and landlords, the allies of Kaledin, Dutov, the slaves of the American dollar, the backstabbers, the right-essers demand in the Constitutional Assembly all power for themselves and their masters—enemies of the people. They pay lip service to popular demands for land, peace, and [worker] control, but in reality they tried to fasten a noose around the neck of socialist authority and revolution. But the workers, peas-

ants, and soldiers will not fall for the bait of lies of the most evil of socialism. In the name of the socialist revolution and the socialist soviet republic they will sweep away its open and hidden killers.[10]

One of the most acerbic reactions to the decision by Vladimir Lenin, Leon Trotsky, Grigory Zinoviev, Nikolai Yakov Sverdlov, and their companions to disband the remains of democracy in Russia came from the jailed Polish-German Marxist thinker Rosa Luxemburg in her manuscript notes on the Russian Revolution. In his trilogy, Leszek Kołakowski quotes Luxemburg's comment: "Freedom only for supports of the government, only for members of the single party, however numerous—this is not freedom. Freedom must always be for those who think differently." Kołakowski accurately captured the thrust of Rosa Luxemburg's criticism of Bolshevism:

> Socialism was a live historical movement and could not be replaced by administrative decrees. If public affairs were not properly discussed they would become the province of a narrow circle of officials, and corruption would be inevitable. Socialism called for a spiritual transformation of the masses, and terrorism was no way to bring this about: there must be unlimited democracy, a free public opinion, freedom of elections and the press, the right to hold meetings and form associations. Otherwise the only active part of society would be bureaucracy: a small group of leaders who give orders, and the workers' task would be applaud them. The dictatorship of the proletariat would be replaced by the dictatorship of a clique.[11]

The European civil war did indeed take place in the twentieth century, but its main stake was not the victory of Bolshevism over Nazism (or vice versa). It was rather their joint offensives against liberal modernity.[12] Both totalitarian movements were intoxicated with "a state of expectancy induced by the intuitive certainty that an entire phase of history is giving way to a new one"—a mood of *Aufbruch* that became the ideological rationale for the totalist project to engineer reality.[13] This explains the readiness of so many Communists to acquiesce in Soviet-Nazi complicity, including the 1939 "nonaggression" pact: the radical militants saw the "decadent" Western democracies as doomed to disappear, and they were therefore willing to ally themselves with the equally antibourgeois Fascists. This is not to say that anti-Fascism was just a propaganda device for the Comintern, or that anti-Marxism was not a central component of National Socialism. The point is that the two movements were essentially and unflinchingly opposed to democratic values, institutions, and practices. German political thinker Karl Dietrich Bracher once memorably stated that "totalitarian movements are the children of the age of democracy."[14] In their most accomplished form, in the Soviet Union and Germany, Leninism and Fascism represented "a ferocious attack on and a frightening alternative to liberal modernity."[15] Their simultaneous experiences situated them in "a 'negative intimacy' in the European framework of 'war and revolution' "[16]—a "mortal embrace"[17] that increased suffering and destruction to a level unprecedented in history.

In my view, clarifying these issues is enormously important for understanding the real political, moral, and cultural stakes of the post–Cold War order, an order that Ken Jowitt assumes to be "without Leninism," but where Leninist and fundamentalist-primordialist legacies continue to haunt political memory and imagination. On the other hand, we live in a world in which not only do post-Communist specters keep resurfacing, but where post-Fascist exclusionary delusions (and their practical consequences) are not fully extinct. The war between liberalism and its revolutionary opponents (and their nostalgia) is not over, and new varieties of extreme utopian politics should not be automatically regarded as impossible.

In a famous scene in his novel *La condition humaine* (translated into English as *Man's Fate*), novelist André Malraux captured the great dream of twentieth-century Communism (or at least the romantic-heroic moments associated with what the French writer once called *l'illusion lyrique,* the lyrical illusion). The scene takes place in China, during the failed Communist insurrection of 1926. Captured by the Kuomintang, a Communist militant is asked what he finds so appealing in the cause he fights for. The answer is "because Communism defends human dignity." "And what is dignity?" asks the tormentor. "The opposite of humiliation," replies the true believer, shortly before his death. I know of many former Communists who joined the cause because of this extraordinary novel, which came out in the early 1930s.

For young Malraux, Communism was a story of purity and regeneration that motivated a fanatical commitment to the still promising future and a visceral opposition to the real or imagined squalor of the old, dying order. In his memoirs, Arthur Koestler described the moral attraction of early Communism, comparing it to the asceticism and martyrdom of the first Christians. But, Koestler hastened to add, in a few short decades Communism declined from the heights of moral idealism to the horrors of the Borgias and the Inquisition. Yet even so lucid a critic of totalitarianism as Raymond Aron was not ready, until the last years of his life, to admit that Communism and Nazism were equally criminal in their very systemic nature. In his influential book *Démocratie et totalitarisme,* based on a course he delivered in 1957–58, Aron pointed to a major distinction between the two totalitarian experiments, referring to "the idea that inspires each of the two undertakings: in one case the final result is the labor camp, whereas in the other it is the gas chamber. In one case we deal with the will to construct the new man and possibly another man by whatever means; in the other there is a literally demonic will to annihilate a pseudo-race." Later, however, in his *Memoirs,* Aron renounced this distinction and wrote an unequivocal indictment of both systems as equally reprehensible: "I abhor Communism as much as I detest Nazism. The argument I once used to distinguish the class Messianism of the former from the race one advocated by the latter does not impress me anymore. The apparent universalism of Communism has become, in last analysis, a mystification."[18] This was a harsh statement that many intellectuals and social activists today are still unready to endorse. The explanation for this reluctance lies, in my view, in the enduring mythologies of anti-Fascism, including those related to the Spanish Civil War, Communist participation in the resistance movements, and a failure to admit that Nazism was not the offspring but the entranced enemy of liberal capitalism.

THE MYTH OF THE PREDESTINED PARTY

The party as the incarnation of historical rationality, with the revolutionary avant-garde elected to lead the otherwise lethargic masses into the Communist paradise, was the hallmark of the Leninist intervention in the political praxis of the twentieth century. Without the party, there would be no Bolshevik revolution and no gulag, one can say. The myth of the party, more than the myth of the leader, explains the longevity and endurance of the Leninist project. The other side, the Fascists, while invoking the commands of historical providence, invested the ultimate center of power less in the institution than in the infallible "genius" of the leader. The party mattered, but there was never the same type of institutional charismatic magnet that Leninist formations represented, particularly in the case of Nazi Germany. In the case of Fascist Italy, when the charismatic leader was deposed in 1943, the party simply could not reinvent itself despite the fact that it successfully managed to reassert its autonomy vis-à-vis the leader by way of the Fascist Grand Council.[19] In Italy proper the party disintegrated, while in the Salo Republic (the part of the country under German control) Mussolini simply became a puppet in Hitler's hands.[20] Mussolini had lost the ability to perform the role of "of a modern *propheta* who offered his followers a new 'mazeway' (world-view) to redeem the nation from chaos and lead it into a new era, one that drew on a mythicized past to regenerate the future."[21] Hitler's myth was much more resilient. Ian Kershaw remarked that his personality cult, as the nexus of "the social expectations and motivations invested in him by his followers,"[22] experienced a "slow deflation rather than the swift puncture."[23]

A note should be made here regarding the possible difference between Italian Fascism and Nazism. As many scholars have already noted, in the German case the institutionalization of charisma was overshadowed by the "Führer principle." Philippe Burrin stresses that in Nazi Germany politics were fundamentally marked by "personalized power—in the double meaning of the term, centered around the person of Hitler and founded upon direct person-to-person relationships." In his classic study, Karl Dietrich Bracher considered that "the creation of the system of terror and extermination and the functioning of the police and SS apparatchiks operating that system rested on this overturning of all legal and moral norms by a totalitarian leader principle which did not tolerate adherence to laws, penal code, or constitution but reserved to itself complete freedom of action and decision-making. Political power was merely the executive of the Leader's will."[24] Ian Kershaw's fundamental analysis of the "Hitler myth" showed the leader as a political entity almost independent of the party, "the motor for integration, mobilization, and legitimation within the Nazi system of rule."[25] In this sense, the attraction of the leader principle, for the case of Germany, comes closer rather to the Lenin cult in the Soviet Union than to the cult of Stalin or Mussolini. Leaving aside its all-out religious aspects, Lenin's cult took the form of a myth of the founding father as the infinite source of ideological rebirth and sustenance for the Communist polity. And indeed the return to "true Leninist principles" repeatedly brought relief for the Soviet regime. The perpetuation and domination of a Khrushchevite understanding of post-Stalinist Communist systems allowed for the invocation of Lenin (the leader without sin, to paraphrase Kershaw) as safeguard of the original utopia, regardless of the latter's terrible toll on the societies that enacted it. Only the consistent failure of such ideological, cultic revivals finally showed the obsolescence of the "Lenin myth," which ultimately crumbled under its violent legacy.

In Mussolini's Italy, Il Duce's myth did not represent the rationale of the Fascist religion. In Gentile's words, "It was created out of the collective experience of a movement that considered itself invested with a missionary charisma of its own, one that was in fact not, in its beginnings, identified with Mussolini. . . . The Mussolini myth came into being within the environment of the Fascist religion once the latter had been institutionalized."[26] Italian Fascism enshrined the leader as an institution potentially independent of Mussolini. An Italian jurist contemporary to those times formulated the problem as follows: "If the new state is to become a permanent way of being, that is a 'life-system,' it cannot do without the role of the Leader because of its hierarchical structure, even if this Leader does not have the extraordinary magnitude of the Man who promoted the revolution in the first place."[27] In 1934, the Sardinian born Fascist intellectual Edgardo Sullis published a book whose title echoed Thomas à Kempis, *Il Duce—Imitatione de Mussolini,* in which he urged the militants to pursue a political life totally dedicated to a radical transformation of society and themselves: "You should imitate Mussolini alone. You should have no other example in life except him."[28] This "totalitarian Caesarism" (to use Gentile's term), or hierocratic Bonapartism, which allowed for the interchangeability of charisma between the leader and the party is strikingly similar to the Soviet formula of the general secretary as the "Lenin of our times" (one often used in other Communist regimes as well). In fact, the struggle between Stalin and his arch-rival Trotsky revolved around the crucial question, Who can legitimately claim to be "today's Lenin"?

The primary form of charisma, in the Soviet case, was that of the party as scientific socialism incarnate, the eschatological agent that stressed "the gap between the proletariat 'in itself' and the proletariat 'for itself' and the creation of an agent charged with closing this gap."[29] Even Stalin's legitimacy, at the peak of the cult of personality, "in the eyes of his fellow party leaders rested in what they saw as his role of guarantor of their collective power of the state."[30] As in Mussolini's case,[31] Lenin remained the founder of Bolshevism, the head of the Soviet state (first workers' state), and the leader of the Soviet peoples. Under Stalinism, "the fact that the party existed as a continuous, integrated hierarchy, which was institutionally and ideologically embedded in the system, meant that it always existed as a resource for correcting and reining in the regime's most extreme policies. The institutional continuity of the party provided the basis for self-containment."[32] Such a specific alignment allowed for successive Leninist reinventions and stagnations in both the Soviet Union and Eastern Europe. One possible explanation for the immensely explosive impact of Nikita Khrushchev's "Secret Speech" (February 1956) was, besides the classical remark about the acceptance of fallibility in the implementation of the party line at the highest level of power, that the revealed crimes were *against* the party. The Stalin myth irreversibly subverted the party's "charismatic impersonalism" (in the words of Ken Jowitt).[33] The bottom line is, for the moment, that both Fascism (in its Italian avatar) and Leninism had the possibility of charismatic regeneration built in regardless of the leadership's persona. What counted for true believers was the salvific promise incarnated in the party—the source of freedom through successful experimentation with history. However, in the Italian case, such a revival of the party after Mussolini's demise proved impossible because of the disastrous situation in which the country found itself as a result of the National Fascist Party's shockingly incompetent administration of the war effort. Historian R.J.B. Bosworth noticed that even during the Salo Republic, "the new regime carefully avoided the word 'Fascist,' opting instead for 'social' as a signal of its revolutionary commitment to a 'new order' at home and abroad." The new *Republica Sociale Italiana* can be perceived as a desperate but doomed attempt to revive the heroic mission of Fascism in Italy.[34]

There was a major distinction between Communism and Fascism in identifying the place of charisma: Leninists worshipped the party (and the leader as the guarantor of the correct party line), whereas Fascists lionized the magnetic personality of a presumably infallible leader. This explains the enduring fascination with Communism among individuals who continued to believe in its promise of a new society and of social, economic, cultural, and political transformation, even after Khrushchev exposed Stalin's abominable crimes. A lingering sentiment that there was after all something moral in Bolshevik utopianism, plus the exploitation of anti-Fascist emotions, led to a persistent failure to acknowledge the basic fact that, from its inception, Sovietism was a criminal system.

I vividly remember a conference in New York in October 1987, when statements by two dissidents (the Russian Eduard Kuznetsov and the Romanian Dorin Tudoran) about Communism as a "criminal civilization" provoked an angry response from Mihailo Marković, the Yugoslavian critical Marxist who in the late 1990s became the main ideologue of the Milošević regime. Simply put, to document and condemn the bestiality of the Nazis was acceptable, but to focus on analogous atrocities perpetrated by the radical Left appeared as primitive anti-Communism. Albert Camus once summarized the moral perplexity provoked by such a consistent barrage of ideologically motivated prejudice: "When I demand justice, I seem to be asking for hate."[35] The revolutions of 1989 and the collapse of the Soviet Union in 1991 changed the situation. The Soviet bloc's efforts to create the City of God here and now, the search for the perfect society, turned out to be an abysmal disaster. The record sheet of these regimes was one of absolute failure, economically, politically, and morally. It is high time for their victims to be remembered. Norman Naimark has formulated a priority for historical scholarship: "In the final analysis, both totalitarian states—Nazi Germany and Stalinist Russia—were perpetrators of genocide, the 'crime of crimes.' In spite of the fall of the Soviet Union and the attendant greater access to information, we know much more about the Nazi atrocities than we do about the Soviet ones, and about those who initiated, organized, and carried them out. The crucial issue of intentionality and criminal culpability in the Soviet case can only be settled definitively with full access to Russian archives and to those responsible, who still survive."[36] Such conceptualization should be extended to the period of "High Stalinism" in China, Albania, Romania, Hungary, and Bulgaria (1949–1953), and even the genocidal terrorism of the Pol Pot regime in Cambodia. In each of these cases one can see how the persistence of the will to sacrifice entire sections of society on the altar of the political myth materialized in a large-scale commitment to violence.[37]

The comparative evaluation and memory of Communism and Fascism were undeniably marked, mediated, and instrumentalized by the tradition of anti-Fascism in the West. At the root of this fundamental intellectual and public ethos lay a flawed and guilty interpretation of the Communist past. The latter was defined, on the one hand, by silence, partiality, or ignorance regarding the crimes and dictatorship of Leninist party-states, and on the other hand, by the difficulty of separating anti-Fascism from the imperialist propaganda of the Soviet Union during the twentieth century (or China, and their various satellites). The case of the Spanish Civil War remains paradigmatic for the entire history of anti-Fascism. François Furet gave an excellent characterization of the grievous misrepresentation that engendered this tradition: "Communist antifascism had two faces, neither of which happened to be democratic; the first face that of solidarity, which had ennobled so many soldiers, perpetually concealed the pursuit of power and the confiscation of liberty." Anti-Fascism functioned for most of its existence on the principle that cohesion had to be defended at all costs, even if this meant, to paraphrase Francis Ponge, taking the party out of things (the original coinage is "le parti pris des choses"). In Furet's words, "In the hour of the Great Terror, Bolshevism reinvented itself as liberty by virtue of a negation."[38]

Subsequently, anti-Fascism was put in the situation of always turning out to be a mere rhetoric of democracy and freedom. It harbored "existential untruths" (to use Diner's term), which it consistently failed to address because of its unflinching dedication to the Communist (i.e., Soviet) core ideology. Anti-Fascism therefore acquired a split personality: "It encompassed the totalitarian satraps of Eastern Europe as well as the political cosmos of the Western European Left from 1945 well into the 1970s."[39] Its proponents (and nowadays its survivors) adopted a hegemonic pretense to socialist utopia's innocence in utter disregard of the criminality of the utopia in power. This anti-Fascist monopoly over the past "afflicted the very past itself."[40]

The anti-Fascist promise failed because of its umbilical connection to the Moscow center. It is difficult, therefore, to agree with historian Geoff Eley, who stated that the 1943–47 moment of anti-Fascist unity lost out because of "the sharpening tensions between the Soviet Union and United States. . . . [A]nd as Stalin hauled the communist parties back to a language of soviets and proletarian dictatorship, this sanctifying of parliamentarianism once again became a key marker of divisions on the left."[41] It failed because of the true nature of the Communist parties and of their leader, Stalin's Communist Party (CPSU). It failed because it accepted the same contract of silence, the one it endorsed during the Great Terror, regarding the Zhdanovist offensive and the already sweeping Sovietization of some Eastern European countries (for example, the extermination camps and mass executions in Bulgaria between 1944 and 1947).[42] Zhdanovism should not be reduced to simply meaning the "two-camp theory" spelled out by Stalin's first lieutenant in September 1947 at the founding conference of the Information Bureau of the Communist and Workers' Parties (Cominform).[43] When referring to the times of Zhdanov (zhdanovshchina), we think of the debate around official philosopher Georgi Aleksandrov's History of West European Philosophy and the condemnation of Anna Akhmatova (slandered as driven by "a sex-crazed mystic longing for Catherine's good old days") and Mikhail Zoshchenko.[44] These key moments of the immediate aftermath of the Second World War triggered in the USSR (and, by default, in the Soviet satellite countries) a new wave of terroristic frenzy under the guise of anticosmopolitanism and ideological remobilization. These domestic dynamics preceded the inception of the Cold War. Also, one should not forget the execution and imprisonment of millions of Soviet citizens scattered across Hitler's Reich (POWs, individuals used as forced labor by the Nazis, or concentration camp inmates) upon their forced return by the Allies to the USSR. Postwar Soviet Union was the antithesis of freedom and democracy; it was indeed "a world built on slavery."[45] After surveying the existent data, Timothy Snyder concludes that "there were never more Soviet citizens in the Gulag than in the years after the war; indeed, the number of Soviet citizens in the camps and special settlements increased every year from 1945 until Stalin's death."[46] With such a system spearheading the anti-Fascist movement, there was no chance for any renewal of the Left.[47] But after the defeat of Hitler, anti-Fascism was entrenched as politicized will, feeding on its own self-righteousness, thrusting blindly forward in a frenzied activism. It thus only worsened a pre-existing fascination with Stalin's "Great Experiment." In this context, as Sydney Hook remarked, "Intellectual integrity became the first victim of political enthusiasm."[48]

To come back to my earlier argument, the comparison between Communism and Fascism has been fundamentally tainted, intellectually and scholarly, both by the claim of the original innocence of Leninism (or the so-called ultimately humane and positive Communist utopia)[49] and by anti-Fascism's long-standing, resounding failure to denounce the murderousness and illiberality of Communist regimes. Additionally, the experience of the Second World War in various Western countries, with its violence, collaboration, treason, and often limited resistance to the Fascist occupier, left a muddled vision of justice. For example, in the case of postwar France, Tony Judt demonstrated convincingly that "the absence of any consensus about justice—its meaning, its forms, its application—contributed to the confused and inadequate response of French intellectuals to the evidence of injustice elsewhere, in Communist systems especially."[50]

Nevertheless, I consider legitimate the questions raised by historian Anson Rabinbach on the legacy of a tradition that is part and parcel of the present European identity: "Is it possible to go beyond a confrontation between antifascism as a state-sponsored myth mobilized to disguise the crimes of the 'first' (Soviet) antifascist regime, and antifascism as a necessary and heroic moment in the history of the West's resistance to totalitarianism in its first phase? Can we come to a different judgment than the mutually exclusive perspectives of 1936 and 1989?"[51] My answer, and the discussion that follows serves as an example, is positive, in the sense that the reassessment of the history of the twentieth century's totalitarianisms provides us with lessons and values for the safeguard of democracy and freedom on both the left and the right. Anti-Fascism and anti-Communism are logical reactions to the experiences and realities of a ravaged century.[52]

THE BLACK BOOK OF COMMUNISM AND ITS IMPACT

One of the most important moments for the reevaluation of the role played by Communism (as both an ideology and a regime type) was the publication of *The Black Book of Communism* and the subsequent debates (in France, Germany, the United States, and so on) generated by this volume and its theses both in the public sphere and among academics. The book initially came out to an enormous success in France, where it sold over 200,000 copies. Its Italian and German translations also became best sellers. The publication of the book in East-Central Europe led to endless polemics and discussions regarding the responsibility for, complicity with, and consequences of Communist crimes. What *The Black Book of Communism* succeeded in demonstrating is that Communism in its Leninist version (and, one must recognize, this has been the only successful application of the original dogma) was from the outset inimical to individual rights and human freedom. As Martin Malia stated in the foreword to the American edition: "The communist regimes did not just commit criminal acts (all states do on occasion); they were criminal enterprises in their very essence: on principle, so to speak, they all ruled lawlessly, by violence, and without regard for human life."[53] In spite of its overblown rhetoric about emancipation from oppression and necessity, the leap into the kingdom of freedom announced by the founding fathers turned out to be an experiment in ideologically driven, unbounded social engineering.[54] The very idea of an independent judiciary was rejected as "rotten liberalism." The party defined what was legal and what was not: as in Hitler's Germany, where the heinous 1935 Nuremberg Laws were a legal fiction dictated by Nazi racial obsessions, Bolshevism from the outset subordinated justice to party interests. For Lenin, the dictatorship of the proletariat was rule by force and unrestricted by any law. His famous reply to Kautsky speaks volumes about the true ethos of his ideology: "The revolutionary dictatorship of the proletariat is rule won and maintained through the use of violence by the proletariat against the bourgeoisie, rule that is unrestricted by any laws."[55]

The class enemy had to be weeded out and destroyed without any mercy. Andrei Vyshinsky, Stalin's hysterical prosecutor in the Moscow show trials of the 1930s, carried this macabre logic to its ultimate consequences when he made the defendants' confessions the main argument for sentencing them to death. In other words, the presumption of innocence was replaced by a universalized presumption of guilt. As for the rhetoric of hatred, comparable to Goebbels's most insanely inflammatory speeches, this passage is worth quoting:

> Shoot these rabid dogs! Death to this gang who hide their ferocious teeth, their eagle claws, from the people! Down with that vulture Trotsky, from whose mouth a bloody venom drips, putrefying the great ideals of Marxism! Let's put these liars out of harm's way, these miserable pygmies who dare to dance around rotting carcasses! Down with these abject animals! Let us put an end once and for all to these miserable hybrids of foxes and pigs, these stinking corpses! Let their horrible squeals finally come to an end! Let's exterminate the mad dogs of capitalism, who want to tear to pieces the flower of our new Soviet nation! Let's push the bestial hatred they bear to our leaders back down their throats![56]

Both totalitarianisms "believed in the ubiquity of maleficent adversaries." Both defined their enemies on the basis of their potential for blocking the realization of the perfect community. Their obsession with eliminating all "objective enemies" on the road to the promised land led first to the replacement of "the suspected offense by the possible crime" (Hannah Arendt), and then to an all-out fixation on universal conspiracies.[57]

Utopian ideals were used to legitimize the worst abuses against "objective" enemies, defined only in connection with the interests of a self-appointed revolutionary vanguard and the leader's fixations. In Nazi Germany, Hitler's Aryan-centered cosmology hyperbolized the imaginary Jew as simultaneously the organizer of market exploitation and the fomenter of Marxist attempts to overthrow it.[58] The mythology of the Judeo-Bolshevik and Judeo-plutocratic plot thrived in the anti-Semitic visions of the East and Central European Far Right (later to reemerge in post–World War II Stalinist anti-Semitism).[59] Paranoia regarding infiltrations, subversion, and treason have been enduring features of all Communist political cultures, from Russia and China to Romania and Yugoslavia. Leninist parties officially playing the democratic parliamentary game (in France and Italy after World War II) were no less intolerant of deviation from the orthodox line than similar formations in power (with the difference that they could not physically liquidate alleged spies and agents). Lenin once famously declared that "an organization of real revolutionaries will stop at nothing to rid itself of an unworthy member."[60]

Perhaps the best book to read for understanding the nature and meaning of Leninism remains Dostoyevsky's novel *Demons*. The great

Russian writer and political-religious thinker grasped the ominous consequences of nihilistic, extremist revolutionary actions undertaken by ecstatic apostles of universal liberation.[61] Indeed, the chapter on Russia in *The Black Book* as well as Martin Malia's foreword show how Bolshevism had deep roots in the culture of apocalyptical extremism of the Russian revolutionary intelligentsia. Its morality was embodied only in the "solid, united discipline and conscious mass struggle against the exploiters" (Lenin). There is only a small step from such destructive dedication to criminal single-mindedness. In August 1919, the organ of the Cheka, *Krasnyi Metch,* provided a vision of red horizons for humanity under the impact of the Great October Revolution: "For us everything is permitted, for we are the first in the world to wield the sword not to oppress and enslave, but to liberate mankind from its chains. . . . Blood? Let blood flow!"[62] This is the very essence of Leninism as a totalitarian movement: the conviction that it was building a new civilization, that it was the repository for the discrimination between good and evil, the interpreter of a new truth.[63]

There was no spectacular revelation in *The Black Book:* after all, whatever has emerged from the secret archives of the former Soviet bloc countries is just a confirmation of the long-held view that Communists everywhere engaged in revolutionary civil war to accomplish the total transformation of man, economy, society, and culture. What was original was the comprehensive and systematic analysis and interpretation of the crimes and repressions associated with Leninist practices in the twentieth century. I commend the nuanced analyses of differences between stages and countries: Poland and Hungary, especially after Stalin's death, were not exactly totalitarian. After all, the Hungarian revolution was initiated by a group of anti-Stalinist reform Communists. There should have been deeper analysis of the Leninist experience in East Germany, including a discussion of currently available data concerning the infamous Stasi universe of fear and intimidation. As a whole, however, the fundamental merit of the *Black Book of Communism,* which set the tone for future discussion, was its endeavor to restore the public memory of Communism's crimes and to oppose revisionist efforts aimed at excusing the Communist vision, if not the practices. The volume showed that, as Michael Scammell excellently pointed out, "what matters is that we understand the *entirety* of this century's terrible history. . . . As a civilization we are obliged to come to terms with that truth [Communism's criminality], and admit our share of culpability, and draw correct conclusions."[64]

The authors of the *Black Book* succeeded in assembling enough information to construct a big picture that maybe for the first time made an undeniable case that the scale of the crimes against humanity committed by Communist regimes *do matter*. Despite arguments to the contrary, Communism *should not* and cannot be studied just like other important events in world history.[65] What is unfortunate, and some of Courtois' controversial introductory statements can be explained on this basis, is that it took too long to learn that "in the sorry story of our century, Communism and Nazism are, and always were, morally indistinguishable." Indeed, as Tony Judt states, this rather belatedly consensual epiphany "justifies a complete recasting and rewriting of the history of our times."[66]

The book came out in France in 1997 and generated tremendous polemics, especially in such publications as *Le Monde, Le Débat,* and *Commentaire.* It was published at a time when the French intelligentsia had passionately discussed the mystifying appeals of Communism, as explored by the late François Furet in his masterful *Le passé d'une illusion.* Statements that were considered acceptable coming from Furet, one of the most respected and highly influential French historians, sounded outrageous to many former leftist intellectuals when presented in a very provocative formulation by the editor of the *Black Book,* Stéphane Courtois, in his introduction. Initially, the introduction was to be written by Furet himself, but when he passed away, Courtois, the editor of the journal *Communisme,* wrote a text that managed to irritate many French historians, political scientists, and journalists.[67] Within a political and academic culture in which the radical Left had long exerted an inordinate influence (one may even use the term *hegemony*), Courtois' blunt and not always very balanced statements regarding the inherent (and, for him, morally mandatory) comparability of Communism and Fascism were perceived as politically charged, a mere simulation of a thoroughgoing historical approach. Furthermore, scholars like Annette Wieworka accused Courtois of an attempt to use this comparison to make Communism look worse than Nazism (at least in terms of the number of victims).[68] Two contributors, Nicolas Werth and Jean-Louis Margolin, decided to dissociate themselves publicly from the main theses of the introduction.

The main problems with Courtois' introduction were a fixation on figures and a failure to highlight not only similarities but also significant distinctions between Communist and Nazi systems of mass terror and extermination. Courtois opened the door to a practice that continues to haunt discussions about the criminality of Communism, especially in the former Soviet bloc: "an international competition for martyrdom" (in the words of Timothy Snyder). Courtois and others who amplified his model of analysis seemed to believe that "more killing would bring more meaning." Indeed, one of the central risks incumbent in the comparison between Fascism and Communism is that it can unleash, if its stakes are gaining the upper hand in a competition over round numbers of victims, what Snyder called "martyrological imperialism." And indeed, as "millions of ghosts of people who never lived"[69] are released in various countries' cultures, the memory of radical evil offers no meaning except for rationalizations in the service of national politics and discourses of historical entitlement.

In comparing the number of victims under Communist regimes (between 85 and 100 million) to the number of people who perished under or because of Nazism (25 million), Courtois downplayed a few crucial facts. In this respect, some of his critics were not wrong. First, as an expansionist global phenomenon, Communism lasted between 1917 and the completion of *The Black Book* (think of North Korea, China, Cuba, and Vietnam, where it is still alive, if not well). National Socialism lasted from 1933 to 1945. Second, we simply do not know what price Nazism would have taken in victims had Hitler won the war. The logical hypothesis (supported by evidence such as the differences between how the Nazis implemented the day-to-day occupation of Poland and how they occupied Holland) is that not only Jews and Gypsies but also millions of Slavs and other "racially unfit" individuals would have died. According to Ian Kershaw, "The General Plan for the east commissioned by Himmler envisaged the deportation over the subsequent years of 32 million persons, mainly Slavs, beyond the Urals and into Western Siberia."[70] And, as the plan for resettling Jews has shown, such designs were themselves genocidal. Christopher Browning and Lewis Siegelbaum excellently summarized, for Nazi Germany, the core post-1941 identitarian mutation that created the potential for cumulative, irradiating racial exterminism: "The Nazi assertion of German identity as the 'master race' meant the destruction of both the freedom and the identity of those whom they ruled. Victory and empire completed the transition of the *Volksgemeinschaft* from the restoration illusion of a unified community of the German people to the Nazi vision of a racial community waging eternal struggle—a *Kampfgemeinschaft*."[71] As for the political opponents of Hitler's reign of terror, suffice it to remember Dachau, Buchenwald, and Sachsenhausen.

Third, in the case of Communism one can identify an inner dynamic that contrasted the original promises to the sordidly criminal practices. In other words, there was a search for reforms, and even for socialism with a human face, within the Communist world, but such a thing would have been unthinkable under Nazism. The chasm between theory and practice, or at least between the moral-humanist Marxian (or socialist) creed, and the Leninist or Stalinist (or Maoist, or Khmer Rouge) experiments was more than an intellectual fantasy. Furthermore, whereas Sovietism and Nazism were equally scornful of traditional morality and legality in their drive to eliminate enemies, one needs to remember that for Lenin and his followers "re-education," cruel and humiliating as it was, could offer at least some chance for survival for either the class enemy or their offspring. Diaries, letters, transcripts of inquiry commissions, and other public and private transcripts have shown the extent to which "speaking Bolshevik" (Kotkin) or becoming "ordinary Stalinists" (Figes) could become a mechanism on social (re)integration. In the words of an author who has extensively dealt with this issue:

> The road to Communist conversion, significantly narrowed during the era of sweeping purges, to be sure, always remained negotiable, though it could be very difficult indeed. The fact that a successful manipulation of the official discourse enabled at least a few to clear their names by distancing themselves from convicted family members points to the importance of the voluntarist kernel in Communism. The right to petition, to write a complaint protesting one's innocence, all this while using public language, did not disappear even during the worst days of the Great Purge. Neither class background nor national origins were an insurmountable obstacle.[72]

This was not the case with the Nazi treatment of the Jews. As Tony Judt puts it, "If we are not to wallow in helpless despair when it comes to explaining why it came to this, we must keep in view a crucial analytical contrast: there is a difference between regimes that exterminate people in the inhuman pursuit of an arbitrary objective and those whose objective is extermination itself."[73] For the Nazis, and for Hitler in particular, the demonization of the Jews, and implicitly their excision, was part and parcel of the regime's millenarian vision of national salvation.[74] Hitler described himself in July 1941 as "the Robert Koch of politics." The Nazi dictator further explained the comparison: "He [Koch] found the bacillus of tuberculosis and through that showed medical scholarship new ways. I discovered the Jews as the bacillus and ferment of all social decomposition. Their ferment. And I have proved one thing: that a state can live without Jews; that the economy, culture, art, etc. can exist without Jews and indeed better. That is the worst blow dealt to the Jews."[75]

The most important pitfall of Courtois' introduction is the fact that, by often turning a blind eye to these differences, his explanation for the flawed anamnesis regarding Communism's criminality opened the door to dubious interpretations. He stated that "after 1945 the Jewish genocide became a byword for modern barbarism, the epitome of twentieth-century mass terror. After initially disputing the unique nature of the persecution of the Jews by the Nazis, the communists soon grasped the benefits involved in immortalizing the Holocaust as a way of rekindling antifascism on a more systematic basis. . . . More recently, a single-minded focus on the Jewish genocide in an attempt to characterize the Holocaust as a unique atrocity has also prevented an assessment of other episodes of comparable magnitude in the Communist world."[76] This is at best a distortion. As Tony Judt, Ian Kershaw, Jürgen Kocka, and other prominent historians have shown, it was only after 1970, or even after 1980, that the Holocaust became a central topic in the analysis and understanding of the Third Reich. The difficulties related to a recognition of Communist mass crimes are due to the long decades of state-controlled information in those countries, the belatedness of archival openings, and the nervous reaction of left-wing circles in Western Europe (especially in France, Greece, and Spain) to what they decry as a political instrumentalization of the past.

There were two types of reaction to Courtois' argument. Reviewers such as Scammell, Judt, Bartov, and Herf admitted that he was justified to a certain extent. Jeffrey Herf, for example, argued that "despite some important exceptions, Courtois has a point: In Western academia, scholars who chose to focus on the crimes of communism were and remain a minority and face the career-blocking danger of being labeled as right-wingers."[77] But, as Scammel and Judt pointed out, this is not a reason for imposing a choice between "our memory of Auschwitz and our memory of the Gulag, because history has mandated that we remember them both."[78] The *Black Book* builds a successful and convincing case for the equation between Communism and *radical evil,* thus placing it in the same category as Fascism. And most recently, this position has been endorsed in the Parliamentary Assembly of the Organization for Security and Co-operation in Europe (OSCE) and discussed in the EU Parliament, during the presentation of the Prague Declaration (signed by, among others, Václav Havel, Joachim Gauck, and Vytautas Landsbergis). For example, the OSCE's "Resolution on Divided Europe Reunited:

Promoting Human Rights and Civil Liberties in the OSCE Region in the Twenty-first Century" states:

> Noting that in the twentieth century European countries experienced two major totalitarian regimes, Nazi and Stalinist, which brought about genocide, violations of human rights and freedoms, war crimes and crimes against humanity, acknowledging the uniqueness of the Holocaust . . . The OSCE Parliamentary Assembly reconfirms its united stand against all totalitarian rule from whatever ideological background . . . Urges the participating States: a. to continue research into and raise public awareness of the totalitarian legacy; b. to develop and improve educational tools, programs and activities, most notably for younger generations, on totalitarian history, human dignity, human rights and fundamental freedoms, pluralism, democracy and tolerance; . . . Expresses deep concern at the glorification of the totalitarian regimes.[79]

Under the circumstances, one can hardly see the point in trying, as Courtois seemed to do (setting the tone for further rationalizations by others in later years), to appropriate the image of ultimate evil. His argument was turned into cannon fodder by those who wished to dismiss *The Black Book* altogether. French journalist Nicolas Weil emphatically declared at the time that the book was "an ideological war machine against the theory of the Shoah's uniqueness" which "minimized the memory of the brown period."[80] One cannot agree with such political coloring of the *Black Book,* but the volume did indeed generate a war of numbers, words, and memories that sometimes, especially in Eastern and Central Europe, had direct or indirect negationist and normalizing tonalities. An implicit causal relationship was established between remembering Jewish suffering and "forgetting" the pain of others, thus setting up a new wave of anti-Semitism in the public sphere.[81]

The comparison between Communism and Nazism had been long sensitive in Russian, East European, and Western analyses. Courtois pointed to the disturbing writings of Vassily Grossman, the author of the novel *Life and Fate,* a masterpiece of twentieth-century literature (and coauthor with Ilya Ehrenburg, in the aftermath of World War II, of *The Black Book of Nazi Crimes against Soviet Jews,* a terrifying report that the Stalinists banned).[82] Both in that novel and in his shorter book *Forever Flowing,* Grossman insisted that the Stalinist destruction of the kulaks was fundamentally analogous to Nazi genocidal politics against groups considered racially inferior. The persecution and extermination of the Jews was as much a consequence of ideological tenets held sacred by the Nazi zealots as the destruction of the kulaks during Stalinist collectivization campaigns. One author with extensive knowledge of the

Soviet archives argued, "It seems that Stalin and his henchmen believed in irredeemable, hopeless individuals who had to be eliminated no less than Hitler did."[83]

CONSTRUCTING THE ENEMY

Millions of human lives were destroyed as a result of the conviction that the sorry state of mankind could be corrected if only the ideologically designated "vermin" were eliminated. This ideological drive to purify humanity was rooted in the scientist cult of technology and the firm belief that History (always capitalized) had endowed the revolutionary elites (of extreme left or extreme right) with the mission to get rid of the "superfluous populations" (as Hannah Arendt put it). Communist regimes tried to permanently excise the segments of the society that it designated as potentially inimical to the realization of utopia. And, as Gerlach and Werth showed in the case of the Soviet Union, "the more defined and precise the Bolsheviks' envisioned order became, the greater the number of those that were forcibly excluded from it." In like manner, they created "a world of enemies, and ultimately there was no other solution to the threat that these imagined enemies posed than their total physical annihilation." In this sense, the two authors conclude by stating that "mass terror was a Soviet variant of the 'final solution.' "[84] Historian Eric Weitz's concept of racialization falls in the same category. He considered it useful in explaining the way Soviet authorities alternated the designation of population categories subjected to terror with direct consequences regarding their imprisonment, execution, deportation, and so on: "It helps capture the malleability of assigned identities, how groups perceived as nations or classes can, in specific historical circumstances, come to be viewed as so utterly distinct from the dominant groups that only the term *race* captures the immense divide that is created. And the term also captures how, in different circumstances, populations can become 'deracialized,' as happened officially to many of the purged nationalities after Josef Stalin's death."[85]

Weitz's approach is just another entry on the long list of scholars who attempted to make sense of "the cycles of violence" (in the words of Nicolas Werth) that became the norm in the Soviet Union. At this point, it became increasingly difficult to ignore the fact that there was an "embarrassing uniformity in the means to salvation advocated by the Nazis and the Communists, namely science (and the practices of reshaping the bodies politic accordingly).[86] The crux of the matter was that in the Soviet Union (as for other Communist regimes) the population was organized based on criteria of exclusion and disenfranchisement according to the ideological imperatives and developmental tasks set up by the party. As Golfo Alexopoulos states, "In the Soviet Union, there were citizens and there were citizens." As in Nazi Germany, citizenship rights increasingly morphed into a boundary between belonging and criminalization, between "the national self and the enemy others," an indicator of friends and foes.[87] The principle of the elect that was at the core of the Leninist theory of the historical subject realizing utopia was reflected in citizenship laws. Those deemed unworthy to hold and exercise the rights assigned to the Soviet body politic were disenfranchised, which in the case of Communist polities equaled de facto denaturalization and statelessness. Moreover, during certain periods in the evolution of these regimes, this rightlessness became an inherited disease. Under Stalin, "the deprivation of rights extended to entire kin groups, as family units were often punished collectively. The Stalinist state viewed enemies of various kinds as defined by ties of kinship; thus entire families lost their rights as a group. Class enemies (Nepmen, traders, kulaks, *lishentsy*) and so-called 'enemies of the people,' as well as enemy nations (Germans, Poles, Koreans, Greeks, Chinese)—both Soviet citizens and foreign subjects—were rounded up as kin groups. The disloyalty of the fathers was thought to be passed down to the sons. Both rightlessness and statelessness became inherited traits."[88]

If one associates such findings with analyses of the camps' population profile or with the nature of terror and victims of mass violence under Communist regimes (such as those provided by the authors of *The Black Book*), then the notion of "class genocide" advanced by Stéphane Courtois (Dan Diner uses the term *sociocide*) gains considerable weight. The victimization, imprisonment, and even execution of "kin groupings" based on a blanket, inheritable identity *exclusively* and *commonly* applied to all its members comes asymptotically close to the type of violence presupposed by the concept of genocide, as it is internationally defined.[89] At times in the history of almost all Communist regimes (what Stephen Kotkin called "re-revolutionizing the revolution"),[90] there are distinct stretches of perpetrating genocide against their subject populations. The crucial difference from Nazism, however, is that these practices were built into the system *by consequence*.[91] Even if one agrees with Halfin that "because guilt in the Soviet Union was always a personal concept, the victim died not as an anonymous number but as a concrete individual convicted for specific actions,"[92] deterministic victimhood *did* become a state norm under Communism. Even the internal debates within the Bolshevik party ruling circles testify to this point.

In 1945, chief ideologue Andrei Zhdanov criticized automatic purges based on class origin: "The 'biological' approach to people is very widespread among us, when the existence of some not entirely 'convenient' relatives or other, frequently long dead, is made a criterion of the political loyalty of a worker. Such 'biologists,' producing their distinctive theory of 'inheritance,' try to look at living communists through a magnifying glass." Even Stalin, in the statement signaling his retreat from the Great Terror, admitted in 1938 the practice of indiscriminate mass purges (which at the time had harrowing consequences for those subjected to them): "It is time to understand that Bolshevik vigilance consists in essence in the ability to unmask the enemy regardless of how clever and cunning he may be, irrespective of how he adorns himself, and not in indiscriminate or 'on the off-chance' expulsions [from the party], by the tens and hundreds, of everyone who comes within reach."[93] The very notion of revolutionary vigilance treaded a thin line between exclusion and physical elimination. At the point of the radicalization of revolutionary utopia in action, the obsession of Lenin and Stalin (and for that matter other Communist dictators) with cleaning and purifying the "human garden," Communism's focus on excision, transmogrified into extermination.[94]

ARGUMENTS FOR COMPARISONS

As a matter of principle, the comparison between Nazism and Communism strikes me as both morally and scholarly justifiable, at least because we can see enough similar as well as dissimilar elements to justify such a comparison. To deny this comparison (which after all inspired one of the great works of political and moral philosophy of the twentieth century, Hannah Arendt's *Origins of Totalitarianism,* and was developed not by right-wingers but by such democratic socialists as the Mensheviks) is a proof of self-imposed intellectual narrow-mindedness.[95] Michael Scammell emphasized that "we cannot choose between our memory of Auschwitz and our memory of the Gulag, because history has mandated that we remember them both."[96] Scholars are not judges, and the confusion between these two roles can make some scholars oblivious to important distinctions. Comparison serves the work of understanding when it is used to highlight both similarities and differences.

François Furet insisted in his correspondence with Ernst Nolte that there is something absolutely evil in Nazi practice, both at the level of original intention and the implementation of utopian goals. This is not to minimize in any way the abominations of Communism, but simply to recognize that, comparable as the two mass horrors are, there is something truly singular about the Holocaust and the manic perfection and single-mindedness of the Nazi Final Solution. Nazi ideology was founded upon what historian Enzo Traverso called "redemptive violence." Its ethos merges anti-Semitism with "a 'religion of nature' based on blind faith in biological determinism to the point where *genocide itself came to represent both 'a disinfection, a purification—in short an ecological measure,' and a ritual act of sacrifice performed to redeem history from chaos and decadence* [my emphasis]."[97]

In the case of the Soviet Union, after the war on the peasants, the Stalinist repressive machine, especially during the Great Terror, attacked all social strata. This form of repression had a distinctive volatile and unpredictable character. Hysteria was universal and unstoppable. Any citizen could be targeted. From this point of view, one could argue that Stalinist terror was more inclusive, amorphous, but also porous because it represents *both* "the extreme penalization of types of social behavior" and victimization based on "political-ideological standards for rooting out deviant language and 'bad' class origins."[98] Starting with Lenin and worsening with Stalin, the comprehensive grasp of state violence in the USSR revealed "an instant readiness to declare war on the rest of society" (as Scammel says). The result was that, according to Nicolas Werth, one in five adult males passed through the gulag. Here, one should also keep in mind the post-1945 campaign against "female thieves" (in reality war widows) or the lowering of the age of criminal responsibility to twelve in 1935.

In Nazi Germany terror was unleashed mainly against minorities (Jews, Roma, the disabled, or gays) and foreign populations. In the Soviet Union, terror brought about two worlds: the Soviet social body, made up of politically validated people, and the gulag, with the party and its repressive institutions mediating between the two realms. While in Nazi Germany the regime sought "its victims mainly *outside* the *Volksgemeinschaft,* the Soviet populace was the main victim of its own regime." In other words, the war conducted by Stalin and the Leninist parties was internal, "a catastrophe ostensibly launched as a social upheaval, appropriating the idiom of class struggle and civil war."[99] Along similar lines,

Richard Overy provides an excellent definition of the gulag, which in his view "symbolizes the political corruption and hypocrisy of a regime formally committed to human progress, but capable of enslaving millions in the process."[100] The state-building Stalinist blueprint, the one that became the core of the "civilizational transfer" implied by exporting revolution or Sovietization, was "dialectically" bent on purification *and* inclusiveness. This paradox is best expressed by the contrast between the 1936 constitution's description of a society made up of "non-antagonistic classes" and Stalin's November 1937 call for eradicating not just the enemies of the people but also their "kith and kin."[101]

One can conclude that, in the Soviet Union at different stages, certain groups were indeed designated targets, but the exercise of terror applied to individuals of all social origins (workers, peasants, intellectuals, party and military cadres, former middle and high bourgeois, priests, even secret police officials). Soviet terror had a distinctly random character, for its sole purpose was the building of Communism through the total homogenization of society. Its rationale was the moral-political unity of the community. From this point of view, the violence inflicted on the population was ideologically functionalized. It never achieved the industrial scope of the Holocaust. It was, however, an end in itself. It was the other face of the Bolshevik regime's "modern agenda of *subjectivization.*" Those individuals who failed to become "conscious citizens engaged in the program of building socialism of their own will," those who failed to understand their obligations as members of "the first socialist state," those who erred in revolutionary vigilance, in other words "the failed hermeneuticists" of the great leap out of the empire of necessity became excess to the needs of the Soviet state. The Bolsheviks were interested in refashioning the human soul. The life of the individual could make sense only if it immersed itself in the "general stream of life" of the Soviet collective.[102] It is no surprise that, as Orlando Figes remarks, the Russian word for *conscience (sovest')* as a private dialogue with the inner self almost disappeared from official use after 1917. On October 26, 1932, Stalin described the full nature of the Bolshevik transformation: "Your tanks will be worth nothing if the soul *(dusha)* in them is rotten. No, the 'production' of souls is more important than the production of tanks."[103]

In the summer of 1937, at the height of the Great Terror, the output of the Bolshevik industry of souls was already on display: over 40,000 participants gathered for a physical culture parade on the Red Square entitled "The Parade of the Powerful Stalin *Breed [plemia]*" (my emphasis). At the end of the celebrations of the first decade of the existence of Fascist Italy, the newspaper *Gioventù fascista* gave an almost archetypical description of the totalitarian body politic: "With Fascism, a crowd has become a harmony of souls, a perfect fit of citizens actively participating in the great life of the State.... [T]his was a crowd with self-knowledge, aware of its obedience, its faith, and its fighting mettle, a crowd serene and secure, trusting in its Leader, in a State.... This was no faceless throng, but an image given shape and order by spirits educated in the epic of these new times; not an amorphous mass, but an amalgam of fresh values and intelligence."[104] The imagery employed by the Italian journalists would have surely been fitting for the rows of thousands of Soviet New Men and Women participating in the parade of the "powerful Stalin breed," expressing the joy of these crowds celebrating their happiness and fortune to be offspring of utopia made reality under the guidance of the beloved Helmsman *(Vozhd)*. What is striking in the passage, from the point of view of our discussion of Fascism and Communism, is the constancy of the signified despite the interchangeability of the key signifiers.

Even when it did not take on a directly exterminist profile (e.g., mass executions, death marches, and state-engineered starvation), Soviet terror took the form of forced labor whose economic utility was highly questionable. I disagree with Dan Diner on this point, for I consider that forced labor in the gulag had a primarily pedagogical and corrective character. In both Nazism and Stalinism, the camps fundamentally served an ideological function; all other aspects that could be assigned to them were epiphenomena to the ideological driving force of the two dictatorships.[105] In the Soviet Union, the labor camps were "a cultural model," a "peculiar wedding of discipline and representation," which ensured that those inside would be trained and those outside terrorized. Most importantly, this negative model of organization within the Communist space was employed for the structuring and disciplining of even positive social milieus, such as factories and universities.[106] Until 1956, the gulag was the blueprint of human management in the USSR. As Orlando Figes notes, it was "more than a source of labor for building projects like the White Sea Canal. It was itself a form of industrialization."[107] I would go even further: the gulag was the normative design at the basis of the Communist project of modernity, the original source of the misdevelopment brought about by *all* Soviet-type regimes.

Exploitation by the state had, indeed, its productive purpose, but it was a consequence and an extension of the institution of the camp and deportation site as places of anthropological transformation. It is true that "the Final Solution was a project annulling even what are broadly considered universally valid standards of self-preservation."[108] But I think it is misguided to force upon Communist terror qualifications on the basis of circumstances and utility while ignoring its purifying and standardizing motifs.[109] To paraphrase Timothy Snyder, Stalinism's project of self-colonization by mass terror was founded upon the indifference to individual human life. Stalinism and Nazism's terror were "built into the world view of each dictator and each dictatorship; it was essential to the system, not a mere instrument of control, and it was practiced at every level of society."[110] Under Communism mass murder became a certainty because of the inevitable violence resulting from the corroboration of the principle of the state *(gosudarstvennost)* and the struggle to create order out of what Leninist leaders perceived as *stikhiinost,* social chaos.[111]

Moreover, Timothy Snyder warns that if we single-mindedly focus on Auschwitz and the gulag, "we fail to notice that over a period of twelve years, between 1933 and 1944, some 12 million victims of Nazi and Soviet mass killing policies perished in a particular region of Europe, one defined more or less by today's Belarus, Ukraine, Poland, Lithuania, and Latvia."[112] Snyder, while stressing the singularity of Nazi atrocities, demonstrates what he calls "the absence of economics": "Although the history of mass killing has much to do with economic calculation, memory shuns anything that might seem to make murder appear rational. . . . What is crucial is that the ideology that legitimated mass death was also a vision of economic development. *If there is a general political lesson of the history of mass killing, it is the need to be wary of what might be called privileged development: attempts by states to realize a form of economic expansion that designates victims, that motivates prosperity by mortality* [my emphasis]."[113] In *Bloodlands* Snyder takes his point further. He argues, in his reassessment of the monstrous chasm generated by the exterminist policies of Stalinism and Nazism, for a revision of our premises for comprehending such cataclysm: "Fourteen million people were deliberately murdered by two regimes over twelve years. This is the moment that we have scarcely begun to understand let alone master."[114] During the twentieth century, "history had truly become a delinquent."[115] Snyder is right: the only solution to this pathology of modernity is "the ethical commitment to the individual." This is also the fundamental lesson of the revolutions of 1989, the legacy of dissidents like Leszek Kołakowski, Jan Patočka, Václav Havel, Jacek

Kuroń, Bronisław Geremek, Adam Michnik, János Kis, and George Konrád. That is exactly why I consider the revolutions of 1989 the end-point of the historical era ruled by utopia.

The most important conclusion to draw from the comparison of ter-ror dynamics in the two cases is that both regimes (radical Leninism or Stalinism and Nazism) were genocidal. Norman Naimark excellently describes this reality: "The two great tyrannies of the twentieth century simply share too much in common to reject out of hand attempts to clas-sify and order them in the history of political systems and genocide."[116] Analytical distinctions between them are certainly important, but their common contempt for the bourgeois state of law, human rights, and the universality of humankind, regardless of spurious race and class distinc-tions, is in my view beyond doubt. Any student of the "age of extremes" would have to acknowledge that Leninism contained all the political and ideological ingredients of the totalitarian order (the party's monopoly on power, ideological uniformity and regimentation, censorship, demoniza-tion of the "people's enemy," a besieged fortress mentality, secret police terror, concentration camps, and, no less important, the obsession with shaping the "New Man"). To paraphrase Dan Diner, Communism and National Socialism, because of the terrible crimes they committed, "em-bedded themselves in the memory of the twentieth century as twins of terror."[117]

For totalitarian experiments to be successful, terror and ideology are mandatory instruments for exerting power. A statement by Boris Sou-varine, the author of a path-breaking and still impressively valid biog-raphy of Stalin published in the mid-1930s, perfectly encapsulates the convergent nature of Communism and Fascism: "In the early years of the Russian Revolution, it was easy to put everything down to the idea of 'Slavic soul'; yet the events that were reputed to be exclusively Slavic phe-nomena have subsequently been witnessed in Italy and Germany. When the beast in man is unleashed, the same consequences are visible every-where, irrespective of whether the man in question is Latin, German, or Slav, however different he may appear on the surface."[118] The cold patho-logical rationality of the Nazi war on the Jews, including the use of mass murder technologies at Auschwitz and the other death factories, could not be anticipated by the Marxist apostate Boris Souvarine in this diag-nosis written in 1937. Nevertheless, he was right in regarding the strange blending of barbarism and derailed modernity in the ideological despo-tisms of the extreme Left and Right.

Again, comparing the two absolute disgraces of the twentieth century, the gulag and the Holocaust, often leads to misunderstandings and injured feelings among victims of one or another of these monstrosities. This is regrettable because, in all fairness, none of these experiences will ever be remembered enough. Yes, as Alain Besançon points out, there is a kind of *amnesia* regarding the Communist crimes, just as there is a *hypermnesia* in relation to the Shoah.[119] But as the French historian shows, this is not because there is an attempt by one group to monopolize the memory of suffering in the twentieth century. The origins of this phenomenon are to be sought after in the fact that Communism was often regarded as progressive, anti-imperialist, and, more important still, anti-Fascist. Communism knew how to pose as the heir to the Enlightenment, and many were duped by this rationalistic and humanistic pretense. So, in my view, the research agenda initially suggested by *The Black Book* presupposed a rethinking not only of Communism and Fascism but also of their opposites, anti-Fascism and anti-Communism. In other words, not all those who resisted Hitler were friends of democracy, and not all those who rebelled against Lenin, Stalin, Mao, or Castro were bona fide liberals. *The Black Book* forced many in France, Germany, the United States, and, if it need be recalled, East-Central Europe to admit that those "who told of the marvels of the Soviet Union served to legitimize the massacre of millions. . . . [They] fooled their own societies into seeing the millions of corpses as a great promise for a better future."[120] The uproar caused by *The Black Book* helped bring to the fore the need both for remembrance of Communism's crimes and for reassessment of the massive killing and dying perpetrated by so many regimes in the name of this ideology with the endorsement of those who preferred to keep their eyes and ears firmly shut.[121]

As far as the anamnesis of Leninist violence, one fundamental problem is that the subjects of trauma mostly belong to social categories rather than national, ethnic ones (as in the case of the Holocaust). This issue is directly connected with the difference discussed above: Communism was at war with its own society. Even under its most moderate avatars (Kádár's Hungary, Gorbachev's USSR, or contemporary China), when a section of society threatened the existence of the system, the repressive (quasi-terroristic) levers were activated to isolate and extirpate the "pest hole." Under the circumstances, Diner's framing of the dilemma is noteworthy: "The memory of 'sociocide,' class murder, is archived, not transmitted from one generation to another as is the case with genocide. . . . How can crimes that elude the armature of an ethnic, and thus long-term, memory be kept alive in collective remembrance? Can crimes perpetrated not in the name of a collective, such as the nation, but in the name of a social construction, such as class, be memorialized in an appropriate form?"[122] It was often the case that such a query was solved through the artificial creation of "ethnic armature." In the former Soviet bloc, Communism was sold as mainly a Russian import, while local leaders fell into a vaguely defined category of collaborators or "elements foreign to the nation." It was just a step from the last coinage to the rejuvenation of the old specter of *Zydokomuna*. But the crux of the problem is that, despite the efforts of Courtois and the other authors of the *Black Book,* a unitary death tool might be possible but a collective, transnational memory of Communism's crimes does not exist. In the early twenty-first century, through the various pan-European documents that have been adopted by the European Union or the Organisation for Security and Co-operation in Europe, the first steps in this direction have been made. The Leninist experiment (that is, the world Communist movement) dissolved into national narratives of trauma and guilt upon the ideology's extinction. Terror and mass murder seem to still keep Communist states separated in terms of both memory and history. And considerable challenges remain in integrating the massive trauma caused by Communist regimes into what we call today European history.

The problem is that most of the crimes are also crimes of *national* Communist regimes; that is to say, the gulag (I use the term here as a metaphor for all mass terror under Communism) is also a *fratricide.* Additionally, these regimes endured for more than a score of years, as they domesticized and entered into a post-totalitarian phase. How to measure accomplished lifetimes against stolen ones? One possible solution is to accept the fact that Leninism is *radical evil,* so that its crimes can be universally (or continentally) remembered and memorialized. This way, unilateral appropriation of trauma, ethnicization of terror, and collective silence can be prevented. Each individual case could maintain its specificities but would, at the same time, be part of a larger historical phenomenon, thus being assimilated to public consciousness. The authors of the *Black Book* condemned what they considered both an institutionalized and informal amnesia about the true nature of Communist regimes. Their accounts were supposed to provoke the necessary intimacy and ineffability for a sacralized memory of the gulag. Since then, some headway has been made along this path, but European identification with sites of its memory (in various countries) is still pending.[123] We should not forget that in 2000, in Stockholm, during the international conference on the Holocaust (commemorating fifty-five years since the liberation of Auschwitz), the participants stated that "the normative basis of a transnational political community is defined by exposing and re-membering inhuman barbarism, cruelty and unimaginable humiliation, which are unthinkable on the background of our collective existence." To paraphrase Helmut Dubiel, the traumatic contemplation of absolute hor-ror and of the total miscarriage of civility legitimizes an ethics that goes beyond the border of any individual state.[124]

To return to the *Black Book,* I wish to emphasize that the key point concerning its legacy is the legitimacy of the comparison between Na-tional Socialism and Leninism. I agree here with the Polish-French his-torian Krzysztof Pomian's approach:

> It is undeniable that mass crimes did take place, as well as crimes against humanity, and this is the merit of the team that put together *The Black Book:* to have brought the debate regarding twentieth century communism into public discussion; in this respect, as a whole, beyond the reservations that one can hold concerning one page or another, it has played a remarkable role. . . . To say that the Soviets were worse because their system made more victims, or that the Nazis were worse because they exterminated the Jews, are two positions which are unacceptable, and the debate carried on under these terms is shocking and obscene.[125]

Indeed, the challenge is to avoid any "comparative trivialization,"[126] or any form of competitive "martyrology" and to admit that, beyond the similarities, these extreme systems had unique features, including the ra-tionalization of power, the definition of the enemy, and designated goals. The point, therefore, is to retrieve memory, to organize understanding of these experiments, and to try to make sense of their functioning, meth-ods, and goals.

Some chapters of *The Black Book* succeed better than others, but as a whole the undertaking was justified. It was obviously not a neutral scholarly effort, but an attempt to comprehend some of the most haunt-ing moral questions of our times: How was it possible for millions of individuals to enroll in revolutionary movements that aimed at the en-slavement, exclusion, elimination, and finally extermination of whole categories of fellow human beings? What was the role of ideological hubris in these criminal practices? How could sophisticated intellectu-als like the French poet Louis Aragon write odes to Stalin's secret po-lice? How could Aragon believe in "the blue eyes of the revolution that burn with cruel necessity"? And how could the once acerbic critic of the

Bolsheviks, the acclaimed proletarian writer Maxim Gorky, turn into an abject apologist for Stalinist pseudoscience, unabashedly calling for experiments on human beings: "Hundreds of human guinea pigs are required. This will be a true service to humanity, which will be far more important and useful than the extermination of tens of millions of healthy human beings for the comfort of a miserable, physically, psychologically, and morally degenerate class of predators and parasites."[127] The whole tragedy of Communism lies within this hallucinating statement: the vision of a superior elite whose utopian goals sanctify the most barbaric methods, the denial of the right to life to those who are defined as "degenerate parasites and predators," the deliberate dehumanization of the victims, and what Alain Besançon correctly identified as the ideological perversity at the heart of totalitarian thinking—the falsification of the idea of good *(la falsification du bien)*.

I have strong reservations regarding theoretical distinctions on the basis of which some historians reach the conclusion that Communism is "more evil" than Nazism. In fact, they were both evil, even radically evil.[128] Public awareness of Communist violence and terror has been delayed by the durability of Leninism's pretense of universality. Because of projection, it took a long time to achieve an agreement that Bolshevism was not another path to democracy and that its victims were overwhelmingly innocent.[129] One cannot deny that Communism represented for many the *only* alternative (in my foreword I discuss a personal family example), especially with the rise of Fascism and of Hitler, at a time when liberal democracy seemed compromised.

Communism was consistently presented as synonymous with hope, but the dream turned into a nightmare: Communism "not only murdered millions, but also took away the hope."[130] Communism was founded upon "a version of a thirst for the sacred with a concomitant revulsion against the profane." The Soviet "Great Experiment's master narrative involves the repurification or resacerdotalization of space."[131] This is why Furet, in his closing remarks to *Passing of an Illusion,* states that upon the moral and political collapse of Leninism we "are condemned to live in the world as it is" (p. 502). With a significantly stronger brush, Martin Malia argued that "any realistic account of communist crimes would effectively shut the door on Utopia; and too many good souls in this unjust world cannot abandon hope for an absolute end to inequality (and some less good souls will always offer them 'rational' curative nostrums). And so, all comrade-questers after historical truth should gird their loins for a very Long March indeed before Communism is accorded its fair share of absolute evil."[132] And, indeed, two important registers of criticism directed toward the process of revealing and remembering the crimes of Communist regimes were that of anti-anti-utopianism and anticapitalism. I will not dwell on the validity of counterpoising Communism with capitalism; it is a dead end. It just reproduces the original Manichean Marxist revolutionary ethos of the *Communist Manifesto*. It is endearing to a certain extent, for one's beliefs should be respected, but it is irrelevant if we seek to understand the tragedy of the twentieth century. The employment of anti-anti-utopianism in the discussion of left-wing totalitarianism is just another way of avoiding the truth. To reject the legitimacy of the comparison between National Socialism and Bolshevism on the basis of their distinct aims is utterly indecent and logically flawed. Ian Kershaw criticizes arguments based on the

> different aims and intentions of Nazism and Bolshevism—aims which were wholly inhumane and negative in the former case and ultimately humane and positive in the latter case. The argument is based upon a deduction from the future (neither verifiable nor feasible) to the present, a procedure which in strict logic is not permissible. . . . The purely functional point that communist terror was "positive" because it was "directed towards a complete and radical change in society" whereas "fascist (i.e., Nazi) terror reached its highest point with the destruction of the Jews" and "made no attempt to alter human behavior or build a genuinely new society" is, apart from the debatable assertion in the last phrase, *a cynical value judgment on the horrors of the Stalinist terror* [my emphasis].[133]

Recognizing Communism as hope soaked in revolutionary utopia is truly a specter to turn away from. This hope materialized as radical evil can only lead to massacre, because "il cherche à s'incarner, et ce faisant, il ne peut faire autrement qu'éliminer ceux qui n'appartiennent pas à la bonne classe sociale, ceux qui résistent à ce projet d'espoir [it looks to take flesh, and doing this, it can only eliminate those who do not belong to the right social class, those who resist this project of hope]."[134] Ronald Suny was right in emphasizing that we should not forget that the original aspirations of socialism "were the emancipatory impulses of the Russian Revolution as well."[135] It is difficult to see how this affects the "duty of remembrance" regarding Leninism's crimes. Not to mention that, as early as 1918, with the Declaration of the Rights of Toiling and Exploited People, the Bolsheviks detailed their ideal of social justice into categories of disenfranchised people *(lishentsy)*, the prototype taxonomy for the terror that was to follow in the later years.[136] Tony Judt puts it bluntly: "The road to Communist hell was undoubtedly paved with good (Marxist) intentions. But so what? . . . From the point of view of the exiled, humiliated, tortured, maimed or murdered victims, of course, it's all the same."[137] Furthermore, such shameful commonalities between socialism and Bolshevism should actually be an incentive to call things by their real name when it comes to the radical evil that Communism in power was throughout the twentieth century. The hope that Bolshevism brought to so many was a lie. The full impact of the lie can only be measured by the nightmare of the millions it murdered. The moral and political bankruptcy of the "pure" original ideals cannot remain hidden just for the sake of safeguarding their pristine state. The uproar provoked by the *Black Book* indicated a "continuing reluctance to take at face value the overwhelming evidence of crimes committed by communist regimes."[138] So many years after the book's publication, some things have changed, but much more remains to be done. To return to Kołakowski's metaphor, the devil not only incarnated itself in history, it also wrecked our memory of it.

Beyond debates about how to remember, compare, and analyze Communism and Fascism, there is a bottom line that all can accept. Perhaps with minimal difficulty all can agree with Emilio Gentile's conclusion that "totalitarian experiments, even if they were imperfect and flawed, involved, conditioned, transformed, deformed and ended the existence of millions of human beings. In no uncertain terms, this was determined by the conviction of the principal protagonists that they were the forebears of a new humanity, the builders of a new civilization, the interpreters of a new truth, the repositories for the discrimination between good and evil, and the masters of the destinies of those caught up in their enterprise."[139] At the end of the day, reflecting on the "why" of the whole Communist experience, one needs to remember that Leninism emerged from the meeting between a certain direction of European revolutionary socialism, one that could in no way come to terms with the established liberal order and the rights of the individual, and the Russian tradition of conspiratorial violence. The mixture of revolutionary anticapitalism and ultranationalist German racism led to Hitler's chiliastic dreams of Aryan supremacy.[140] At a speech in the Berlin Sports Palace on February 10, 1933, Hitler formulated with religious fervor his "predestined mission" to resurrect the German nation: "For I cannot divest of my faith in my people, cannot dissociate myself from the conviction that this nation will one day rise again, cannot divorce myself from my love for this, my people, and I cherish the firm conviction that the hour will come at last in which the millions who despise us today will stand by us and with us will hail the new, hard-won and painfully acquired German Reich we have created together, the new German kingdom of greatness and power and glory and justice. Amen."[141] Similarly, Mussolini confessed in *My Autobiography* that "I felt the deep need for an original conception capable of bringing about a more fruitful rhythm of history in a new period of history. It was necessary to lay the foundation of a new civilization." Fascism for Mussolini was the solution to "the Spiritual Crisis of Italy."[142] The same frenzy for "a new temporality and nomos," alternative and opposite to that of liberal modernity, was also at the core of Communism. Such a sense of mission was apparent at the Congress of Victors (the Seventeenth Congress of the Communist Party of the Soviet Union) in January–February 1934, as the Soviet regime entered the second five-year plan and finalized the Cultural Revolution, after Stalin had murdered, starved, and deported millions of kulaks in Ukraine and forcibly resettled several ethnic groups, and as he consolidated his position as undisputed leader of the Bolshevik party. At such a "glorious moment," almost two and a half years before the beginning of the Great Terror, Politburo member Lazar Kaganovich praised Stalin as the creator "of the greatest revolution that human history has ever known."[143]

The plight of Communism's millions of victims (many of whom had once espoused the generous promises of the Marxian doctrine) cannot be explained without reference to the Leninist party and its attempt to forcibly impose the will of a small group of fanatics over reticent and more often than not hostile populations. Mikhail Bakunin put it most aptly in an angry letter disavowing Sergey Nechaev's apotheosis of destructive violence and psychological terrorism: "Out of that cruel renunciation and extreme fanaticism you now want to make a general principle applicable to the whole community. You want crazy things, impossible things, the total negation of nature, man, and society!"[144] Communism and Fascism believed that fundamental change was possible. They engineered radical revolutionary projects in order to answer this belief.[145] However, they enacted their utopias with complete disregard for individual human life. Their frantic acceleration of human development engendered the materialization of radical evil in history.

CHAPTER 2

Diabolical Pedagogy and the (*Il*)logic of Stalinism

I am too busy defending innocents claiming their innocence
to waste my time with guilty individuals claiming their guilt.

—Paul Éluard, refusing to sign a petition against the hanging of
Czech surrealist poet Zášvis Kalandra (in Stéphane Courtois,
The Black Book of Communism)

Lucreţiu Pătrăşcanu died as a soldier serving his political
ideals which he pursued through darkness, underground, and
palaces, tenaciously, fiercely and fanatically.

—Petre Pandrea, *Memoriile Mandarinului Valah* (Memoirs of
a Wallachian Mandarin)

With ascetic rigor towards itself and others, fanatical hatred
for enemies and heretics, sectarian bigotry and an unlimited
despotism fed on the awareness of its own infallibility, this
monastic order labors to satisfy earthly, too "human"
concerns.

—Semyon Frank, *Vekhi* (Landmarks)

It's not only the word "impossible" that has gone out of
circulation, "unimaginable" also has no validity anymore.

—Victor Klemperer, *I Will Bear Witness*

One of the main distinctions between the Nazi and Stalinist tyrannies
was the absence in Germany of permanent purges of the ruling party elite
as a mechanism of mobilization, integration, and scapegoating. In fact,

Slovene philosopher Slavoj Žižek is right to observe that there were no Moscow-style show trials in Hitler's Germany (or for that matter in Mussolini's Italy).[1] The explanation lies in the differences between the centrality of the charismatic party in Bolshevik regimes and the prevailing status of the leader in Fascist dictatorships. This is not say that the leader (whether Stalin, Mao, Mátyás Rákosi, Gheorghe Gheorghiu-Dej, Klement Gottwald, or Enver Hoxha) was not an omnipotent figure under Leninism, but his cultic power derived from the apotheosis of the party as the carrier of history's behests. The absence of show trials in Nazi Germany did not eliminate purges as a means to consolidate the Führer's power.[2] The Blomberg-Frisch affair, when Hitler entrenched his dominance over the army leadership, and the elimination of the Ernst Röhm SA faction during the Night of the Long Knives in 1934, were, according to Ian Kershaw, "stepping-stones in cementing Hitler's absolute power."[3]

In order to understand the dynamics of the Stalinist experiment in Eastern Europe, one must take into account the paramount role of direct Soviet intervention and intimidation.[4] Local Communist formations were pursuing the Stalinist model of systematic destruction of non-Communist parties, the disintegration of the civil society, and the monopolistic occupation of the public space through state-controlled ideological rituals and coercive institutions.[5] The overall goal was to build a passive consensus based on unlimited commitment to the ideocratic political program of the ruling elite. The true content of the political regime was described by the "cult of personality." Stalin, as the *Egocrat* (to use Solzhenitsyn's term), was the ultimate figure of power. Echoing earlier critiques of the Leninist vertical-authoritarian logic by Leon Trotsky and Rosa Luxemburg, French political philosopher Claude Lefort points out that this principle presupposed a specific "logic of identification": "Identification of the people with the proletariat, of the proletariat with the party, of the party with the leadership, of the leadership with the Egocrat. . . . The denial of social division goes hand in hand with the denial of a symbolic distinction which is constitutive of society."[6] The personalization of political power, its concentration in the hands of a demigod, led to his forcible religious adoration and the masochistic humiliation of its *subjects*. British journalist George Urban described this system as "a paranoia of despotism" that boasted its own (*il*)logic. It looks now and did then "like a form of madness to *us*, observing it as we are from the outside, but did not seem so to anyone identifying himself with the context in which Stalin operated. *Within* that context Stalin pursued his objectives relentlessly *and* rationally."[7] In the context of such absolute inversion of the life-world, Old Bolshevik Nikolai Bukharin's letter to Stalin on December 10, 1937, a few months before his public trial and execution as an "enemy of the people" in March 1938, can make sense. Bukharin, like Karl Radek, another Bolshevik luminary, was the proto-type of the character Nikolai Salmanovich Rubashov in Arthur Koestler's masterpiece *Darkness at Noon* (it was Radek who spoke of the "algebra of confession").[8] As historians J. Arch Getty and Oleg V. Naumov point out, "According to Stalin's formula, criticism was the same as opposition; opposition inevitably implied conspiracy; conspiracy meant treason. Algebraically, therefore, the slightest opposition to the regime or failure to report such opposition was tantamount to terrorism."[9]

Once Stalin's close friend and supporter, ousted under charges of "right-wing deviation" in 1929 and reinstated into the Central Committee in 1934, Bukharin had been described by Lenin in his "Testament" as the party's "favorite child."[10] He had bowed to Stalin's supremacy and was in fact one of the authors of the 1936 Stalinist Constitution. The same year, Bukharin traveled to Paris to retrieve the Marx-Engels Archive from the exiled German social democrats. In spite of old friends' warnings (among them veteran Mensheviks Fyodor Dan and Boris Nikolaevsky) that back in Moscow he would be arrested, Bukharin refused to remain abroad. He was imprisoned after the notorious February 1937 Central Committee Plenum when Stalin spelled out his theory of the sharpening of class struggle as the USSR advanced toward socialism. Bukharin was forced to publicly confess to surreal charges. However, he refused to acknowledge having participated in a plot to arrest Lenin in 1918. Stalin's outstanding biographer, Robert C. Tucker, best describes Bukharin's contradictory stance: "He pleaded guilty to 'the sum total of the crimes committed by this counter-revolutionary organization,' but thereupon suggested that not only did he not take part in but he even lacked knowledge of 'any particular act' involved."[11]

During the last days of his trial, Bukharin wrote a letter to Stalin. In it he claimed "personal intimacy" with the Soviet leader, actually reaffirming his unswerving faith in the party's vision of social utopia and the Bolshevik revolutionary cause. Furthermore, this love for the party translated into an almost neurotic desire to reassure Stalin of his unbending dedication to the infallible leader himself. This document (which Stalin kept in his personal drawer until his death in March 1953) bears testimony to the mystical underpinnings of the Bolshevik belief system and its reverberations in the interpersonal relations within the top party elite. It is therefore worth quoting extensively from Bukharin's letter:

This is perhaps the last letter I shall write to you before my death. That is why, though I am in prison, I ask you to permit me to write this letter without resorting to officialese [*ofitsial'shchina*], all the more so since I am writing this letter to you alone: the very fact of its existence or nonexistence will remain entirely in your hands. I have come to the last page of my drama and perhaps of my very life. I agonize over whether I should pick up pen and paper—as I write this, I am shuddering all over from this quiet and from a thousand emotions stirring within me and I can hardly control myself. But precisely because I have so little time left, I want to *take my leave* of you in advance, before it's too late, before my hand ceases to write, before my eyes close, while my brain somehow still functions. . . . Standing on the edge of a precipice, from which there is no return, I tell you on my word of honor, as I await my death, that I am innocent of those crimes which I admitted to at the investigation. . . . So at the Plenum I spoke the truth and *nothing but the truth* but no one believed me. And here now I speak the absolute truth: all these past years, I have been honestly and sincerely carrying out the party line and have learnt to cherish and love you wisely. . . . There is something *great and bold about the political idea* of a general purge. It is a) connected to the pre-war situation and b) connected with the transition to democracy. This purge encompassed 1) the guilty; 2) persons under suspicion; and 3) persons under potential suspicion. This business could not have been managed without you. Some are neutralized one way, others in another way, and the third group yet another way. . . . For God's sake, don't think that I am engaged here in reproaches, even in my inner thoughts. I wasn't born yesterday. I know all too well that *great* plans, *great* ideas, and *great* interests take precedence over everything, and I know that it would be petty to place the question of my own person *on a par* with the *universal-historical* tasks resting, first and foremost, on your shoulders. But it is here that I feel my *deepest* agony and find myself facing my chief, agonizing paradox. . . . My head is giddy with confusion, and I feel like yelling at the top of my voice. I feel like pounding my head against the wall: for, *in that case,* I have become a cause for the death of others. What am I to do? What am I to do? Oh, Lord, if only there were some device which would have made it possible for you to see my soul flayed and reaped open! If only you could see how I am attached to you, body and soul. . . . Well, so much for "psychology"—forgive me. No angel will appear now to snatch Abraham's sword from his hand. My fatal destiny shall be fulfilled . . . Iosif Vissarionovich! In me you have lost one of your most capable generals, one who is genuinely devoted to you . . . but I am preparing myself mentally to depart from this vale of tears, and there is nothing in me toward all of you, toward the party and the cause, but a great and boundless love. I am doing everything that is humanly possible and impossible. . . . I have written to you about all this. I have crossed all the t's and dotted all the i's. I have done all this in *advance,* since I have no idea at all what condition I shall be in tomorrow and the day after tomorrow, etc. . . . Being a neurasthenic I shall perhaps feel such universal apathy that I won't be able even so much as to move my finger. But now, in spite of a headache and with tears in my eyes, I am writing. My conscience is clear before you now, Koba. I ask you one final time for your forgiveness (only in your heart, not otherwise). For that reason I embrace you in mind. Farewell forever and remember kindly your wretched. N. Bukharin[12]

Bukharin's letter can be taken at face value or with a grain of salt. He obviously was trying to save his young wife and child; the letter was a last desperate attempt in this sense. Such an argument does not, however, explain the exaltation in the letter. Bukharin died as a true believer committed to achieving Bolshevik utopia. Furthermore, it is still questionable if he perceived his death as a last service made to the party, as suggested by Koestler's *Darkness at Noon*. Stephen E. Cohen, Bukharin's quite empathetic biographer, considered that he wanted to protect "Bolshevism's historical legacy by refuting the criminal indictment" rather than accepting it.[13] Robert C. Tucker argued for a more nuanced reading of Bukharin's transcript: "Bukharin thus had a twofold objective in the trial—to comply with Stalin by confessing and at the same time to turn the tables on him. He wants to make two trials in one." According to Tucker, "there was an active effort on Bukharin's part to transform the trial into an anti-trial. The fight he put up against Vyshinsky was entirely dedicated to this purpose."[14] Undoubtedly Bukharin, in his final public appearance, was trying to make a last political statement against Stalin and the system the latter had created. One should not forget that during a fateful meeting of the Central Committee on February 23, 1937, Bukharin warned Stalin that "I am not Zinoviev or Kamenev, and I will not tell lies about myself." After this event, he wrote a letter entitled "To a Future Generation of Party Leaders," which he asked his wife to memorize, in which he ominously noted, "I feel my helplessness before a hellish machine, which . . . has acquired gigantic power, fabricates organized slander, acts boldly and confidently." He then accused Stalin: "By political terrorism, and by acts of torture on a scale hitherto unheard of, you have forced old Party members to make 'depositions.'"[15]

All things considered, the case of Bukharin cannot be read solely as the heroic tale told by Cohen or as Koestler's self-immolation *only* in service of the party. What remains is a paradox: on the hand, Bukharin was committed to the Bolshevik cause while knowing full well Stalin's "theory of sweet revenge";[16] on the other hand, his letter to Stalin reveals that he preserved an uncanny attachment to his former ally and friend.

Upon being devoured by the utopia that he had helped build, his last moments were a mixture of obedience, opportunism, fear, and most important, faith. Last but not least, Cohen's and Tucker's interpretations of his last stand at the trial were formulated *without* any knowledge of Bukharin's letter to Stalin.

Bukharin, however, was not the only case of faith in the party and the Communist cause in the face of an impending exterminatory purge. In June 2010, I delivered a lecture in Bucharest on secular religions and totalitarian movements, focusing on the meanings of purges and show trials. I quoted extensively from Bukharin's letter. Immediately after I finished my presentation, a Romanian historian approached me and mentioned the existence in the National Council for the Study of the Securitate Archives of a strikingly similar letter addressed to the party by veteran communist Mirel Costea (Nathan Zaider), head of the Party Cadres Department, before he committed suicide during the heyday of Stalinist terror in Romania (June 1951). Costea's brother-in-law, engineer Emil Calmanovici, had been one of the Romanian Communist Party's main financial backers during the underground years. Closely associated with people involved in the Lucreţiu Pătrăşcanu affair, he was arrested and charged with treason. Having to choose between the "objective" logic of his unflinching devotion to the party and his subjective understanding of Calmanovici's innocence, Costea decided to take his own life. In his last massage to his comrades, Costea wrote:

> A communist must maintain faith in the Party and must be the happiest person in the world when he feels that a Party trusts him. I was happy, I enjoyed the Party's trust and I say that I deserved it because I did not mislead the Party. Since 1939, I had no other life than for the Party. I hated and I hate the enemies of the working class, its traitors. . . . I cannot bear the thought that the Party lost its trust in me. For this reason I kiss my Party card which I have never sullied before I had it in this form of hereafter. I give in to the Party. I thank the Party for the trust showed to me up to a certain moment. This [committing suicide] is not the gesture of the communist, I have not learned these gestures from the Party, it is a leftover of bourgeois education and morality. I would have been able to bear tortures in the cells of the *Siguranta* [interwar Romanian political police], but I cannot bear the agony that I have lost the trust of my Party. My last thought goes to comrade Stalin, to the Central Committee of the Romanian Workers' Party, to comrade Gheorghiu-Dej.

I also found in the Securitate archives Mirel Costea's last letter to his daughters, Rodica and Dana, written a few minutes before he shot himself:

Your daddy, whom you have loved and who has loved you apologizes that he needs to leave. When you grow older you will understand that the most precious good for an honest human being is to enjoy the trust of the Party. Until recently I have enjoyed this trust; until recently, and this is something I cannot bear. My life has been for the Party, without its trust it has no meaning. I beg you to live well and to love each other as we have loved you, me and your mother. Keep in mind that your father was an honest man, faithful to the Party. However, if you ever find out that the Party thinks differently about me, then you should believe what the Party says. Your mother will take care of you and will educate you in the spirit of love for comrade Stalin, for the USSR, for our Party, for the beloved leaders of our Party, as I have educated you.[17]

The symbolic vehicle for this moral and political regimentation was the Stalinist definition of internationalism as unbounded allegiance to the USSR (the "touchstone theory"). To keep strict control over all mechanisms that guaranteed social reproduction and preserved the matrix of domination in such a system, the party had to play the central role. Based on my research in the Romanian Communist Party's archives, it appears that no segment of the body social, economic, or cultural, as well as no repressive institution, escaped continuous and systematic party intervention. Even during the climactic terrorist period (1948–53), the secret police served as the party's obedient instrument and not the other way around. Indeed, as one scholar stated, "The USSR, in other words, did not keep two sets of books, at least on ideological questions."[18] Ideological purity and revolutionary vigilance were imposed as main political imperatives. Political police, cast in the Soviet mold and controlled by Soviet advisers, took care to fulfill the ideological *desiderata*. The political content of that ideological dictatorship in its radical incarnation (the first five years) was sheer terror and permanent propaganda warfare waged within a personalized dictatorship embodied by local "little Stalins."

What these countries experienced was not merely an institutional import or imperial expansion. They went through what one could label, using Stephen Kotkin's formulation, a "civilizational"[19] transfer that transplanted a secular eschatology (Marxism-Leninism), a radical vision of the world (capitalist encirclement and the touchstone theory of proletarian internationalism[20] spelled out by Stalin in the 1920s), and ultimately, an alternative idea of modernity (based upon anticapitalism and state-managed collectivism) self-identified as infallibly righteous—in other words, Stalinism. Kotkin's characterization of Stalinism as civilization comes very close to the comparison by Anthony Stevens, a Jungian analyst, to National Socialism. According to Stevens, "Nazism had its

Messiah (Hitler), its Holy Book *(Mein Kampf),* its cross (the Swastika), its religious processions (the Nuremberg Rally), its ritual (the Beer Hall Putsch Remembrance Parade), its anointed elite (the SS), its hymns (the 'Horst Wessel Lied'), excommunication for heretics (the concentration camps), its devils (the Jews), its millennial promise (the Thousand Year Reich), and its Promised Land (the East)."[21] Both Stalinism and Nazis were radical, revolutionary civilizations that aimed at establishing an alternative, illiberal modernity by instrumentalizing the political religion that lay at their core.

Stalinism was a self-sufficient, pre-established plan to restructure society, in the name of which the movement dispensed with as many human lives as needed while frantically engineering radical transformation.[22] The personality cult (and the growing Russianization of the Stalinist system during and after World War II) combined with the intrinsic and increasingly orthodox outlook of Communism (as "a lived system")[23] exacerbated the exclusionary logic in the "people's democracies." As in the Soviet Union, in Eastern Europe Stalinism itself was the revolution:[24] it broke through the already frail structures of the ancien régime and laid the groundwork of state socialism in each of the region's countries. It created an all-pervasive party-state that tried and in most cases succeeded in extending its tentacles into all walks of life.[25] In the words of the director of the French Institute in Tallinn, Jean Cathala, in 1940 the process of Sovietization meant "the incorporation into another world: into a world of institutions, of practices and ways of thinking, that had to be accepted as a bloc, because the spiritual and the temporal, doctrine and the state, the regime and methods of government, the homeland and the party in power were all mixed together in it."[26]

At the same time, Sovietization was "part of an imperialist conception, whereby a system of domination and subjugation was effected and rationalized, and whereby a subaltern identity was ascribed to the subjected peoples."[27] The main weakness of this system, however, was its chronic deficit of legitimacy. Under mature Stalinism, both in the Soviet Union and in Eastern Europe, autocratic despotism ruined the functioning of the party as an autonomous institution, its potential for "charismatic impersonalism" inherent in Leninism as an organizational model. This phenomenon explains the neotraditionalist features of Stalinism. If one follows Ken Jowitt's argument, the mutation of the definition of revolutionary heroism (initially belonging to the party, but now the prerogative of one) cancelled the fundamental characteristic of novelty in Leninism as an ideo-political form of aggregation.[28] In this monolithic structure dominated by the revolutionary phalanx, plans to reshape man, nature, and society were frantically pursued. Stalinism as a political religion overturned traditional morality: good and evil, vice and virtue, truth and lie were drastically revalued. The goal was to create a system that unified victim and torturer, that abolished traditional moral taboos and established a different code, with different prescriptions and prohibitions. The dramaturgy of show trials with their "infernal pedagogy" (Annie Kriegel) was the main component of a system based on universal fear, duplicity, and suspicion.

The "oceanic feeling," the ecstasy of solidarity, the desire to dissolve one's autonomy into the mystical supra-individual entity of the party, aptly described by Arthur Koestler, was the emotional ground for a chiliastic type of revolutionary commitment.[29] In his conversations with Czesław Miłosz, Polish poet Aleksander Wat formulated a memorable evaluation of the phenomenon: "Communism is the enemy of interiorization, of the inner man. . . . But today we know what exteriorization leads to: the killing of the inner man, and that is the essence of Stalinism. The essence of Stalinism is the poisoning of the inner man so that it becomes shrunken the way headhunters shrink heads—those shriveled little heads—and then disappears entirely. . . . The inner man must be killed for the communist Decalogue to be lodged in the soul."[30] Community, defined in terms of class, was the antipode of the execrated petty egotism of the bourgeois individual. The self had to be denied in order to achieve real *fraternité*. Generations of Marxist intellectuals hastened to annihilate their dignity in this apocalyptical race for ultimate certitudes. The whole heritage of Western skeptical rationalism was easily dismissed in the name of the revealed light emanating from the Kremlin. The age of reason was thus to culminate in the frozen universe of quasi-rational terror. Paradoxically, in the aftermath of World War II, Georg Lukács, a paragon of Marxist philosophy and staunch supporter of Bolshevism, wrote a whole treatise accusing Western philosophy of having abandoned humanist traditions in favor of an overall attempt to destroy Reason.[31]

The subject, the human being—totally ignored at the level of philosophical discourse—was eventually abolished as a physical entity in the vortex of the "great purges." Historian Jochen Hellbeck accurately remarked in his analysis of diaries during Stalinism that "an individual living under the Bolshevik system could not conceivably formulate a notion of himself independently of the program promulgated by the Bolshevik state. An individual and the political system in which he lived cannot be

viewed as two separate entities."[32] These images were more than metaphors, since metaphor suggests an ineffable face of reality, whereas what
happened under Stalin was awfully visible and immediate. Even those
diarists who were targets of political campaigns or whose close relatives
were victims of the purges tried to align their thought with the official
line:

> Stalin-era diarists' desire for a purposeful and significant life reflected a
> widespread urge to ideologize one's life, to turn it into the expression of a
> firm, internally consistent, totalizing *Weltanschauung*. . . . The regime was
> thus able to channel strivings for self-validation and transcendence that
> emerged outside the ideological boundaries of Bolshevism. In this light, the
> Soviet project emerges as a variant of a larger European phenomenon of the
> inter-war period that can be described as a two-fold obligation for a per-
> sonal world view and for the individuals' integration into a community. . . .
> The power of the Communist appeal, which promised that those who had
> been slaves in the past could remold themselves into exemplary members of
> humanity, cannot be overestimated.[33]

Under Stalin, the process of establishing one's identity was fundamentally conditioned by the party-state's project of radical transformism.

It can be hardly denied that Fascist and Communist regimes were the
antithesis of the Western humanist legacy. In the words of Hungarian
critical Marxist philosopher Ferenc Fehér, the all-embracing telos of
Nazism was "universal conquest which can only conclude either in a
collective of the 'race' or in the irrelevance of the objective itself when
the conquest becomes truly universal." As for the characteristics of the
Communist bestiarum, Fehér listed the following: the everyday drab-
ness of the gulag, the moblike rudeness of its personnel, rudeness as a
general atmosphere, a false kind of atheism, and the Jacobin element.
Writes Fehér:

> It is a strange dialectic that many refined aspects of the Jacobin project serve
> as a foundation of the outright animal indifference of the bestiarum. The
> first of them is the legitimation of all inhuman acts in the name of the "fu-
> ture generations," whose happiness is allegedly at sake. This is a good anti-
> dote against the vestiges of a personal conscience. The second is the collec-
> tive moral slandering of the enemy: belonging to a non-accepted group
> becomes here a sin which also has the useful side-effect of eliminating the
> remnants of Christian compassion. . . . The extension of the bestiarum in
> "real socialism" cannot be reasonably reduced to the scope of the Gulag
> proper. The culture created by Stalin, attenuated but left fundamentally un-
> altered by his heirs and successors, is barbaric precisely in the sense that in it
> there is no line of demarcation between the bestial and the non-bestial. . . .
> Therefore it is not accidental that the only cultural creation in this society

has been coming for decades now only from dissidents who are writing about the bestiarum and whose outraged question is precisely this: what have you done to our people?[34]

At the same time, François Furet and Pierre Hassner were right to emphasize the nature of Leninism/Stalinism as pathology of universalism, a derailed *(devoyé)* offspring of the Enlightenment. Naturally, it would be preposterous to restrict ourselves to mere ethical condemnation. But it would not be by any means commendable to gloss over the moral implications of Stalinism or, echoing a famous essay by the young Georg Lukács, the dilemmas of "Bolshevism as a moral problem." It is important, when pondering the fate of Marxism in the twentieth century, to grasp the split of personalities, the clash between lofty ideals and palpable practices, the methods of the Stalinist terrorist pedagogy in its endeavor to produce a new type of human being whose loyalties and beliefs would be decreed by the party. The revenge of history on its worshippers—thus could be depicted the terrorist psychosis of the Stalinist massacres. To quote sociologist Alvin W. Gouldner's perceptive interpretation, "The central strategy of the Marxist project, its concern with seeking a remedy to *unnecessary* suffering, was thus in the end susceptible to a misuse that betrayed its own highest avowals. The root of the trouble was that this conception of its own project redefined pity. . . . The human condition was rejected on behalf of the historical condition."[35]

As Koestler once pointed out (in his 1938 letter of resignation from the exiled German Communist Writers' Union), for Lenin it was not enough to smash his enemy—he wanted to make him look contemptible. László Rajk, Lucrețiu Pătrășcanu, Rudolf Slánský, Ana Pauker, Vladimir Clementis, Traicho Kostov, Bedřich Geminder, Artur London, Rudolf Margolius—all of them had to be portrayed as despicable scoundrels and scurrilous vermin. Yesterday's heroes had become today's scum.[36] To a certain extent, Robert C. Tucker is right to point out that "the show trials of 1936–1938 . . . for Stalin were a dramatization of his conspiracy view of the Soviet and contemporary world. . . . The Stalinist terror was in large part an expression of the needs of the dictatorial personality of Stalin, and these needs continued to generate the terror as long as he lived."[37] However, at the core of Lenin's vision of a new society lay an exterminist ethos. Bukharin, whom Cohen labeled the "last Bolshevik" and who considered himself the true heir of Lenin, emphasized in his volume *Economics of the Transition Period,* published in 1920, that "proletarian coercion in all of its forms, beginning with shooting and ending with labor conscription, is . . . a method of creating communist mankind out of the human materials of the capitalist epoch." By the beginning of the 1930s, Bukharin had shifted to a theory of "growing into socialism." However, as he had wisely been warned by Trotsky, "The system of apparatus terror cannot come to a stop only at the so-called ideological deviations, real or imagined, but must inevitably spread throughout the entire life and activities of the organization."[38] The Great Terror might have been Stalin's doing and might have reflected his "warfare personality" (as Tucker argues), but the principle of widespread excisionary violence against those opposed or alien to dictatorship of the proletariat was encoded at the heart of Leninism.

Especially after 1951, Stalinist anti-Western, anti-intellectual, and anti-Titoist obsessions merged with an increasingly rabid anti-Semitism:

> Stalin feared that other peace champ countries would follow the independent Yugoslav model and break away from the influential sphere of the Soviet Union. He instigated the terror of political trials to uncover "enemies" within each Communist Party in order to discourage dissent. Victims were sought out and accused of connection with Tito's opposition attitudes and treachery. In later cases, the Soviets turned to Zionism and its supposed link with Western imperialism as the cause of the Communist betrayal. The show trial was a propaganda arm of political terror. Its aim was to personalize an abstract political enemy, to place it in the dock in flesh and blood and, with the aid of a perverted system of justice, to transform abstract political-ideological differences into easily intelligible common crimes. It both incited the masses against the evil embodied by defendants and frightened them away from supporting any potential opposition.[39]

Among the East European Stalinist legal frame-ups, the Slánský trial in Prague, in the fall of 1952, symbolized the ultimate conversion of Bolshevism into an emerging version of Communist-Fascism. The selection of the defense (eleven of the fourteen were prominent Communists of Jewish descent); the vicious brutality of the interrogations, which included crude anti-Semitic slurs; the hysterical anti-Zionist media campaigns in Czechoslovakia and the other Communist countries; the rabidly racist indictment uttered by the chief prosecutor, Josef Urválek; the direct involvement of Stalin's envoys in the concoction of this mega-provocation—all these elements conjured up an unprecedented chain of broken illusions, bitter vendettas, and betrayed loyalties. In the words of Artur London, one of three survivors of the trial and a veteran of the Spanish Civil War and the French anti-Nazi *maquis*, who was at the moment of his arrest in 1951 deputy foreign minister of Czechoslovakia: "Every physical and moral torture was carried to an extreme. I had been forced to walk on continuously. . . . [I]t went on for months, and was made all the worse by my having to keep my arms to my sides. My feet and legs became swelled. The skin round my toenail burst, and the blisters became suppurating wounds."[40] The son of Margolius, one of the defendants, imagines his father's thoughts the night before the trial opened at the High Court in Pankrác on November 20, 1952:

> Rudolf recalled reading Søren Kierkegaard's *The Concept of Anxiety* written in 1844, where the great philosopher stated: "The individual becomes guilty not because he is guilty but because of his anxiety about being thought guilty." Rudolf felt it was his duty to perform as demanded; he was not guilty but the Party asked him to support it in its hour of need . . . ironically it was exactly like Koestler's *Darkness at Noon,* which [Pavel] Tigrid [a major figure of the Czech democratic exile] had lent him. [Karol] Bacilek [the Stalinist minister of state security, 1952–53] sounded like Gletkin, who told Rubashov: "Your testimony at the trial will be the last service you can do to the party." The Party denied the free will of the individual—and at the same time, exacted his will in sacrifice. Except all that had been fiction: Rudolf was in the real world.[41]

On the second day of the Slánský trial, Bedřich Geminder, a former Comintern official and chief of the International Department of the Czechoslovak Communist Party, was subjected to unspeakable deprecations linked to his German-Jewish origin:

Judge Novák: "What nationality are you?"

Defendant Geminder: "Czech"

Judge Novák: "Can you speak Czech well?"

Defendent Geminder: "Yes."

Judge Novák: "Do you want an interpreter?"

Defendant Geminder: "No."

. . .

Prosecutor Urválek: ". . . you never really learned to speak Czech well, not even in 1946 when you came back to Czechoslovakia and occupied important posts in the Communist Party?"

Defendent Geminder: "No, I didn't learn to speak Czech properly."

. . .

Prosecutor Urválek: "You cannot really speak any language properly, can you? You are a typical cosmopolitan. As such you sneaked into the Communist Party."[42]

"Rootless cosmopolitanism" was a Stalinist code word, a counterpart to Julius Streicher's vicious anti-Semitic propaganda. The vilified Geminder, born into a German-Jewish family in Moravia in 1901, had joined a Zionist youth group before he became a member of the Communist Party in 1921. In 1928, he was elected to the Executive Committee of the Communist International of Youth (KAM). Following the Munich Pact of 1938, Geminder moved to the Soviet Union, where he joined the Comintern as head of its Press and Information Service under the nom de guerre G. Friedrich.[43] For his revolutionary services he was given the Order of Lenin. He was married to Irene Falcon, a Spanish Communist and personal secretary to the general secretary of the Spanish Communist Party, the legendary Dolores Ibarruri, la *Passionaria*.[44] Sentenced to death on November 27, 1952, Geminder was shot on December 3. On March 6, 1953, Stalin passed away.[45]

The magic impact of power in classical Stalinism would have been unthinkable in the absence of ideology. They feed each other; power derives its mesmerizing force from the seductive potential of ideology. Man is proclaimed omnipotent, and ideology supervises the identification of abstract man with concrete power. Veneration of power is rooted in contempt for traditional values, including those associated with the survival of reason. It is important, therefore, to resist the temptation of critical thought, since reason is the enemy of total regimentation. To quote one of Stalin's most important (and vicious) accomplices, Lazar Kaganovich, "Treachery in politics always begins with the revision of theory."[46] In one of his late aphorisms, Max Horkheimer hinted at the philosophical revolution provoked by Marxism. Defending the dignity of the individual subject becomes a seditious undertaking, a challenge to the prevailing myth of homogeneity: "However socially conditioned the individual's thinking may be, however necessarily it may relate to social questions, to political action, it remains the thought of the individual which is not just the effect of collective processes but can also take them as its object."[47] Political shamanism, practiced by alleged adversaries of mysticism, thwarts attempts to resist the continual assault on the mind. Marxism-Leninism, which was the code name for the ideology of the *nomenklatura,* aimed to dominate both the public and private spheres of social life. Man, both as an individual and as a *citoyen,* had to be massified. The cult of violence and the sacralization of the infallible party line created totally submissive subjects for whom any crime ordered by the upper echelons was justified in the name of "glowing tomorrows." Like the ideologically driven Eichmann, Stalin's "willing executioners" acted on the base of what Hannah Arendt called "thoughtlessness."[48]

A climate of fear is needed to preserve monolithic unity. To cement this frail cohesion, the Stalinist "warfare personality" contrived the diabolical figure of the traitor: "The characteristically paranoid perception of the world as an arena of deadly hostilities being conducted conspiratorially by an insidious and implacable enemy against the self finds highly systematized expression in terms of political and ideological symbols that are widely understood and accepted in the given social milieu. Through a special and radical form of displacement of private affects upon public objects, this world-image is politicized. In the resulting vision of reality, both attacker and intended victim are projected on the scale of large human collectivities."[49] In René Girard's sense, scapegoating[50] fed a utopia freed of exploitation, antagonism, and the imperative of necessity. The origin of this exclusionary logic is of course Lenin's combatant, intransigent Manichaeism, us versus them, who will get rid of whom *(kto kogo).*[51] Or, to return to Bukharin's 1920 volume, *Economics of the Transition Period,* revolutionary force is "midwife" to the transition from the ancien régime to the new order: "[It] must destroy the fetters on the development of society, i.e., on one side, the old forms of 'concentrated force,' which have become a counterrevolutionary factor—the old state and the old type of production relations. This revolutionary force, on the other side, must actively help in the formation of production relations, being a new form of 'concentrated force,' the state of the new class, which acts as the lever of economic revolution, altering the economic structure of society."[52] For Bukharin, as for Lenin or Stalin, "the dismantled social layers" of the old were recombined by a proletarian state through the etatization, militarization, and mobilization of the production forces. Subsequently, the author of *The ABC of Communism* concluded that "the process of socialization in *all of its forms* [my emphasis]" was "the function of the proletarian state."[53] As already shown, in the process of eliminating the ambivalences of the Soviet society, the Bolsheviks introduced indiscriminate state violence in the functions of the proletarian state. Terror was a central mechanism of *ordering* the new polity.

Who are the enemies? Where do they come from? What are their purposes? Providing answers to these questions was the main function of the show trials. Maintaining vigilance, stigmatizing the presumed villains, and preserving the psychology of universal anguish were the tasks Stalin assigned to the masterminds of successive purges. No fissures were admitted in the Bolshevik shield, no doubt could arise that did not conceal mischievous ploys aimed at undermining the system. Time and again the refrain was repeated by spineless sycophants: we are surrounded by sworn enemies, we are invincible only inasmuch as we stay united. Expressing dissenting views necessarily meant weakening the revolutionary avant-garde. Breaking ranks was considered a mortal sin, and suspiciousness was the ultimate revolutionary virtue. In fact, when acquiescence is the golden rule, it takes great moral courage to rebel. In the homogenous space of totalitarian domination, opposition amounted to crime and opponents were treated as mere criminals. They incarnated difference and were therefore seen as outcasts. Ostracism led ultimately to mental emancipation, the autonomy of the mind acquired by Aleksandr Solzhenitsyn's *zeks*, the population of Stalin's gulag. The barbed wire was thus the symbol of a new kind of boundary between absolute victims and relative accomplices of evil. The whole tragedy of Communism lies in this hallucinating statement: the vision of a superior elite whose utopian goals sanctify the most barbaric methods; the denial of the right to life to those who are defined as "degenerate parasites and predators," the deliberate dehumanization of victims.

The image of man as a mechanism, put forward by French philosophes, found its strange echo in this all-pervading technology of socially oriented murder. This was the acme of radical utopianism, when nothing could resist the perpetual motion of foul play. Marxist eschatology was imposed through Stalinist demonology. The purge functioned as a panopticon where sinners and their secrets came into the open. It was a ritual of self-deprecation and ultimate submission to the party's sacrosanct will. Criticism and self-criticism were party rituals of *certitudo salutis* for the inner-worldly vocation of its members: "The party appeared as a *panopticon* which could discover at 'open meetings of the nuclei' the 'moral corruption and discreditable conduct on the part of Party members. The required self-criticism and criticism of the party cadres was used as medium to reach their inner conscience, and therefore to convert and to convince them to show self-discipline and 'self-sacrificing work for the benefit of communism.'"[54] Within this construct, morality was defined in terms of loyalty to a sense of ultimate historical transcendence. Igal Halfin eminently presented the process by which, through cyclical purges in the Soviet Union (one can consider their embryonic stage as 1920–21), Marxist eschatology morphed into a demonology that reached its discursive, exacerbated, and criminal maturity with the Second Socialist Transformation triggered by the *pyatiletka* unleashed to build socialism in one country.[55] Public discourse was saturated with frightening images of deviators, heretics, spies, agents, and other scoundrels. By the mid-1930s, one can see under Stalinism a process that bears a strong resemblance to terror practices under Nazism: "the desubjectification of the victim" became "a programmed precondition for his/her victimization, a precondition enabling the perpetrator's enactment of the narrative program of extermination."[56] A phenomenology of treason was devised to justify carnage, and there was no paucity of intellectuals to support this morbid scenario. In other words, perpetrators successfully defined victims in their own terms. A lingering sentiment that there was after all something moral in Bolshevik utopianism, plus the exploitation of anti-Fascist emotions, led to a persistent failure to acknowledge the basic fact that from its inception Sovietism was a criminal system.

In Stalin's mind the purges were means of political consolidation and authority-building, a springboard for newcomers and time-servers. They would secure the human basis for effective control over society. One of the foremost biographers of Stalin commented on the function and consequences of the Great Purge: "He wanted to achieve an unrestricted personal dictatorship with a totality of power that he did not yet possess. . . . Emerging from the events of 1936–38 as a personal dictator in what was now a truly totalitarian system of power, Stalin had achieved the international political purpose of the Great Purge."[57] In one of his most poignant essays, published before World War II in *Partisan Review,* Phillip Rahv put forward a thorough interpretation of the mechanism that led to the "great terror": "These are trials of the mind and of the human spirit. . . . In the Soviet Union, for the first time in history, the individual has been deprived of every conceivable means of resistance. Authority is monolithic: property and politics are one. Under the circumstances it becomes impossible to defy the organization; to set one's will against it. One cannot escape it: not only does it absorb the whole of life but it also seeks to model the shapes of death."[58] Without the purges the system would have looked radically different. Both victims and beneficiaries of the murderous mechanism were lumped together by this sacrificial ritual. For some of the Bolshevik militants liquidated or deported during the great purge, the terrorist ordeal amounted to *necessary* self-deprecation and self-abasement. Moreover, it was an opportunity to attain the long-expected absolution for those moments of "derailment" when they had dared to oppose Stalin. Zbigniew Brzezinski synthetically listed long ago the main objectives of the purge: "The cleansing of the party, the restoration of its vigor and monolithic unity, the elimination of enemies, and the establishment of the correctness of its line and the primacy of the leadership."[59] An entire phenomenology of mystical servility came about in the process of massacring society, and it was irresponsibly (and enthusiastically) reproduced by many intellectuals who had accepted this emasculation of their critical faculties. Residual hopes for elusive crumbs of morality within the Communist utopia combined with a Machiavellian exploitation of anti-Fascist sentiment led to a tragic failure to acknowledge the criminal nature of the Soviet experiment. Still, one needs to mention those who saw the reality and refused to remain silent. Among these voices of lucidity, one should mention Panait Istrati, Boris Souvarine, Ignazio Silone, Carlo Roselli, George Orwell, and other intellectuals who challenged the Big Lie.[60]

The problem with Leninism was the sanctification of ultimate ends, and thus the creation of an amoral universe in which the most terrible crimes could be justified in the name of a radiant future. In practice, the elimination of politics seemed a logical terminus, for the party was the embodiment of an extremist collective will.[61] This fixation on ends and the readiness to use the most atrocious means to attain them are features of many ideological utopias, but in the Leninist experience they reached grotesquely tragic limits. Lenin's ultradeterministic belief in the coming of the proletarian order functioned after 1917 as a nihilistic mechanism for bringing the world in line with such millennialism. The old order needed to be smashed, so its human embodiments were demonized and became targets for merciless persecution. In his manifesto against the Mensheviks, *One Step Forward, Two Steps Back* (1904), Lenin proclaimed that "it would be *the most criminal cowardice* to doubt even for a moment the inevitable and complete triumph of the principles of revolutionary Social-Democracy, of proletarian organization and Party discipline [my emphasis]."[62] Bertrand Russell noticed as early as 1920 that there was a central duality within Bolshevism that contained the movement's doom: there was, on the one hand, "its commitment to a certain conception of modernization," and, on the other hand, "an ideological commitment to an ideological world view shaped by ideological zeal and intolerance of other world views, which was a denial of the Enlightenment to rational discourse."[63] In other words, Bolshevism was pregnant with its own Inquisition from the beginning.

No less important, the appeal of Communism was linked to the extraordinary power of its ideology (and the core myth of the party as the carrier of reason in history). No other revolutionary movement has been as successful as Leninism in turning a gnostic creed into a self-hypnotizing weapon. Leninist militants worldwide believed in the myth of the party with an ardor comparable only to the illuminates of religious millennial sects. It is important to insist on both the ideological and institutional foundations of Leninism when we try to fathom the mystery of Leninism's endurance in the twentieth century. The myth of the party as the repository of historical wisdom and rationality is the key to grasping the dynamics and finally the decay and extinction of Leninism. Leninism, in its various phases, was what Ken Jowitt described as a "Catholic moment" in history, when "a universal 'word' becomes institutional 'flesh,' an authoritatively standardized and centered institutional format dominates a highly diverse set of cultures." The Althusserian interpretation remains valid only if one performs a phraseological inversion: Leninism was a new praxis of philosophy. The explanation of its longevity in the twentieth century can therefore be found in "the promise of the Great October Revolution . . . of the Soviet Union as socialist hierophany."[64]

The biographies of the ideological elites in Soviet-type regimes were usually colorless and lacked any moment of real distinction. In Eastern Europe, the ideological watchdogs were recruited from the Muscovite factions of the ruling parties. In Hungary, József Révai, once one of Georg Lukács's promising disciples, became a scourge of intellectual life. Révai was a member of the Hungarian delegation to various Cominform meetings and enthusiastically implemented the Zhdanovist strategy. In Romania, the tandem of Iosif Chişinevschi and Leonte Răutu forced the national culture into a mortal impasse. Similar denials of genuine national traditions and an apocryphal sense of internationalism were promoted by ideological bureaucracies in Czechoslovakia (Vilem Kopecky, Jiři Hendrich)[65] and East Germany (Gerhart Eisner, Albert Norden, Kurt Hager).[66] All devices were convenient when it came to uprooting vicious deviationist temptations. "Bourgeois nationalism" was fused with "rootless cosmopolitanism" in the diabolical figure of the malignant enemy. In the meantime, socialist nationalism was thriving. The members of the ideological army were willingly officiating in the rites of the cult. Deprived of their own personality, they were glad to identify with and invest in Stalin's superpersonality. After the terrorist dissolution of the ego, it was normal for the apparatchiks to project themselves into Stalin's myth as an institutionalized superego.

The Cominform emerged in September 1947 as the first attempt to institutionalize the *satellitization* of Eastern Europe. It represented an initiative to contain and annihilate the centrifugal trends within world Communism (the "domesticist" temptation and the search for a "national path to socialism" championed by militants as different as

Gottwald, Gomułka, and Pătrăşcanu). It laid the foundation for future frameworks of supragovernmental domination and ideological hegemony from the Soviet Communist Party. Paradoxically, the Cominform brought about the first instance of dissent and revisionism from a party-state (the Titoist "heresy"). In Tito's case there was a significant level of ambivalence: he supported enthusiastically Stalin's new orientation (Zhdanov's "two camp theory") but thought the moment was propitious for furthering his own hegemonic agenda in the Balkans. One could call such a strategic syndrome *parallel hegemonism*. The irony of the situation was that the break between the two leaders happened at a time when Soviet and Yugoslav visions of class struggle at the world level mirrored each other. In 1947–48, Tito underestimated the total monopoly of power achieved by the Kremlin tyrant, and he fancied himself the beneficiary of some leverage in regional decision-making. Historian Ivo Banac correctly diagnosed the paradox: "The dramatic denouement of 1948 was directly connected with Stalin's fears that Yugoslavia began to take on a role of regional communist center and the inherent potential provocations against the West that such a position entailed."[67] Indeed, the leader of the League of Communists in Yugoslavia (until 1952 the Yugoslav Communist Party) carried along unabated with his plans of creating a Communist Danubian confederation (which was to incorporate Yugoslavia, Bulgaria, and Romania)[68] while simultaneously persevering in the assimilation of the Albanian Communist Party (which in 1948 became the Albanian Party of Labor).

The conflict with Yugoslavia and Tito's excommunication from the Cominform in June 1948 signaled the beginning of dramatic purges in Eastern Europe Communist parties. It also indicated that Moscow's hegemony could not completely suppress domestic tendencies even in the most pro-Soviet Communist factions. Nevertheless, in Stalin's view, at such a dangerous time, when the imperialists had decided to intensify their aggressive actions against the budding "people's democracies," and the threat of a new world war loomed large, no country or leader could be allowed to engage in national Communist experiments. Those identified as nationalists could be charged with the most fantastic sins. After all, the sole principle of legitimation for the ruling Communist parties in the Soviet bloc was their unreserved attachment to the Soviet Union, their readiness to carry out unflinchingly all of Stalin's directives. The harshness of Stalin's reaction can be explained by the fact that the Soviet Communist Party leadership reactivated the geopolitical motif of "capitalist encirclement." In this vein, the end of the Second World War triggered a new imperialist offensive against Communism that, according to Stalin, signaled an imminent world-scale armed conflict. Under the circumstances, any national Communism temptation had to be crushed in the bud. Therefore, within the countries of the Soviet bloc, party leaders would be allowed to enjoy the adoration of their subordinates, but their cults were only echoes of the true faith: unswerving love for Stalin. In the words of Władisław Gomułka, the cult of the local leaders "could be called only a reflected brilliance, a borrowed light. It shone as the moon does."[69]

Links with Tito were used as arguments to demonstrate the political unreliability of certain East European leaders (e.g., László Rajk in Hungary, who fought in the Spanish Civil War and had maintained friendly relations with members of Tito's entourage). It is worth discussing in this context the analysis of forced confessions proposed by Erica Glaser Wallach, Noel Field's foster daughter, whose parents were members of the medical units associated with the International Brigades in Spain:

> That depends on you, confess your crimes, cooperate with us, and we shall do anything in our power to help you. We might even consider letting you go free if we are satisfied that you have left the enemy camp and have honestly contributed to the cause of justice and progress. We are no man-eaters, and we are not interested in revenge. Besides you are not the real enemy; we are not interested in you but in the criminals behind you, the sinister forces of imperialism and war. You do not have to defend them; they will fight their own losing battle. People like you we want to help—and we do frequently—to find their way back to a normal life and a decent place in society. . . . You want to know what a capitalist snake looks like? Take a look at her, at that bag of filth standing over there. You will never see such a low and abominable creature. . . . Take that dirty smile off your face, you American stooge. . . . You are a prostitute! That's what you are. Worse than that: prostitutes sell only their bodies: you sold your soul. For American dollars, stinking American dollars.[70]

Domesticism, according to Zbigniew Brzezinski, was an exaggerated if frequently unconscious "preoccupation with local, domestic communist objectives, at the expense of broader, international Soviet goals."[71] It was not an elaborated philosophy of opposition to Soviet hegemony, but a conviction on the part of some East European leaders, like Gomułka in Poland, Lucreţiu Pătrăşcanu in Romania, and Traicho Kostov in Bulgaria, that national interests were not necessarily incompatible with the Soviet agenda and that such purposes could therefore be pursued with impunity. Henceforth, the Cominform's main task—if not its only task—was to suppress such domestic ambitions. The fulfillment of the Stalinist design for Eastern Europe included the pursuit of a singular strategy that could eventually transform the various national political cultures into carbon copies of the "advanced" Soviet experience. Local Communist parties, engaged in frantic attempts to imitate the Stalinist model, transplanted and sometimes enhanced the most repulsive characteristics of the Soviet totalitarian system. The purpose of the show trials that took place in the people's democracies was to create a national consensus surrounding the top Communist elite and to maintain a state of panic in the population. According to George H. Hodos, a survivor of the 1949 László Rajk trial in Hungary, those frame-ups were signals addressed to all potential freethinkers and heretics in the satellite countries. The trials also "attempted to brand anyone who displayed differences of opinion as common criminals and/or agents of imperialism, to distort tactical differences as betrayal, sabotage, and espionage."[72] However, one needs to emphasize that these trials were not a simple repetition of the bloody purges that had devastated the Soviet body politic in the 1930s. Between 1949 and 1951 the main victims of the trials were members of the "national Communist elites," or "home Communists," as opposed to doctrinaire Stalin loyalists. Koçi Xoxe, Traicho Kostov, Lucrețiu Pătrășcanu, Władysław Gomułka, and László Rajk had all spent the war years in their own countries participating in the anti-Nazi resistance movement. Unlike their Moscow-trained colleagues, they could invoke legitimacy from direct involvement in the partisan movement. Some of these "home-grown" Communists may have even resented the condescending attitudes of the "Muscovites," who traded on their better connections with Moscow and treated the home Communists like junior partners. Stalin was aware of those factional rivalries and used them to initiate the permanent purges in the satellite countries.

In the early 1950s, Stalin became increasingly concerned with the role of the Jews as carriers of a "cosmopolitan worldview" and as "objective" supporters of the West. For the Communists, it did not matter whether an individual was "subjectively" against the system; what mattered was what he or she might have thought and done by virtue of his or her "objective" status (for instance, coming from a bourgeois family, having studied in the West, or belonging to a certain minority). While there is a growing and impressive literature dealing with Stalin's anti-Semitism during the later years of his reign, there is a regrettable scarcity of analysis of anti-Semitism as a defining feature of post-1948 political culture in the East European satellites. In a assessment from 1972 of anti-Semitism in the Soviet Union, William Korey made an interesting observation:

> Anti-Jewish discrimination had become an integral part of Soviet state policy ever since the late thirties. What it lacked then was an official ideology rationalizing the exclusion of Jews from certain positions or justifying the suspicion focused upon them. First during 1949–1953, and then more fully elaborated since 1967, the "corporate Jew," whether "cosmopolitan" or "Zionist," became identified as the enemy. Popular anti-Semitic stereotyping had been absorbed into official channels, generated by chauvinist needs and totalitarian requirements. . . . The ideology of the "corporate Jew" was not and is not fully integrated into Soviet thought. It functions on a purely pragmatic level—to fulfill limited, though clearly defined, domestic purposes. This suggests the possibility that it may be set aside when those purposes need no longer be served.[73]

In Stalin's mental universe, Jews were associated with the Mensheviks, but even more seditiously with the intraparty opposition headed in the 1920s by Leon Trotsky, Lev Kamenev, and Grigory Zinoviev. While Stalin championed the interests of the Communist apparatus, the oppositionists were portrayed as reckless adventurers deprived of commitment to the building of "socialism in one country." In the 1930s, in a famous interview with the Jewish Telegraphic Agency, Stalin defined anti-Semitism as a latter-day form of cannibalism. It may well have been that strong anti-Semitic feelings developed in his mind, especially after World War II, during the campaigns to assert Russian priorities in culture and science and restore complete ideological regimentation.

Timothy Snyder argues that the anti-Semitism in postwar Stalinism was tightly connected to the affirmation of Russians as the "safe base" of the regime after 1945. The starting point of this process was, of course, Stalin's famous victory toast to "the Great Russian nation" just after the end of the war. However, as Snyder stressed, "war on the Soviet territory was fought and won chiefly in Soviet Belarus and Soviet Ukraine, rather than in Soviet Russia." But "Soviet Russia was much less marked by the Holocaust than Soviet Ukraine or Soviet Belarus, simply because the Germans arrived later and were able to kill fewer Jews (about sixty thousand, or about one percent of the Holocaust). In this way, too, Soviet Russia was more distant from the experience of the war." In the operation of insulating "the Russian nation, and of course all of the other nations, from cultural infection . . . [o]ne of the most dangerous intellectual plagues would be interpretations of the war that differed from Stalin's own."[74] The tragedy of the Jews in the Soviet Union

> could not be enclosed within the Soviet experience, and was thus a threat to postwar Soviet mythmaking. About 5.7 million Jewish civilians had been murdered by the Germans and Romanians, of whom some 2.6 million were Soviet citizens in 1941. This meant not only that more Jewish civilians were murdered in absolute terms than members of any other Soviet nationality. It also meant that more than half of the cataclysm took place beyond the postwar boundaries of the Soviet Union. From a Stalinist perspective, even the experience of the mass murder of one's peoples was a worrying example of exposure to the outside world. . . . Precisely because extermination was a fate common to Jews across borders, its recollection could not be reduced to that of an element in the Great Patriotic War.[75]

The outcome of the new founding myth of Stalin's Soviet Union had an ominous impact upon the memory and role of the Jews in the new polity: "The murder of the Jews was not only an undesirable memory in and of itself; it called forth other undesirable memories. It had to be forgotten."[76] Under the circumstances, the Soviet Jews rapidly became enemies "masquerading in the guise of Soviet people."[77]

Chief ideologue Andrei Zhdanov played a major role in the campaign, including the notorious Central Committee resolutions regarding literary journals, philosophy, and music. Initially a supporter of the formation of the State of Israel, Stalin developed strong misgivings regarding the presumed "divided loyalty" of Soviet Jewish citizens to their homeland. Members of the Jewish Anti-Fascist Committee (a Soviet propaganda arm during the war) were arrested under hallucinating charges of conspiracy to disband the Soviet Union and to create "a Jewish state in Crimea." Among the victims of this anti-Semitic witch hunt were major Yiddish language poets (among them Peretz Markisch and David Bergelson), Old Bolshevik intellectuals, a former member of the Central Committee and deputy minister of foreign affairs, Solomon Lozovsky, and academician Lina Shtern, a prominent physician who had come to the USSR as a political refugee from Nazi Germany. The defendants, including Lozovsky, refused to confess. With several exceptions recruited among secret political police informers, they were sentenced to death and executed in the summer of 1952 (Lina Shtern was the exception, probably because of her prestige among German Communists).[78]

Stalin's final paranoia consisted in the designation of Jews—in the USSR as well as in East Central Europe—as the new "enemies of the people," as treacherously villainous as the Trotskyists in the 1930s. No one was spared suspicion: even the most loyal Communists could be spies and renegades, double-dealers and wreckers, especially those who might nourish hidden Zionist propensities. This Judeophobic cosmology included real and imagined Zionists but no real enemy of the Soviet Union. During the last month of Stalin's life, the anti-Semitic campaign reached its climax with thousands of layoffs of Jews in major Soviet institutions and the arrest of Kremlin doctors, mostly Jewish, who were accused of having poisoned or deliberately applied wrong treatments to such Stalinist luminaries as Andrei Zhdanov, Aleksander Scherbakov, and Marshall Ivan Konev.[79] The propaganda department was instructed to obtain public endorsements from highly recognized Jewish personalities in support of imminent decisions to punish those suspected of disloyalty and treason. Among those approached by Central Committee emissaries were writer Ilya Ehrenburg and historian Isaac Mints, a member of the Soviet Academy of Science. Although a flamboyant supporter of Stalinist peace campaigns, the former refused to sign a letter meant to be published in the party daily, *Pravda*.[80] The latter did it, probably after heartbreaking agony:

> Mints's daughter said that her father was deeply frightened and troubled by the accusations against him, and news of the Doctor's Plot only exacerbated his fears. She still remembers how pale he was when, after Stalin's death, he brought her the newspaper announcing that the so-called plot had been a fabrication. He spoke not a word, just showed her the headline. But Mints may also have felt that he was acting within the prescribed norms of Bolshevik academic culture. Mints could accept his public denunciation and participate in an obvious fabrication of Jewish sentiments because these were part of a cultural process and lexicon that he knew well. It was part of the standard public ritual that one had to go through to be a Bolshevik and to show one's commitment and loyalty.[81]

While the specter of a massive pogrom loomed over the Soviet Jewish population, in the people's democracies, the struggle against "rootless cosmopolitanism" allowed certain local leaders to engage in an elite purge against the "Muscovite" factions dominated by Communists of Jewish extraction (many of whom had fled Fascism and had sought refuge in the Soviet Union between the two wars).[82] The elimination of those otherwise totally loyal Stalinists reached a spectacular level in Czechoslovakia, where the chief defendant was Rudolf Slánský, who until September 1951 had been the general secretary of the ruling Communist Party and in that capacity had presided over the ruthless persecution of Communists and non-Communists. Since the trial had to confirm Stalin's conviction about the existence of a worldwide conspiracy threatening the Communist bloc, there was no way to exonerate any of the defendants. Furthermore, the anti-Semitic charges were bound to appeal to pro-Communist chauvinistic prejudices in the whole region. The numerous instances of anti-Semitism under so-called state socialism cannot be simply disregarded as aberrations. As Vassily Grossman rightly pointed out, since under totalitarian regimes there is no civil society, "there can only be *state* anti-Semitism."[83] Under Communism, the Jews became a target of policies of exclusion, isolation, and punishment on the basis of their ethnicity, were deemed potentially disloyal ("enemies of the people") and inherently bourgeois ("class enemies"). Jewish identity turned at times under Communism into an innate, invariable, and even hereditary source of otherness that called for state-engineered excision.

In addition, postwar Stalinist anti-Semitism forced Jewish Communists to persevere in the denial of their own identity. Very few maintained their Jewish names (Ana Pauker, Jakub Berman), while most adopted names attuned to ethnic majorities (Mátyás Rákosi, Roman Zambrowski, Leonte Răutu). Generally speaking, Jewish Communists abjured their background, proudly severed all links with their ancestors' traditions, and engaged in vitriolic attacks on "Jewish bourgeois nationalism." They were, to use Isaac Deutscher's term, "non-Jewish Jews." After 1945, though, "Jewish Stalinists . . . were caught between Stalinist anti-Semitism in Moscow and popular anti-Semitism in their own country." For example, Timothy Snyder remarks that in Poland "Jewish communists had to stress that their political identification with the Polish nation was so strong that it erased their Jewish origins and removed any possibility of distinct Jewish policies."[84] Under the circumstances, Stalinist anti-Semitism was both criminal and conducive to an entire community's erasure from the recognized grand narratives of the postwar order under Communism.

A direct consequence of the Slánský events in Czechoslovakia was the purge trial of Paul Merker, a member of the Central Committee of the Socialist Unity Party (SED) since 1946. His initial downfall came about because of his relationship during the Second World War with Noel Field and Otto Katz (part of the group tried and executed in Prague in 1951). However, the crux of the accusations against Merker concerned his opinions and positions on the Jewish question in post-1945 Germany. In 1952, the SED's Central Party Control Commission produced a document that detailed Merker's errors. Unsurprisingly, it was entitled "Lessons of the Trial against the Slánský Conspiracy Centre." The commission insisted that Merker was involved in "the criminal activity of Zionist organizations," which, allied with "American agents," aimed to destroy the "people's democracies" in Eastern Europe. Additionally, it claimed that Merker tried "winning over SED comrades of Jewish descent."[85] During interrogation (both by the Stasi and the People's Commissariat for Internal Affairs), Merker was stamped as a *Judenknecht* ("servant of the Jews"). In an interesting twist, even after the 1954 resolution of the Noel Field case, Merker was not released. On the contrary, now his whole trial was focused on his alleged collaboration with Jewish capitalist and cosmopolitan circles. He was sentenced in 1955 to eight years in prison but was released in 1956 without ever being fully rehabilitated. Nevertheless, Merker and his spouse never attempted to flee to West Germany. Taking an exemplarily Rubashov-like approach, Merker stated, "In the trial against me, I did without a defense lawyer in order to help keep the proceedings absolutely secret." Again, the (il)logic of Stalinism was at work: "He had made efforts to prevent 'enemies of the DDR' from using his case, and he and his wife had been and would remain silent about the case."[86] His trial, sentence, and interrogation minutes were indeed kept secret, emerging only after the fall of the Berlin Wall.

In May 1952 the Romanian media announced the elimination of three members of the Politburo, two of whom had been the leaders of the party's Moscow émigré center during World War II. All three had been party secretaries and had shared absolute power with the leader of the domestic faction, Gheorghe Gheorghiu-Dej. Ana Pauker, a veteran Communist leader who long had been lionized by international propaganda as an impeccable Communist fighter, lost her job as minister of foreign affairs and was put under house arrest. Her Muscovite ally, the Hungarian-born Vasile Luca, was accused of economic sabotage during his tenure as minister of finance and of collaboration with the bourgeois police during the party's underground activity. Luca was arrested and died in prison in the early 1960s. The third member of the group, Teohari Georgescu, a home Communist and former minister of internal affairs whose principal fault consisted in his close association with the Pauker-Luca faction, was also jailed but soon released, though never reinstated in party positions. The Romanian case is a perfect example of country dynamics determined by party factionalism and sectarianism. It can be said that the more marginal and less historically representative a Communist party was, the more profound its sectarianism was. The Romanian Communist Party (RCP), torn apart by internal struggles among its three centers[87] during the underground period, preserved a besieged fortress mentality even after World War II. Given that in the pre-1945 period mutual accusations had usually resulted in the expulsion of the members of the defeated faction, once the party was in power, the effects of the continued struggles were catastrophic. Once established as a ruling party, the RCP projected a vision based on exclusiveness, fierce dogmatism, and universal suspicion at the national level.

The mystique of the party called for complete abrogation of its members' critical faculties. As Franz Borkenau put it, Communism, "a Utopia based upon the belief in the omnipotence of the 'vanguard,' cannot live without a scapegoat, and the procedures applied to detect them, invent them, become only more cruel and reckless."[88] For all practical purposes, the political history of the international Communist movement is the history of continual purges of different factions branded by the victors as "anti-party deviations." Those defeated in party power struggles were labeled factionalists, whereas the winners were lionized as champions of the "holy cause" of party unity.

Whereas the Slánský trial and the "doctor's plot" seem to represent the limits of the Stalinist system's irrationality, the purge of the Pauker-Luca-Georgescu group is primarily an expression of domestic revolutionary pragmatism. This process involved massive purges of the Jewish Democratic Committee and the Hungarian Committee, suggesting a concerted campaign of weakening the Moscow faction. In the Byzantine schemes that devoured the Romanian Communist elite, the mystical internationalism of the Comintern period was gradually replaced by a cynical position embellished with nationalist, even xenophobic, motifs. Gheorghiu-Dej and his acolytes not only speculated about Stalin's anti-Semitism but did not hesitate to play the same card.[89] The stakes were absolute power, and the Jewishness of rivals was an argument that could be used with the Soviet dictator. If the national Stalinists were the prime beneficiaries of Stalin's warning not to transform the party from a "social and class party into a *race* party,"[90] they were neither its initiators nor its architects. No less caught up in the same perverse mechanism of self-humiliation than their Polish and Hungarian colleagues, the Romanian Stalinists—Gheorghiu-Dej, Chişinevschi, and Ceauşescu as much as Ana Pauker and Vasile Luca—were willing perpetrators of Stalin's designs. They were allowed by the Soviet dictator to gain autonomy not from the center but from another generation of the center's agents. It was indeed a sort of moment of emancipation, but one that signaled Moscow's sanctioning of the coming of age of a new Stalinist elite in

Romania. The history of the Stalinist ruling group in other East-Central European countries is strikingly similar. There is the same sense of political predestination, the same lack of interest in national values, the same obsequiousness vis-à-vis the Kremlin.

An indicator of the *continuous* Stalinist nature of the Romanian regime, of its permanent purge *mentalité*, is Leonte Răutu's fateful longevity in the highest power echelons as the high priest of a cultural revolution *à la roumaine*.[91] A prominent party veteran of Bessarabian-Jewish origin, perfectly fluent in Russian, he was the architect of anti-cultural politics of Stalinism in Romania. Until his removal from the Political Executive Committee in the summer of 1981, he epitomized a *perinde ac cadaver* commitment to the Marxist-Leninist cause. He was the most significant figure of the "party intellectuals," who produced, reproduced and instrumentalized ideological orthodoxy. A professional survivor prone to the most surreal dialectical acrobatics, Leonte Răutu adjusted and took advantage of the regime's gradual systemic degeneration, making a successful transition from professional revolutionary to cunning and slippery bureaucrat always ready to hunt down heretics among party ranks and within society as whole. Born in 1910, Răutu joined the RCP in 1929 (while a student in mathematics at Bucharest University) and in the 1930s became head of the propaganda and agitation department. In Doftana Prison he came in contact with Gheorghiu-Dej and Nicolae Ceauşescu. In the following years he became the editor of *Scînteia,* the party's illegal newspaper. In 1940 he left Romania and took refuge in the USSR, becoming the director of the Romanian section of Radio Moscow. He returned to the country with Ana Pauker, Vasile Luca, and Valter Roman, and initiated a domestic version of Zhdanovism. In one of his most vehemently Zhdanovite speeches, "Against Cosmopolitanism and Objectivism in Social Sciences,"[92] Răutu declared war on everything that was worthy in the national culture: "The channels by which cosmopolitan views become pervasive, especially among intellectuals, are well known: servility to and kowtowing to bourgeois culture, the empty talk of the so-called community of progressive scientists and the representatives of reactionary, bourgeois science, national nihilism, meaning the negation of all that is valuable and progressive for each people in his culture and history, the contempt for the people's language, hatred of the building of socialism, the defamation of all that is new and developing, replacing the *partiinost* with bourgeois objectivism, which ignores the fundamental difference between socialist, progressivist culture and bourgeois, reactionary culture."[93]

After 1953, he pursued a seemingly more balanced approach, as a defense mechanism in the context of de-Stalinization. His main weapon in these changing times was that of *manipulation*. The individual was always a tool with no distinct personality (rather being a complex of acquired or ascribed features); when s/he displayed the will for autonomous action, s/he became a victim of the diabolical logic of the purge (an excellent example is the career of Mihai Beniuc, the "little tyrant from the Writers' Union," as veteran Communist poet Miron Radu Paraschivescu once called him). Răutu's cynicism and opportunism were flagrant in 1964, when the same individual who had directed the Sovietization of Romanian culture initiated a strident campaign against academia, which he unmasked and accused of "having forgotten true national values" and of "shamelessly showing fealty to even the slightest Soviet achievement." Leonte Răutu's career was fundamentally characterized by an extraordinary capacity for siding with those in power within the RCP. He first became a favorite of Ana Pauker and Vasile Luca, obtaining his position at Radio Moscow and his initial nominations in Romania because of this connection. By 1952, he jumped into Dej's boat, being, along with Miron Constantinescu, the author of the May-June Plenary Session resolution, the text on which the purge proceedings were based (what came to be known as "the June nights"). His inquisitorial contribution to the Pauker case was not the first (see his involvement in unmasking Pătrășcanu's intellectual "crimes") and wouldn't be the last such activity. In 1957, he was again on the prosecutor's bench during the party action against Chișinevschi-Constantinescu (these events are often labeled in Romanian historiography "a failed de-Stalinization"). After the downfall of these two, who had been direct competitors in the struggle to administer the cultural front, Răutu became the unchallenged patriarch of the Communist politics of culture. With the exception of the period when he shared power with Grigore Preoteasa, Răutu created an apparatus manned by mediocre individuals, whose ego equaled their incompetence (e.g., Mihail Roller and Pavel Țugui). The biography of Leonte Răutu is the perfect expression of the perverse game of Stalinist masks. Dissimulation, ethical promiscuity, and hypocrisy were the only constants of the apparatchik's existence, a full-blown retreat from any moral imperative. Răutu was the incarnation of the diabolical antilogic of Stalinism: an individual experiencing an irresistible process of personal decline based upon unswerving subordination to the party leader beyond considerations such as reason, honor, and dignity.

The mind of the Stalinist elites in Eastern Europe was impressively revealed by the Polish journalist Teresa Toránska in a series of interviews conducted in the early 1980s with some former leaders of the Polish Communist Party. The most illuminating of these interviews is with the former Politburo member and Central Committee secretary Jakub Berman, who tried to defend the actions of his political generation. According to Berman, Polish Communists were right in championing Stalin' policies in Poland because the Soviets guaranteed his country's social and national liberation. The leaders of the Soviet-bloc Communist parties were convinced, like Lenin at the moment he founded the Bolshevik party, that the people needed an external force to enlighten them, that without such a vanguard party there was no hope of true emancipation. Berman was convinced that a day would come when mankind would do justice to this chiliastic dream of global revolution, and all the atrocities and crimes of Stalinism would be remembered only as passing incidents: "I am nonetheless convinced that the sum of our actions, skillfully and consistently carried out, will finally produce results and create a new Polish consciousness; because all the advantages flowing from our new path will be borne out, must be borne out, and . . . there will finally be a breakthrough in mentality which will give it an entirely new content and quality."[94]

In his absolute belief that history was on his and his comrades' side, Berman was not alone. His was a mindset characteristic of the Communist elites in all Soviet satellite countries. Such (il)logic explains the frenzy of submission syndrome: the readiness to engage in any form of self-debasement and self-deprecation as long as such gestures were required by the party. The East European Communist leaders were seasoned militants for whom Stalin's personality was an example of correct revolutionary conduct. They admired the Soviet leader's intransigence and his uncompromising struggle against oppositional factions, and they shared his hostility to the West. They believed in the theory of permanent intensification of the class struggle and did their best to create a repressive system where critical tendencies could be immediately weeded out. Their minds were Manichean: Socialism was right, capitalism was wrong, and there was no middle road. During their Communist underground service, the Soviet-bloc Communists had learned to see Stalin's catechistic formulations as the best formulations of their own thoughts and beliefs. They fully internalized a diabolical pedagogy based upon a belief in being ordained as both juror and executioner, for their legitimacy drew from a fanatical obedience to the *vozhd*. When Stalin died, his East European disciples were orphaned: more than their parties' supporter, they lost their protector, the embodiment of their highest dreams, the hero they had come to revere, the symbol of their vigor, passion, and boundless enthusiasm.

The logic of Stalinism excluded vacillation and hesitation, numbed critical reasoning and intelligence, and instituted Soviet-style Marxism as a system of universal truth inimical to any form of doubt. The permanent purge, the basic technique of Stalinist demonology, was the modern equivalent of the medieval witch hunt. It was eagerly adopted by Stalin's East European apprentices and adapted to their own purposes. Echoing Stalin's fervid cult, East European leaders engineered similar campaigns of praise and idolatry in their own countries. The party was identified with the supreme leader, whose chief merit consisted in having correctly applied the Stalinist line. The solutions to all disturbing questions could be found in Stalin's writings, and those who failed to discover the answers were branded "enemies of the people." Members of the traditional political elites, members of the clergy, and representatives of the nationalist intelligentsia who had refused to collaborate with the new regimes were sentenced to long prison terms following dramatic show trials or cursory camera trials. That was the first stage of the purge in Eastern Europe. After 1949 the purges fed upon the Communist elites themselves, and through them many faithful Stalinists experienced firsthand the effects of the unstoppable terrorist machine they had helped set in motion.

Societies under Stalinism were restructured by a reimagining of class community, which in itself reflected these regimes' visions of all-out conspiracies both internally and externally. As Sheila Fitzpatrick judiciously notes, it took only one step and "the imagined *class* basis of the conspiracy would fall away."[95] Class guilt frequently overlapped with national profiling during Stalin's reign. Erik van Ree explains that for Stalin "national characters were shared by all members of the nation; they formed a 'mentality *[dukhovnyi oblik]* of the people who come together in a nation.' This 'stable' mentality was furthermore transmitted over time, as a 'psychological makeup *[psikhicheskii sklad]* that was formed among them from generation to generation as a result of identical conditions of existence.' "[96] Such an approach to the nationalities problem allowed Stalin to indulge in national stereotypes, which he superimposed upon Bolshevism's ultrarationalistic vision of social engineering. In this worldview, Russians and other nationalities became the heroes storming any fortress, while those who were perceived as unwilling to dedicate themselves to Stalin's "heroic modernity" were stigmatized as a decadent species spoiled by a profit-seeking mentality. This form of political romanticism played upon existing stereotypes in the population at large. No wonder that in the letters sent to *Pravda* in early 1953, most speakers agreed that "it was high time to purge Jews from the Party and from leading positions in state service and the professions." The solution to the perceived treacherousness of the Jews was their "education through labor."[97]

Thus a central aspect of post-1945 purges both in the Soviet Union and Eastern Europe was Stalinist anti-Semitism. This phenomenon was rooted in Stalin's own mentality, in the immediate aftermath of the war, and in the prejudices of majority populations in these countries. Even if some of its origins lay in the 1930s (after all, many of the Old Bolsheviks who were eliminated by Stalin were of Jewish origin), Stalinist anti-Semitism was a direct product of the Soviet leader's post-1945 worldview. It may not have had the same murderous results as the Great Terror, but "it confused the European past": "Stalinist anti-Semitism haunted Eastern Europe long after the death of Stalin. It was rarely a major tool of governance, but it was always available in moments of political stress. Anti-Semitism allowed leaders to revise the history of wartime suffering (recalled as the suffering only of Slavs) and also the history of Stalinism itself (which was portrayed as the deformed, Jewish form of communism)."[98] Indeed, anti-Semitism resurfaced often during the existence of the Soviet bloc. In some cases, it was part and parcel of the building of socialist nations. As I discussed elsewhere, national Stalinism in Romania or in Poland or East Germany was characterized, among other things, by reaffirmation of the Jew among the archetypical *Others* of the dominant ethnic group.[99] But the most destructive legacy of Stalinist anti-Semitism is its obfuscation of the Holocaust. Timothy Snyder excellently formulates this paradox: "So long as communists governed most of Europe, the Holocaust could never be seen for what it was."[100] In other words, Stalin's mystification of the mass murder of the Jews set up the competitive regimes of memory in post-1989 East and Central Europe. On the one hand, for decades the Holocaust had not been remembered and the truth about the genocide of the Jews had remained hidden. On the other hand, the dimensions of the crimes of Stalinism and of the various Communist regimes were only surfacing to their true extent. Taking Snyder's point a bit further, the silence about both the gulag and the Holocaust in Eastern Europe ensured that these radically traumatic historical experiences are yet to fully be a part of the common history of Europe.[101]

To return to the more general problem of Stalinism's exterminism, I agree with Leszek Kołakowski, who believed the purges had an integrative function, contributing to the destruction of the last vestiges of subjective autonomy and creating a social climate where no one would even dream of criticism. According to the great Polish philosopher, "The object of a totalitarian system is to destroy all forms of communal life that are not imposed by the state and closely controlled by it, so that individuals are isolated from one another and become mere instruments in the hands of the state. The citizen belongs to the state and must have no other loyalty, not even to the state ideology."[102] Communist victims belonged to a category described by Stalinist legal theory as "objective enemies." They were people who once in their lives might have expressed reservations about the sagacity of Soviet policies or, even worse, might have criticized Stalin personally. Stalinism functioned on the basis of an exhaustively repressive strategy displaying pedagogical ambitions and vaunting itself as the triumph of ethical spirit and egalitarian collectivism. Nicolas Werth enunciates, along these lines, the following diagnosis: "Throughout Stalin's dictatorship of a quarter of a century, repressive phenomena varied, evolved, and took on different forms and scope. They reflected transformations of the regime itself in a changing world. This adaptable violence was characterized by various levels of intensity, continual displacements, shifting targets, often unpredictable sequences, and excesses that blurred the line between the legal and extralegal."[103] Maniacal purging consummate with self-devouring was both the praxis and the theoretical legitimation of this extremist and exterminist system. To paraphrase the title of a famous novel of Stalin's era, this is *How the Steel Was Tempered*.

CHAPTER 3

Lenin's Century

Bolshevism, Marxism, and the Russian Tradition

The use of inhumane methods to achieve impossible ends is
the essence of revolutionary utopianism.
—John Gray, *Black Mass*

Created by Lenin and refined by Stalin, the one-party
dictatorship and command economy would be Russian's
most consequential bequest to twentieth-century history.
—Steven G. Marks, *How Russia Shaped the Modern World*

Marxism was, as Leszek Kołakowski once said, the greatest philosophical fantasy of modern times. It was a gigantic Manichean political
myth, a major script of political modernity that contrasted the forces of
reaction, barbarism, and decay to those of historical progress, reason,
and human liberation. It promised salvation via the destruction of a system based on domination, exploitation, and alienation. The proletariat,
in this soteriological vision, was the universal redeemer or, as young
Marx put it, the messiah-class of history.[1] Feverishly appealing to what
historian Norman Cohn called highly emotional mass movements, both
Leninism and Fascism created millenarian sociological and psychological
constellations. Both were militant chiliasms that energized extraordinary
ardor among unconditionally committed followers. Focusing on revolutionary messianism in medieval and Reformation Europe and its reverberations in modern totalitarian experiences, Cohn pointed out that there
was no call "to distinguish overmuch between what so far had been the
two major forms of totalitarianism, Communism on the one hand and
German National Socialism on the other." He continues: "Admittedly it

87

seems a far cry from the atavism, the crude tribalism, the vulgar irrationalism and open sadism of the Nazis to the ostensibly humanitarian
and universalistic, scientific, and rational outlook of the Communist—
and still it is true that both these movements shared certain features
so extraordinary as to suggest the emergence of a form of politics
vastly different from any known in the past."[2]

VIOLENCE AND THE QUEST
FOR THE PERFECT COMMUNITY

National Socialism never achieved a level of theoretical coherence and
conceptual sophistication comparable to the Marxian paradigm and its
offshoots. It would be impossible to speak seriously about Nazi philosophy. Even Stalin's thought was more intellectually structured that Hitler's nebulous vagaries. Yet the inner core of deep anticapitalist, antiliberal, and antidemocratic obsessions could be found in both of these
otherwise inimical doctrines.[3] Leninism and National Socialism (or more
generically, Fascism) were founded upon programs of total societal mobilization intended to achieve a radical transformation of the body politic.
The first step in the revolutions promoted by Leninism and Fascism (German and Italian) was the takeover of power. The mode of takeover was
fundamentally exclusionary in relation to all other political formations
or adversaries. For Lenin, once imposed via the Bolshevik insurrection,
the "dictatorship of the proletariat" was irreversible and unrestrained by
any law. In March 1933, Hitler announced, "The government will embark upon a systematic campaign to restore the nation's moral and material health. The whole educational system, theatre, film, literature, the
press, and broadcasting—all these will be used as means to this end."[4]
Indeed, during the trial of the army officers imprisoned for their involvement with National Socialism in Leipzig in 1930, Hitler had declared
that he aimed at a "legal revolution," which meant entering "the legal
agencies and in that way [making] our Party the determining factor."
However, like the Bolsheviks' stance in 1917, this method only opened
the gates for the Nazi Party's absolute dictatorship. In Hitler's words,
"Once we possess the constitutional power, we will mould the state into
the shape we hold suitable."[5]

This approach was disturbingly reminiscent of the Bolshevik precedent. Lenin believed that any wavering in taking power was a criminal
act. Political historian Stephen Cohen gave an excellent characterization of the path to government of Lenin's party: "A minority party to

the end (they received about 25 percent of the votes for the Constituent Assembly in November), the Bolsheviks neither inspired nor led the revolution from below; but they alone perceived its direction and survived it."[6] Just like the Nazis and Italian Fascists, Bolsheviks knew that they wanted to rule because each believed in a perceived historical, transformative, and redemptive mission. And to attain this end, all means were justified. To quote Lazar Kaganovich, one of Stalin's henchmen, "Comrades, it has long been known that for us Bolsheviks democracy is no fetish."[7] Fascists and Communists alike believed in the imperative of creative destruction of the old world in order to create new civilizations based upon new men, new social systems that in their turn would generate a new international order. To paraphrase Roger Griffin, these two political movements were utterly consumed with palingenetic, revivalist fervor.

Leninism's belief in the purifying effect of shattering the world was founded upon the writings of the founding fathers—Karl Marx and Friedrich Engels. According to Marx, what was unique about "the Revolution was not just that no further event was to follow it, but that no other event need follow it, because in the Revolution the whole purpose of History was to be fulfilled."[8] Marxism was first and foremost a Promethean attempt to get rid of an abhorred bourgeois order based on market relations (private property), transcend reified social relations, and organize revolutionary social forces for the ultimate confrontation, which would result in a "leap from the kingdom of necessity into the kingdom of freedom."[9] Marx's strong demarcation of his revolutionary thought in contrast to other versions of socialism (Christian, reactionary-feudal, petty-bourgeois, critical-utopian) is intimately linked to his firm belief, especially after 1845, that he was in the know (the postulate of epistemic infallibility), and that his *Weltanschauung* was essentially scientific, that is, nonutopian. For Marx, the conviction that history was governed by laws, a Hegelian viewpoint that he consistently promoted, meant that once these laws were grasped, reason (thought) and revolution (action) would coincide in the global proletarian liberation.[10] The understanding of social and natural forces allowed for the full realization of the transformative ethos: "Once we do understand them [social and natural forces], once we grasp their action, their direction, their effects, it depends only on ourselves to subject them more and more to our own will, and by means of them to reach our own ends."[11] Subsequently, in the name of proletarian (authentic) democracy, formal liberties could be suspended, even suppressed. To achieve a higher version of morality, emancipated from the bondage of bourgeois hypocrisy, traditional morality could be abrogated.[12] Marxism perceived itself as science rather than ethics, and therefore the revolution it preached was "part of a historical mechanism: hence, purged of values."[13] As Raymond Aron points out:

> Marxism is a Christian heresy. As a modern form of millenarianism, it places the kingdom of God on Earth following the apocalyptic revolution in which the Old World will be swallowed up. The contradictions of capitalist societies will inevitably bring about this fruitful catastrophe. The victims of today will be the victors of tomorrow. Salvation will come through the proletariat, that witness to present inhumanity. It is the proletariat that, at a time fixed by the evolution of productive forces and by the courage of the combatants, will turn itself into a class that is universal and will take charge of the fate of mankind.[14]

It was indeed the fate of Marxism to pretend to be in charge of the destiny of humanity by impersonating, in a simultaneously tragic and optimistic way, the solution to mankind's millennia-long agonies, fears, and terrors. Never was a political doctrine so ambitious, never a revolutionary project so much imbued with a sense of prophetic mission and charismatically heroic predestination.

MARXIST DREAMS, LENINIST EXPERIMENTS

All its radical hubris notwithstanding, Marxism would have remained a mere chapter in the history of revolutionary ideas had Vladimir Lenin not turned it into a most potent political weapon of ideological transformation of the world. The twentieth century was Lenin's century. In fact, Leninism was a self-styled synthesis between Marxian revolutionary doctrine and the Russian tradition of nihilistic repudiation of the status quo. Yet one should not forget that Lenin was a committed Marxist, who intensely believed that he was fulfilling the founding fathers' revolutionary vision.[15] For Lenin, Marxism was "a revelation to be received with unquestioning faith, which admits of no doubt or radical criticism."[16] This is the meaning of Antonio Gramsci's comparison between Lenin and Saint Paul: Lenin transformed the Marxian salvationist *Weltanschauung* into a global political praxis. The Bolshevik revolution was applied eschatological dialectics, and the Third International symbolized the universalization of the new revolutionary matrix. Lenin's crucial institutional invention (the Bolshevik party) and his audacious intervention in the praxis of the world socialist movement enthused Hungarian philosopher Georg Lukács, one of Max Weber's favorite disciples, who never abandoned his deep admiration for the founder of Bolshevism. Referring to Lukács's enduring attachment to Lenin's vision of politics, Slovene political theorist Slavoj Žižek writes, "His Lenin was the one who, à propos of the split in Russian Social Democracy into Bolsheviks and Mensheviks, when the two factions fought over a precise formulation of who can be a Party member as defined in the Party program, wrote: 'Sometimes, the fate of the entire working class movement for long years to come can be decided by a word or two in the party program.' "[17]

We need to remember that Leninism, as an allegedly coherent, monolithic, homogenous, self-sufficient ideological construct, was a post-1924 creation. It was actually the result of Grigory Zinoviev and Joseph Stalin's efforts to delegitimize Leon Trotsky by devising something called "Leninism" as opposed to the heresy branded as "Trotskyism." At the same time, Bolshevism was an intellectual and political reality, a total and totalizing philosophical, ethical, and practical-political direction within the world revolutionary movement.[18] It was thanks to Lenin that a new type of politics emerged in the twentieth century, one based on elitism, fanaticism, unflinching commitment to the sacred cause, and the substitution of critical reason for faith for the self-appointed "vanguards" of illuminated zealots (the professional revolutionaries). Leninism, initially a Russian and then a world-historical cultural and political phenomenon, was the foundation of the system that came to an end with the revolutions of 1989 and the demise of the USSR in December 1991.[19]

Whatever one thinks of Lenin's antibureaucratic struggle during his last years, or about his initiation of the New Economic Policy (NEP), the thrust of his action was essentially opposed to political pluralism. The nature of the Bolshevik "intraparty democracy" was inimical to free debate and competition of rival political views and platforms (as Lenin himself insisted, the party was not a "discussion club"). The March 1921 "ban on factions" resolution, directly related to the crushing of the Kronstadt sailors' uprising, indicated the persistent dictatorial propensity of Bolshevism. The persecution of such foes as the left-wing Socialist Revolutionaries and Mensheviks confirms that for Lenin and his associates, the "dictatorship of the proletariat" meant continuous strengthening of their absolute control over the body politic. Tolerance for cultural diversity and temporary acceptance of market relations were not meant to disturb the fundamental power relationship—the party's monopolistic domination and the stifling of any ideological alternative to Bolshevism.[20] In this respect, there were no serious differences among the members of Lenin's Politburo—Trotsky, Zinoviev, and Bukharin included. To put it briefly, if there had been no Lenin, there would have been no totalitarianism—at least not in its Stalinist version.

The October 1917 Bolshevik putsch (later elevated to the status of revolution) was *the* event that irreversibly changed the course of Western civilization and world history. In claiming to unify humanity under the banner of a collectivist and egalitarian ideal, Bolshevism actually ignited the insurrection of the masses in politics. It annihilated the mechanisms of limited government, as envisaged by the liberal tradition, and it founded a despotic system defined by an unprecedented disregard for the individual and the rule of law. It was a gigantic historical adventure meant to bring about heaven on earth, to materialize utopia.[21] According to Claude Lefort, Lenin renounced the principle of *consensus juris* as a precondition for the regime's cultivation of lawlessness. Instead, Leninism "promises to release the fulfillment of law from all action and the will of man; and it promises justice on earth because it claims to make mankind itself the embodiment of the law."[22]

Therefore, post-Communism means a continuous struggle to overcome the "remains of Leninism" or "the Leninist debris," a term I proposed as an elaboration of Ken Jowitt's illuminating concept of the Leninist legacy as a civilizational constellation that includes deep emotions, nostalgias, sentiments, resentments, phobias, collectivist yearnings, and attraction to paternalism and even corporatism.[23] Jowitt is among the few political scientists who accurately understood the deep appeals of Leninism as directly related to the emergence of the vanguard party as a substitute for traditional charismatic, religious-type reference frameworks in times of deep moral and cultural crisis: "Leninism and Nazism were each, in different ways, perverse attempts to sustain and restore a heroic ethos and life in opposition to a liberal bourgeois individualistic system . . . . [T]he defining principle of Leninism is to do what is illogical, and that is to make the impersonal charismatic. Charisma is typically associated with a saint or a knight, some personal attribution, and what Lenin did was remarkable. He did exactly what he claimed to do: he created a party of a new type. He made the party charismatic. People died for the party."[24] Thus Jowitt's definition of Leninism links ideological, emotional, and organizational components in a comprehensive dynamic constellation: "Leninism is best seen as a historical as well as organizational syndrome, based on charismatic impersonalism; a strategy based on an 'ingenious error' leading to collectivization/industrialization; and an international bloc led by a dominant regime, with the same definition as its constituent parts, acting as leader, model and support."[25]

Leninism as a political and cultural regime, or as an international system, is undoubtedly extinct. On the other hand, the Leninist-Stalinist model of the highly disciplined, messianic sect–type organization based on the rejection of pluralism and the demonization of the Other has not lost its appeal—suffice it to remember Lenin's diatribes against the Mensheviks, the Socialist Revolutionaries, the kulaks, the aristocrats, the "bourgeois intellectuals," and so on. In his view, their place, even when they disguised themselves as individuals unaffiliated with the party, was in jail or, if they were lucky, in exile.[26] This quasi-rational, in fact almost mystical, identification with the party (conceived as a beleaguered fortress surrounded by vicious enemies) was a main psychological feature of Bolshevism before what Robert C. Tucker defines as its deradicalization (what Jowitt would call the rise of the Aquinas temptation, in the figure of "modern revisionism," as Mao Zedong quite accurately defined Titoism and Khrushchevism). To be a Leninist meant to accept the party's claim to scientific knowledge (grasping the "laws of historical evolution") as well as its oracular pretense. Doubting the party's omniscience and omnipotence was the cardinal sin (as finally admitted by the Old Bolshevik Nikolai Rubashov, Arthur Koestler's hero in *Darkness at Noon*).[27] For Lenin, the party member was dispensable human capital in the revolutionary struggle. The individual was a simple particle, a *zero* compared to the *infinity* of the cause.[28] On this point, he closely followed—although he would have never admitted it—Russian terrorist Sergey Nechaev's ruthless fanaticism, as formulated in the *Revolutionary Catechism*:

Paragraph 1. The revolutionary is a lost man he has no interests of his own, no cause of his own, no feelings, no habits, no belongings; he does not even have a name. Everything in him is absorbed by a single, exclusive interest, a single thought, a single passion—the revolution

Paragraph 2. In the very depths of his being, not just in words but in deed, he has broken every tie with the civil order, with the educated world and all laws, conventions and generally accepted conditions, and with the ethics of this world. He will be an implacable enemy of this world, and if he continues to live in it, that will only be so as to destroy it more effectively. . . .

Paragraph 4. He despises public opinion: he despises and hates the existing social ethic in all its demands and expression; for him, everything that allows the triumph of the revolution is moral, and everything that stands in its way is immoral.

Paragraph 5. The revolutionary is the lost man; with no pity for the state and for the privileged and educated world in general, he must himself expect no pity. Everyday he must be prepared for death. He must be prepared to bear torture.

Paragraph 6. Hard with himself, he must be hard towards others. All the tender feelings of family life, of friendship, love, gratitude and even honor must be stifled in him by a single cold passion for the revolutionary cause. For him there is only one pleasure, one consolation, one reward, and one satisfaction—the success of the revolution. Day and night he must have one single thought, one single purpose: merciless destruction. With this aim in view, tirelessly and in cold blood, he must always be prepared to die and to kill with his own hands anyone who stands in the way of achieving it.

Paragraph 7. The character of the true revolutionary has no place for any romanticism, sentimentality, enthusiasm or seduction. Nor has it any place for private hatred and revenge. This revolutionary passion which in him becomes a daily, hourly passion, must be combined with cold calculation. Always and everywhere he must become not what his own personal inclination would have him become, but what the general interest of the revolution demands.[29]

THE MYSTICISM OF THE PARTY

Bolshevik humanism was by definition concrete, hinging upon the success of the cause. The individual's existence maintained its weight in the world insofar as it contributed to the construction of the revered social utopia. In this ideologically defined universe, the only agent capable of fulfilling and thereby ending history by bringing humanity to the promised land of classless society was the party. Two pronouncements by Yury Piatakov, one of Lenin's favorites in the younger generation of the Bolshevik Old Guard, spelled out this cosmic, or mystical, identification with the party in the most dramatic terms: "In order to become one with this great Party he would fuse himself with it, abandon his own personality, so that there was no particle left inside him which was not at one with the Party, did not belong to it."[30] The former Central Committee secretary (in 1918) added, "Yes I shall consider black something that I felt and considered to be white since outside of the party, outside accord with it, there is no life for me."[31] Or, in Marxian lingo, the party was the medium through which the individual erased the duality between self and the reified social being. The Bolsheviks were harbingers of the beginning of true history.

Ideological absolutism, worship of the ultimate goal, voluntary suspension of critical faculties, and the cult of the party line as the perfect expression of the general will were imbedded in the original Bolshevik project. The subordination of conventional moral criteria to the ultimate end of achieving a class society was the main problem with Leninism. It shared with Marxism what Steven Lukes calls "the emancipated vision of a world in which the principles that protect human beings from one another would no longer be needed."[32] One of the best descriptions of the Communist mind can be found in the testimony of Lev Kopelev, the model for Aleksandr Solzhenitsyn's character Rubin in *The First Circle*: "With the rest of my generation I firmly believed that the ends justify the means. Our great goal was the universal triumph of Communism, and for the sake of that goal everything was permissible—to lie, to steal, to destroy hundreds of thousands and even millions of people, all those who were hindering our work or could hinder it, everyone who stood in the way. And to hesitate or doubt about all this was to give in to 'intellectual squeamishness' and 'stupid liberalism,' the attributes of people who "could not see the forest for the trees.'"[33] Political philosopher Steven Lukes was therefore correct in emphasizing the structural-generative ideological and emotional matrix of Communism that made its crimes against humanity possible: "The defect in question causing moral blindness at a heroic scale was congenital."[34] This same point is emphasized by novelist Martin Amis, for whom Lenin "was a moral aphasiac, a moral autist."[35] Lenin, once in power, "set about placing History on a large gauge railway track altogether, where it would be pulled by the locomotives of a revolutionary design."[36]

The magic evaporated once the historically anointed leader ceased to be the custodian of absolute truth. This makes Khrushchev's onslaughts on Stalin at the Twentieth Congress of the Communist Party of the Soviet Union (CPSU) on February 25, 1956, crucially important (as admitted by Mikhail Gorbachev in his conversation with former Prague Spring chief ideologue Zdeněk Mlynář.[37]) At the same time, it was precisely charismatic impersonalism, as Jowitt argues, that provided the antidote to desperation at the moment when Khrushchev exposed Stalin's crimes. This feature, indeed, crucially distinguished Bolshevism from Nazism: "The leader is charismatic in Nazism; the program and (possibly) the leader are charismatic in Leninism."[38] Lenin's ultimate goal was the elimination (extinction) of politics through the triumph of the party as the embodiment of an exclusionary, even exterminist general will.[39]

In the context of monastic certitude, recognition of fallibility was the beginning of the end for any ideological fundamentalism. During "heroic" times, though, such as War Communism and the "building of socialism," the unity between *party* and *vozhd* (leader) was, no less than terror, key to the system's survival. Homo sovieticus was more than a propaganda concoction. In her acceptance speech for the Hannah Arendt Award of 2000, given jointly by the city of Bremen, the Heinrich Boll Foundation, and the Hannah Arendt Association, Elena Bonner stated, "One of Hannah Arendt's key conclusions was 'The totality of terror is guaranteed by mass support.' It is consonant with a later comment by Sakharov: 'The slogan "The people and the Party are one," painted on every fifth building, are not just empty words.' "[40] This is precisely the point: the internalization of Leninist forms of thinking by millions of denizens of the Sovietized world, and their readiness to accept paternalistic collectivism as a form of life preferable to risk-driven, freedom-oriented experiences. In my view, the major cleavage in today's Russian political culture is between the Leninist heritage and the democratic aspirations and practices associated with Andrei Sakharov and Russia's human rights movement. To quote Elena Bonner again, "In the preamble to his draft of a Soviet Constitution, Sakharov wrote: 'The goal of the people of USSR and its government is a happy life full of meaning, material and spiritual freedom, well-being and peace.' But in the decades after Sakharov, Russia's people have not increased their happiness, even though he did everything humanly possible to put the country on the path leading to the goal. And he himself lived a worthy and happy life."[41]

As a political doctrine (or perhaps as a political faith), Bolshevism was a synthesis between radical Jacobinism or Blanquism (elitism, minority rule distinguished as "dictatorship of the proletariat," exaltation of the heroic vanguard), unavowed Russian "Nechaevism" (a radical-conspiratorial mentality), and the authoritarian-voluntaristic components of Marxism.[42] Bolshevism emphasized the omnipotence of the revolutionary organization and nourished contempt for what Hannah Arendt once called "the little varieties of fact"—such as Lenin and Trotsky's fierce attacks on the "renegade" Social Democrat theorist Karl Kautsky, who had dared to question the Bolshevik repudiation of all "formal" liberties in the name of protecting the "dictatorship of the proletariat," never mind that Lenin borrowed from Kautsky his "injection of consciousness" theory.

Lenin, in contrast to Marx, emphasized the organizational element as fundamental to the success of revolutionary action. For Marx, class consciousness was an organic result of the political and ideological development of the proletariat. I am thinking here, for example, of Engels's thesis on "the German proletariat as the heir of classical German philosophy," or the statement of young Marx regarding the dialectical relationship, which was therefore mutually binding, between "the critic of weapons" and "the weapon of the critique" during the process of overcoming/abolishing/conserving philosophy—*Aufhebung*). The revolutionary intellectuals were those who developed the doctrine, but the proletarians were not perceived as an amorphous mass toward which a self-appointed group of "teachers" had the duty of injecting consciousness of "historical truth." Marx did not put forth the thesis of the party as a total institution and did not consider fanatical activism to be the sine qua non of political efficacy. Marx did not conceptualize a revolutionary sect deriving its power "not from the multitudes but from a small number of enthusiastic converts whose zeal and intolerance make each one of them the equal in strength of a hundred indifferentists."[43] Rather, Lenin created an organization in which "deracinated intellectuals and the occasional worker would be baptized into the proletarian vanguard."[44] Marx's emphasis on human emancipation as the conscious absorption of society by the individual and his equation of social antagonisms with class conflict led him to advocate the elimination of intermediaries (laws, institutions, etc.) regulating the relationship between civil society and the state. Therefore, as Kołakowski brilliantly argued, "If freedom equals social unity, then the more unity there is, the more freedom. . . . The concept of negative freedom presupposes a society of conflict. If this is the same as a class society, and if a class society means a society based on private property, then there is nothing reprehensible in the idea that the act of violence which abolishes private property at the same time does away with the need for negative freedom, or freedom *tout court*. And thus Prometheus awakens from his dream of power."[45]

Marx assigned great importance to social unity but failed to give instructions on its achievement. This discrepancy left the field open for Lenin's creative understanding of necessity, which led to the Bolshevik version of man's salvation of himself. The party became the slayer of alienation and therefore the true messiah of human freedom. The combination of Marxism and state power "set the Russian body politic onto a course of self-purification."[46] In the Soviet experiment, the Marxian principle of social unity was transformed into Lenin's "unity of will," which, under Stalin, became what Erik van Ree called "the organic theory of the party." If, in Lenin's case, unity was a solution to factionalism, for Stalin it was an instrument for "the *Gleichschaltung* of the member minds." In the midst of the December 1923 struggle for supremacy, Stalin stated that "it was wrong to see the party only as 'something like a complex of a whole series of institutions with lower and higher functionaries.' Instead, it was a 'self-acting *[samodeiatel'nyi]* organism.' He described it as 'actively thinking' and 'living a lively life.'" The vision of the revolutionary leading body combined with the imposition of the practice of repentance for one's past incorrect political views (at the Fifteenth Party Conference in 1927) opened the door to murderous campaigns to remove the sores from the party organism so that the latter wouldn't fall ill.[47] The struggle to sustain and further the Bolshevik miracle turned into fighting the degeneration of the body politic. In this context, the unity of the party became the moral-political unity of the people. Society under Stalin transformed itself into an "organism engaged in a struggle for survival. [It] develops various instruments—such as productive technology, a class system of property, and language—attuned to the need of increasing its own viability."[48] Lenin's purposeful fashioning of all aspects of human existence in the context of a life-or-death class struggle grew, under Stalin, into what Erik van Ree called "Marxist Darwinism."[49]

LENIN'S UNBOUNDED RADICALISM

As a political gnosis, Bolshevik philosophy proposed the opposite of the young Marx's emphasis on the relatively spontaneous revolutionary development of class consciousness. For Marx, as the young Lukács showed, the revolutionary class symbolized the viewpoint of totality, thereby creating the epistemic premises for acceding to historical truth. For Lenin, the party was the totality—and dialectical logic served to render this oxymoron palatable to committed militants.[50] This was the origin of the major conflicts between Lenin and Luxemburg and one of the main distinctions between Soviet and Western Marxism. Rosa Luxemburg anticipated the path taken by the Bolsheviks toward the totalization of power when she wrote that the development of their revolution "moves naturally in an ascending line: from moderate beginnings to ever-greater radicalization of aims and, parallel with that, from a coalition of classes and parties to the *sole rule of the radical party* [my emphasis]."[51] In the same criticism of the Russian Revolution, Luxemburg issued a strong warning concerning the methods of preserving power adopted by Lenin and his party. She cautioned that the elimination of democracy, with its institutions that though cumbersome did prevent abuses of power, would lead to the mortification of the first workers' state: "To be sure, every democratic institution has its limits and shortcomings, things which it doubtless shares with all other human institutions. But the remedy which Trotsky and Lenin have found, the elimination of democracy as such, is worse than the disease it is supposed to cure; for it stops up the very living source from which alone can come the correction of all the innate shortcomings of social institutions. That source is the active, untrammeled, energetic political life of the broadest masses of the people."[52] Luxemburg's words were echoed later by one of Lenin's closest collaborators, Nikolai Bukharin, who, in the aftermath of the Bolshevik victory in the civil war, concluded that the notion that "all tasks . . . can be solved by Communist decree" was "Communist conceit."[53] A few years later he added that "we do not carry out experiments, we are not vivisectionists, who . . . operate on a living organism with a knife; we are conscious of our historic responsibility."[54] This thinking, however, did not prevent Bukharin from purging individuals perceived as deviationists within the party. Despite moderation, his behavior essentially reflected the organizational ethos of Leninism: dictatorship over and uncompromising struggle against the the party's enemies and heretics. No wonder that in 1927 Bukharin was denounced by an old comrade as the "jailer of the best Communists."[55]

The Communist Manifesto foreshadowed this fundamental schism by advancing in two directions that would be further elaborated in mature Marxian theory: on one hand, it emphasized the self-development of class consciousness; on the other, it glorified violence. The bastardization of Marxism in Lenin's experiment cannot be dissociated from the attacks on bourgeois rights and the criminalization of private property in the founding fathers' writings. This was of course legitimized by high historical necessity, the ultimate end that would somehow justify the cruelty of the means: "In place of the old bourgeois society, with its classes and class antagonisms, we shall have an association, in which the free development of each is the condition for the free development of all."[56] Moreover, one need go no further than the famous opening lines of part 1 of the *Manifesto* for evidence of this monism: "The history of all hitherto existing society is the history of class struggles. . . . Our epoch, the epoch of the bourgeoisie, possesses, however, this distinct feature: it has simplified class antagonisms. Society as a whole is more and more splitting up into two great hostile camps, into two great classes directly facing each other—Bourgeoisie and Proletariat."[57]

From the outset, the *Manifesto* announced what the influential Russian Marxist Georgi Plekhanov called a "monist view of history," according to which all historical conflict is reducible to class conflict and all political debate is reducible to the question of which class you represent or support.[58] In *History and Class Consciousness* Georg Lukács reads the thought of Marx as an "expression" of "the standpoint of the proletariat." Lukács offers an ingenious interpretation of Marxism as the unfolding "truth" of the class struggle. And in reducing questions of truth or falsity and right or wrong to questions of "class standpoint," he is simply following the lead of the *Manifesto*. For it was Marx himself who declared, "The theoretical conclusions of the Communists are in no way based on ideas or principles that have been invented, or discovered, by this or that would-be universal reformer. . . . They merely express, in general terms, actual relations springing from an existing class struggle, from a historical movement going on under our very eyes."[59] The intellectual distance separating this formulation from the Bolshevik idea that the Communists are in possession of "politically correct" insight into the movement and the *meaning* of history is not far. Moreover, Marx himself consistently showed an obvious unwillingness to tolerate those socialists who did not agree with him or questioned his authority. The energy he spent denouncing such "heretics" indicates the presence of an authoritarian personality.

In the passionately incandescent lines of the *Communist Manifesto,* one can decipher the whole tragedy that was to follow: Lenin's forcing of the pace of history, the genesis of Bolshevism as a matrix for generalized terror, the Stalinist horrors, and the universe of the concentration camp. Nations were murdered to carry out Lenin's utopian desiderata. Social classes were victimized in the name of his abstract speculations and moral revolt. The question, therefore, is what connection exists between the Leninist exterminist project and the original Marxian salvationist fantasy. In retrospect, one can argue that Marx's oracular monism, defined by his hyperdeterministic approach, scientism, and positivism, took revenge on the ethical-libertarian dimension and laid the foundation for intolerance and repression. To elaborate on a dichotomy proposed by Karl Popper, it can be said that the moral radicalism of Marxism survived in contemporary varieties of democratic socialism. Political radicalism, with its mixture of historicism and positivism, culminated in Leninist conspiracy and dictatorship.[60] Essentially, the Bolsheviks' revolutionary subjectivism was defined by the conception of parties as "oligarchies of scholars and organizers, assemblies of people who change the world through their wills, while constantly obeying the laws of history."[61]

REDEMPTIVE MYTHOLOGIES

Is this all over? Far from it—and this applies not only to the countries once ruled by Leninist parties, but also to nationalist-socialist parties like Baath and charismatic fundamentalist, neototalitarian movements, including Osama bin Laden's Al Qaeda.[62] The Leninist (Bolshevik) mental matrix was rooted in a political culture suspicious of open dialogue and democratic procedures, and hostile to spontaneous developments from below. Leninism was not only an ideology but also a set of precepts and techniques meant to inspire revolutionary global activism and militantism opposed to bourgeois liberalism and democratic socialism. Both Leninism and Fascism were discourses of domination that achieved effectiveness by functioning as "closed rhetorical systems that determined content as well as limits of political consciousness."[63] This is precisely the similarity but also the main distinction between these two onslaughts on liberal individualism: Fascism was a pathology of romantic irrationalism, and Bolshevism was a pathology of Enlightenment-inspired hyperrationalism. I don't want to be misunderstood: as an offspring of nineteenth-century antibourgeois, often antimodern, ideologies of resentment, Fascism did not need Bolshevism in order to emerge and mature (as demonstrated in Isaiah Berlin's fascinating essay on Joseph de Maistre and the origins of Fascism).[64] The cult of race, the blending of pseudoscientism (social Darwinism) with the neopagan worship of blood and soil, and the resentful rejection of liberal values as "soulless arithmetic" predated Leninism. On the other hand, it is hard to deny that the triumph of Bolshevism and the intensity and scope of the Red Terror, together with the traumatic effects of World War I and the widespread sentiment that "the world of yesterday" (to quote Stefan Zweig) had irretrievably come to an end, mobilized the Fascist offensive against the universalistic traditions of the Enlightenment.

Fascism was no less a fantasy of salvation than was Bolshevism: both promised to rescue humanity from the bondage of capitalist mercantilism and to ensure the advent of the total community. Fascism was a type of hysteria rooted in pseudopoetic heroic nostalgias, in militant collectivism, and above all, in the programmatic abhorrence of the fundamental values of liberal democracy. Its potential for emotional identification originated in myth, in the obsessive invocation of supposedly pristine origins, in the excessive cult for what Sigmund Freud once called "the narcissism of small differences."[65] Fascism aimed at homogenization through the sublimation of the body politic to the common denominator of its imagined genetic bedrock. Its fundamental nature is expressed in the principle that "in order for the national phoenix to arise, everything and everyone that stands in its way first has to be brunt to ashes, literally if necessary."[66] In the aftermath of the First World War, Italo Balbo, one of the main ideologues of Italian Fascism, expressed the ethos of this new political movement by contrasting it to the old order, which he deemed effete, corrupt, degenerate, and decaying. Rather than helping to restore prewar society, Balbo emphatically declared, "No, better to deny all, destroy all, renew all, from the base."[67] Contempt for the old bourgeois order and fascination with the utopian new one were attitudes shared by Communists and Fascists.

Both Leninism and Fascism were creative forms of nihilism, extremely utilitarian and contemptuous of universal rights. The essential element of their *modus vivendi* was the "sanctification of violence."[68] They envisioned society as a community of "bearers of beliefs," and every aspect of their private life and behavior was expected to conform with these beliefs. Upon coming into power and implementing their vision of the perfect society, the two political movements established dictatorships of purity in which "people were rewarded or punished according to politically defined criteria of virtue."[69] Dario Lupi, an undersecretary of the Ministry of Education in Fascist Italy, warned menacingly that "he who joins us either becomes one of us in body and soul, in mind and flesh, or he will inexorably be cut off. For we know and feel ourselves in possession of the truth. . . . [W]e know and feel ourselves to be part of the only movement in marvelous harmony with the history time. . . . For ours is the only movement that faithfully reflects the innermost layers of the souls and feelings of our own kind."[70] Similarly, Hitler considered that the movement he led was a necessary creative destruction generated by the imperative of reestablishing the chosen community on the right track of history. On July 1934, Hitler stated that "when a deathly check is violently imposed upon the natural development of a people, an act of violence may serve to release the artificially interrupted flow of evolution to allow it once again the freedom of natural development."[71]

Both Leninism and Fascism presented themselves as revolutionary breakthroughs to a new life. Their novelty lay in the shrill ideological sacralization of revolutionary power. They preconditioned reconstruction by unleashing destruction. Oblivious to any independent moral dimension, both stressed "force and guile in shaping history," exposing "hypocrisy, the absurdity of human condition," while simultaneously preaching a political zeal that was supposed to "construct meaning, and sought, through political organization and action, to bring it into being." Each of them was, as A. E. Rees showed, forms of a "revolutionary Machiavellian conception of politics. . . . More precisely, Nazism and Bolshevism might be defined as the Machiavellianism of parties which claimed to rule in the name of the masses."[72] To paraphrase Eugen Weber, in the case of both Leninism and Fascism, the locomotives that dragged them across history were their tactics. Leninism was therefore based on a "goal rationality," which implied "the validity of its demands." In this mental framework, "compliance is claimed to be based on a rational relationship between the ultimate goal of communism and the specific tasks assigned to social units, and individuals' rationality relates to the appropriateness of the means used . . . to the goals set."[73]

Such a radically utilitarian, transformist conception of politics ultimately materialized in the divinization of a mythical state holding the right of life and death over its subjects. Or as the Catholic intellectual Adolf Keller wrote, "A superhuman giant, claiming not only obedience, but confidence and faith such as only a personality has the right to expect."[74] In this conception, the state was beyond moral limitations, for it was the *only* producer of morality. However, as sociologist Michael Mann underlines, Fascism and Communism, despite the presence of party or leader despotism, "ruled more as a fluid, continuing revolutionary movement than as an institutionalized state." They were, according to Mann, "regimes of continuous revolution."[75] These political movements were fueled by their projected heroic perpetual dynamism. In the case of Communism, stagnation and ultimately demise developed as its "shrill confidence in the history-making mode of action dissipated . . . in light of what experience had revealed."[76]

The leader, of course, played an essential role in such movements.[77] As Leszek Kołakowski puts it, "Party mindedness, the political principle revered by all Leninists, resulted in the infallible image bestowed on the general secretary."[78] Paul Berman explains: "Lenin was the original model of such a Leader—Lenin, who wrote pamphlets and philosophical tracts with the confidence of a man who believes the secrets of the universe to be at his fingertips, and who established a weird new religion with Karl Marx as god, and who, after his death, was embalmed like a pharaoh and worshipped by the masses. But il Duce was no less a superhuman. Stalin was a colossus. About Hitler, Heidegger, bug-eyed, said: 'But look at his hands.' "[79] Peter Ehlen makes the insightful observation that Lenin "redefined the ground upon which the Communist renewal would be based. Henceforth, it would be the will of the leader." In this context, power would become "absolute power and knows to lend itself a quasi-numinous appearance."[80] In other words, Leninism was also vitally premised on the apotheosis of the leader. An amusing but telltale example of the weight of this founding element of Leninism is Comrade Lazurkina's intervention at the Twenty-second Party Congress in Moscow. In October 1961, during discussions about the expulsion of Stalin from the Lenin Mausoleum, an Old Bolshevik, Comrade Lazurkina, "who had spent 17 years in prisons and camps, reported that Lenin had appeared to her repeatedly in a dream. Lenin had demanded that his successor be removed from his mausoleum. And so it came to pass."[81] The ghost of one leader could not bear that of his successor anymore. The pantheon of Bolshevism had only one master—Lenin. Another matter related to the insertion of the will of the leader into the practice of Leninism was the "continuing inability of the party's leading legislative organs—the congress, CC [Central Committee] and Politburo—to develop a strong sense of institutional integrity and coherence," according to Graeme Gill. Gill shows how the organizational basis of Stalin's power in the aftermath of Lenin's death, and even earlier, was "the absence of a major commitment of leading political figures to strengthen the organizational norms and identity of these bodies, inertia and the methods of action adopted by the party leadership."[82] For Gill, the weaknesses of Leninism evident in the 1920s set the stage for Stalin's autocratic rule over the party and over the Soviet Union.

Spontaneity *(stikhiinost')* has always been the Leninists' nemesis (think of Lenin's polemics on the relationship between class and party, first with Rosa Luxemburg, then with the left-wing Communists). Its counterpart was the obsession with *partiinost'* (partisanship), the unbounded acceptance of the party line (philosophy, sociology, and aesthetics had to be subordinated to party-defined "proletarian interests," hence the dichotomy between "bourgeois" and "proletarian" social science). However, in the context of the Russian proletariat's underdeveloped class consciousness, Lenin, on the occasion of the 1905 revolution, revealed, according to Ana Krylova, "the 'true nature' of the working class ... not through workers' conscious revolutionary initiative, as had been expected, but through an 'instinctive urge' that the workers 'felt' for open revolutionary action." His discovery lay in the fact that the workers had the ability to "sense history and act in accordance with its objective needs without necessarily understanding them."[83] To close the circle, this reading of the December uprising reinforced Lenin's belief that behind the party, under proper leadership, the workers would fulfill their class mission despite an insufficient understanding of their historical role. This allowed him to justify both the voluntarism of Bolsheviks' takeover of power and the Enlightenment mission the party embarked on once in power.

Moreover, this insertion of "class instinct" in the equation of *stikhiinost'-partiinost'* explains to a large extent Lenin's theory of the common struggle (alliance) between the workers and the peasants *(smychka)*. Its fundamental presupposition was that the Bolsheviks could awaken the peasants' class instincts, thus winning them over to the side of the revolution. According to Lenin, "The more enlightened the peasantry becomes the more consistently and resolutely will it stand for a thoroughgoing democratic revolution."[84] This is what Ken Jowitt called "the ingenious error of Leninism"—transplanting class struggle to the countryside: "The ideological-conceptual map with which Leninists work leads them to see economic differences as evidence of social polarization and the existence of 'class allies' in the villages, and it enables them to do politically what nationalists can do only analytically—that is, distinguish and oppose competing social bases and conceptions of the nation-state. Working with such a paradigm, Leninists attack the institutional bases, not simply the elite organization of peasant society."[85] And if Bukharin's model of the gradual growth of private property in socialist agriculture does not happen (and it did not during the New Economic Policy), then Leninism's vision of a spontaneous class "transformist" commitment and interests opened the door to collectivization. This amounted to an all-out attack on the foundation of the peasants' institutional and private lives, the rural counterpart to the urban socialist revolution. In their pursuit of this goal, the Bolsheviks had no limits, no pangs of conscience, no scruples. The result was genocide.

Much of Leninism's dogmatism stemmed from Russian authoritarian traditions and the lack of a culture of public debate. Remember Antonio Gramsci's reflections on Russia's "gelatinous" civil society and the omnipotence of the bureaucratic state? Wasn't Lenin himself, by the end of his life, terrified by the resurgence of the time-honored traditions of rudeness, violence, brutality, and hypocrisy that he had lambasted and against which the revolution was presumably directed? As one author remarked, "Lenin was a direct heir to the tradition of revolutionary Machiavellianism in Russian history and to the Jacobin tradition in the European revolutionary movement."[86] On the one hand, as we have already discussed, Lenin believed that revolution was essential and inevitable, and that it would, of necessity, be violent; he considered any other approach to be conciliatory and doomed to failure.[87] On the other hand, his Jacobinism was "a metaphor for revolutionary energy, incorruptibility and a willingness to push forward as far as possible in the interests of the working masses." It was founded on his dedication to plebeian politics, "and the twentieth century plebeians were of course the class of wage-laborers. Hence consistent proletarian socialists had to be Jacobins."[88] Or, to use Lenin's formula, the Bolsheviks were Jacobins working for the proletariat.[89]

Lenin was conscious that his most difficult trial was the transition from revolutionary action to governance and the preservation of state power. The success of the October Revolution seemed to confirm that he had successfully merged "the elemental destructive force of the masses" and "the conscious destructive force of the organization of revolutionaries." But how was the newly won power to be consolidated? The initial drive toward democracy from below and self-empowerment of the masses, was replaced in 1917 by emphasis on the reconstructed state machine that according to Lenin was indispensable for defending the revolution and pursuing its main goals. In form, Lenin said, this was a dictatorship, but in substance, because it represented the interests and aspirations of the large majority of the population, it was the true, substantive democracy. The main problem with Lenin's concept of the dictatorship of the proletariat was his contempt for the rule of law. For him, the revolutionary dictatorship of the proletariat "is power won and maintained by the violence of the proletariat against the bourgeoisie, power that is unrestricted by any laws."[90] This was the central point of Rosa Luxemburg's criticism of the Russian Revolution. She argued that "[Lenin] is completely mistaken in the means he employs. Decree, dictatorial force of the factory overseer, Draconic penalties, rule by terror—all these things are but palliatives. The only way to a rebirth is the school of public life itself, the most unlimited, the broadest democracy and public opinion. It is rule by terror which demoralizes." With great foresight, Luxemburg warned that the path taken by the Bolsheviks would lead to "the brutalization of public life."[91]

The restoration of state prerogatives was for Lenin a "necessary evil," and he tried to justify the notion of a proletarian dictatorship by defining it as the dictatorship of the majority of the population (poor peasants included), and therefore not exactly a dictatorship. Lenin was convinced, however, that these exceptional measures, including the persecution of dissidents and banning of all political parties but the Bolsheviks, were needed for the survival of the revolution in Russia. In the long run, however, he hoped that the revolution would triumph in the West and a certain political and economic relaxation would become possible. Lenin saw this as a temporary stage; he never accepted the idea that the Russian Revolution would be the *sole* proletarian revolution for decades to come. At the end of the day, though, Lenin imposed two fundamental elements on the Bolshevik conception of politics: law as an epiphenomenon of revolutionary morals and the heteronomy of individual action. In this sense, Lenin opened the door to the realization of radical evil, for the latter, if one is to follow Hannah Arendt, means "making human beings as human beings superfluous. . . . This happens as soon as all unpredictability—which, in human beings, is the equivalent of spontaneity—is eliminated."[92] Here lies the essential ambivalence in interpreting Leninism: was it a form of Russian *Sonderweg* (special road) on the path to implementing modernity or was it a Marxist *Sonderweg* in the accomplishment of socialist revolution?

Whatever one thinks of the final disintegration of Leninism, it was a quite successful experiment in reshaping political community according to a certain interpretation of Marxist socialism.[93] How does one make sense of the fact that, unlike all other Eastern European societies, Russia is the only one that seems unable to restore pro-Communist traditions and parties? Where are the Socialist Revolutionaries, Kadets, or Mensheviks? The answer is that Lenin produced "the end of politics" via the ultimate triumph of political will.[94] In fact, this meant that a sect of self-appointed revolutionary pedagogues managed to coerce a large population to accept their obsessions as the inexorable imperative of history. Using the example of the implementation of surveillance (considered one of the practices of "institutionalizing modernity"), Peter Holquist shows that its enforcement was not "a specifically Bolshevik, Marxist, or even totalitarian practice—it was a modern one." In his opinion, what gave the Soviet regime its singularity was "the intersection

of a particular ideology with the simultaneous implementation of a particular modern understanding of politics—put succinctly, an understanding that views populations as both the means and the goal of some
emancipatory project." With its specific Marxist conception of politics,
society, and history in the background, Leninism developed "a closed,
rather than open, model of historical progress."[95]

Communism and Fascism were sustained by the historical-political
sense of historical urgency and their willingness to act in a radical mode.
The vanguards that brought these political movements to power and
kept them there were mobilized and vindicated by the ethical-political
change that they considered themselves uniquely prepared to spearhead
because of their postliberal consciousness, as well as their spirit, will,
discipline, self-sacrifice, and willingness to act.[96] Imposing the dictatorship of the Communist Party as the sole instrument for history-making
action, the Bolsheviks successfully exhausted the political sphere, eliminating all alternative visions of the body politic. Lenin, and later Stalin,
transformed the political system into "the central and sacralized arena
for the self-salvation and self-sacrifice of revolutionaries striving to im-
plement the utopian designs which have to be realized in the present and
on earth."[97] Considering that the Soviet Union survived for over seventy
years, the operation of making sense of the pre-Communist past logically faces a historical hiatus. The various trajectories of Russian political thought must overcome either an utter lack of domestic continuity or
the thorny issue of synthetic reinterpretation. In the final analysis, it is
difficult to recuperate tradition into the twenty-first century, when the
country's only version of mature modernity was Leninism.

This statement, however, takes us to another ramification of the dilemma of the *Sonderwegs*. The major theme of the Richard Pipes–
Martin Malia controversy is important not only for our interpretation
of Russian modern history but also for the discussion of the nature and
future of left-wing, socialist politics in the twentieth century: was it Russia that destroyed (compromised) socialism, as Pipes and, earlier, Max
Weber put it, or rather was it revolutionary socialism that, because of its
political, indeed metaphysical, hubris, imposed immense sufferings on
Russia?[98] Objecting to the young Georg Lukács's celebration of Lenin's
takeover of power in Russia, Weber insisted on the impossibility of building the socialism Karl Marx had envisioned in the absence of genuine
capitalist, bourgeois market developments: "It is with good reason," he
wrote, "that the *Communist Manifesto* emphasized the *economically
revolutionary* character of the bourgeois capitalist entrepreneurs. No

trade-unions, much less state-socialist officials, can perform this role for us in their place."[99] Earlier than many critics of Sovietism, Weber concluded that the Leninist experiment would discredit socialism for the entire twentieth century.[100]

REENACTING LENIN?

So, is there a reason to consider Lenin's political praxis a source of inspiration for those who look for a new political transcendence? Is it a blueprint for a resurrected radicalism, as suggested by Slavoj Žižek, who proposes the revival of the Leninist 1917 revolutionary leap into the kingdom of utopia? Reenacting Lenin's defiance of opportunistic or conformist submission to the logic of the status quo is for Žižek the *voie royale* for restoring a radical praxis:

> *This* is the Lenin from whom we still have something to learn. The greatness of Lenin was that in this catastrophe situation *he wasn't afraid to succeed*—in contrast to the negative pathos discernible in Rosa Luxemburg and Adorno, for whom the ultimate authentic act is the admission of the failure, which brings the truth of the situation to light. In 1917, instead of waiting until the time was ripe, Lenin organized a pre-emptive strike; in 1920, as the leader of the party of the working class with no working class (most of it being decimated in the civil war), he went on organizing a state, fully accepting the paradox of the party which was to organize—even recreate—its own base, its working class.[101]

Compare this exalted vision of Lenin to that of a former Communist ideologue, the apostate Alexander Yakovlev's indictment of Lenin's essential role in the establishment of a dictatorial regime in which the working class was to suffer as much as other social strata the effects of utopian social engineering.[102] Can Leninism be separated from the institution of the vanguard party and be conceived as a form of intellectual and moral resistance to the conformist debacle of the international Left at a moment of civilization collapse (World War I)? The debate on Leninism bears upon the possibility of radical-emancipatory practice and the need to reconstruct areas of autonomy in opposition to the logic of instrumental rationality. The burning question remains whether such efforts are predestined to end in new coercive undertakings, or whether Leninism was a peculiar, sui generis combination of Marxism and an underdeveloped political and economic structure. Indeed, as Trotsky insisted, the defeat of "world revolution"—after all, the main strategic postulate on which Lenin had built his whole revolutionary adventure—made the rise of Stalinism a sociological and political necessity. Here we may remember Isaac Deutscher's analysis: "Under Lenin, Bolshevism had been accustomed to appeal to reason, the self-interest, and the enlightened idealism of 'class-conscious' industrial workers. It spoke the language of reason even when it appealed to the *muzhiks*. But once Bolshevism had ceased to rely on revolution in the West, once it had become aware that it could only fall back on that environment and dig itself in, it began to descend to the level of primitive magic, and to appeal to the people in the language of that magic."[103]

At this point, the last element of our dilemma comes into play. If one is to even partially accept the validity of the Russian *Sonderweg* thesis, the next problem is how much this Russian distortion was Stalin's. What needs to be discussed is not only Deutscher's claim that Stalinism was "the language of magic," but also Robert C. Tucker's theory of *reversion.* The latter consists of the claim that under Stalin one can identify "the revival of certain features which belonged to the past, especially the more distant past, and had receded or been abolished (like serfdom) in nineteenth century Russia, but re-surfaced in the Stalin period." Tucker takes this analysis even further as he labels Stalinism Russian National Bolshevism, a blend of Leninist Marxism and Russian nationalism.[104] His thesis is consonant with more recent views advocated by authors such as Terry Martin and David Brandenberger, who emphasize a neotraditionalist turn in the process of building socialism in one country. During mature Stalinism, "Soviet patriotism" became an apology for national authenticity, pride, and loyalty. At the same time, the Soviet Union, "a state with no ambition to turn itself into a nation-state—indeed with the exact opposite ambition," became a site of large-scale ethnic cleansing.[105] Moreover, the society was a hierarchy on the basis of "Stalinist *soslovnost.*" According to Sheila Fitzpatrick, "*soslovnost*' provides a framework within which it becomes immediately comprehensible that the 'classes' of the Stalinist society should have been defined, like *sosloviia,* in terms of their relationship to the state rather than, like Marxist classes, in terms of their relationship to each other."[106] This whole array of developments originated in Stalin's development of a new, non-class, "popular" form of mobilization. As David Priestland points out, "The unified *narod,* now no longer divided by class, embodied socialism, and was to achieve heroic feats in the struggle against largely external enemies."[107] Subsequently, the USSR itself became "the avant-garde of the international communist movement and the dynamic centre of world politics."[108] This phenomenon was symptomatic for the Soviet experiment, where "the sense of collectively creating socialism was more important than the use of class categories and the assumption of proletarian privilege."[109] In the context of building socialism in one country, for Stalin the body social was the chosen community bringing into *state*-reality Lenin's social utopia.[110]

What this "mutation" of Marxist orthodoxy tells, though, is that the ultimate aim of Stalin's policies *remained* Communism. Even his cult of personality functioned as "a unifying mechanism," "a personification of socialist state-building."[111] Graeme Gill simply states that "the Stalin cult grew upon the edifice of Leninist orthodoxy." In his study of K. Popov's article "The Party and the Role of the Leader," one of the pieces theoretically underpinning the cult, Gill pointed to "three main grounds for recognition of the *vozhd*": the leader "armed with Marxist-Leninist revolutionary theory, hardened by many years experience of the struggle for Leninism, hand in hand with Lenin"; the ability to endure 'those difficulties which befell the narrow circles of selfless revolutionaries" by way of exceptional organizational talent; and "the will of an individual leader [that] could personify the will of the proletariat."[112] Indeed, Lenin was the embodiment of the theory, the struggle, and the party. This was his model of successful radical revolutionary transformation. In 1930, Stalin claimed to be the personification of this heritage of Lenin. He upheld this assertion of supremacy over his rivals by organizational power, thus creating an environment fundamentally inimical to any form of opposition. Like Lenin, but to an exaggerated degree, by the end of the 1930s, Stalin managed to become synonymous with the party itself.

Stalin also emulated Lenin's creativity in his approach to the political thought of the founding fathers. In 1941, Stalin warned the authors of the commissioned *Short Course of Political Economy,* "If you search for everything in Marx, you'll get off track . . . . In the USSR you have a laboratory . . . and you think Marx should know more than you about socialism." By 1950, his attitude toward Marxism resembled Lenin's famous remark from the *Philosophical Notebooks:* "Half a century later none of the Marxists understood Marx." Stalin wrote in *Pravda:* "In the course of its development Marxism cannot help but be enriched by new experience, by new knowledge; consequently, its individual formulas and conclusions must change with the passing of time, must be replaced by new formulas and conclusions corresponding to new historical tasks. Marxism does not recognize immutable conclusions and formulas obligatory for all epochs and periods."[113] Ultimately, Stalin's rehashing of Marxism (and) Leninism could be read in a more general key. It should be placed in the original interpretative ethos of Bolshevik "substitution-ism." Georg Lukács justified Lenin's theory of the revolution based on the idea of "ascribed class consciousness," that is, "the appropriate rational reactions 'imputed' to a particular typical position in the process of production."[114] Why would we not accept the same ascription for the building of state socialism? Both for Lenin and for Stalin, the state that seemed to stubbornly refuse to wither away remained the ultimate test for "the *real* understanding and recognition of Marxism."[115]

Going back to the ambivalence of Leninism, I think that what we need to stress, beyond the debates about its Marxist, Russian, or reified core (by Stalin), is that "its goal is to transcend any particular politics . . . and to realize a philosophical project over the heads (or behind the backs) of the participants. Its justification lies in its claim to transcend their (alienated) self-consciousness in the name of the really real truth. It is politics as antipolitics."[116] From this point of view, regardless of distinctions between party persuasion and coercion (in Tucker's formulation) or the language of reason versus that of magic, it is undeniable that Lenin was the one who created the possibility for the culmination of "Marx's hypothesis that the working class has a privileged knowledge of the final purpose of history in the assertion that Comrade Stalin is always right."[117] Lenin produced and implemented a charismatic doctrine of universal human regeneration, a New Faith (as Czesław Miłosz called Bolshevism) based on "the archetypal human faculty for imbuing the home and the community, and hence the new home and the new community, with suprahuman, ritual significance."[118] In the final analysis, Leninism was the child of three mothers: the Enlightenment with its focus on reason and progress; Marx's social theory and project of world historical transformation; and the Russian revolutionary tradition with its utilitarian nihilism and a quasi-religious socialist vision of the transformation of mankind.

With this intellectual pedigree in mind, one needs to be very cautious in writing Leninism's definitive obituary. Yes, as a Russian model of socialism it is exhausted, but there is something in Leninism—if you want, its antidemocratic, collectivist pathos associated with the invention of the party as a mystical body transcending individual fears, anguishes, despair, loneliness, and so on—that remains with us. All political figures in post-Soviet Russia—all parties, movements, and associations—define themselves, and must do so, in relationship to Lenin's legacies. In this respect, as an organizational principle but not as a worldview, Leninism is alive, if not well. Ideologically it is extinct, of course, but its repudia-

tion of democratic deliberation and contempt for "sentimental bourgeois values" has not vanished. This is because the cult of the organization and the contempt for individual rights is part and parcel of *one*
direction within the "Russian tradition." Russian memory includes a
plurality of trends, and one should avoid any kind of Manichean taxonomy. It is doubtless that, as Christian existentialist philosopher Nikolai Berdyaev noticed, there is something deeply Russian in the love for
the ultimate, universally cathartic, redeeming revolution, which explains
why Lenin and his followers (including the highly sophisticated philosophers Georg Lukács and Ernst Bloch) embraced a certain cataclysmic,
messianic, absolutist direction within the Marxist tradition.[119] The Bolshevik revolution was indeed the expression of Russian intellectuals'
obsession with "a version of a thirst for the sacred with a concomitant
revulsion against the profane, a contest of values that can be seen in an
early paradigm, the story of Christ's throwing the money changers out
of the temple."[120] In his revolutionary praxis, Lenin, as famously formulated by Robert C. Tucker, "married the old image of two warring
Russias with Marxism."[121] Leninism was "not solely a revolutionary
response to the inequities of the Tsarist state and the social injustice
endemic to capitalist liberalism, but also a response to the crisis of
modernity."[122]

At the same time, one should place Leninism in contradistinction to
other versions of Marxism, which were at least as legitimate if not more
legitimate than the Bolshevik doctrine. It is not at all self-evident that
one can derive the genocidal logic of the gulags from Marx's universalistic postulates, whereas it is quite clear that much of the Stalinist system
existed in embryo in Lenin's Russia. Together with Robert C. Tucker, we
should admit the heterogeneous nature of the Bolshevik tradition itself
and avoid the temptation of "retrospective determinism." Thus Stalin's
Lenin was only one of the possibilities implied in the Leninist project.

Now, in dealing with the impact of Russian ideas and practices on
the West, there is always a problem: what Russian tradition do we refer
to?[123] The Decembrist or the czarist-autocratic one? Cernyshevsky or
Herzen? Chaadaev or Gogol? Turgenev or Dostoyevski? The humanists
who opposed the pogroms and the blood libel or the Black Hundreds?
The liberal writer Vladimir Korolenko or the czarist reactionary Konstantin Pobedonostsev? The Bolshevik apocalyptical scenario or the
Menshevik evolutionary socialism? The Nechaev-style terrorist rejection
of the status quo, the intelligentsia's perpetual self-flagellation and outrage, or the dissident vision of a tolerant polis? Even within the dissident

culture, there has always been a tension between the liberals and the nationalists, between the supporters of Andrei Sakharov and those of Igor Shafarevich, between Solzhenitsyn's Slavophile inclinations and Sergey Kovalev's democratic universalism.[124] All these questions remain as troubling now as they were one hundred years ago. Once again, Russia is confronted with the eternal questions "What is to be done?" and "Who are to be blamed?" And whether they admit it or not, all participants in the debate are haunted by Lenin's inescapable presence. Lenin was the most influential Russian political personality of the twentieth century, and for Eastern Europeans, Lenin's influence resulted in the complete transformation of their life worlds. It would be easy to simply say that Leninism succumbed to the events of 1989–91, but the truth is that residual Bolshevism continues to be a major component of the hybrid transitional culture of post-Soviet Russia (and East Central Europe).

To return to our initial dilemma about the proper interpretation of the Soviet experiment, one needs to draw one final line and ask, What was Lenin's unique, extraordinary innovation? What was the substance of his transformative action? Here I think that Jowitt rather than Žižek gave the accurate answer. The charismatic vanguard party, made up of professional revolutionaries, was invented by Lenin over one hundred years ago, in 1902, when he wrote his most influential text, *What Is to Be Done?* Lars Lih disagrees with the "textbook interpretation" of Leninism (the predestined-pedagogical role of the revolutionary vanguard, i.e., the Communist Party) and insists that many, if not most, Social Democrats at the beginning of the twentieth century were convinced of the need to bring consciousness to the class from "without."[125] According to Lih, the thrust of the criticism from other socialists was aimed not at *What Is to Be Done,* but rather at his "Letter to a Comrade," written in September 1902, and especially *One Step Forward Two Steps Backwards,* published in the spring of 1904. But this "injection approach" (bringing consciousness from the outside, awakening a dormant proletariat) was not the thrust of Lenin's main revision of classical Marxism: it was not educational action per se, but rather the nature of the pedagogical agent that mattered in the story. This "party of a new type" symbolized what Antonio Gramsci later called the "New Prince": a new figure of the political that absorbs and incorporates the independent life of society up to the point of definitive osmosis or asphyxiation.

BOLSHEVISM AS POLITICAL MESSIANISM

Lenin created a mystique of the party as the ultimate repository of strategic wisdom, a "community of saints" dedicated to bringing about the cataclysmic millenium: it was *the* historical agent, for it encompassed the professional revolutionaries, those who, by reuniting their acting and thinking faculties, regained "the grace of the harmonious original being."[126] One statement speaks volumes about the totemic entity he wished to create: "We believe in the party, we see in her the reason, the honor and the conscience of our epoch . . . the only guarantee for the liberation movement of the working class."[127] For the Bolsheviks, "like Christ, the party was, at one and the same time, a real institution and an incarnated idea. The formation of the Party was the First Coming; not fully appreciated by an immature working class, it heralded a Second Coming and the apotheosis of workers' consciousness at which point all workers would join the Party, thereby rendering it superfluous. The eschatological significance of the Party explained the zeal with which the Marxists guarded its purity."[128] Lenin developed an exclusivist vision of party unity founded on unflinching adherence to the established doctrinal line and *not* on a consensual agreement about the main ideological tenets. For him, it was "the unity of Marxists, not the unity of Marxists with the enemies and distorters of Marxism."[129] As I have shown, this unwillingness to compromise over the interpretation of history is one of the fundamental features of the sacralization of politics.

Leninism was a form of modern messianism intolerant of realities escaping its ideological panorama. It was a production recipe for *The Communist Manifesto*'s "scenario for the drama of millenarian redemption."[130] The professional revolutionaries who made up "the party of a new type" were, according to Yury Piatakov, "men of miracles" bringing into life "that which is considered impossible, not realizable and inadmissible. . . . [W]e are people of special temper, without any equivalents in history precisely because we make impossible possible."[131] Therefore, the party was the embodiment of historical reason and militants were expected to carry out its orders without hesitation or reservation. Discipline, secrecy, and rigid hierarchy were essential to such a party, especially during clandestine activities (like those in Russia). The main role of the party was to awaken proletarian self-consciousness and instill revolutionary doctrine (faith) into the dormant proletariat. This was the party's salvific mission, and because of it the party was the embodiment of freedom. Instead of relying on the spontaneous development of consciousness among the industrial working class, Leninism saw the party as a catalytic agent bringing revolutionary knowledge, will, and organization to the exploited masses.[132] Futurist poet Vladimir Maya-kovsky was right when he said:

> When we say Lenin
> We mean the Party
> And when we say Party
> We mean Lenin.[133]

First Leninism, then Stalinism, codified the total commitment to an apocalyptic scenario dedicated to bringing about not only a new type of society but also a new type of human being.[134] With its ambition to initiate an anthropological revolution, Marxism can be regarded as a form of utopian radicalism—utopian because it is basically future oriented and overlooks the perennial features of the human condition, radical inasmuch as it aims to transform the body politic and establish a form of social organization totally different form all previous ones. Moreover, in its Bolshevik application, this utopian radicalism turned into "a set of values and beliefs, a culture, a language, new forms of speech, more modern customs and new ways of behaving in public and in private." And the name under which all this came together was Stalinism—a self-identified separate and superior civilization.[135] Marxism-Leninism as mythology therefore relied on two mutually conditioning myths: a sustaining one (the first workers' state with its corollary the Great October Revolution) and an eschatological one (the realization of Communism).[136] According to these myths, Marx's collectivity of self-determined, quasi-divine beings undergoing "perpetual becoming that knows no limits and continually striving forwards anew" entered its *kairos,* accomplishing the ultimate destiny prefigured by history. This triumphant tale of humanity's renewal was provisioned only by surrender and self-sacrifice to the will of the leader (unqualified yet).[137] It was the "scientific" answer to the paradox of *theodicy* intrinsic to Marxism: the eschatological subject was identified, but its coming of age needed leadership—the Kautskyan intervention from without, Lenin's party of a new type and, why not, ultimately Stalin's revolution from above. Marxism-Leninism was the formula used to reconcile the ever-expanding rational mastery of the world with the aspiration for individual liberation.

The Leninist party is dead (it is quite ironic that the Gennady Zyuganov–style epigones of the Communist Party of the Russian Federation combine Slavophile orthodoxy, xenophobia, imperialism, and Bolshevik nostalgia in a baroque nationalist-cum-egalitarian collectivistic blending).[138] But the cult of the party as a sacred institution, the sectarian vision of a community of virtuous, ascetic, righteous individuals selflessly committed to improving the life of humanity and erecting Nikolai Chernyshevky's "Crystal Palace" *here and now* is not extinct.[139] It explains the nature of the post-Communist transitions where initiatives from below are still marginal and the center of power remains, in many cases, as conspiratorial, secretive, and nondemocratic as it was in pre-Leninist and Leninist times. Is this bound to stay the same? My answer is tentatively negative; after all, the monolith is broken, the dream of Communism as the secular kingdom of God has failed. The challenge remains, however, of coming to terms with Lenin's legacies and admitting that Sovietism was not imposed by extraterrestrial aliens on an innocent intelligentsia but rather found its causes, origins, and most propitious ground in the radical segments of Russian political culture.[140] To put it simply, the Third International and the major schism within the world Marxist movement were the consequences of Lenin's defiant gesture, his seizure of power in the fall of 1917. His determination to force socialist revolution upon the czarist empire, and implicitly upon the world, triggered the beginning of the epoch of totalitarian politics. And his single-mindedness would be emulated by others. Rosa Luxemburg again anticipated the significance of the Bolshevik push for state power: "Their October uprising was not only the actual salvation of the Russian Revolution: it was also the salvation of the honor of international socialism."[141] Indeed, until 1989, the October Revolution remained the central symbolic pillar of the world Communist movement.

The two letters Lenin sent to the Bolshevik Central Committee on September 15, 1917 (*The Bolsheviks Must Assume Power* and *Marxism and Insurrection*), sum up the voluntaristic pathology of the political that was to plague the rest of the century: "History will never forgive us if we do not assume power now. . . . We shall win *absolutely* and unquestionably. . . . Our victory is assured for the people are close to desperation and we are showing the entire people a way out. . . . The majority of the people are *on our side*. . . . It would be naïve to wait for a 'formal' majority; no revolution ever waits for that."[142] Hitler shared this self-entitlement, for he too was convinced that mundane politics were to be sacrificed on the altar of the total revolution: "We are avid for power, and we take it wherever we can get it. . . . Wherever we see a possibility to move in, we go! . . . Whoever has us clinging to his coattails can never get rid of us again."[143] To paraphrase Claude Lefort, both Leninism and Fascism identified with the revolution as an irreversible moment breaking with the past and creating a totally new world. In this sense they are cosmic mutations of symbolic structure.

The Bolshevik takeover of power in October 1917 inaugurated a period of global ideological warfare that may have come to an end only with the collapse of the USSR in 1991 (the "age of extremes," as Eric Hobsbawm calls this epoch or, to use George Lichtheim's term, later adopted by Ernst Nolte, "the European civil war"). Because of Lenin, a new type of politics was born in the twentieth century, one founded upon fanaticism, elitism, unflinching commitment to a sacred cause, and total submission of critical reason by means of faith to a self-appointed "vanguard" of militant illuminati.[144] Clara Zetkin's exalted proclamation at the Third Party Congress of the KPD (the German Communist Party) in 1923 reflected the ethos of a new political religion being born: "Take off your shoes! The ground on which you stand is holy ground. It is ground sanctified through the revolutionary struggle [and] the revolutionary sacrifices of the Russian proletarian."[145] With Lenin, the activist turned into a professional revolutionary (regardless of background, intellectual or proletarian—Heinz Neumann or Ernst Thälmann in the KPD; Gheorghiu-Dej, Ana Pauker, David Fabian, or Lucrețiu Pătrășcanu in the RCP). Henceforth, the revolutionary fanatic sought deliverance in the elevation of mass movements.[146] S/he was a soldier acting out a newly acquired, virtuous identity validated by the righteousness of the world mission.[147]

In an important book, Claude Lefort, the distinguished French political philosopher,[148] proposes a deliberatively controversial thesis. Engaging in a polemic with François Furet and Martin Malia, Lefort maintains that Bolshevism (or, in general, twentieth-century Communism) was not simply an ideological mirage.[149] Ideology mattered enormously, as demonstrated by Solzhenitsyn, about whom Lefort wrote extensively. But ideological passion alone or the will to impose a utopian blueprint cannot explain the longevity and intensity of the Communist phenomenon. In the spirit of French sociology (Emile Durkheim and Marcel Mauss), Lefort contended that it would be fruitful to regard Communism as a "total social fact." The totalitarian system can be seen not only as an emotional-intellectual superstructure but also as an institutional ensemble inspired by these passions. In other words, it is not the original Marxism constituted in the Western revolutionary tradition that explains the Soviet tragedy but rather the mutation introduced by Lenin.

There is, undoubtedly, an authoritarian temptation at the heart of the Marxian project, but the idea of the ultracentralized, sectarian, extremely militarized party, composed of a minority of knowledgeable "chosen ones" who possess the gnosis while preaching egalitarian rhetoric to the masses, is directly linked to Lenin's intervention in the evolution of Russian and European social democracy. Lenin's revolutionary novelty consists in the cult of the dogma and the elevation of the party as the uniquely legitimate interpreter of the revealed truth (a trait of right-wing revolutionary totalitarian movements): "Even when it was still neither a monolithic party nor a single party, it potentially combined these two characteristics because it represented the Party-as-One, not one party among others (the strongest, most daring among them), but that party whose aim was to act under the impulse of a single will and to leave nothing outside its orbit, in other words, to merge with the state and society."[150] Moreover, Lefort emphasized the prescriptive role of the supposedly revealed Word as a defining characteristic of left totalitarianism: "The *Text [Écrit]* was supposed to answer all questions emerging in the course of things. Presenting itself at once as the origin and the end of knowledge, the *Text* required a certain kind of reader: the Communist Party member."[151] Indeed, Lenin carried to an extreme the idea of a privileged relation between "revolutionary theory" and "practice." The latter constitutes (substantiates) itself in the figure of the presumably infallible party, custodian of an omniscience ("epistemic infallibility," to use Giuseppe di Palma's term) that defines and exorcises any doubt as a form of treason. The party was invested with demiurgic characteristics practically substituting for the revolutionary class—an elite invested by history with the mission of the salvation of humanity via revolution. Robert C. Tucker correctly diagnosed Lenin's invention: "Revolutions do not simply come, he was contending, they have to be made, and the making requires a properly constituted and functioning organization of revolutionaries. Marx proclaimed the inevitable and imminent coming of the world proletarian socialist revolution. Lenin saw that the coming was neither inevitable nor necessarily imminent. For him—and this was a basic idea underlying the charter document of his Bolshevism, although nowhere did he formulate it in just these words—there was no revolution outside the party. *Nulla salus extra ecclesiam.*"[152]

In opposition to those authors who are still ready to grant Marxism and even Leninism a certain legitimacy in their claims to liberal-democratic pedigrees, it is essential to recognize (together with Lefort)[153] that

Bolshevism was inherently inimical to political liberties. It is not an accidental deviation from the democratic project but its logical, direct and unequivocal antithesis. Thus Lefort quotes Alexis de Tocqueville: "To grant the epithet of democratic to a government that denies political freedom to its citizens is a blatant absurdity." The annihilation of democracy within Leninist practice is determined by the nature of the party as a secular substitute for the unifying totalizing mystique in the political body of the absolute sovereign (the medieval king). In other words, the Leninist model breaks with the Enlightenment tradition and reasserts the integral homogenization of the social space as a political and pragmatic ideal. According to Lefort, the fundamental organizational principle of Communism was "the People-as-One"—the golden rule of unity of the new society: "It is denied that division is constitutive of society. In the so-called socialist world, there can be no other division than that between the people and its enemies: a division between inside and outside, no internal division. After the revolution, socialism is not only supposed to prepare the way for the emergence of a classless society, it must already manifest that society which bears within itself the principle of homogeneity and self-transparency."[154] Under the circumstances, it is difficult to see a way to democratize Leninist regimes, precisely because the doctrine's original intention was to organize total domination. Communism was indeed a deviant, though very real, version of modernity, an attempt to realize a new world-space *(espace-monde)* where the difference between I and Thou dissipated into the party, "the only concretion of the social" (to quote Lefort).

Here lies the essence of the Leninist (or Communist) question: the institution of the monolithic, unique party that emerges as a "besieged fortress" after 1903 (the great schism between Bolsheviks and Mensheviks) acquired planetary dimensions after 1917. Marxism, converted and adjusted by Lenin, ceased to be a revolutionary doctrine intended to grasp or conceive *(begreifen)* reality and became an ideological body that requires from militants a discipline of action that makes them "members of a collective body." Thus Bolshevism added to nineteenth-century revolutionary mythologies something new: the inclusion of power in a type of representation that defines the party as a magical entity. It is thus important to keep in mind the significance of the political and symbolic structures of Leninism, the underpinnings that ensured its success as an ideological state *(Weltanschauungstaat)*. No matter how we look at it, Lenin's celebration of the party's predestined status, together with his obsessive insistence on conspiratorial forms of organization (revolutionary "cells") and the cult of fanatic regimentation, have initiated a new form of political radicalism, irrevocably opposed to the Western individualistic liberal tradition or, for that matter, to antiauthoritarian, democratic (liberal) socialism. Leninism's *Weltanschauung* was as intolerant and exclusivist as that of Fascism: it demanded "complete recognition as well as the complete adaptation of public life to its ideas."[155] In the twentieth century, Leninism and Fascism brought about an unprecedented "enlargement, intensification, and dynamicization of political power"[156] with the purpose of radically transforming the world.

With this in mind, I would conclude that Slavoj Žižek's proposed "return to Lenin" means simply a return to a politics of irresponsibility, the resurrection of a political ghost whose main legacies are related to the limitation, rather than the expansion, of democratic experimentation. After all, it was Lenin who suppressed direct democracy in the form of councils, disbanded the embryonic Russian parliament, and transformed terror into a privileged instrument for preserving power. Žižek seems to adopt, and truly enjoy, the role of Thomas Mann's character, the Jesuit dialectician Leo Naphta: an oracle of the resurrection of what one might call *le désir de révolution*. In his defense of Leninism, Žižek actually advocates the rehabilitation of chiliastic experiences, secular soteriologies, and visionary messianism, all for the sake of regaining the "authentically apocalyptical Paulinian atmosphere." Simultaneously, though, he (and others who imitate his plea) does not seem to mind the mass graves that people keep discovering wherever the Leninist ideal, in one form or the other, has been implemented. When Hitler destroyed the Weimar constitutional system and abolished all "bourgeois freedoms," he imitated the Bolshevik precedent of the permanent emergency as a justification for legitimizing the destruction of legality and eliminating (including physical annihilation) all those regarded as "objective" obstacles to building a perfect, organic community. Despite their pretense of rationality, the Bolsheviks, "unconstrained by concerns of legality or any usual checks on executive power, were particularly prone to resort to naked force."[157]

In the Soviet Union, Fascist Italy, and Nazi Germany, the abolition of the prerevolutionary state created "the institutional precondition for cumulative radicalization. Flexible, extra-legal; and extra-bureaucratic agencies institutionalized the terror against fictitious enemies; the fiction of a future civilization and a new moral sense that legitimized it."[158] The new order of the utopia in power opened the door to a sort of "institutional Darwinism" defined by "political activism occurring on its own, or at least without immediate direction" from the power center (the leader or party).[159] This process can account for both the escalation of terror and the organizational corruption and ultimate demise of these totalitarian political movements. The fundamental difference with National Socialism (but not so much with Mussolini's Fascism, considering that it did survive for at least two decades) was that Lenin and Stalin "achieved not only a social revolution but the conditions of a stable political order."[160] Bertrand Russell in *The Practice and Theory of Bolshevism,* written upon his return from the Soviet Union in 1920, diagnosed the murderous reality lying at the heart of Lenin's political invention, the specter that contemporary prophets of irresponsibility such as Žižek choose to ignore: "I felt that everything I valued in human life was being destroyed in the interests of a glib and narrow philosophy, and that in the process untold misery was being inflicted upon many millions of people."[161] Once victorious in 1917, Lenin opened a Pandora's box. By the end of the twentieth century, all we found was tyranny and bloodshed anywhere his world-historical exploit was emulated, from Shanghai to Rostock.

Dialectics of Disenchantment

Marxism and Ideological Decay in Leninist Regimes

The Western system may be flawed in many social respects, but it is, after all, a fully operational democratic system, not a dictatorship. I would certainly agree that the Western democracies, too, are now without a universally accepted value-system, but whereas the loss of such a system in a live democracy is balanced by the interaction of a broad variety of democratic institutions, the loss of ideology in a totalitarian society means the complete collapse of the morale of that society, because the sole justification of totalitarian rule *is* the ideology on which it rests.

—Zdeněk Mlynář (in George Urban, ed., *Communist Reformation*)

Communist regimes were partocratic ideocracies (as discussed by authors such as Leonard Schapiro, Alain Besançon, Martin Malia, Richard Pipes, Orlando Figes, and Stephen Kotkin). Their only claim to legitimacy was purely ideological, that is, derived from the organized belief system shared by the elites and inculcated into the masses that the party benefited by special access to historical truth. If this interpretation is correct, then deradicalization, the decline of self-generated energy, primarily in the field of ideological monopoly, leads to increased vulnerability. The demise of the supreme leader (Stalin, Mao, Enver Hoxha, or Tito) has always ushered in ideological anarchy and loss of self-confidence among the rulers. Kenneth Jowitt correctly pointed out that "there is a constant tendency in Leninism toward strong executive leaders."[1] Sometimes, though, Communist parties invoke also the leadership of a messiahlike prophet, a charismatic guide.[2] The cases of Stalin and Mao are the most obvious, but Nicolae Ceauşescu, Enver Hoxha, Ho Chi Minh, Kim Il-sung, and others come to mind as well. Building upon Jowitt's argument, we can observe the following trend: in an attempt to permanently confirm and sustain the "charismatic impersonalism" of the party under Communism (particularly in its Stalinism avatars), magic, miracle, and mysticism blended in totalitarian regimes that were apparently scientifically justified. In fact, they were chiliastic ideologies, redemptive doctrines shrouded in rationalistic disguise, political religions based on their own sense of original sin, the fall of mankind, historical torment, and final salvation. Attempts to restore the "betrayed values" of the original project (Nikita Khrushchev, Mikhail Gorbachev) resulted in ideological disarray, a change of mind among former supporters, desertion of critical intellectuals from the "fortress," criticism of the old dogmas, awakening, a break with past, and eventually apostasy. If we compare the Leninist experiments with Fascist revolutionary utopias, the absence of a revisionist temptation within Fascism is striking. With very few exceptions, like the brothers Gregor and Otto Strasser (early Nazis who broke with Hitler's regime soon after the takeover), there were no disenchanted Nazis. The plot against Hitler in 1944 was fomented by conservative aristocrats and military luminaries who wanted to avoid a crushing defeat by the Allies and a much feared occupation by the Red Army.[3]

This chapter looks into the adventures of critical Marxism in Soviet-style regimes and its corrosive impact on the Moscow center during the 1970s and particularly the 1980s. Furthermore, I conceptualize the Gorbachev phenomenon as a culmination of the revisionist ethos in the socialist bloc, which implicitly turns the focus of my contribution on the inherent paradoxes and fallacies of perestroika. The latter is perceived to be inherent in the incompleteness of East European Marxist revisionism's promise for change. Nevertheless, by no means do I deny the role of this fascinating period of intellectual and political history in providing a fundamental lesson about the role of ideas in the disintegration of authoritarian regimes of Leninist persuasion. Such a self-critical development would have been unthinkable under the Nazi regime, as already shown in previous chapters.

My point is that the impact of Marxist revisionism and critical intellectuals can hardly be overestimated and that this impact is one of the main distinctions between Communism and Fascism. The adventure of revisionism led these intellectuals beyond the once-worshipped paradigm, critical Marxism turned into post-Marxism and even, as in the case of Kołakowski, into liberal anti-Marxism. In his gripping book about the postwar Soviet intelligentsia, historian Vladislav Zubok concludes that the story of this group, which is crucial to understanding the fate of Leninism in the twentieth century, was about "the slow and painful disappearance of their revolutionary-romantic idealism and optimism, their faith in progress and in the enlightenment of people." He emphasizes that "the children of Zhivago spent their lives on 'a voyage from the coast of Utopia' into the turbulent open sea of individual self-discovery."[4]

Among Soviet and Eastern European intelligentsia, Marxism was found wanting in its most powerful ambition, to respond in a positively engaging way to the challenges of democratic modernity, to restructure democratic imagination itself:

> With one resolute gesture of contempt, therefore, Marx swept away all particularities: the interests of the peasants, of middle classes, of nations, and of colonialism. This absolute universalism made Marx particularly insensitive to political questions in general, and to democratic politics in particular. Democratic politics is one of the basic components of modernity, and, when Marx failed to cope with this problem, his pioneering theory of modernity was drastically curtailed. One could only speculate as to why a man of genius, who discovered and analyzed so many basic features of modernity, was not to the slightest degree superior to any of his socialist contemporaries whenever he embarked in discussing political problems. When it came to politics, his genius invariably failed him. The bombastic style of his political writings, the vagueness of his political ideas, the open bias of his judgments, and the mythologization of his favorite heroes shift Marx back to a period and its guises, the epoch of the French Revolution and Bonapartism, precisely that period the ideological customs of which Marx had so vigorously sought to debunk.[5]

I argue that only the reinvention of politics operated by the dissident movement could offer the *possibility* of achieving genuine democracy and full liberty in Eastern Europe and the Soviet Union. The proposed analysis represents a revisiting and development of my theses on the role of ideological disillusionment in the ultimate decline (deradicalization) of Leninist regimes as formulated in the 1980s and early 1990s.[6]

Several generations have come of political age in Eastern Europe and the Soviet Union by assimilating a radical promise of universal redemption, genuine equality, and emancipation. The civilization built and exported by the Bolsheviks had a totalizing ambition encompassing all spheres of life. In the early 1980s, exiled dissident writer Andrei Sinyavsky argued that this alternative illiberal modernity was "a durable, stable . . . structure, . . . [which] arouses the interest and attention of the world as, perhaps, the most unusual and awe-inspiring *[groznoe]* phenomenon of the twentieth century. It is awe-inspiring because it makes claims to the future of all mankind and . . . considers itself as an ideal and as the logical conclusion of the development of world history."[7] This construct of Leninism was first and foremost erected on faith. Emancipation from such radically transformative conviction became an odyssey synonymous with the history of Communism. As one Soviet philosopher put it, "I resisted long and fiercely, until I had to surrender *before . . . life itself* [my emphasis]."[8]

Marxism in its Leninist avatar was imposed as the philosophy par excellence, the unique scientific worldview, the spiritual complement of the technological-industrial evolution of the society. It jealously guided, inspired, and motivated the political-intellectual development of East European societies. It regulated their main political, philosophical, ethical, and aesthetic corpus of hypotheses, theses, values, norms, and opinions. Moreover, under the specific circumstances of the Stalinist period, Marxism was converted into dialectical materialism *(Diamat)*, a simulacrum of dialectical jargon combined with pseudoscientific claims. The latter was gradually instituted into a monopolistic orthodoxy imagined according to the requirements of self-sufficient, noncontradictory, and a priori infallible religious dogmas. Conceived as such, it brought about a continual stiffening of spiritual life in Eastern European countries, as well as a normal, absolutely logical counterreaction of refusal and dissatisfaction with the prevalent ideas.

The Stalinist functionalist-pragmatic *Weltanschauung* succeeded in emphasizing as altogether certain and genuinely axiomatic a number of theses from Karl Marx's early writing, *The German Ideology* (such as economic determinism and the assumption that the dominant ideas within a social organization are the ideas of the hegemonic group). It also took on several naïve materialist positions defended and promoted by Lenin in *Materialism and Empiriocriticism,* above all Lenin's vulgar representation of the philosophical parties. Under Stalin, dialectics suffered a strange metamorphosis, a process of *refunctionalization,* the result of which was its transformation into a mere ideological weapon, a mythological instrument supporting each political step of the regime, each tactical turning. Robert C. Tucker, in his attempt to understand Stalin's urge to master the supposedly objective laws of socioeconomic development, pointed to his adoption of "a legislative attitude toward reality. . . . [W]hat he referred to as 'objective scientific laws' were an externalization of his inner policy dictates; they were a projection upon Soviet history of the formulas for socio-economic development generated in his own mind. *His own ideas appeared to him as natural necessities governing the development of society* [original emphasis]."[9]

THE UTOPIAN IMPULSE

Stalin's projection of his own ideas as natural law was, however, the result of the structural challenges of utopia in power (adoption, fulfillment of ideals, and adaptation to the world). To follow Klaus-Georg Riegel, under Stalin Soviet rule became the "hierocratic domination of the church-dispensed grace." In the physical absence of Lenin, the numinous leader incarnating the absolute power of the party, "the imagined community of Leninist disciples"[10] had to reinvent itself by founding its charisma in the scriptures of the founding fathers. The invented tradition of Marxism-Leninism was then thrust upon the party ranks as a means of purification or, rather, to stabilize the unquestionable normative identity of the party. However, Stalin's obsession with strengthening the party was not far from Lenin's dictum that "a party becomes stronger by purging itself."[11] Indeed, to prevent diffuseness of dogma and weakness among the cadre, Stalin pronounced that "the more drastic the purge, the more likelihood is there of a strong and influential Party arising."[12]

The climax of this mode of operation, its most glaring and outrageous consequence, involved the "dialectical confessions" during the Stalinist show trials, those abject self-flagellations meant to give the totalitarian political order moral legitimacy: if all opponents (real or invented) were nothing but scoundrels, loathsome agents of the West, despicable traitors, and infamous saboteurs, then the Stalinist leadership, benefiting from a perfect political purity, was entitled to invoke the alibi of an "objective" historical rationality.[13] These "poetics of purge" regulated ideological space within the body social and politics of the Soviet-type polity, redefining the "elect" within the community and reemphasizing their messianic role. Accordingly, the sacred history of the movement was heroically rewritten by blood and exclusion. Conceived by its founding fathers as an antistatist philosophy, Marxism culminated in the Soviet apotheosis of the party and state machine (partolatry and statolatry). The legitimacy of the Bolshevik elite derived primarily from its relationship to Marxist doctrine. Arcane as they sounded to external observers, the squabbles of the 1920s touched on the most sensitive points of what Czesław Miłosz has called the New Faith, an ideology "based on the principle that good and evil are definable solely in terms of service or harm to the interests of the Revolution."[14] The revolution was hyperbolized as a cathartic event, the advent of a new age of social justice. Marxism's claims of scientific infallibility were added into the mix. The result was a gnostic vision that explained history and society in almost geometric formulas whose deep secrets were accessible only to a select group of ideological guardians. All these factors revealed the process of intellectuals being seduced by allegedly ironclad determinism in an age of political extremes. In other words, to quote from a highly influential book of the 1930s, *The ABC of Communism,* "what Marx prophesized is being fulfilled under our very eyes."[15]

The social promises and regenerative spirit of Bolshevism were invoked as arguments against those who deplored violence by dictatorial power. Many intellectuals, including some famous names like Maxim Gorky, André Gide, Arthur Koestler, Manès Sperber, Romain Rolland, André Malraux, and Ignazio Silone, were fascinated by what seemed to be a heroic historical adventure. The Bolshevik revolution was, to use the words crafted by the socialist politician Jean Jaurès for the French one, "a monstrous cannon, which had to be maneuvered on its carriage with confidence, swiftness and decisiveness."[16] Moreover, the Soviet Union was, for them, clearly a model for ideas and institutions, the source of a new socialist ethos, of a novel humanism, at the time when liberal, representative democracy was perceived as having failed to rise to the challenges posed by modern societies. Some of them grew disappointed with the cynicism of the Communist commissars and left the Leninist chapels; others, like Pablo Neruda and Louis Aragon, refused to abjure their faith and remained attached to hackneyed Communist tenets. Moreover, upon the Sovietization of Eastern Europe, Leninism became an *alternative* for national rebirth. For example, Communist doctrinaire Václav Kopecký argued in January 1948 that "the ideology of the new Czechoslovakia will be the ideology of the new People's Democratic Republic and the ideology of transition on the road from capitalism to socialism."[17] Many such examples can be found in the newspapers of those years in each of the countries in the region.[18] The Communist "moral elite" claimed an exclusive mandate of salvation and historical truth in fulfilling its world mission.[19] Or, in the words of Jean-Paul Sartre in 1961, "Nothing is clearer; whatever its crimes, the USSR has over the bourgeois democracies this redoubtable privilege: the revolutionary objective. . . . [The Soviet Union was] incomparable with other nations; it is only possible to judge it if one accepts its cause and in the name of that cause."[20]

STALINISM AS A POLITICAL MYTH

The Short Course of History of the CPSU, published in 1938, represented the paradigm of Bolshevik intellectual debasement: "It not only established a whole pattern of Bolshevik mythology linked to the cult of Lenin and Stalin, but prescribed a detailed ritual and liturgy. . . . The *Short Course* was not merely a work of falsified history but a powerful social institution—one of the party's most important instruments of mind control, a device for the destruction both of critical thought and of society's recollections of its own past."[21] Turned into a gospel for the international Communist movement, this parody of Marxism was extolled as the pinnacle of human wisdom. Stalinist ideology brought to fruition the pauperization of Marxist theoretical practice and actually functioned as an effective counterdoctrine to emasculate the originally emancipatory momentum of negative dialectics and to substitute for it an opportunist-positivistic sociology deliberately situated beyond traditional moral borders. Through the *Short Course,* Leninism became a "true book religion" (in the words of Riegel). This "Stalinist revolution of belief" provided unitary guidance and unity of will among the cadres involved in building socialism in one country, in the Soviet modernization project. It was the literary reflection of the "monopoly of the legitimate use of hierocratic coercion" (as Max Weber put it) exercised by Stalin in the show trials. To paraphrase Souvarine, the *Short Course* paradigm officially transformed Leninism into a *religion d'état.*[22] The human being that Stalinism envisaged was supposed to repudiate the classical distinctions between *good* and *evil,* scornfully discredited as obsolete through exposure to another moral code, in many points suggestive of the Nazi *Übermensch.* Its ideology was rooted in hatred and resentment and developed into a logic of *manipulation, domination,* and *survival.* The main task of propaganda was to purify the mind; it was like an exorcising ritual through which the regime attempted to eliminate all the vestiges of Western culture and to create the human instrument of perfect social reproduction. Its content consisted in a few mechanically reiterated themes; its method was symbolic aggression, ideological violence. In 1929, Stalin had proclaimed the "year of the great break" *(god velikogo pereloma),* which, according to Bernice Glatzer Rosenthal, connoted "the Marxist leap from 'necessity' to 'freedom' . . . a complete rupture with the accursed old world. . . . Under Stalin's leadership, the masses were building an earthly paradise."[23] What was really happening at the time was an annihilation of free will, total intoxication, moral dereliction, and thereby absolute identification with the system. It was the Soviet version of an individual *Gleichschaltung*.

Stalinism's modus operandi was excess in matters such as bureaucratization, police terror, absence of democracy, and censorship: "Not, for example, merely coercive peasant policies, but a virtual civil war against the peasantry; not merely police repression, or even civil war–style terror, but a holocaust by terror that victimized tens of millions of people for twenty-five years; not merely a Thermidorean revival of nationalist tradition, but an almost fascist-like chauvinism; not merely a leader cult, but deification of a despot."[24] After the Soviet occupation of Eastern Europe, the same form of Leninism—they never dared call it Stalinism—was decreed the unique interpretation of Marxism. Stalin's death was "a necessary prerequisite of post-Stalin change and, indeed, as the essential first act of 'de-Stalinization.'"[25] After Nikita Khrushchev's fulminating attack on Stalinism at the Twentieth Congress of the CPSU in February 1956, certain changes became inevitable within the rigid structure of Soviet dogma. In addition to institutional innovations, de-Stalinization meant dedogmatization, the end of the boundless worship of sacred texts written by or attributed to Stalin. As one author remarked, with de-Stalinization, "the relations between the party-state and society underwent significant changes, with a new emphasis on mediation through soft controls, inducements and strategies of incorporation. But the monolithic structure of the party-state rule and of economic management remained fundamentally unchanged."[26]

THE BROKEN MONOLITH

The post-1953 political relaxation, often referred to as the "Thaw," ushered in an era of doubt and criticism. Gone were the times of absolute certainties dictated by a presumably infallible supreme leader. Totalitarian imagery that had functioned for decades through "*tremendum et fascinosum* (the alternation of fear and hope, terror and salvation)"[27] found its spell radically questioned. In spite of its limitations, Khrushchev's Secret Speech, one of the most important political documents of the twentieth century, revealed, to a limited extent, the crimes against the party. But its significance lay in the fact that it "stretched the limits of unbelief in postwar Soviet Russia."[28] Most importantly, the first wave of de-Stalinization put an end to terror as an instrument of governance: "The reforms to criminal justice, especially the amnesties, and the debunking of the Stalin cult in the Secret Speech stand as lasting achievements of the period, for they ensured that full re-Stalinization—of the Gulag, and of the Stalin cult—would never again be possible."[29] As early as March 1953, K.P. Gorshenin, the minister of justice, argued in *Pravda* that the amnesty decree, which released a total of 1,201,738 people, was evidence of "Soviet humanity." He advocated for "socialist legality" as the correct way to ensure the country's "transition from socialism to communism."[30]

However, de-Stalinization advanced reforms that "threw up more questions than they answered."[31] In the realm of culture and public life, de-Stalinization generated a panoply of initiatives aimed at moving away from the petrified doctrine toward the origins of Marxism as a philoso-phy, toward the so-called young Marx as the archetype of a pure, non-adulterated socialist impetus. In the Soviet Union, but also Eastern Eu-rope, "de-Stalinization did not mean the end of the communist ideal. To the contrary, it meant a rejuvenation of the idealism and the intellectual identity of the pre-Stalin period." Or, in the words of acclaimed Soviet poetess Bella Akhmadulina, "The Revolution isn't dead; the Revolution is sick, and we must help it."[32] Consequently, the political emancipation (de-Bolshevization) of Soviet and East European intellectuals coincided with—and was catalyzed by—the wave of liberalization touched off by Nikita Khrushchev's historical revelations.[33] While the campaigns that followed the Soviet leader's Secret Speech "set out to emancipate the popular consciousness from the Stalin cult, it also inadvertently risked the 'de-Sovietization' of public opinion, as swathes of the Soviet popula-tion reacted in violent, unpredictable and 'anti-Soviet' ways to de-Stalinization."[34] All the Stalinist theoretical and political constructions had been denounced as a horrible hoax: the illusions could no longer cover the squalid reality. The dogmas had proved their total inanity. Yearning for moral reform of Communism was the basic motivation for the neo-Marxist revival in the Soviet Union and Eastern Europe. Indeed, "it was a Marxism that led back to a European tradition of social-democratic reformism."[35] The intellectuals' rebellion against totalitarian controls threatened the endurance of Soviet-type regimes. The terror-tainted legitimacy of Sovietism was questioned by critics who could not be accused of belonging to the defeated social classes. With their outspo-ken advocacy of humanism and democracy, they contributed to eroding the apparently monolithic consensus.

In a certain way this movement had been anticipated by Yugoslav theorists (Moša Pjade, Milovan Djilas, the Praxis group) who felt com-pelled, by the very logic of the political conflict with the Soviet Stalinist elite, to rediscover the initial impulses of Marxist anthropology, sociology, and philosophy.[36] Those most active, however, in the struggle against Stalinist obscurantism were Hungarian and Polish intellectuals, the exponents of a radical political outlook that inflamed the masses throughout the hectic months after the Twentieth Congress of the Communist Party of the Soviet Union. This fact has to be related to the traditions of the Left in those countries, but also to the existence of a confusion within the Communist *nomenklatura* heightened by the growing antibureaucratic radicalism of the working class. We have to take into consideration, in this respect, the evolution of the class consciousness of both the working class and the intellectuals and the existence of a certain psychoemotional communication, even osmosis, between these two social groups. I stress these facts in order to suggest an explanation—beyond the sheer force of the political police—for the relative political passivity of the working class in other Communist countries (such as Romania and Bulgaria) and for the astonishing neutrality of the Czech and Slovakian intellectuals during the Hungarian and Polish revolts in 1956.

THE SAGA OF REVISIONISM

More than a decade after Stalin's death, the East European and Soviet intelligentsia was experiencing a period of ethical reconstruction, an invitation to rehabilitate the whole historical evolution of Western Marxism and to a critical approach to "institutional dialectics." Georg Lukács, an "enigmatic heretic inside his Church" (to quote Ferenc Fehér) invited to participate in the debates of the Petöfi Circle in Budapest, was perceived as the representative of *another Marxism* than the ossified Diamat preached by the Stalinist doctrinaires; Marxist intellectual Geza Losonczy was the soul of the discussions concerning freedom of the press; Leszek Kołakowski was launching his long fight for the humanization of the "State-socialist" Polish society, appealing to the potential of a presumed Socialist New Left. In his 1957 manifesto, "Permanent vs. Transitory Aspects of Marxism," Kołakowski made the seminal distinction between institutional Marxism and intellectual Marxism. While the first was mere religious dogma manipulated by those in power, the second was characterized by "radical rationalism in thinking; steadfast resistance to any invasion of myth in science; an entirely secular view of the world; criticism pushed to its ultimate limits; distrust of all closed doctrines and systems . . . a readiness to revise accepted theses, theories and methods."[37] Freedom had again become the highest good for human

beings released from the asphyxiating dependence on the party's definition of truth. In the Soviet Union, the *shestidesiatniki*, "the people of the
sixties," formed a community that "had 'the ability and desire to think, to
reflect about life and its complexities.' They sought to understand the reality 'behind every word.'"[38] A "spirit of revisionism" came about in the
Soviet bloc that would fundamentally mark the political and cultural
dynamics of the region in the late 1950s and 1960s. In this context, revisionism, a term coined by neo-Stalinist orthodoxies to stigmatize critical
currents of thought and the main adversary encountered by ruling bureaucrats since the factional struggles of the mid- and late 1920s, became
the main foe of the neo-Stalinist ideological construct.[39] One should note,
however, that revisionism *was not* a social movement; rather, it was "a
diffuse ideological current that articulated itself in equal parts in official
and unofficial fora and which was of a highly various character in different countries."[40]

The favorite theme in the discourses of East European philosophers,
sociologists, and men of letters in general was the return to an idealized
Marx: the attempt to detect those elements in Marx's original design that
could justify the politically liberating changes within the system. Moreover, that endeavor was conceived as a *rediscovery* and *reinterpretation*
of Marx's early works, of the whole Marxian philosophical legacy detested by the Stalinist ideologues. The concept of *alienation* became the
basis of the most impassioned philosophical controversies, fostered the
case for liberalization, and provided the theoretical basis for political
criticism. In fact, the "dictatorship of the proletariat" was felt as exactly
the opposite of the "bright future" promised by the founders of Marxism.
It was viewed as a caricature of the project of emancipation announced
by the *Communist Manifesto*.

The immediate effect of the general intellectual unrest was the con-
figuration of a fundamentally *radical* answer to the obvious structural
crisis of the East European Soviet-type societies. One of the most interesting expressions of this phenomenon was the 1964 *Open Letter of the
Basic Party Organization of PZPR (Polish United Workers' Party) and
to Members of the University Cell of the Union of Socialist Youth at
Warsaw University* written by two left-wing antibureaucratic intellectuals, Jacek Kuroń, an assistant professor of pedagogy, and Karol Modzelewski, a member the History Department at the University of Warsaw,
son of Zygmunt Modzelewski, a Communist old-timer and the first foreign minister of Communist Poland. The document, a striking example
of critique of the party from the antitotalitarian Left, claimed to uphold

the true principles of Marxism-Leninism against the fictitious party democracy, to defend workers' rights against top-down decision-making.[41]
The same year, Czech legal scholar Zdeněk Mlynář drafted *The State
and the Individual* (an anticipation of his 1968 "Towards a Democratic
Political Organization of Society"), in which he tried to reconcile democracy and socialism. In this document, the author (a former room-
mate of Mikhail Gorbachev during their student years at Moscow
State University in the early 1950s who became the main ideologue of
the Prague Spring in 1968) reasserted the role of social organizations in
the process of democratization. Moreover, he emphasized workers' self-
management bodies in the factories in order "to overcome the system of
planning by decree and to establish the socialist enterprise as an autonomous agent that would be able to enter the market in that capacity."
Moreover, the leading role of the party could be maintained, according
to Mlynář, only if it was made up of a "conscious vanguard" in service
to the "overall interests and socialist goals of the entire society," and it
didn't take for granted its leadership but led by "tireless persuasion."[42]

It was an exhilarating search for the "realm of freedom" prophesized
by Marx, an explosion of what Hegel called *unglückliches Bewusstsein*
(unhappy consciousness), a revolt of the libertarian undercurrents that
had survived the mortifying experience of Stalinism. The theoretical manifestations of these undercurrents provided a *new semantic horizon,* the
coalescence of a new emotional and intellectual infrastructure that was
translated into a resurgence of repressed philosophical topics, above all
humanism as a privileged metaphysical concern. The crushing of the
Hungarian Revolution and the attempt to tame the Polish intelligentsia,
the hardening of the political line in East European countries between
1957 and 1961, and the harsh antirevisionist campaign after the publication of the program adopted by the Communist League of Yugoslavia
could not obstruct the creative philosophical openings nor hinder the
antidogmatic impetus that resulted in the humanist-ethical outlook execrated by the impenitent Stalinists and neodogmatics. Revisionism was
suppressed because of its commitment to values fatally perverted through
official manipulation. It was a fallacious strategy based on wishful
thinking and a doomed yearning for moral regeneration of the ruling
elite. It foolishly demanded dialogue with those who valued only brutal
force. Detlef Pollack and Jan Wielgohs accurately defined its ideological
character as "system-immanent." In the same vein, Adam Michnik aptly
described the inescapable dilemma of neo-Marxist revisionism in East-
Central Europe: "The revisionist concept was based on a specific intra-

party perspective. It was never formulated into a political program. It assumed that the system of power could be humanized and democratized and that the official Marxist doctrine was capable of assimilating contemporary arts and social sciences. The revisionists wanted to act within the framework of the Communist party and Marxist doctrine. They wanted to transform 'from within' the doctrine and the party in the direction of democratic reform and common sense."[43]

The dominant ideological apparatus in the East European Communist Parties tried to maintain control over, and eventually to paralyze, all these potentially dangerous spiritual developments. From the beginning, de-Stalinization raised the crucial dilemma of "the prerogative to direct and control social and cultural change. . . . Even in its most populist, radical moments, however, the party continued to believe in the party's unimpeachable authority over the people."[44] Ideological hacks viciously attacked the very idea of the *reforms from below* that would go beyond the party-approved struggle against bureaucratization and for increased productivity. The "revisionist" claim for a profound, inclement analysis of the Stalinist system and of the whole tragic texture of events and situations euphemistically designated by the Communist parties as the "cult of personality" provoked ambivalent reactions. In October 1961, at the Twenty-second Congress of the Communist Party, Khrushchev unleashed a second onslaught on the memory of the defunct tyrant. Stalin's embalmed body was removed from Lenin's mausoleum, the sanctum sanctorum of Bolshevism. This new thaw, indeed a short-lived and inconclusive liberalization, stopped short of in-depth political and economic reforms: "As the party grew more confident in publicizing its iconoclastic narratives about the Stalinist past, it also, paradoxically (although perhaps necessarily) reduced its commitment to de-Stalinizing the Soviet public sphere."[45] The party leaders rapidly became aware of the subversive implications of the Marxist "return to the source" and discovered the negative-libertarian appeal of such concepts as alienation, humanism, self-managed democracy, human rights, and freedom of the subject. They also grew increasingly weary of "the potential new forms of interaction between state and society, and between individual citizens."[46]

Subsequently, revisionism became an obsessive projection of Stalinist ideologues, the embodiment of their secret anguish. To paraphrase Leszek Kołakowski, the jester could not avoid the confrontation with the intolerant reaction of the wrathful priests; he had to radicalize his "attitude of negative vigilance in the face of any absolute."[47] The nervousness of the Kremlin leadership regarding the increasingly daring behavior of young

Soviet intellectuals radicalized by the new wave of de-Stalinization is best exemplified by Nikita Khrushchev's furious reprimand of Soviet poet Andrei Voznesensky. In March 1963, at the amphitheater of the House of the Unions during a meeting with the Soviet cultural elite, Khrushchev, upon hearing Voznesensky praise Vladimir Mayakovsky despite the fact that the latter had not been a party member, exploded:

> Why are you so proud that you are not a Party member? We will sweep you off clean! Do you represent our people or slander our people? . . . I cannot listen calmly to those who lick the feet of our enemies. I cannot listen to the agents. Look at him. He would like to create a party of noncommunists. Well, you are a member of the party, but it is not the same one I am in. . . . The Thaw is over. This is not even a light morning frost. For you and your likes it will be the *arctic* frost *[long applause]*. We are not those who belonged to the Petöfi Club. We are those who helped smash the Hungarians *[applause]*. . . . They think that Stalin is dead and anything is allowed . . . No, you are slaves! Slaves! Your behavior shows it.[48]

A NEW FREEZE

By the end of Khrushchev's rule in the fall of 1964, it was quite clear, both in the USSR and Eastern Europe, that systemic reform from within by a free-thinking intelligentsia operating within the party-defined boundaries of the permissible had ceased to be a viable option. At the same time, the epistemological priority of revisionism in the Soviet bloc consisted in focusing Marxist historical methodology on Marxism itself. In other words, the *historicity* of Marxism, the moment of the Marxist self-consciousness was central to *reinventing* the true value of negativity as a new space for the affirmation of *particularity* against the spurious *universality* glorified by the system. The Hegelian-Marxist direction seemed the most appropriate for assuming a metaphysical legitimacy, that spiritual source which expressed and symbolized the same ambitions, obsessions, anxieties, and hopes. During the sharp polemics of the 1930s, Karl Korsch postulated clearly the significance and seditious content of Marxist dialectics, and East European critical Marxists did not hesitate to adopt his stance, even to go beyond the positions crystallized in *Marxismus und Philosophie:* the Marxist thinker had the obligation to emphasize the philosophical dimension of Marxism, the negative nerve of dialectics, "in contrast with the contempt previously manifested, in different forms but with the same result, by the various currents of Marxism, toward the revolutionary philosophical elements of the doctrine created by Marx and Engels."[49]

The champions of the neodogmatic theology were, of course, the Soviet and East German official philosophers who specialized in hunting down the slightest sign of heterodoxy: in the GDR, from the party's chief theoretician, Kurt Hager, to people like Manfred Buhr or Wilhem-Raymund Bayer, the East German ideologues missed no opportunity to combat and eradicate the revisionist heresy.[50] From this point of view, I believe it would be inaccurate to consider, with Kołakowski, that the traditional exclusive-dogmatic mentality was almost completely replaced by a cynical, strictly pragmatic approach specific to the new type of Communist bureaucrat. Certainly, the most intolerant generation of ideological clerks vanished after 1960, but one should not suspect the subsequent cohorts of apparatchiks of liberal or humanistic leanings. Morally and psychologically, they belonged to a generation different from the "priests" once evoked by Kołakowski. They had not been personally involved in the Stalinist crimes and had no reason to look for historical rationalizations, but politically they must have shared the same values as their forerunners. They were "objectively" prisoners of the same fallacious logic.[51] The indifferent, amoebic ideological apparatchiks, with their simulated axiological aloofness, were actually an efficient element of the smoothly functioning authoritarian-bureaucratic superstructure: they had nothing in common with Marxist philosophy or Socialist ethics; they superbly ignored embarrassing problems of historical responsibility. To paraphrase Engels, their main task was to correct the logic of conflicting facts, to fashion and expound upon history, against all hope, as immutably marching toward Communism. They had only one faith, one absolute credo; they paid tribute only to one God; they honored but one political value: their own bureaucratic survival, their enduring access to power, their right to dominate, to dictate, and to terrorize. They abandoned all pretense of credible, trustworthy communication of faith, thereby undermining the sustaining and eschatological myths of Marxism-Leninism. Nevertheless, for instance among the Soviet leaders grouped around Leonid Brezhnev, "the enduring influence of Marxism-Leninism as the source of legitimacy and language of politics, together with an ingrained Stalinist outlook, produced a deep distrust of the West and a lasting susceptibility to 'revolutionary' appeals and expansionist policies."[52] The neo-Stalinist *nomenklatura* preserved deep loyalty to a radically simplified version of Marxist-Leninist holy writ: "[Brezhnev] thought that to do something 'un-Marxist' now was impermissible—the entire party, the whole world, was watching him. Leonid Ilyich was very weak in [matters of] theory and felt this keenly."[53]

In this respect, the late Soviet dissident and philosopher Aleksandr Zinovyev was right to delineate a perfect continuity from the first Stalinist generation—those people who perpetrated the crimes or supported the whole terrorist system—to the contemporary distant, cold, pseudo-sophisticated cultural (ideological) clerk making use of Marxist rhetoric to cover a moral and intellectual vacuum. However, it is difficult to sympathize with Zinovyev's simplistic attempt to identify Marxism with Stalinism and his total lack of interest in the "heretic" tradition of Marxism. Zinovyev banished as irrelevant all "revisionist" developments, the entire Hegelian-Marxist heritage and the contemporary negative-dialectical currents, as well as the para-Marxist criticism of totalitarian bureaucracy. He refused the possibility of "critical-genuine" Marxism, rejected as hypocritical and logically inconsistent any position attempting to separate original doctrine from adulterated practice: "Stalin was the most genuine and the most devoted Marxist. . . . Stalin was perfectly adjusted to the historical process which engendered him."[54] Zinovyev's negative attitude toward Western Marxism, his skeptical approach to negative dialectics and generally to any hypostasis of philosophical radicalism, should be related to the general metaphysical malaise Soviet and East European intellectuals expressed in their dissatisfaction with the "democratic illusions" and Socialist strategies promoted by the "radical humanist opposition" in the advanced industrial societies. At any rate, he showed a certain short-sightedness, ignoring the libertarian dimension of critical reason and underrating the absolute divorce between this outlook and the bureaucratic-institutional orthodoxy. To reject *de plano* the validity and relevance of the antitotalitarian Marxist arguments meant suppressing a valuable segment of the necessary criticism of neo-Stalinist régimes and erasing a whole tradition of utopian emancipatory thought.

The publication of the young Marx's philosophical contributions had a tremendous impact in East European societies, because they were perceived as a true manifesto of the freedom of subjectivity, the emancipation of revolutionary praxis, and an unbounded approach to the social, economic, political, and cultural problems of Soviet-type regimes. The young Marx was a precious ally of liberal forces against the political conservatism of the dominant bureaucracies of Eastern Europe; a sensitive reading of these writings revealed irrefutable arguments against the oppressive prevailing order. To use Dick Howard's formulation, "Marx did announce that the specter of democracy is haunting Europe." In rediscovering Marx, East European revisionists discovered the democratic implications of his theory.[55]

The entire unorthodox Marxist tradition was eventually summoned to participate in the struggle against sclerotic social and economic structures: from Rosa Luxemburg to Trotsky, form the young Lukács and Karl Korsch to Wilhelm Reich and Erich Fromm, from Gramsci to Sartre to the Frankfurt School, a whole intellectual thesaurus was invoked and developed in this offensive against the authoritarian bureaucracies. It was like the unexpected revival of a forgotten tradition, an evanescent osmosis with the *impossible utopia,* a tragic endeavor to re-create a mentality altogether opposed to the self-satisfactory, philistine logic of the monopolistic Communist elite. In partaking of this revolutionary and Marxist tradition, revisionist intellectuals had yet to renounce socialism. The young Marx's impulse was thereby unified with the rebellious legacy of classical German idealism; the *unhappy consciousness* was breaking loose from bureaucratic coercion. It was, therefore, logical that the counterreaction of the ideological apparatus consisted in supporting regimented philosophical and sociological investigations, those research areas that avoided the collision with the power monopoly of the Communist Party. Paradoxically, the watchful guarantors of official doctrine became supporters of the epistemological, praxiological, and logical researches, openly encouraging the once abhorred *wertfrei* approaches.

Avoiding any simplifying scheme, we can distinguish three fundamental levels of ideological-spiritual stratification within the East European "bureaucratic-collectivist" societies in the 1960s and 1970s. First of all, there was the official ideological party apparatus, whose main concern was to preserve the purity and the integrity of the apologetic dominant doctrine and to ensure its hegemony. There were, of course, differences among the East European regimes: in Hungary the party bureaucrats spoke about the *hegemony* of Marxism, whereas in Romania or the GDR Marxism, or more precisely, the party interpretation of Marxism, was supposed to enjoy a total cultural-philosophical monopoly. The second level comprises the intellectuals trusted by the party apparatus, who shared the dominant values and myths of the regime. The party recruited many future apparatchiks from within their ranks, especially in the cultural field, thus bringing about a new social structure of the political elite. The third level was represented by those whose subversive and antisystemic voices become gradually more articulated from the ranks of the silent intellectual majority. This stratum was that of the *challenging subgroup of dissidents* and was made up both of all-out anti-Communists and of those who started along the path of revision but through disenchantment found the door open to apostasy. The interaction between these three camps, especially in the last decade of the Soviet bloc, represents one of the most important keys in explaining the sudden and shocking end of Communist regimes. Their respective positions set up the trajectories for liberalization and democratization in the region.

Turning back to a general assessment of critical Marxism, one must stress that this phenomenon signified more than just resurrection of the original humanist-emancipatory drive of the philosophy of praxis. It brought about a new sense of intellectual responsibility, rejuvenating the *critical* dimension of spiritual action. In this respect, providing a different matrix than its counterpart in the Western world, the critical Marxist paradigm developed by East European radical thinkers offered the main epistemological and historical-political categories and concepts necessary for a comprehensive criticism of authoritarian-bureaucratic institutions and methods and provided as well the prerequisites for a project of essential change. That was the reason for the angry attack on Rudolf Bahro in the GDR, for the unexpected rage of the Kádár regime regarding the theoretical conclusions worked out by Konrád and Szelény, the denunciation of the Prague Spring efforts to humanize socialism, or the "moderate" persecution of the Budapest School. In the words of historian Vladislav Zubok, "The regime, as before, did not want to encourage an autonomous civic spirit or share its control over the cultural sphere with intellectuals, writers, and artists."[56]

The ideological state apparatuses in Soviet-type regimes had no greater fear than the crystallization of the interior resistance, the structuring of a critical social consciousness, the radicalization of the intelligentsia. The latter was perceived as the most perilous evolution, a menace to the stability of the dominant institutions and values. East European critical Marxism attempted to counterbalance the inept official "dialectical triumphalism," the conservative-dogmatic functionalism promoted by the ruling Communist parties. Its project was to offer the spiritual weapons for criticism of the system in order to engender a more humane, less asphyxiating, eventually democratic socio-political order. Ultimately, it succeeded, as correctly shown by Ferenc Fehér, in transforming "the semantic potentialities of their vocabulary into the language of an actual politics of dissent."[57]

The most significant theoretical achievement of critical Marxism in the Soviet bloc was the enhancement of the humanist, antitotalitarian potential of dialectics, the illumination of the *negative-emancipatory* substratum neglected and occulted by the official triumphalist-apologetic doctrine, and the revelation of the latent radical tendencies within the *bureaucratic continuum*. The philosophical and sociological researches undertaken by Kołakowski, Karel Kosik, or the Budapest School contributed to the revival of the *qualitas occulta* of dialectics, the *renaissance of negativity* in a social universe that seemed saturated with a distressing positivity. Yugoslav critical Marxism does not enter the area encompassed by this study, for many reasons, at once historical, economic, sociological, and cultural. Nevertheless, the philosophical and sociological investigations carried out by the Praxis group (Mihailo Markovič, Svetozar Stojanovič, Gajo Petrovič, Predrag Vranicki, and others) furthered the theoretical consolidation of the humanist criticism of Soviet-type authoritarian-bureaucratic regimes. Their main objective was to establish a metaphysical and sociological humanism as a counterpedagogy that would have both therapeutic and prophylactic consequences. Another very important function of the Praxis group was their distillation of revisionist thinking from across Eastern Europe in the pages of their journal. The latter became the most important platform of antibureaucratic opposition in the region. At the same time, Praxis succeeded in developing collaborations with anti-Communist thinkers such as Ernst Bloch, Lucien Goldmann, Erich Fromm, and André Gorz.[58] One should mention, however, that the relationship between certain East European critical Marxists and the Western New Left was rather contradictory. The latter was suspected of despotic-terrorist temptations and accused, more than once, of messianic sectarism. Kołakowski's merciless criticism of utopian millenarianism in his *Main Currents of Marxism* expressed more than a dissatisfaction with the desperate powerlessness of negative dialectics: it was an invitation for critical Marxists to go beyond their ideological and emotional attachments, to assume the basic ambivalence of their doctrine, to honestly examine Marxist false consciousness, and to transcend the metaphysical paradigm of Hegelian-Marxist radicalism.

HUMANISM AND REVOLT

From France to Czechoslovakia, from Germany to Poland, from Spain to Italy, from the United States to the Soviet Union, the second half of the sixties was defined by the challenges of redefining oppositional politics, with varying degrees of participation and representation in efforts to assert the awakening of society as a response to a perceived crisis of the state. The fundamental difference among these movements was their attitude toward *utopia,* with crucial consequences for the reconceptualization of the *political* in all these countries. Some were anti-ideological, others were against established structures of authority, but all were variants of an activism advocating the new societal differentiations developed in the aftermath of the Second World War. The circumstances of bipolarism imposed, nevertheless, a significant difference in rationale: in the West, the logic of 1968 was of politically emancipating spaces previously exempt from public scrutiny; in the East, it was about humanizing Leninism, breaking its ideologically driven monopolistic grip on society.[59] Or, to invoke Milan Kundera, the Parisian May was "an explosion of revolutionary lyricism," while the Prague Spring was "an explosion of post-revolutionary skepticism."[60]

In the Soviet bloc, the crushing of the Prague Spring, the March events in Poland, and the turmoil in Yugoslavia brought about the "death of revisionism" (as Adam Michnik put it). In the West, the inability to articulate a coherent vision of an alternative order and the incapacity to sustain revolutionary action generated a departure from what Arthur Marwick called the "Great Marxisant Fallacy."[61] Tony Judt accurately notes that despite its claims of novelty and radical change, the sixties were still very much dominated by one grand master narrative "offering to make sense of everything while leaving open a place for human initiative: the political project of Marxism itself."[62] The movement of 1968 was a blessing in disguise because through its failures it revitalized liberalism. Agnes Heller perceptively summarized the essential impact of these momentous events: they strengthened the center.[63] For the first time in the twentieth century, the hegemony of radical thought among European intellectuals was in retreat.

The year 1968, in the Soviet bloc, signaled the retreat from revisionism and the inception of the dissident movement, a large-scale, cross-regional "goodbye to Marx." With historical hindsight, one can also identify it as the threshold for the gradual decomposition of the Communist regimes. The system had lost its initial totalizing drive; stagnation and immobility were its main characteristics. The increasingly routinized mechanization of ideology laid open the cracks in the system's edifice for easier exploitation by the opposition (e.g., "new evolutionism" or the Charter '77 movement). The Prague Spring of January through August, the Polish March student upheaval, the April student protests in Belgrade (and the later Croatian Spring of 1970–71, an all-out contestation of this country on national bases), and the Soviet intellectuals' reaction to the

Sinyavski-Daniel trial all represented a fundamental challenge to the Stalinist foundations of the Soviet bloc.[64] The failure of these movements left an enduring disenchantment with state socialism and the loss of any hope of reforming these regimes. In other words, "it underscored the political and moral sterility . . . of the attempt to marry the Soviet project to freedom without a return to private property and capitalism."[65] Moreover, as one of Gorbachev's future advisors remarked, one side effect of the Soviet Union's reassertion of hegemony was that the Western Communist parties "without confessing it, came to understand the irrelevance of the Communist movement either for the majority of the countries where it was formally present or, even more important, for the Soviet Union itself."[66] The reaffirmation of the status quo and the systemic stagnation in the Soviet bloc signaled an irreversible "disenchantment with the (Communist) world." Despite the fact that the Berlin Wall came tumbling down in 1989, "the soul of Communism had died twenty years before: in Prague, in August 1968."[67]

The West, on the other hand, experienced an upsurge of "romantic anticapitalism," a rebirth of radicalism fed by the reenchantment with utopia. In the context of the shock produced by the Tet offensive in Vietnam and the identity crisis of the former colonial powers, 1968 "began [for the New Left] with the scent of victory in the air" (in the words of Jeffrey Herf), for, as Paul Auster reminisced, "the world seemed headed for an apocalyptic breakdown."[68] The second half of the 1960s marked both a return to Marx and a rejection of the existing practices of democracy (with the notable exception of Spain and Portugal, where, between 1966 and 1968, civil unrest targeted the right-wing dictatorships of Salazar and Franco). The influence of the New Left, the Chinese Cultural Revolution, the Vietnam War, the Latin American *guerilleros,* and the decolonization movements combined, in a amorphous blend, with the generational clash, an institutional crisis (the occupation of the Sorbonne, the nearly two-year-long paralysis of Italian universities), and a wave of recession (signaled by workers' strikes and *autogestion* projects). This mix produced what some authors later called *les années 1968.* The sixty-eighters claimed to have developed a critique of the ideological bases of the West in the context of the Cold War (also against older self-representations of the Left) and a spontaneous "direct action" against the "hidden oppression" of the liberal-capitalist establishment. The "anti-politics" of 1968 were, to a certain extent, a topsy-turvy expression of the attempt to reconcile theory with praxis *(Theoriewut).* The extreme radicalization of certain sectors within the student movement and the cultivation of violence as a cathartic instrument led to a divorce between left-wing post-Marxist thinkers such as Adorno, Horkheimer, and Habermas, and those whom they suspected of "Red Fascist" inclinations. In France, Raymond Aron proposed a scathing critique of the new search for redemptive revolutionary paradigms.

Ultimately, 1968 effected, both in the West and the East, an anti-ideological reaction that was the premise of "the project of a global civil society." Or, as Tony Judt put it, "a 180-year cycle of ideological politics in Europe was drawing to a close."[69] The 1968 movement was indeed one of the world-historical events of our age, *la brèche,* the cleavage that set up a course of events that seem to have yet to run their course.[70] Charles Maier eminently summarized the transformation: "1968 closed an epoch as surely as it opened one."[71] To paraphrase Paul Berman, the imaginary panoramas deployed across the world by the rebellious youth of the West gradually gave way to the new realities of reformed democratic societies.[72] In the East, decade-long futile attempts to find ways of reforming Communism from within were replaced by an emphasis on human dignity and the inviolability of human rights.[73] As Communist regimes declined under the burden of their own ineffectiveness and the elites lost their sense of historical predestination, it became possible for the long-silent civil society to reorganize itself and to launch a battle for the reconstitution of the public sphere. The upheavals of the late sixties and their aftermath had a formative effect on the Soviet intelligentsia, and particularly on the new cohort of experts, the so called *mezhdunarodniki,* "those policy analysts, journalists, scholars, and others mainly concerned with foreign affairs."[74] According to Fyodor Burlatsky, "Analyzing [East European] reforms . . . we concluded that many of them could be . . . adopted in our country. We studied the rapid integration of Western Europe, deeply envious of the Common Market and its contrast with the slow, bureaucratic functioning of CEMA [Council for Economic Mutual Assistance]. We thought about acquiring . . . modern technology and joining in the greatest achievements of world culture. In other words, we dreamed of reforming Russia."[75] In other words, if for some revisionist intellectuals in Eastern Europe and the Soviet Union the conclusion of the events of 1968 led them toward liberal opposition, for others, especially in the Moscow center, the lesson was a different one. Those who would later lay the foundation of the perestroika reforms came to believe that "reforms *were* possible, but only under an enlightened leader that many 'awaited as if for the coming of the Messiah.'" Robert English accurately commented on this position: "Their naïveté—if only leaders had the will, then reforms would 'work without a hitch'—would be a severe handicap to a later leader's search for 'socialism with a human face.'"[76]

THE REVISIONIST CZAR

Under these circumstances, the antinomies of the East European Marxist project were most obvious in the last decade of the Soviet Union, when the tribulations of the "Gorbachev phenomenon" were perfect examples of the failure of ideological reform. The fundamental question here, identical in its nature with the one that kick-started revisionist thinking, was, could the Soviet system reform itself into something really different without ceasing to be the Soviet system?[77] On the one hand, by the late 1980s, Gorbachev and his followers had a clear idea of what they were trying to reform: "a system that suffocated individuals, a totalitarian regime, a State monopoly over everything," one not merely imposed by the Cold War, because "there was also, within it, a dominant group that sought embitterment, pursued utopia, yearned for War Communism, and thought it could govern with continued repressions."[78] However, the revitalization of the USSR's status on the world stage and the relegitimization of socialism (both domestically and internationally) were dependent, in Gorbachev's view, on a successful systemic transformation of the Soviet state. In other words, the Soviet leader rejected "the option of muddling through" characteristic of his predecessors.[79] Ultimately, his staunch belief in the possibility of simultaneously dismantling "Stalinist socialism" (a formula used by the weekly *Literaturnaya gazeta* in May 1988) and refounding the Soviet polity lies at the heart of the paradoxes that brought about the collapse of the Moscow center. Retrospectively, this approach, which proved fatally contradictory, leaves us with a historical image of Gorbachev best described by political scientist Stephen Hanson in 1989: "A pure revolutionary romantic, believing absolutely in the creative power of the masses, unable to countenance in principle any concrete institutionalization of revolutionary politics that might stifle this creativity, and therefore doomed to be defeated by others who had no such scruples."[80]

One can therefore safely say, as Archie Brown did throughout his work, that Gorbachev was in fact a genuine Marxist revisionist, who, while paying lip service to Lenin's iconic figure, moved away from

Bolshevism as a political culture based on fanaticism, sectarianism, and voluntarism toward a self-styled version of Marxist revisionism. In the Russian tradition of reforms from above, Gorbachev's attempt to restore the moral impetus of Communism was based, however, on a miscalculation: the gradual elimination of the party's control over society opened the door to autonomous alternatives. The Russian literary critic Igor Dedkov spelled out in his diary the new horizons brought forth by Gorbachev's ascendance in the Kremlin: "A man of our generation has come to power. A new cycle of Russian illusions is about to begin."[81] The politics of glasnost unleashed pluralism, with its own dynamics that would transgress the focus of Gorbachev's reform project.

When trying to understand the complex picture of perestroika, its context and consequences, one must not overlook the role that ideas played in the course of events. In itself, the prehistory of East European revisionism was, along with the mythical "original Leninist moment" (the 1917 Soviets or the NEP period), a stepping stone for the Soviet 1980s. Moreover, the successes of the dissent movement in the region (greatly aided by Gorbachev's commitment to "non-intervention") heightened the sense of revolutionary transformation among the actors involved in the process of change. I mentioned earlier in this chapter the three layers of the intellectual establishment in a Soviet-type system (ideological apparatchiks, party technocrats/intellectuals, and dissidents). In the 1980s, these three groups influenced each other to the extent of provoking a wholesale alteration of the discursive horizon, the conceptual pool employed, and the expectations both at the level of policy-making and of the public space. It could be argued that by the last decade of Leninism, there was a general consensus within Soviet intellectual milieus regarding the imperative of *rethinking* the possible solutions to the USSR's problems. Here lies the oddity of the situation: the Soviet polity was indeed on the decline (especially as a leader of the world Communist movement), but it was far from being in turmoil. According to Stephen Kotkin, "Nationalist separatism existed, but it did not remotely threaten the Soviet order. The KGB crushed the small dissident movement. The enormous intelligentsia griped incessantly, but it enjoyed massive state subsidies [that were] manipulated to promote overall loyalty."[82] Gorbachev's biographer, political scientist Archie Brown, formulated this argument in an even more straightforward fashion: "In the Soviet Union reform produced crisis more than crisis forced reform. The fate of the Soviet system and of the Soviet state did not hang in the balance in 1985. By 1989 the fate of both did."[83]

The mixture of a fading and compromised international status (the U.S. challenge, the post-Helsinki embarrassments, the Third World adventures, the Afghan quagmire, or even Euro-Communism), the obvious lack of legitimacy of the East European Communist regimes (and their glaring inability to counter dissident movements without widespread violence), and the almost unanimous belief among large sections of the party elite in the necessity of proposing reform (in the aftermath of the Brezhnevite "stagnation" and of the Konstantin Chernenko debacle) produced an environment where Gorbachev and his followers' ideas could turn into a political program. In other words, it was time for revisionism to come to power at the very center of the empire. Herein lies the difference between the 1980s in the USSR and 1956 or 1968 in Central Europe. In 1968 Europe, critical Marxism officialized into policy was a response to chronic delegitimation of and turmoil within the respective regimes; in the former, it functioned rather as a preemptive measure and as a perceived need for systemic revival.[84] In the Soviet Union, the "new thinking," as the epitome of the leadership ranks' mindset, "did not merely signal a reconsideration of policy efficacy or recalculation of ends and means, but reflected instead a long-term and wholesale revision of beliefs, values, and identity."[85]

The group of party intellectuals who rallied around the CPSU general secretary informed and influenced his political thought and major choices. These advisors and associates not only shared Gorbachev's reformist drive but also contributed to its radicalization.[86] They were the "children of the Twentieth Party Congress," individuals who benefited from the opening of possibilities, both domestically and internationally, facilitated by de-Stalinization: "Inadvertently, Khrushchev's policies of peaceful coexistence [and later Brezhnev's détente] and cultural competition, as well as his rhetoric, helped resurrect a major phenomenon familiar to the older Russian intelligentsia: the idea of the outside world, above all the West, as a measuring stick for Russia's progress or backwardness. . . . The discovery of other worlds was still linked in the minds of many intellectuals to the future of the Soviet communist experiment, its progress or failure."[87]

The glasnost campaign notwithstanding, some things never changed in the structure of the Soviet propaganda rituals. The general secretary was still the dominant voice authorized to express the revealed truth. The limits of the discussion and the scope and objectives of openness were prescribed by the ideological *nomenklatura*. Even important figures such as Alexander Yakovlev were confronted with vilification by hard-core Communists, KGB top brass, and Great Russian xenophobes for being Gorbachev's "evil spirit" and archtraitors to socialism. Other such representatives of the reformers' group who got into the crosshairs of those threatened by the "Gorbachev phenomenon" were philosopher Ivan Frolov (for a while CPSU Central Committee secretary); political scientist Georgiy Shakhnazarov (president of the Political Sciences Academy); Gorbachev's foreign policy advisor Anatoly Chernyaev; Otto Latsis, deputy editor-in-chief of the CPSU theoretical journal *Kommunist;* Georgii Smirnov, the director of the CPSU Institute of Marxism-Leninism; Ivan Voronov, the head of the Central Committee's Cultural Department; and many others.[88] Some of them had worked in Prague in the 1970s as editors of the monthly *World Marxist Review* and were attracted to ideas that within the general atmosphere of *zastoi* were unorthodox, if not altogether heretical.[89] What remains crucial regarding the "young policy-academic elite" surrounding Gorbachev was that the bond which brought it together was a common experience of acculturation in reform. Robert English identified two levels in the process of learning a new identity: "*Comparative-interactive learning,* whereby foreign ties facilitate a shift in intellectuals' essential 'self-categorization' of the nation among allies and adversaries; and *social learning,* in which growing numbers of intellectuals from diverse professions are drawn into an informal domestic community."[90] People such as Yakovlev, Alexei Arbatov (department head of the Institute of the World Economy and International Relations of the Academy of Sciences of the USSR), Abel Aganbegyan, Evgeny Velikhov, Chernyaev, Shakhnazarov, and others became the proponents of a "new thinking" in international politics that rejected the Soviet tradition of capitalist encirclement or permanent revolution in favor of integration with "the common stream of world civilization." They brought about what conservatives called the "conspiracy of academicians," which engineered the volte-face that brought an end to the Cold War.[91] They were also among the first to attack the reality of *Brezhnevschina*— political paralysis accompanied by moral disarray, intellectual despair, and a continuous erosion of the ruling ideology. Robert C. Tucker rightly described pre-Gorbachev Soviet Union as a profoundly troubled society: "People en masse have stopped believing in the transcendent importance of a future collective condition called 'communism.' They have stopped believing in the likelihood of the society arriving at that condition and the desirability of trying to achieve it through the leading role of the Communist party, or through themselves as 'builders of communism,' which is how the official party program defines Soviet citizens. In a society with an official culture founded on just those beliefs, this spells a deep crisis."[92]

The whole ethos of the Soviet political class thus suffered a process of slow and apparently irreversible dissolution. Not surprisingly, the regeneration of Soviet political culture emerged as a widely shared concern among the elite stalwarts. Gorbachev's 1989 unpublished manuscript in which he delineated the main directions for an overall pluralist renewal of the Soviet system can be considered an answer to those who expressed skepticism about his determination to go beyond the boundaries of a revamped Leninism (including many Soviet dissidents as well as Western academics and politicians). By promoting the idea of a system based on the rule of law, Gorbachev did in fact unleash an unstoppable political process with world-historical effects. In February 1990, Gorbachev convinced the Central Committee to accept the principle of a multiparty system and to relinquish the Communist Party's constitutional privilege: "The party in a renewing society can exist and play its role as vanguard only as a democratically recognized force. This means that its status should not be imposed through constitutional endorsement."[93] One can see that Gorbachev was actually restating a 1968 pronouncement by his friend Zdeněk Mlynář on the two conditions of validity for the preservation of the leading role of the party.[94] According to many authors, even this approach was just the tip of the iceberg, in the sense that from 1987 until 1991, Gorbachev and his entourage jostled with the idea of splitting the CPSU in the search for greater legitimacy and wider support for the perestroika version of the USSR.[95]

In 1988, Brown argues, a major shift occurred in Gorbachev's intellectual awakening. By that time, he had already publicly condemned Stalin's "unforgettable and unforgivable crimes." For all practical purposes, he converted to a version of Marxist revisionism directly inspired by Eduard Bernstein's evolutionary socialism. In the words of Anatoly Chernyaev, Gorbachev was going through a process of "sweeping de-ideologization."[96] The Twenty-seventh Party Congress in 1986 had already replaced the iron law of class struggle with "a new doctrine emphasizing the priority of 'universal human values,' including human rights and self-determination."[97] By denouncing Stalin's reign of terror, Gorbachev was effectively bidding farewell to Lenin's ideology-driven partocratic system. Contrary to those who consider civil pressure as the major cause of perestroika, Brown underlines that "with the principal exception of Poland, it is doubtful that the growth of civil society should be seen as a source of fundamental political change in the communist world rather than as a consequence of it."[98] It was "institutional amphibiousness"[99] that caused most of the transformations. In other words, institutions designed to foster and legitimize the system (ideological departments, the party academy, theoretical journals, and think tanks) came to undermine the role they were supposed to play. This point indeed clarifies the unexpected intellectual trajectories within the *nomenklatura*, including some spectacular apostasies that were responses to the system's insoluble moral and cultural crisis. Gorbachevism tried to offer antidotes to the rampant pathologies of cynicism, corruption, and cronyism. The last years of the Soviet Union were fundamentally characterized by a process of national iconoclasm, with the major mythological foundations of the existing system falling apart one after the other.

Ultimately, however, Gorbachev's inability to overcome the old ideological dramaturgy affected the extent of change within the Soviet system. Whereas Yakovlev came to the conclusion that Stalinism was inseparable from the Bolshevik tradition, which needed to be jettisoned entirely, Gorbachev could not breach a certain mental horizon determined by his attachment to the existing system. He held back for tactical reasons, but also because of his deep inner convictions. For Yakovlev, Lenin was guilty of crimes against humanity, a stance that Gorbachev would consistently evade. A seasoned Marxist-Leninist yet a fundamentally honest human being, Yakovlev came to understand the Soviet Union, the historical product of Leninism, in its essence as a state defined by proscription. Gorbachev could not overcome his perception of it as a realm of possibility.[100]

Yet Gorbachev's break with Leninism, less strident than Yakovlev's, was real. At the end of the day, one can see Gorbachev as a combination of Imre Nagy and Alexander Dubček: unable to fully abandon the outworn Leninist model, desperately searching for "socialism with a human face," torn between nostalgia for old ideals and the tragic awareness of their hollowness. More than a neo-Menshevik or a Western-style Social Democrat à la Willy Brandt (whom he admired), Gorbachev remains the last and most influential of those East European Leninist leaders who tried to humanize an inherently inhuman system. Yakovlev, for his part, was the prototypical case of the apparatchik turned apostate in the terminal stages of Bolshevism. His volume of dialogues with Lilly Marcou tried to point to a "democratic potential" of Leninism. At the time, he argued,

Through the return to universal values and the process of European integration, the socialist idea is taking root in Europe. The way out of this dead end that was the Cold War will be through *perestroika* in the USSR and through the evolution in the other East European nations. . . . For the moment, the people are refusing socialism: the idea has stumbled on the real conditions of East European countries; it was destroyed by the Stalinist counterrevolution. Now that the Stalinist model has been eliminated, we will see the emergence of a post-Thermidor socialism. This new socialism, which will no longer know bureaucratic oppression, will be made in the name of mankind.[101]

Of course, after 1992, the break was complete, allowing him to become the president of the Commission for the Rehabilitation of Stalinism's Victims. His book, *A Century of Violence in Soviet Russia,* bears witness to his journey from dogma to democracy.

The need for a dramatic divorce from the past was nevertheless recognized by the most radical partisans of perestroika. The *Declaration of Moscow Conference of Socialist Clubs,* issued in August 1987, formulated the following demands: legal status for independent organizations and associations; the right to initiate legislation and to secure the fulfillment of party decisions aimed at democratizing the electoral system; the right for social organizations to nominate their own representatives to all levels of the Soviets of People's Deputies without restrictions and with free access of candidates to the mass media; a legal distinction between criticism of the shortcomings of the existing system and antistate activity; and, in accord with the first point of the Russian Social-Democratic Labor Party program, citizen rights to prosecute in court officials responsible for illegal acts, independent of complaints made at administrative levels.[102]

As the perestroika policies advanced, political mobilization from below in the Soviet Union focused on the elimination of the counterweights preventing the realization of true democracy. These counterweights, according to Stephen Cohen, infringed on what he calls "the institutions of a representative democracy [existent already in the Soviet polity]—a constitution that included provisions for civil liberties, a legislature, elections, a judiciary, a federation."[103] Their removal seemingly would have finally unveiled the long-awaited "reformed Soviet socialism." The USSR's rapid collapse combined with the political reorientation of large sections of the federation's population argue against Cohen's thesis. As Archie Brown notes, perestroika did not succeed in overcoming systemic limbo. The transition from one system to another was never completed, thus reinforcing the increasingly widespread perception of the Soviet polity's unreformability.[104] Both Karen Dawisha and Stephen Hanson indicate that what Gorbachev envisaged as reform became, in the context of the last decade of the Moscow center, "a (counter)revolutionary self-destruction of the party-state." To paraphrase Karen Dawisha, perestroika, through its policies, publicly acknowledged the elephant in the "communal apartment"—there was a critical and fatal error at the core of the Communist project for building a new civilization.[105]

The ruling elites in Communist countries failed because of their inability to function within political pluralism. The principal function of Communist bureaucracy was to exert dictatorship over mind and body. The Communist bureaucratic ethos involved a strong esprit de corps, a solidarity developed through common existential experience, continued paternalism, and a jealously guarded monopoly of power. It can be argued that Gorbachev was too conscious of the revolution from above that he had initiated. The policy of glasnost was, for him, primarily an instrument for clearing the ranks of state and party bureaucracy. The acceptance of the imposed degree of economic reform and democratization continued to torment the Soviet ruling elite.

Gorbachev seemed perplexed by the popular reaction and extrapolation of his policies, as he focused primarily on eliminating his rivals (from Ligachev to Yeltsin). He thus facilitated what Stephen Hanson calls "a breakdown of elite unity" that left the door open to "damaging, short-run opportunistic behavior by lower-level agents of the state bureaucracy throughout the USSR."[106] Gorbachev indeed triggered a revolution from above but missed the revolutionary effect it would have upon the population. His ultimate commitment to a Soviet state under the rule of the CPSU, another avatar of the old revisionist fancy of ideological craft from within with supposedly preexisting tools, is another explanation for his downfall. This commitment is key to his vacillations in early 1991, when he briefly approached the hard-liners in the party (sacrificing, among others, Yakovlev) and his dubious stand on the use of force in Latvia, Lithuania, and Azerbaijan. It also explains the January 1991 CPSU resolution that advocated "the export of energy sources to Eastern Europe as the most important instrument" for "reestablishing our [Soviet] 'presence' in the region" in order to "neutralize or at least diminish the anti-Soviet tendencies in the East European countries."[107] Even the famous abandonment of the CPSU's constitutionally guaranteed leading role in society (Article 6) came three days after a 100,000-strong demonstration in Moscow against the Communist Party.

Reading Gorbachev and Mlynář's dialogue in "What to Do with the Party?" it is obvious that the Soviet leader was utterly confused as to how to bring about political pluralism while sustaining state socialism. He correctly took the first step by digging up the Great October slogan "All Power to the Soviets!" in order to secularize power and decision-making in the USSR. In this way, he attempted to place party officials under the control of society. The original slogan of the 1917 revolution meant "freedom from party dictates not only for elected government bodies but also for executive bodies established by those legislative bodies. It meant a law-based separation of government powers." The parallel structures created could not fully develop into bodies of representative democracy while preserving Article 6 of the CPSU Constitution, which maintained the power monopoly of the Communist Party. Gorbachev's description of the events shows how the protracted negotiations within the Central Committee did produce change, but only under pressure from the 1990 republican elections. He admits that *only* in July 1991 did the leading body of the party succeed in producing "a program of democratic socialism in the modern sense of the word." Political pluralism for Gorbachev meant a rather dubious "development of the party into a social organism, that is, to regroup and reshape the millions of Communists who were not part of the *nomenklatura*."[108] He apparently maintained a belief in the inner-worldly vocation that characterized the *virtuosi* of the early years of Bolshevism. A question therefore lingers, one I initially raised in 1990: Did Gorbachev's revolution have the potential to be an anti-Leninist revolution? His plans do seem to have maintained the features of a movement-regime defined by an encompassing socialist spirit. He attempted to formulate a new social contract based on mutual trust and respect between leaders and citizens. The party as a collective intellectual in the Gramscian sense, its relegitimation through intellectual competence and moral authority, never succeeded, however, in becoming a viable alternative to the political and national pluralism or fragmentation of the Leninist twilight.

Following Archie Brown, one can identify three main causes for the failure of the Gorbachev experiment: first, he did not champion economic reforms in the direction of a market economy; second, he reacted late and often in self-defeating ways to the rise of centrifugal nationalist and separatist movements; third, he underestimated the *nomenklatura*'s capacity for retrenchment and delayed an alliance with genuine democratic forces. It was Boris Yeltsin who knew how to capitalize politically on the tempestuous rise of civil society in Russia. Nonetheless, it was thanks to Gorbachev and the Gorbachevites that the USSR moved from a state based on contempt for the individual and the rule of law to one in which human and civil rights were taken seriously. Whatever one thinks of Gorbachev's post-Leninist political philosophy, it is certain that he dissociated himself from the obnoxiously despotic features of the old regime. Gorbachev's problem was that he and his followers advocated what Jacques Levesque called "an ideology of transition" permeated by "a Promethean ambition to change the existing world order, based on new, universal values." It provided the justificatory basis for Soviet foreign policy and created the legitimacy that held in check and ultimately defeated the conservative forces within the CPSU.[109] It also fueled a two-fold illusion: the capacity to control change in the context of a society ravaged by the workings of the Marxist-Leninist political religion and a belief in the society's will for socialist transformation despite doctrinal competition and political pluralism. In other words, Gorbachevism did not realize at the time that no phoenix could be reborn from the ashes of "the first workers' state."

The dissolution of civil society and the preservation of an atomized social space, the sine qua non features of Soviet-type totalitarianism, engendered widespread moral indifference and intellectual corruption. In the words of Archie Brown, "there were almost certainly more true believers in a radiant future during the worst years of mass terror than forty years later."[110] The official language was second nature, a protective shield against outbursts of spontaneity. People simulated loyalty to the system, generating a flourish of ritualistic behavior rather than of sentimental attachment. As Václav Havel put it, "Because of this dictatorship of the ritual, however, power becomes anonymous. Individuals are almost dissolved in the ritual. They allow themselves to be swept along by it and frequently it seems as though ritual alone carries people from obscurity into the light of power. . . . The automatic operation of a power structure thus dehumanized and made anonymous is a feature of the fundamental automatism of this system."[111]

WHAT REMAINS

Citizens of socialist countries were master practitioners of double-talk and double-think. The life of the mind was split, and the result of this excruciating process was that not even the Soviet general secretary was entirely convinced of what the party proclaimed. Ideology functioned more as a residual institution than as a source of mystical identification with the powers that be. After the CPSU's Twentieth Congress and the Hungarian Revolution, official slogans sounded like a succession of senseless sentences. The only effect of ideological sermonizing was an all-pervasive ennui. Ironically, ideological imperialism resulted in simulacra of faith that were merely camouflage for an ideological vacuum. At the moment this imposture was exposed, the whole castle fell apart. In Havel's words, "Ideology, as the instrument of internal communication which assures the power structure of inner cohesion is, in the post-totalitarian system, something that transcends the physical aspects of power, something that dominates it to a considerable degree and, therefore, tends to assure its continuity as well. It is one of the pillars of the system's external stability. This pillar, however, is built on a very unstable foundation. It is built on lies. It works only as long as people are willing to live within the lie."[112] In every society citizens need a set of guiding values whose observance ensures tranquility and worldly achievements. Soviet-type regimes ignored this and forced the individual to divide his or her soul between the public and the private person. Person and citizen were different entities in these societies. The outcome was apathy, disgust with politics, drug addiction, interest in exotic cults, or even fascination with Nazism, as in the case of certain Soviet youth groups. One can therefore regard the extinction of mystical ardor as the major liability of Communist political systems. These systems experienced a perpetual ideological crisis, as their promises had long ago lost any credibility. Gorbachev's injunctions received lukewarm support from those he wished to mobilize. It was no surprise that it was the liberals and the radical Westernizers who ousted Gorbachev from power.

The CPSU leader became a victim of his own policies because he underestimated the detachment between the will for revolutionary change in the Soviet bloc and the preservation of the organizational big picture in the area. He overlooked what I would call, employing Mark Kramer's terminology, "the demonstration effects" of empowerment. Gorbachev undercut Marxist-Leninist ideology. He internalized the vulnerability of the Soviet regime. He diminished his leverage on curbing unrest within both the bloc and the federation. He misinterpreted the East European civil societies' visions of regime-transformation and then was taken aback by the contagiousness of democratization—essentially an alternative to his vision. Following Michnik's statement, "the perestroika virus" was indeed the last ingredient necessary to open the floodgates of dissent. But also, the virus of the East European reinvention of politics irreparably subverted "the Gorbachev phenomenon," amounting to a permanent challenge that in the end pushed systemic change into collapse of the system. The transnational, intrabloc, cross-border "demonstration effect" of social movements, political platforms, and state policies accelerated the crystallization and articulation of nonviolent revolutionary consciousness, first among the intelligentsia and then in the population at large. In contrast to earlier crises in the socialist camp, during the 1989–1991 events, people both knew what was being demonstrated and understood the ideas diffused. Mark Kramer points to the fact that this situation fostered parallels, analogies, and conscientiousness among those mobilized in the revolutionary process. The "tightness" of the socialist camp, which was previously enforced by a Soviet interventionist regime (under the Brezhnev doctrine), now proved the catalyst for the lightning speed of change and for the flux of ideas about it:

> Having begun as a largely unidirectional phenomenon in 1986–1988, the spillover became bidirectional in 1989 but then shifted back to a unidirectional pattern in 1990–1991. Unlike in 1986–1988, however, the direction of the spillover in 1990–1991 was mainly *from* Eastern Europe *into* the Soviet Union. . . . The paradox of the changes that occurred under Gorbachev is that, from 1989 on, this same structure *facilitated* rather than impeded the spread of political unrest and democratizing influences from Eastern Europe into the USSR—the very sorts of influences that eventually undermined the Soviet regime and the Soviet state.[113]

Revisionist intellectuals who have done so much to subvert the ideological façade of Communist regimes ultimately abandoned their illusions about the reformability of the system from within the ruling party. Given the density of the Soviet–East European environment, their apostasy created the premises for seeing democracy beyond any arrangement that a revolution from above could bring. They turned instead toward rediscovering the virtues of dialogue and the advantages of civil discourse. According to Zubok, the formation of the human rights movement in the Soviet Union was a breakthrough caused by a shift of consciousness "from the idealization of the 'golden age of Bolshevism' and praise of 'Leninist norms' to the embrace of 'universal moral principles.'"[114] Members of the newborn democratic opposition advocated the need to create an alternative politics. Hungarian writer George Konrád spoke of the emergence of antipolitics as a challenge to the apocryphal version of politics embodied by the system: "The ideology of the democratic opposition shares with religion the belief that the dignity of the individual personality (in both oneself and the other person) is a fundamental value not requiring any further demonstration. The autonomy and solidarity of human beings are the two basic and mutually complementary values to which democratic movement relates other values."[115]

Bitter experiences in Poland, Hungary, and Czechoslovakia convinced these critics that the crux of the matter was to go beyond the logic of the system. Revisionism's crucial contribution to putting an end to Marxist-Leninist self-satisfaction was undeniable, but its main weakness was submission to the rules dictated by officialdom. The new radical opponents of totalitarianism saw revisionism as a half-hearted plea for change, though it was heretical to the regimes' ideological zealots. These writings were esoteric, especially if contrasted with dissident literature, and they held little appeal to the large public. However, the most important fallacy of revisionism was that it generated a criticism that was still encoded in the language of power and the logic of Soviet-type dictatorships. There was no doubt, however, that the revisionist ideas of the 1960s catalyzed the emergence of the counterculture of dissent. Disenchantment with Marxism was an opportunity to rethink the radical legacy and reassess Jacobin ideals of total community.

In the struggle between the state and civil society, it was the latter's task to invent a new principle of power that would respect the rights and aspirations of the individual. This counterprinciple was rooted in the independent life of society, in what Václav Havel aptly called the power of the powerless. A new epoch came of age. It was the inception of the all-out debunking of the duplicitous infrastructure of Communist power. First Solzhenitsyn, then East and Central European dissidents announced their decision to restore the normative value of truth. Refusing official lies and reinstating truth in its own right has turned out to be a more successful strategy than revisionist criticism from within. Dissent in East Central Europe subverted Leninism using two trajectories: "the self-conscious creation of a site of resistance," also called "parallel *polis*," "second society," "antipolitics," and so on, and "the twin strategies of new evolutionism and non-violence" (such as Jacek Kuroń's "self-limitation" or János Kis's "radical reformism").[116] For the first time in the twentieth century, dissidents rejected emergency revolutionary status (privilege) as a justification for (state) violence in societal transformation. In the process, they also forced Western intellectuals to face their own illusions rooted in the totalitarian fascination with armed utopia. Furthermore, the dissident movement irreversibly destroyed the self-constructed, self-blinding, and utterly obsolete veil of ignorance concerning the human cost of revolution. In the case of France, the land of seemingly unending engagement with revolutionary privilege, "in overwhelming, searing detail, Solzhenitsyn's *Gulag Archipelago* was the indictment that, in the words of Georges Nivat, 'broke us.'"[117]

The ultimate goal of Communism, overcoming politics in a fully unified body social—the celebrated "leap into the kingdom of freedom"—was challenged by a moral imperative of political responsibility. Concepts such as central planning, the leading role of the party, the principle of class struggle on the world stage, and the pyramid of soviets were legitimated in historical terms, "a process that was greater than what they, as temporal forms of organization, represented."[118]

In a sense, Gorbachev hoped the party would recapture its soul in the struggle for the modernization of Soviet political culture but found that the times made such endeavors futile. Only when it was too late, in July 1991, at a moment of devastating ideological disarray within the CPSU, did he urge "a decisive break with outmoded ideological dogmas and stereotypes." He failed to look for solutions outside the party. He refused to adopt the roundtable strategy—the symbol of the 1989 Central European peaceful revolutions. He envisaged transition to democracy by means of socialism (yet incoherently articulated), but in a pluralistic society his vision was not the only one competing in the public square. It is now obvious that the main strength of Communist regimes was their ability to maintain a climate of fear and hopelessness; their main weakness was a failure to muzzle the human mind. I do not underestimate the intrinsic economic problems of these regimes, but their main vulnerability was the failure to generate confidence. Glasnost was an attempt to solve the insoluble, a desperate effort to create a less suffocating environment without changing the principle of party domination. The upheavals of 1989 and 1991 showed that the fabric was perhaps softer, but the straitjacket had remained unchanged, generating the ultimate stand—complete popular systemic rebuke.

The Hungarian dissident philosopher G. M. Tamás expressed a widespread feeling among East European independents when he refused to consider Gorbachevism as heaven-sent: "I don't agree . . . with the complacency of most Western observers, especially now with the advent of Gorbachev, who would confine us within the limits of a mildly reformed communist system where power still lies with the Party, but where some other people can also shout a bit. If people don't have to suffer for their views but nevertheless have no real influence over what happens, the

longer such a situation continues the greater the difference develops between words and deeds. We cannot develop a normal life for the future
on such a basis."[119] Or, as political thinker and dissident Miklós Haraszti put it in the afterword to the American edition of his book on artists under socialism: "For decades Hungary has been a textbook model
of a pacified post-Stalinist neo-colony. This fact has not been lost on Mr.
Gorbachev as he attempts to wrap more velvet on the bars of his prison
in order to create a less primitive and more manageable order in the
heart of his empire."[120]

The disruptive effects of this ideological relaxation were felt not only
in the Soviet Union but also in East Central Europe. It did allow for a
redistribution of the constellation of power as a consequence of social
self-organization. The experience of the Workers' Defense Committee
(KOR) in Poland demonstrated that a tiny nucleus of committed intellectuals could fundamentally change the post-totalitarian political
equation.[121] KOR contributed to the climate of cooperation between the
radical core of the intelligentsia and the militant activists of the working
class. Neither a political party nor a traditional trade union, *Solidarnosc*
prefigured a synthesis of nonutopian language for a rational polis and an
emancipated community. The pace of reform in the Soviet Union held a
vital importance for the fate of East European nations. The intensification of dissent activities in 1987–89 in Poland, Hungary, Czechoslovakia,
and the GDR anticipated the daring, all-out challenge to the Communist
regimes in these countries. The October 1986 statement signed by dissidents from Poland, Hungary, Czechoslovakia, and the GDR inaugurated
a new chapter in the history of antitotalitarian struggles. It showed that
international actions could and should be undertaken to emphasize the
values and the goals of the opposition. It was the historical calling of
critical intellectuals to counter the strategy of cooptation and assert the
primacy of those values the system stifles.

At the moment when genuine independent social movements co-
alesced, intellectuals did provide an articulate program for political
change, the exact alternative that revisionism failed to create. In their
seminal volume *Dictatorship over Needs,* Heller, Fehér, and Márkus offer
a thoughtful explanation of the demise of Marxism-Leninism: "A social
order is legitimated if at least one part of the population acknowledges it
as exemplary and biding and the other part does not confront the existing social order with the image of an alternative one as equally exemplary. Thus the relative number of those legitimating a system may be
irrelevant if the non-legitimating masses are merely dissatisfied."[122] In

his turn, Archie Brown, rather than advocating a vantage point from above, argues that the collapse of Communism can be explained by a combination of "new ideas, institutional power (the commanding heights of the political system having fallen into the hands of radical reformers), and political choices (when other options could have been chosen)."[123]

So, why did Communist regimes collapse? The answer is multicausal and requires grasping the many origins and implications of the world-shattering events of 1989–91. If I were to start the list of causes, however, I would say that Communist regimes disappeared because they lost their ideological self-confidence, their hierocratic credentials. Their ritualized hegemony was successfully challenged by the reinvention of politics brought about by dissent. The existence of an alternative in a space previously imbued with myth and ideology triggered a process of individual and collective self-determination. The logic of consent, of emancipation within "ideocratic" limits, was replaced by the grammar of revolt, self-affirmation, and freedom. The Communist project of modernity oriented toward "an integrated accumulation of wealth, power, and knowledge" while relying on the "embedded phantasm of a shortcut to affluence through total social mobilization"[124] was rejected on moral grounds. The crystallization of a critical theory focusing on subjectivity and negativity reasserted the central position of the human being in the symbolic economy of Central and East European politics. Ironically, the Soviet warning, "Either we destroy revisionism or it will destroy us!" seems now stunningly prescient. Thanks to critical intellectuals relying upon the tradition and grounds established by revisionist Marxism, revolts ultimately morphed into revolutions.

CHAPTER 5

Ideology, Utopia, and Truth

Lessons from Eastern Europe

Any social Utopia which purports to offer a technical
blueprint for the perfect society now strikes me as pregnant
with the most terrible dangers. I am not saying that the idea
of human fraternity is ignoble, naïve, or futile; and I don't
think that it would be desirable to discard it as belonging to
an age of innocence. But to go to the lengths of imagining
that we can design some plan for the whole society whereby
harmony, justice and plenty are attained for human engineering is an invitation for despotism. I would, then, retain
Utopia as an imaginative incentive . . . and confine it to that.
The point where despotism differs from totalitarianism is the
destruction of civil society. But civil society cannot be
destroyed until and unless private property, including the
private ownership of all the means of production, is
abolished.

—Leszek Kołakowski (in George Urban ed., *Stalinism*)

More than in any other period of human history, individuals in the
twentieth century were tempted by the promises of revolutionary messianism rooted in grandiose teleological fantasies imagined by prophets
who mostly wrote their manifestos during the previous century.[1] Or to
use the formulation of Czech philosopher and dissident Jan Patočka, the
last century experienced the rise of "radical super-civilizations" that
sought forms analogous to that of a "universal church." According to
him, they were "geared toward the totalizing of life by means of rationalism; we deal with a yearning for a new center, 'from which it is possible

to gradually control all layers all the way to the periphery.' "[2] From both extreme left and right, the quest for an absolute reshaping of the human condition inspired frantic endeavors to transcend what appeared to be the philistine carcass of liberal institutions and values.[3] Many Bolsheviks, including Aleksandr Bogdanov, Anatoly Lunacharsky, and quite likely even Lenin found Nietzsche's proclamation regarding the advent of the *Übermensch* (superman) exhilarating or at least intriguing. This type of influence "touched a deep chord in the Russian psyche that continued to reverberate long after his [Nietzsche's] initial reception. . . . Ideas and images derived from his writings were fused, in various ways, with compatible elements in the Russian religious, intellectual, and cultural heritage, and with Marxism."[4]

In Communism and Fascism, ideology was there to justify violence, sacralize it, and to discard all opposite views as effete, sterile, dangerous, and fundamentally false. In the ideological binary logic (Lenin's *kto-kogo*, who-whom principle) there was no room for a middle road: the enemy—always defined by class (or race) criteria—lost all humanity, being reduced to the despicable condition of vermin. Stalinists and Nazis proudly avowed their partisanship and abolished human autonomy through loyalty to the party/leader/dogma. The main purpose of revolutionary ideological commitment was to organize the mental colonization (heteronomy) of individuals, to turn them into enthusiastic builders of the totalitarian utopia. In brief, totalitarianism as a project aiming at complete domination over man, society, economy, and nature, is inextricably linked to ideology.[5] The ideologies of Communism and Fascism held in common a belief in the plasticity of human nature and the possibility of transforming it in accordance with a utopian blueprint: "What totalitarian ideologies therefore aim at is not the transformation of the outside world or the revolutionizing transmutation of society, but the transformation of human nature itself."[6] Ideology cut across all regime dynamics, "grounding and projecting action, without which governance, violent action, and socialization were impossible."[7] Both Leninism and Fascism have inspired unflinching loyalties, a fascination with the figure of the perfect society, and romantic immersion in collective movements promising the advent of the millennium.[8]

THE ENDURING MAGNETISM OF UTOPIA

Despite Leninism's decline, the utopian reservoir of humanity has not been completely exhausted: refurbished ideologies have resurfaced, among them populism, chauvinism, and fundamentalism of different shades. The ghost of the future conjured up by young Karl Marx in the *Communist Manifesto* has been replaced with revamped specters of the past, summoned into the present by disconcerted political actors unable to come to terms with the hardships of the democratic project and the challenges of (post)modernity. To the soulless "Europe of butter" lambasted and decried by various neoromantics, they often contrast the myth of the original communal democracy of the agrarian societies. In short, the end of Communism, the revolutions of 1989, and the disturbing Leninist legacies have created a world full of dangers, in which traditional lines of demarcation have completely disintegrated and new forms of radicalism simmer under the carapace of pseudostability. With the breakdown of Leninism a crucial threshold was crossed, but the readiness to indulge in ideological fallacies is not totally extinct. This is the reason for Kołakowski 's wry conclusion to the new epilogue of his masterful trilogy: "No one can be certain whether our civilization will be able to cope with the ecological, demographic, and spiritual dangers it has caused or whether it will fall victim to catastrophe. So we cannot tell whether the present 'anti-capitalist,' 'anti-globalist,' and related obscurantist movements and ideas will quietly fade away and one day come to seem as pathetic as the legendary Luddites at the beginning of nineteenth century, or whether they will maintain their strength and fortify their trenches."[9]

Marxism was a protean political movement, but what distinguished it as a movement were its grandiose and ideologically driven political ambitions.[10] According to Jan Patočka, the systematization of man and history, culminating in Marx, made evident "that, in a full working out of the spirit of metaphysics that means man, as historical and as social, placing himself in the position once reserved for the gods and for God, myth, dogma, and theology were reabsorbed into history and flowed into a philosophy that discarded its time-honored name of a simple love of wisdom in order to become a scientific system."[11] Once this scientific pretense ceased to inspire genuine commitment, the spell of Marxism as a promise of earthly salvation started to dissipate. The eclipse of Marxism as a strategy for social transformation ended an age of radicalism and justified a number of reflections regarding the destiny of utopian thought in this century. One can agree with Ferenc Fehér's masterful obituary of "Marxism as politics," but we still need to discuss Marxism's utopian component, which Marxism has never acknowledged.[12] On the contrary, Marx and his followers were convinced that they possessed access to the hidden laws of historical development and that their historical waver was meant to result in an immanent kingdom of freedom.

With characteristic nineteenth-century hubris, Marx declared his social theory the ultimate scientific formula, as exact and precise as the algorithms of mathematics or the demonstrations of formal logic. Not to recognize their validity was for Marx, as for his successors, evidence of historical blindness, ideological bias, or "false consciousness," which were characteristic of those who opposed Marxist solutions to social questions. Prisoners of the bourgeois mentality, alienated victims of ideological mystifications, and non-Marxist theorists—all purveyors of false consciousness—were scorned and dismissed as supporters of the status quo. At the opposite pole, the proletarian viewpoint, celebrated by Marx and crystallized in the form of historical materialism, was thought to provide ultimate knowledge and the recipe for universal happiness. Thanks to proletarian class consciousness, the doctrine maintained, a revolution would occur that would end all forms of oppression. Mankind would undertake the world-historical leap from the realm of necessity (scarcity, injustice, torments) into the realm of freedom (joy, abundance, and equity). This would end humanity's prehistory and begin its real history. All human reality was thus subordinated to the dialectical laws of development, and history was projected into a sovereign entity, whose diktat was beyond human questioning.

Here lies a fatal methodological error in Marxism: its rendering of history as a *gesetzmässig* (law-governed) succession of historical formations, and the corollary of this rendering: the dogma of class struggle as the engine of historical progress. In this theory, individuals are nothing more than hostages of forces whose workings they can scarcely understand. This combination of philosophy and myth, so persuasively explored by Robert C. Tucker,[13] prevented the German radical philosopher and his disciples throughout the decades from grasping the subjective dimension of history and politics. The main difficulty with the Marxian project is its lack of sensitivity to the psychological makeup of mankind. This obsession with social classes—what French sociologist Lucien Goldmann once referred to as the viewpoint of the transindividual historical subject (a Lukácsian formulation, to be sure)[14]—the failure to take into account the infinite diversity of human nature, the eagerness to reduce history to a conflict between polar social categories, this is indeed the substratum of an ideology that, wedded to sectarian and fanatic political movements, has generated many illusions and much grief throughout the twentieth century. With its cult of totality, this social theory, which purports to be the ultimate explanatory archetype, set the stage for its degeneration into dogma and for persecution of the heretics that were to punctuate Marxism once it was transfigured into Leninism.

An example of this dogma is the *Communist Manifesto*'s thesis of the inherent internationalism of the proletarian class, that famous assertion according to which proletarians have no fatherland. In this thesis, metaphysically deduced from the proclamation of the proletariat as the social embodiment of Hegelian reason, Marx bestows on the working class a universalist mandate with no empirical validity (as it was borne out in the outburst of nationalism during World War I, to the dismay of the Zimmerwald Left and other Marxist internationalists). Marx imagined an ideal proletariat, ready to renounce all social, communitarian, and cultural bonds. What really happened was precisely the opposite of Marx's prophesy: the proletariat failed to initiate the apocalyptical breach, the cataclysmically chiliastic cleavage so powerfully heralded in the *Manifesto*.

The *Communist Manifesto* was perhaps the most inflammatory and impassioned text ever written by a philosopher. In this scathing, vitriolic, and incandescent pamphlet, Marx (in coauthorship with his loyal friend Friedrich Engels) at once pilloried and glorified a whole social class—the bourgeoisie—and a whole social order—capitalism—and prophesied the objective, inexorable necessity of their overthrow by a higher form of society. Written in the middle of the nineteenth century, the *Manifesto* became in the twentieth century the charter of the Bolshevik oracular creed. Marxism, for all its scientific aspirations, from the beginning represented a secular substitute for traditional religion, offering a totalizing vocabulary in which "the riddle of history" was solved, and envisioning a leap from the realm of oppression, scarcity, and necessity to a realm of freedom. Its chiliasm helps to explain its magnetism, its capacity to elicit romantic-heroic behavior, to generate collective fervor, to mobilize the oppressed, to incite political hostility, and to inspire both social hope and mystical delusions. Precisely because of its deliberately simplified rhetorical devices, the *Manifesto* became the *livre de chevet* for generations of professional revolutionaries. It was the political counterpart to the eleventh of Marx's Theses on Feuerbach, in which he assigned philosophy an urgent transformative task by proclaiming that the issue was not how to interpret the world but how to change it.

The *Manifesto* does more than articulate a grand historical narrative of the progressive rise and fall of classes. It designates the proletariat as the ultimate collective agent, destined to bring the story of class struggle to a close. At the same time, it reduces all questions of morality to questions of class power. The story of capitalism is a story of how the bourgeoisie expropriated feudal property, made the modern "bourgeois" state its own, and wielded political power to enhance the process of capital accumulation, unwittingly calling into existence its own "grave-diggers"—the industrial proletariat. As the proletariat evolves, it comes to an increasing awareness of its "mission" as the only "really revolutionary class," to abolish—indeed, to "destroy"—not simply private property but human oppression itself.

The *Manifesto* presented proletarian empowerment and human emancipation not as contingently related but as essentially the same thing. And it described this empowerment in strikingly Manichean terms, complete with "decisive hours" of conflict, "despotic inroads" on property, and the "sweeping away" of outmoded historical conditions. In their frantic opposition to the bourgeois status quo and its ideological superstructures, including forms of false consciousness, Marx and Engels underrated the persistent power of traditional allegiances, including the potential of nationalism: "The working men have no country. We cannot take from them what they have not got. Since the proletariat must first of all acquire political supremacy, must rise to be the leading class of the nation, must constitute itself *the* nation, it is, so far, itself national, though not in the bourgeois sense of the world. National differences and antagonisms between peoples are daily more and more vanishing. . . . The supremacy of the proletariat will cause them to vanish still faster."[15] It could be said that in laying out this historical trajectory Marx intended merely to describe and not to prescribe. And yet the pamphlet was laced with moral outrage and denunciation, buoyed by a vision of ultimate liberation ("the free development of each . . . the free development of all"). More to the point, it heaped scorn on any reservations on the part of other Communists or Socialists—much less "the bourgeoisie"—regarding the morality or justice of class struggle. According to the *Manifesto*, "the Communists disdain to conceal their views and aims. They openly declare that their ends can be attained by the forcible overthrow of all existing social conditions. Let the ruling classes tremble at a Communist revolution. The proletarians have nothing to lose but their chains. They have a world to win. WORKING MEN OF ALL COUNTRIES UNITE!"[16]

To identify these texts in the *Manifesto* is not to imply that this is all that is there, but these are central texts, and they articulate what Marx maintained was most distinctive about "Communism" as a political formation distinct from the socialists and utopians that he disparages—that it unsentimentally, resolutely, and presciently both comprehends and apprehends the "real movement" of history, a movement heretofore marked by exploitation, expropriation, and violence, at the same time that it now, finally, stands at the threshold of a new dispensation. "In depicting the most general phases of the development of the proletariat," Marx and Engels wrote, "we traced the more or less veiled civil war, raging within existing society, up to the point where that war breaks out into open revolution, and where the violent overthrow of the bourgeoisie lays the foundation for the sway of the proletariat."[17]

Marx did not articulate a "Leninist" theory of the "vanguard party." Indeed, he insisted that "the Communists do not form a separate party opposed to other working-class parties." But he also emphasized that the Communists alone possess a proper and historically privileged understanding of the total interests of the proletarians as a class:

> They have no interests separate and apart from those of the proletariat as a whole. They do not set up any sectarian principles of their own by which to shape and mould the proletarian movement. The communists are distinguished from other working-class parties by this only: (1) In the national struggles of the proletarians of different countries, they point out and bring to the front the common interests of the entire proletariat, independently of all nationality. (2) In the various stages of development which the struggle of the working class against the bourgeoisie has to pass through, they always and everywhere represent the interests of the movement as a whole. . . . The theoretical conclusions of the Communists are in no way based on ideas or principles that have been invented or discovered, by these or that would-be universal reformers. They merely express, in general terms, actual relations springing from an existent class struggle, from a historical movement going on under our very ideas."[18]

For Marx, communism united ideological superiority, political militancy, and an unflinching and resolute appreciation of historical tasks. The distance separating Marx from Lenin on this score was barely perceptible. It is thus easy to see how Lenin later could claim that the *Manifesto* contained the idea of the dictatorship of the proletariat even though Marx and Engels had yet to name that idea. For Lenin, the book's central theme was clearly "the proletariat organized as the ruling class." Because political power was the organized power of one class or another, and because the state "is an organization of violence for the suppression of some class," for Lenin it made perfect sense that the proletariat must seize state power and use it "to crush the resistance of the exploiters." Such a politics, he insisted, was absolutely irreconcilable with Menshevik-style reformism. And there is more. For the "truth" of this perspective is only manifested by radicalized, uncompromising Communism. In her prescient critique of Lenin's neo-Jacobin, potentially dictatorial organizational philosophy, Rosa Luxemburg wrote in 1904:

> Ultracentralist tendency . . . the central Committee is the only active nucleus in the party and all the remaining organizations are merely tools for implementation . . . absolute blind submission of the individual organs of the party to their central authority . . . a central authority that alone thinks, acts, and decides for everyone. The lack of will and thought in a mass of flesh with many arms and legs moving mechanically to the baton. . . . Zombie-like obedience *[kadavergehorsam]* . . . absolute power and authority of a negative kind . . . sterile spirit of the night watchman . . . strict despotic centralism . . . the straight-jacket of a bureaucratic centralism that reduces the militant workers to a docile instrument of a committee . . . an all-knowing and ubiquitous Central Committee."[19]

And thus the foundation for a violent tutelary dictatorship was laid. Stalin would extend the premises put forward by the founder of Bolshevism, exalting party-mindedness *(partiinost')* as an antidote to "bourgeois scientific neutrality" and other such illusions: "The omnipotence of the Lie was not due to Stalin's wickedness, but was the only way of legitimizing a regime based on Leninist principles. The slogan constantly met with during Stalin's dictatorship, 'Stalin is the Lenin of our days,' was thus entirely accurate."[20] Reviewing *The Black Book of Communism,* Anne Applebaum judiciously noted that "it is possible now, in a way it would not have been a few years ago, to trounce once and for all the myths of a more promising 'early period' of communist history, or of 'better' regimes which deviated from the general rule. . . . Without exception, the Leninist belief in the one party state was and is characteristic of every communist regime, from Russia to China to Cuba to Mozambique. Without exception, the Bolshevik use of violence was repeated in every communist revolution."[21]

The revolutionary subject refused to perform its allegedly predestined role. The proletariat, in this soteriological vision, was the universal redeemer or, as the young Marx put it, the messiah class of history. The concept of class struggle, as elaborated in the *Manifesto,* was foundational for the whole Marxian revolutionary cosmology. And as Raymond Aron, Alain Besançon, Robert Conquest, Leszek Kołakowski, and Andrzej Walicki have shown, in its emphasis on struggle, the Marxian project sanctified historical violence (a viewpoint unapologetically affirmed by a range of Marxist texts, from Leon Trotsky's *Their Morals and Ours* to Maurice Merleau-Ponty's *Humanism and Terror*). In the Marxian perspective, violence of the oppressed against the oppressors was justified as a means to smash the bourgeois state machine and ensure the irreversible triumph of the proletariat. Marx drew this conclusion from the defeat of the Paris Commune in 1871, which he attributed to the lack of determination on the side of the Communards to establish their own dictatorship of the proletariat. Later, Leninism used and abused this philosophy of revolutionary historical *Aufhebung,* celebrating the role of the vanguard party and deriding concerns about the absence of a mature proletariat in industrially underdeveloped Russia. For Lenin, the Bolshevik regime had to resort to any means, including mass terror, to "form a government which *nobody* will be able to overthrow."[22] In his 1972 address upon receiving the Nobel Prize for Literature, Aleksandr Solzhenitsyn stressed the upward spiral of degeneration involved in the Communist project: "At its birth violence acts openly and even with pride, [but later] it cannot continue to exist without a fog of lies, clothing them in falsehood."[23]

There are *two* trajectories laid out in the *Communist Manifesto,* foreshadowing further elaborations in mature Marxian theory. On one hand there is the emphasis on the self-development of class consciousness, which lends itself to a more or less social democratic politics of proletarian self-organization and political empowerment—what the American Socialist Michael Harrington called "the democratic essence." On the other hand, there is the privileging of an ideologically correct vanguard committed to a totalizing revolution by any means necessary (for, in the words of Leon Trotsky's famous aphorism, you can't make an omelet without breaking some eggs). Yet even the more "humanistic" version of Marxism was deeply Manichean, centering on capitalist exploitation as the fundamental injustice and on proletarian counterhegemony as the agent of its transcendence. This dialectic of class struggle—what C. Wright Mills ironically called a "labor metaphysic"—is the core principle of all versions of Marxism. And its prominence explains why the more elitist and violent form of Marxism that came to dominate the politics of the twentieth century—Bolshevism—can be seen as a legitimate heir of Marxism's emancipatory project, even if it is not the only legitimate heir.[24] We can perhaps imagine other worlds in which a different realization of Marxian ideas might be possible. But in the real world of historical actuality, there was only one successful effort to "overthrow the bourgeoisie" and institute the "sway of the proletariat." And it laid waste to the eastern half of Europe.

A range of political intellectuals writing in the 1940s and 1950s first identified a "totalitarian temptation" within Marxism. Authors such as Boris Souvarine, Czesław Miłosz, Karl R. Popper, Isaiah Berlin, Hannah Arendt, and Albert Camus hardly converged on a single political perspective. But they shared a sense that Communism was "a God that failed" miserably, and that in important respects this failure could be traced to deficiencies in the thought of its humanistic founder, Karl Marx. The intellectual history of the twentieth century can be written as a series of political disenchantments with a doctrine that promised universal emancipation and led instead to terror, injustice, inequality, and abysmal human rights abuses.[25] In this reading, the main weakness of Marxist socialism was the absence of a revolutionary ethic, the complete subordination of the means to the worshipped, nebulous end. The numerous traumatic breaks with Communism of some of the most important European intellectuals of the twentieth century did not necessarily imply a farewell to Marxism. They were nevertheless most exacting emotional experiences. In the words of Ignazio Silone, "One is cured of communism the way one is cured of a neurosis."[26]

As I came of age politically in the Romania of the "Great Helmsman," Nicolae Ceaușescu, these authors—and more contemporary ones, such as François Furet, Leszek Kołakowski, the Praxis group, the Budapest neo-Marxist School, (Ferenc Fehér, Agnes Heller, György Márkus, Mihaly Vajda)—helped me understand the genealogy of the Leninism that held my country (and the whole region) in thrall. While some left-wing critics might argue that this antitotalitarian critique of Marxism is simply an artifact of Cold War liberalism, I would remind them that the Cold War liberalism with which I identified centered not on the foreign policy of the United States but on the challenges of trying to live freely as a subject of an ideologically inspired dictatorship. This is the thrust of the argument made by Agnes Heller and Ferenc Fehér in the 1980s when they insisted on the need to discover a common language between critical intellectuals of the East and the West. In other words, in spite of the real uses and manipulations of the term *totalitarianism* during the Cold War, for East European neo-Marxists this was a sociologically, politically, and morally adequate concept.[27] To get a better sense of how such authors perceived the realities of the politics of utopia instrumentalized by Com-

munist regimes, one should remember Václav Havel's still cogent characterization of what he called the *post*-totalitarian order:

> The post-totalitarian system touches people at every step, but it does so
> with its ideological gloves on. This is why the life in the system is so thor-
> oughly permeated with hypocrisy and lies: government by bureaucracy is
> called popular government; the working class is enslaved in the name of
> the working class; the complete degradation of the individual is presented
> as his ultimate liberation; depriving people of information is called making
> it available; the use of power to manipulate is called the public control of
> power, and the arbitrary abuse of power is called observing the legal code;
> the repression of culture is called its development; the expansion of impe-
> rial influence is presented as support for the oppressed; the lack of free
> expression becomes the highest form of freedom; farcical elections become
> the highest form of democracy; banning independent thought becomes the
> most scientific of world views; military occupation becomes fraternal
> assistance.[28]

THE SHIPWRECK OF UTOPIA

The revolutions of 1989–91 dealt a mortal blow to the ideological pretense according to which human life can be structured in accordance
with scientific designs proposed by a general staff of revolutionary doctrinaires. These movements countered the apotheosis of bureaucratic
domination with the centrality of human rights. "Seeing like a state" (to
use James C. Scott's formula) turned out to be a strategy with catastrophic consequences.[29] Some acclaimed these revolutions precisely
because they were non-Jacobin, nonteleological, and nonideological.
They were anti-utopian precisely because they refused to pursue any
foreordained blueprint. In emphasizing the non-utopian character of
Charter 77, Havel tellingly described the foundation upon which the
resistance that fueled the 1989 upheaval was built: "An essential part of
the 'dissident' attitude is that it comes out of the reality of the human
here and now. It places more importance on often repeated and consistent concrete action—even though it may be inadequate and though
it may ease only insignificantly the suffering of a single insignificant
citizen—than it does in some abstract fundamental solution in an uncertain future."[30] The answer to the pervasiveness of a spuriously revolutionary ideology was to fill the gap between the public and the private
existence by way of reestablishing "authentic human relations, which
would preserve the direct and genuine communication of the private

life, being at the same time politically influential as a counterweight to the oppressive, bureaucratic state."[31]

With the exception of some vaguely defined concepts like civil society, return to Europe, and popular sovereignty, these revolutions occurred in the absence of and in opposition to ideology. Precisely because ideology had become the justification of state-sponsored lies, coercion, terror, and violence, dissidents, from Solzhenitsyn to Havel, insisted on the need to overcome the schizophrenic ideological chimeras and rediscover the galvanizing power of concepts such as dignity, identity, civility, truth, transparence, trust, and tolerance. For example, Czech philosopher Jan Patočka, himself a victim of Communism because of his central role in the creation of Charter 77, considered that Russian dissidents Andrei Sakharov and Aleksandr Solzhenitsyn shared "a sense of *the truth of their own humanity* that outweighed any material advantage or dogmatic slogan that could be offered to them" [my emphasis].[32] In response to the totalist pretension of a totalitarian movement, dissidents reaffirmed what Patočka conceptualized as "care for the soul"— that "which makes whatever is properly human in us possible: morality, thought, culture, history. It is the most sacred thing in us, something through which we become connected to that which is eternal, yet without having to leave this world."[33] Or, "the attempt to embody what is eternal within time, and within one's own being, and at the same time, an effort to stand firm in the storm of time, stand firm in all dangers carried with it."[34] Communism was therefore faced with individuals who rejected both living a lie and messianic posturing. One author even remarked that this could also be an explanation for the aftermath of 1989: "Václav Havel's idea of living in truth, as well as Adam Michnik's new evolutionism, George Konrád's antipolitics and other dissident conceptions, are actually long-term strategies of resistance—not instructions to civil societies after the reestablishment of liberal democracies."[35]

In the aftermath of the demise of the Leninist order, the moral landscape of post-Communism was marred with confusion, venomous hatreds, unsatisfied desires, and endless bickering. This is the bewildering, often terrifying territory in which political mythologies make a return. In Václav Havel's words: "The fall of communism destroyed this shroud of sameness, and the world was caught napping by an outburst of the many unanticipated differences concealed beneath it, each of which— after such a long time in the shadows—felt a natural need to draw attention to itself, to emphasize its uniqueness, and its difference from others."[36] The ideological extinction of Leninist formations left behind a vacuum that has been filled by syncretic constructs drawing from the region's pre-Communist and Communist heritage (nationalism, liberalism, democratic socialism, conservatism, populism, neo-Leninism, and an even more or less refurbished Fascism). Ethnocentric ideology, as mendacious as the Communist one, has become a new salvationist creed, a quasi-mystical source of identification: "When the nationality conflict obliterates all else and the high priests of the intelligentsia support their nation's obsession with romantic platitudes, we have what can be called political hysteria."[37] Moreover, Patočka argued that during the twentieth century, and especially under Communism, individuals had to be "shaken" into "an awareness of their own historical nature, their own possibilities for freedom via the assumption of a self-reflective stance and the rejection of ideology."[38] Dissidents themselves were "a community of the shaken," but they were hardly the majority of the population. The persistence of ideological ruins within post-Leninist societies and the echoes of the last century's totalitarian temptations made East Europeans vulnerable to resurgent specters of alternative or derivative salvationisms (e.g., clericalism, ethnocentric conservatism, and populism). Havel warned that ideology was "a specious way of relating the world. It offers human beings the illusion of identity, of dignity, and of morality while making it easier for them to *part* with them."[39]

At the very core of Marxism one finds a millenialist myth about justice, fraternity, and equality, a social dream about a perfect world where the ancient conflict between man and society, between essence and existence, would be transcended. More than anything else, Marxism represented a grandiose invitation to human beings to engage in a passionate search for the City of God and to construct it here and now. Leninism relied on its utopian aspect, as it proposed what Eric Weitz describes as a "capacious vision" of historical development: "By clearing the rubble of the past, they believed they would open the path to the creation of the new society that would permit the ultimate efflorescence of the human spirit."[40] This human adventure has failed, but the deep needs that Marxism tried to satisfy have not come to an end. According to Leszek Kołakowski, "Marxism has been the greatest fantasy of the twentieth century." The professed unity between theory and praxis that Marxism found was its historical *cul-de-sac:* its practical failure was the confirmation of its theoretical fallacies. In other words, a philosophy that proclaimed praxis as the criterion of truth and maintained that concrete reality is the test of validity was dramatically belied by the practical impossibility of its implementation as originally designed and

174 | Lessons from Eastern Europe

by the human costs linked to its Leninist and post-Leninist revisions and experiments. As Leszek Kołakowski concluded in his unsurpassed trilogy, *"The self-deification of mankind, to which Marxism gave philosophical expression, has ended in the same way as all such attempts, whether individual or collective: it has revealed itself as the farcical aspect of human bondage* [my emphasis]."[41]

In Andzej Walicki's view, Marx's double-faceted concept of freedom was the conceptual grounding for Stalinism. One the one hand, there was freedom as "conscious, rational control over economic and social forces"; on the other, the notion of that individual freedom is to be replaced by "species freedom"—the liberation of mankind's communal nature.[42] Subsequently, the fundamental utopian element of this totalizing polity was the drive toward fulfilling such a free society. Leninism argued for a *telos* of "democratic dictatorship" (allegedly the only real democracy) and for communism, with the party as the magical entity injecting the necessary consciousness and offering the type of leadership for the completion of this journey.[43] Neil Robinson argues:

> This telos was transcendental because, although communism could be described, it was separate from experience and was immutable. It performed an ontological function because it acted to make sense of general experience for all: all real phenomena could be judged against it and were ascribed value, form and essence in its light. It therefore acted, as a kind of "super" or "main" discursive convention: it determined what could be claimed as being good (that which was conducive to communist construction) and what had to be rejected as bad (that which was harmful to the process of communist construction). In performing this ontological function, the *telos* therefore provided the party with an idea of the meaning of the material world. This idea was unchallengeable and kept the discourse from fragmenting. . . . there could be no commentary on the way in which the system was structured for such commentary would be a denial of the truth of the telos, a denial of the idea that the actions taken to secure historical development were appropriate and legitimate.[44]

Such a conceptual framework for ideological discourse, combined with what Rachel Walker labels "the invariate conventions governing it" (that is, dogmatism as opposed to defending the purity of Marxism-Leninism),[45] provided a continuous but variable narrative of emancipation, a source of incessant re-enchantments with state socialism as utopia in action. It comes as no surprise, then, that the revolutions of 1989 brought about for the Western Left what Jan-Werner Müller identified in the German case as "the loss of utopia."[46] Writing shortly before his death in 1983, Raymond Aron concluded his lifelong endeavor to analyze Marxism by pointing to its colossal theological and practical failure: "The prophecy, contradicted by both the evolution of capitalism and by the experience of so-called socialist regimes, remains as empty as it was at the beginning: How would the proletariat become the ruling class? Why would the proletariat become the ruling class? Why would collective ownership suddenly produce unprecedented efficiency? What magic wand would accommodate authoritarianism and centralized planning to personal freedom and democracy? What was to replace the market economy other than bureaucratic planning? The mystification began with Marx himself when he called his prophecy scientific."[47]

This is indeed the way Marxism appears in the aftermath of the convulsive twentieth century: a hidebound and often abstruse millennialism, having little to do with the reality and challenges of industrial civilization and unable to offer as remedies for human suffering anything other than empty slogans and ossified dogmas. As the "opium for the intellectuals," it is almost extinct. This twilight is, at least in its implications, a grandiose *fin de partie:* we see the final agony of a hopeless attempt to overcome the limits of human nature by imagining a total break in the chain of those often strange and inexplicable occurrences that for want of a better term we have come to call "history." The waning of utopian radicalism does not mean, however, the demise of an enduring yearning for social engineering. Historical hubris has not vanished; anguishes and malaise are here and can lead to new follies: "The communist ideology seems to be in a state of rigor mortis, and the regimes that still use it are so repulsive that its resurrection may seem to be impossible. But let us not rush into such a prophecy (or anti-prophecy). The social conditions that nourished and made use of this ideology can still revive; perhaps— who knows?—the virus is dormant, waiting for the next opportunity. Dreams about the perfect society belong to the enduring stock of our civilization."[48]

The question of Marxism's culpability has not receded in importance in the wake of the fall of the Berlin Wall. Indeed, it is an essential question of modern historical self-understanding, especially in Eastern Europe and the former Soviet Union, because at the present moment—over twenty years after the revolutions of 1989—Leninist legacies endure, and there are forces in both East and West that maintain that the Communist catastrophe was essentially exogenous to the generous pledges of Marxist humanism. This is true, for instance, of the prominent Romanian Marxist philosopher Ion Ianoşi, for whom the text of the *Manifesto* and its historical consequences should not be amalgamated for "partisan reasons."[49] Comparing Marx to Nietzsche, Ianoşi wrote about "culpables without culpability." In the same vein, Hungarian former dissident (and briefly Straussian) thinker G.M. Tamás has lately (after 2000) become increasingly vocal in criticizing liberal values (not only liberalism) and championing the need to resurrect working-class political radicalism. Former Romanian dissident thinker Andrei Pleşu responded bitterly to this idealized view of the Marxist legacies in the region, insisting that for the denizens of the former Soviet Bloc, these are not abstract speculations but tragic facts of life.[50] Recently, I engaged in a polemical exchange over G.M. Tamás's espousal of French philosopher Alain Badiou's irresponsible exaltation of revolution as the ultimate *évènement*, a cataclysmic moment in which an anarchic, inchoate version of liberty allegedly triumphs over the mediocrity (or, in Žižek's neo-Leninist terms, the cretinism) of liberalism.[51] Another interesting case is Lukács's former disciple, István Meszáros, a student of the Hegelian-Marxist concept of alienation, whose enduring anticapitalist convictions have been enthusiastically acclaimed as a paradigm of *pensamiento critico* by Venezuela's "Bolivarian socialist" Hugo Chávez.[52] In all the former Communist countries, the Far Left and the Far Right tend to share animosities, idiosyncrasies, neuroses, and phobias. What unites these two trends is that they are both "far": they resent the "grayness" of liberal democracy and abhor the "philistine mediocrity" of bourgeois existence.[53] The neoromantic hostility to the challenges of a globalized economy generates new salvationist mythologies, including utopian flights into agrarian reveries and the cult of the unadulterated, pristine, archaic *völkisch* community. Disciples of Marx and Lenin close ranks in the company of frantic admirers of Carl Schmitt and Julius Evola, the Italian Fascist mystical philosopher.[54]

One of the main effects of Marxist deradicalization in East-Central Europe was a need to redefine the relations between the Western intelligentsia and the liberal tradition, including the legacies of Western humanism. The post-Marxist, that is, postideological, age allowed for reconsideration of the political and moral responsibilities of intellectuals, including a refusal to indulge in long-cherished fantasies of repudiating the liberal democratic status quo.[55] The fate of Marxism in Eastern Europe highlights the role of awakening, apostasy, and metanoia: it was precisely disenchanted Marxists who decisively contributed to the erosion of the ideocratic-partocratic systems. As I emphasized in the previous chapter, Marxist revisionism represented a major corrosive force in dissolving the Leninist ideological hubris. By contrasting the official pretense to the abysmal realities and offering the concept of alienation as an interpretive key for understanding bureaucratic authoritarianism, the revisionists offered alternative discourses of emancipation. The very fact that they had belonged to the Communist "family" made their critique poignantly explosive and exasperatingly annoying for the *nomenklaturas*. The destiny of East European revisionism[56] illustrates a noble tradition of moral dignity, the reclaiming of the concept of alienation from the totalitarian Moloch, and a phenomenology of honor and resistance that played a crucial role in the constitution of dissident movements and the demise of state socialist systems. Their approaches have converged with Western anti-authoritarian post-Marxism,[57] illustrated by attempts to rediscover the social imagination and new horizons for emancipatory practice beyond the ossified and rigid ideologies of the past. Post-Marxism therefore meant renunciation of the apocalyptical visions of revolutionary catharsis, acceptance of the new challenges in the era of global communications, internet networks, and new social movements, and widespread concern regarding growing inequalities. Post-Marxism recognized the persistence of the traditional socialist agenda but admitted the waning of redemptive forms of political radicalism. Post-Marxism confronted the need to acknowledge the incontrovertible fact that "Marxism as a doctrine cannot be separated from the history of the political movements and systems to which it led."[58]

THE FATE OF A POLITICAL RELIGION

More than other political theologies, Marxism was able to deter for many decades the emergence of critical questioning, and to nourish an ardent, even fanatical attachment on the part of the normally skeptical Western intellectuals. The disintegration of the Stalinist gnosis as a self-sufficient system of authoritarian norms and quasi-mystical precepts impelled revisionist intellectuals toward the construction of what Kołakowski called an agnostic Marxism, actually a quixotic attempt to salvage the humanistic kernel of the doctrine lest the whole Marxist utopia fall apart. Critical Marxism was therefore an attempt to regenerate the moral dimension of political praxis. Revisionism pondered the relation between means and ends and arrived at the conclusion that no goal could justify the manipulation and degradation of the individual.[59] Ethical relativism was exposed as a most harmful deception, and moral values were again postulated as transcendent values, independent of contingent circumstances and selfish interests. Less idealistic than their unorthodox adversaries, the ideological supervisors knew better. Committed to a cynical realpolitik, they saw no reason to let the genie out of the bottle. Reified in the figure of ideological power, Marxism was doomed to survive as a disembodied symbolic ceremonial. Trying to revive and to secularize it, as the revisionist thinkers did, amounted eventually to intellectual narcissism. The point was not to recapture a presumed original libertarian thrust, but to formulate the conditions for the invention of a liberated social space. Milovan Djilas presciently identified in the early 1980s the bureaucratic degeneration of Marxism as one of the main causes of the ultimate debacle: "With the extinction of this utopian faith, communism has lost its soul, its *raison d'être*. Maintained largely by a relatively well-paid apparatus of officialdom and the imperialist ambitions of the Soviet oligarchy, it has metamorphosed into an ever more banal lust for power, thereby losing its revolutionary strength and, to a large degree, its volcanic force as well. In doing so, communism has been reduced to its power-hungry, monopolistic essence and thereby condemned itself to destruction."[60]

Some Western philosophers—primarily Cornelius Castoriadis and Claude Lefort—unlike many East European thinkers, predisposed to the traditional reformist illusions, understood that, in order to gain credibility, the discourse of the opposition had to be de-Marxisized.[61] Dialectical (ideological) trump cards had to be debunked and taken for what they indeed were: convoluted justifications for the humiliation of the human being. From the revisionism of the late 1950s and early 1960s to the dissidents' skeptical treatment of Marxism or even outward anti-Marxism, there was a whole odyssey of ruined hopes and failed illusions. Instead of indulging in what Hegel called a "litany of lamentations," dissident thinkers have tried to clarify the causes of this abortive end of the romance between Marxism and intellectuals. One cause was a growing awareness of the inherent ambivalence of the Marxian message, a discontentment with pragmatic utopianism. The mentor of the dissidents associated with Charter 77 in Czechoslovakia, philosopher Jan Patočka, simply rejected Marxism's claim to a revolutionary prerogative over history: "Humans do not invent morality arbitrarily, to suit their needs, wishes, inclinations, and aspirations. Quite the contrary, it is morality that defines what being human means."[62]

In the aftermath of 1956, but especially after 1968, the post-totalitarian phase of state socialism brought about a system of power based on conformity, co-optation, cynicism, and inclusive, privilege-based regimentation. Reflecting on the hollow-ritualistic nature of the ideological reproduction of state socialism, Václav Havel provides an excellent description of the internalization mechanisms that replaced the terrorist methods:

> Part of the essence of the post-totalitarian system is that it draws everyone into its sphere of power, not so that they may realize themselves as human beings, but so that they may surrender their human identity in favor of the identity of the system, that is, so that they may become agents of the system's general automatism and servants of its self-determined goals, so they may participate in the common responsibility for it, so they may be pulled into and ensnared by it, like Faust into Mephistopheles. . . . What we understand by the [post-totalitarian] system is not a social order imposed by one group upon another, but rather something which permeates the entire society and is a factor in shaping it.[63]

Mental co-optation was a crucial systemic goal; its achievement meant the perpetuation of endless ideological symbolic performances. The main purpose of this policy was to cauterize any sense of *historical transcendence,* to preclude any independent nuclei of thought and action. The very concept of truth had long since been distorted (and negated) by Lenin with his Manichean view of philosophical partisanship: for the Leninists, truth is what serves the interests of the proletariat, themselves defined by a self-appointed elite made up of revolutionary zealots. After 1956, however, the dogmatic core started to crumble. Full-fledged totalitarianism never reached perfection, but it was the main ambition during the revolutionary stages of both Nazism and Stalinism. In the Soviet case, the Secret Speech led to disillusionment and ushered in *detotalitarianization.*[64] Ideological lip-service was all-pervasive, but true believers had long since vanished. In fact, with very few exceptions, nobody believed in the bombastic rhetoric of the existing socialism. Still, although everybody knew that it was the incarnation of a huge lie, the system continued to operate, pathetically stifling (or stiflingly pathetic). The Solidarity movement was a major breakthrough, but the real beginning of the end came, as I have shown, when Gorbachev decided in 1987–88 to jettison ideology in favor of frankness and truth.

The ideological camouflage of serfdom was the main underpinning of the post-totalitarian order. In this sense one can argue for the *continuous* totalitarian ethos of these regimes, despite their reformist vagaries: "When we speak of totalitarian regimes we have in mind not systems that have reached perfection, but rather those which are driven by a never-ending *effort* to reach it, to swallow all channels of human communication, and to eradicate all spontaneous social life forms [emphasis in the original]."[65] The profile of the regimes in former Eastern Europe was determined by the specificities of the ideological content (one might even say hubris) filling the gap between their self-representation and their practice.[66] Therefore, following Lefort, their nature was determined by their "*self*-understanding as a 'distinctive' project,"[67] in the context of a neotraditionalist degeneration of the socialist system, where "the party's combat ethos was ritualized," its agents were transformed into "Party principals," and the issue of *political equality* was consistently sidestepped and displaced.[68] In Arendtian terms, Communism as a regime was permanently beset by a resilient conflict between power and reality.

Generally speaking, Leninism attempted to encompass and filter through its ideological matrix all that had potential for public discourse, to mediate any self-defining narrative. It created a "new type of cultural hegemony" that aimed to carry out "an 'anthropological revolution' through the use of an essentially ritualistic and transformative politics."[69] The demise of Communism generated the space for alternative "semiotic sacralizations" (Roger Griffin), which determined a proliferation of what I previously called *fantasies of salvation:* ideological surrogates whose principal function was to unify the public discourse and provide citizens with an easily recognizable source of identity as a part of a vaguely defined ethnic (or political) community. These mythologies minimized individual rights and emphasized instead the need to maintain an organic supra-individual ethos, which in turn determined the boundaries between good and evil, true and false. Indeed, they were not ideologies, but they shared with ideology the appearance of a coherent narrative.

The evolution of democracy in post-Leninist Eastern Europe has shown that large social strata resented Communist ideology but not the state socialist guarantees of security and stability. Existing inventories of historical heritage and culture brought forth from under the Leninist debris provided the reservoir for the justification of the new/old political actors' intentions. In the past, for denizens of the Communist world, the myth of the classless society could serve such a purpose. In the post-Communist present, Communist nostalgia idealized "heroic mobilization," seen as both the expression of a lost unity and disappeared community, and as disaffection with democratic pluralism and the market economy.[70] In a period characterized by weakness of social capital, loss of solidarity among members of the political community, the disorientation, decline, or inertia of civil society, and rampant erosion of traditional authority, the checks and balances for myth-making inflation were seriously weakened. The history of the region's first two post-Communist decades is a story of the quest for cohesive citizenry in the face of the grievous fragmentation typical of the Leninist legacy (in Jowitt's sense).[71]

In the context of the routinization (and sometimes deradicalization) of Communist regimes and of the exhaustion of the Marxist revisionist alternative, a new type of political thought developed in East and Central Europe. It was both a reaction to the collectivistic, pseudo-egalitarian logic of Communist regimes and an inspiration for both moral reform and social change in this region from the 1970s on. The dissidents' writings, the stances of critical intellectuals, provided a composite oppositional complex that emphasized morals, tolerance, civility, and self-scrutiny. This body of thought reasserted the centrality of the individual. To paraphrase Jan Patočka, the locus of change was the soul of the individual—"the spiritual person." Dissidence represented the return to what sociologist Alvin Gouldner called the "culture of critical discourse," while also introducing the criterion of normative truth as the only valid one in a praxis meant to resist new forms of oppression. For example, for the signatories of Charter 77, the "hope for politics was that citizens could learn to act as free and responsible persons, and that government would recognize this orientation by respecting the moral dimension of political life."[72]

As the regimes declined under the burden of their economic ineffectiveness and moral numbness, as the elites lost their sense of historical predestination and showed signs of incurable disarray, it became possible for the long-silent civil society to reorganize itself and to launch a battle for reconstitution of the public sphere. Moreover, critical intellectuals not only rejected regimentation but also signaled their disenchantment with Marxist theory and proclaimed the revolutionary nature of truth-telling. Leszek Kołakowski gave full expression to the newly acquired understanding of the intimate connection between the Marxist worldview and the practice of Communism in the twentieth century: "It would be absurd to maintain that Marxism was, so to speak, the efficient cause of the present-day communism; on the other hand, communism is not a mere "degeneration" of Marxism but a possible interpretation of it and even a well-founded one, though primitive and partial in some respects. . . . The self-deification of mankind, to which Marxism gave philosophical expression, had ended in the same way as all such attempts: it has revealed itself as the farcical aspect of human bondage."[73] In 1968, as the Czechoslovak experiment of "socialism with a human face" was in its last days, Russian dissident and eminent scientist Andrei Sakharov published in samizdat his memorandum *Reflections on Progress, Coexistence, and Intellectual Freedom*. In this document, the author abandoned and condemned the ideological Manicheanism that functioned as a cardinal principle to both Marxism and Leninism: "'The division of mankind threatens it with disaster,' he began, and 'in the face of these perils, any action increasing the division of mankind, any preaching of the incompatibility of world ideologies and nations is madness and a crime.'"[74]

REINVENTING POLITICS

The creation of civil society in East and Central Europe, or what I call the reinvention of politics in a non-Machiavellian way, was centrally premised upon a rebellion against the mortifying role of ideology: "Because the regime is captive to its own lies, it must falsify everything. It falsifies the past. It falsifies the present, and it falsifies the future. It falsifies statistics. It pretends not to possess an omnipotent and unprincipled police apparatus. It pretends to respect human rights. It pretends to fear nothing. It pretends to pretend nothing."[75] The moral anesthesia of the population was the most important ally of post-totalitarian Communist power, and one should hasten to add, *it is the ally of any bureaucratic-alienating structure.* The system worked as long as the prevailing lie was accepted and tolerated by the individual, as long as the average citizen— the greengrocer posting in the shop's window the meaningless sign "Workers of the World, Unite!"—continued to endorse the ideological nonsense, even though he was aware that all this verbiage was nothing but a collection of lies. When Solzhenitsyn asked his fellow Soviet writers to cease lying, that is, to abandon ideology, his point was that moral life starts at the moment we refuse to lie. The world may be full of injustice, but let me not add to it. The problem, therefore, was not simply to identify the source of oppression in the government but also to realize how each individual was tied to the power structure and that it was in his power to emancipate himself. Upon reading Solzhenitsyn's *Gulag Archipelago*, Russian intellectuals heard "a trumpet calling to the terrible court of history."[76] The pain of millions recounted in the book shook off the cynicism and the hypocrisy perpetuated by the post-totalitarian order in the East or by ideological folly in West.[77] At the same time, Soviet leaders realized the potentially irreversible caesura generated by *The Gulag Archipelago*. In 1974, at a Politburo meeting, none other than Leonid Brezhnev straightforwardly asserted that "we have every basis to imprison Solzhenitsyn, for he has encroached on what is most sacred—on Lenin, on our Soviet system, on Soviet power, on everything that is dear to us."[78] Indeed, the revelations spelled doom; as one letter to the Soviet Politburo stated, "The *Gulag Archipelago* is the indictment with which your trial at the hands of the human race begins."[79] Solzhenitsyn, along with those who followed his example, undermined, as one party hack put it in 1988, "the foundations on which our present life rests."[80]

According to Havel, the system's ability to turn its victims into accomplices made post-totalitarianism different from classical dictatorships. The very idea of change had vanished, and the individuals were faced with the imperative of coming to terms with what appeared to them as the only possible form of life. Emancipation, the birth of an alternative to the all-pervasive lie, came not as an exogenous benefit bestowed by others, but at the moment when some individuals decided to put an end to grotesque forms of self-denial. His or her decision to break the enchanted circle of complicity with the power-that-be and to utter his or her own truth was the premise for the civil society to resurrect itself. Therefore, Havel (along with George Konrád, János Kis, Jacek Kuroń, Adam Michnik, Martin Palouš, Miklós Haraszti, and others) advanced an alternative discourse on individuality that created the potential for a reconstruction of community and a redefinition of subjectivity. It was to become the embryonic state of a willingness to assume responsibility for one's own actions, to take risks, and to question institutions on the basis of a necessary accountability. Echoing the teaching of his mentor Jan Patočka, Havel asserted that "an act is right not because it is likely to lead to favorable results (utilitarianism) nor because it is the universal duty of the agent to behave thus under the circumstances (deontology), but because it is the essentially human thing to do, a genuine aim of life."[81] The Central European dissidents provided an identity conceptualization opposed both to the manipulative inclusion of "really existing socialism" and to the "chiliastic trope of the New Man" at the core of Leninism.[82] Moreover, in post-Communism, the legacy of their writings provided a durable check on "pseudo-chiliastic" fantasies of salvation, based upon the exclusion and marginalization of the very category of otherness; it provided a safety-net against such destructive and stigmatizing collective vanities. It was a critique of those "cows that proclaimed themselves for decades as holy," thus rejecting "any divine principles" buttressing their sacredness.[83]

Havel emphasized one fundamental aspect of this notion of individuality: "[The notion of human *responsibility*] has begun to appear as the fundamental point from which all identity grows and by which it stands or falls; it is the foundation, the root, the center of gravity, the constructional principle or axis of identity, something like the 'idea' that determines its degree and type. It is the mortar binding it together, and when the mortar dies out, identity too begins irreversibly to crumble and fall apart."[84] He proposed an "existential revolution" that aimed to "expose the totalitarian colonization of post-traditional identity at the level of its very formation." It was based upon a vertical interpretation of identity, which was shaped ethically, "constituted in responsibility to the other." This vertical ethics, inspired by French philosopher Emanuel Levinas, was, according to Martin Matustik, "suspicious towards totalitarian ambitions of ecological freedom; towards historical projection of the ego on revolutionary identity; towards conservative nostalgia for the ego of the nation, party, totem, or the church."[85] The revolt of the powerless did not have an explicit political dimension. The politics of antipolitics consisted of a discreet, unobtrusive, almost Mozartian attempt to restore the dignity of the individual. It confronted totality from within, preparing the ground for the actual revolution: "Given the complex system of manipulation on which the post-totalitarian system is founded and on which it is also dependent, every free human act or expression, every attempt to live within the truth, must necessarily appear as a threat to the system and, thus, as something which is political by excellence."[86] This ethical insurrection took place "in the real sphere of potential politics in the post-totalitarian system," outside the perverse and perverting circle of power. The touchstone of a countersociety was the individual's decision to proclaim his or her inner independence. Commitment to those "eternal values" derided and subverted by Communist (or Fascist) ideocratic dictatorships did become the main strategy for reasserting freedom as a constitutive human and social possibility.

Ultimately, the crucial problem with the projects of the New Man and of Marxian freedom and with post-Communist fantasies of salvation "was not that they were centered on Faith, but that they were centered on Faith pretending to be *knowledge*."[87] In the light of the analysis of Havel's "existential revolution," Marxism (-Leninism) and post-1989 political mythologies share the quality of "moral blindness" (S. Lukes). They promised to free humankind from specific conditions of morality: from scarcity, from the selfishness or partiality of conflicting individuals and groups, from nonconvergent and incompatible values, and from the anarchy and opacity of a world not subject to collective human control. In pursuing the accomplishment of their promises, they discarded the already existent principles that protect human beings from one another.[88] Any source of failure was externalized, responsibility existing only at an intergroup level, as the *ur*-community (e.g., proletariat or nation) pursued its historical mission in counterdistinction to the *other*-categories (e.g. bourgeoisie, peasantry, Jews, enemy-nation).

Václav Havel and other Eastern European dissidents proposed an alternative in his project of "moral politics," which would "teach both ourselves and others that politics does not have to be the art of the possible, especially if this means the art of speculating, calculating, intrigues, secret agreements, and pragmatic maneuvering, but it can also be the art of the impossible, that is the art of making ourselves and the world better."[89] The demise of Leninism made it possible to change all the established political paradigms. Nevertheless, the legacy of the twentieth century into the twenty-first is the imprint of the totalitarian ethos lurking under the surface of our daily interactions. I am referring to the symptoms of ur-Leninism or ur-Fascism. They are two sides of the same coin: the temptation of palingenesis and that of the chosen agent of history (i.e., the search a new proletariat or the return to the perfect ethnic community).[90] The specific nature of these specters should reinforce our agreement on the centrality of Havel's quest: how to exit the castle? His answer is as simple as it is difficult to enact: by regaining the authenticity of human existence. Following Patočka, Havel considered that living in truth was premised on the care of the soul, which in its turn gave the latter a clear sense of order, self-consistency, and inner beauty.[91]

The transition from state socialism took place against the background of a universal disparagement of conventional political dichotomies, including a widespread crisis of self-confidence on the part of Western liberalism. In my view, the main ideological successor to Leninism and the principal rival to liberalism was ethnocentric nationalism. One could argue that, taking into account most of the twentieth-century tradition of conceptualizing power in Eastern Europe, the ideal of instituting a society on the basis of procedural norms and against a neutral backdrop of minimal rights and duties had little chance to materialize. On the contrary, a "thick" notion of citizenship based on ideals that require allegiance to the community because of a presupposed "pre-political commonness of its members" seemed more likely to take shape.[92] In the struggle between gemeinschaft and gesellschaft, the former had a considerable head start. After two decades of post-Communism, in what concerns the dominant visions of membership and identity in Eastern Europe, the results are mixed.

No political myth in the twentieth century has proved more resilient, protean, and enduring than nationalism. A comprehensive and potentially aggressive constellation of symbols, emotions, and ideas, nationalism also offers a redemptive language of liberation for long-subjugated or humiliated groups. It would therefore be simply misleading to reduce nationalism to one ready-made interpretation. Conductor Leonard Bernstein used to say that whatever statement one makes about Gustav Mahler's music, the opposite is equally true. This is also the case with nationalism. It is often described as archaic, antimodern, traditionalist, in short reactionary. Other interpretations see it as a driving force of modernizing liberation, an ideology of collective emancipation, and a source of human dignity and pride. Overall, it can be said that nationalism "offers a kind of collective salvation drama derived from religious models and traditions, but given a new activist social and political form through political action, mobilization, and institutions."[93] Whatever one thinks of it, its ubiquitous presence at the end of the last century and the beginning of the new one is beyond any doubt. The problem, therefore, is to find ways to reconcile it with the democratic agenda. Once the nation becomes the master symbol of identitarian narratives, structures of power and regimes of knowledge are determined by *who defines* and *how are defined* the communalities perceived to represent the bedrock of that particular community of people. In other words, how can one tame that violent propensity which a Georgian political philosopher aptly called "the illiberal flesh of ethnicity"?[94]

The return of ethnocentric politics, especially during the 1990s, the agonizing search for roots, and the obsession with identity were major trends of the turn of the twenty-first century in Eastern Europe. They often collided with the inclusive, civic values advocated by former dissidents such Havel or Michnik. The post-Communist first wave of primordial passions and the appeals of the new exclusionary discourses remind us that neither the premises nor the outcomes of modernity have been universally accepted. As tragically demonstrated in the former Yugoslavia, the revival of this specific form of politics can prove noxious to civic-liberal development in the post-communist societies. In most of East and Central Europe ethno-nationalism has fundamentally altered the left-right ideological spectrum.

Usually, it was intellectuals who manufactured discourses that justified nationalist identifications and projections, then the mobilized masses gave these discourses the validation of practical realities. This is, to employ for a moment Pierre Bourdieu's terminology, a process of the naturalization of a nation-centered *habitus,* meaning a "system of durable, transposable dispositions, structured structures predisposed to function as structuring structures, that is as principles which generate and organize practices and representation." This way, nationalism, understood as both structures of power and a regime of knowledge, is transformed into self-reproducing and self-referential reality. Nationalism becomes the "the obvious way of doing and thinking about things."[95] The community ordered in such fashion will not only be "known and imagined; it will also be deeply felt and acted out."[96] While in the 1960s nationalism appeared at least in the West as an extinct myth, the end of Communism and the new era of international ethnic conflict that followed the Cold War have made nationalism the main competitor to liberalism and civil society. Its most important strength comes precisely from its ability to compensate for the loss of certainties and to offer immediate explanations for failure, confusion, and discomfiture. Nationalism caters to painful collective anxieties, alleviates angst, and reduces the individual to the lowest common denominator: the simple fact of ethnic belonging. At its core lies a revivalist myth (or, to use Roger Griffin's term, a palingenetic one). As many scholars have shown, such a myth is "an archetype of human mythopoeia which can express itself in both secular and religious forms without being 'derived' from any particular source or tradition." Its most important function is to provide the groups employing it in cultural and political practice with new sources of meaning and social function. The main danger inherent to its activation is that it can bring forth an "organically conceived nation to be cleansed of decadence and comprehensively renewed."[97]

SPECTERS OF NATIONALISM

Romanian exiled writer Norman Manea, who survived the Holocaust as a teenager only to be later persecuted because of his Jewishness and nonconformist ideas under the Ceauşescu regime, gave a powerful description of this ethnocentric temptation as the main rival to the civic vision of the community associated with modernity and liberalism:

> The increased nationalism all around the world, the dangerous conflicts
> among minorities in Eastern Europe, and the growing xenophobia in West-
> ern Europe emphasize again one of the main contradictions of our time, be-
> tween centrifugal, cosmopolitan modernity and the centripetal need (or at
> least nostalgia) for belonging. . . . The modern world faces its solitude and
> its responsibilities without the artifice of a protective dependency or a fictive
> utopian coherence. Fundamentalist and separatist movements of all kinds,
> the return of a tribal mentality in so many human communities, are expres-
> sions of the need to reestablish a well-ordered cohesion which would protect
> the enclave against the assault of the unknown, of diversity, heterogeneity,
> and alienation.[98]

Ethnic nationalism appeals more often than not to primary instincts of
unity and identification with one's own group: foreigners are often seen
as vicious destabilizers, dishonest breakers of traditions, and agents of
dissolution. Nationalism, indeed, sanctifies tradition, once described by
Gilbert K. Chesterton as the "right to vote granted to the dead people."
Especially in times of social frustration, foreigners tend to be demonized and scapegoated. A Ukrainian nationalist, for instance, would see
Russians (or Jews) as forever conspiring to undermine Ukraine's independence and prosperity. A Romanian would regard members of the
Hungarian minority as belonging to a unified body perpetually involved
in subversive and irredentist activities. A Croatian militant nationalist
would never trust Serbs, while Serbian ethnic fundamentalists would
invoke Croatia's alliance with Nazi Germany as an argument against
trust and ethnic coexistence. Estonian, Latvian, or Lithuanian national-
isms are colored by the memory of the Soviet (and previously Russian)
occupations of the Baltic states. National discourses not only preserve a
sense of ethnic identity but also continuously "reinvent the tradition"
(Hobsbawm), regenerate historical mythology, infuse an infrarational,
transcendental content into the sense of national identity. During imperial collapse, nationalism becomes an ideological balm used to calm
sentiments of despondency and rage.

With its shattered identities and wavering loyalties, the post-
Communist world allowed delusional xenophobic fantasies to thrive and
capture the imagination of millions of disaffected individuals. National
homogenization became the battle cry of political elites, for whom unity
and cohesion were the ultimate values. The Leninist exclusionary logic
("us" versus "them") has been replaced by the nationalist vision, which
sanctifies the ethnic in-group and demonizes "aliens." Those who criticize
this trend are immediately stigmatized as a "fifth column" made up of
"inside enemies." For the late Croatian president, Franjo Tudjman, for

instance, it was only the intellectuals supportive of the "national spirit and self-determination" who deserved the name of intelligentsia. All others, he maintained, were just Pharisees.[99] The continuous invention of enemies and hatreds aggravates the climate of insecurity and makes many honest individuals despair about the future of their societies.

In this context, it is no surprise that post-Communism was, and still is, defined by a lasting tension between national(ist) consciousness and the emphasis on "post-conventional identities" (Habermas), continuing the project of universalization of rights that was unleashed in the eighteenth century.[100] There is still a scarcity of "social glue," because existing political formations have failed to foster the consensus needed for the sustenance of a constitutional patriotism *(Verfassungpatriotismus)*.[101] Contemporary ethnic nationalism is less a resurrection of the pre-Communist politics of intolerance than an avatar of the Leninist effort to construct the perfectly unified body politic. To be sure, the past is often used to justify the resentful fantasies of nationalist demagogues. This "return of history" is, however, more of an ideological reconstruction meant to respond to present-day grievances than a seemingly primordial destiny of nations destined to continuously fight with and fear each other.[102] The strange synthesis of national ambition and ideological monism explains the intensity of nationalist passions in the post-Communist world: ethnic exclusiveness is a continuation of the Leninist hubris, of its adversity to anything smacking of difference, uniqueness, or otherness. Antiliberalism, collectivism, and staunch anti-intellectualism blend together in the new discourses of national self-aggrandizement.

Nevertheless, the Europeanization of Eastern Europe, without being the illusory end of politics, can be envisioned as the first clear break with the last century's dreadful cycle of ideology and utopia in this region. Indeed, a substantive democracy, which takes truth and emancipation as its core values, can also be defined as post-democracy: "By post-democracy I mean nothing more, and nothing other, than a democracy that has once again been given human content, which is to say that it is not just formal, not just institutional, not just an elegant mechanism to ensure that although the same people govern, it appears as though the citizens are themselves choosing them again."[103] The pedagogical dictatorship of Marxism turned out to be a false solution to the dilemmas of Enlightenment and modernity, with catastrophic consequences. French Marxist structuralist thinker Louis Althusser once wrote that Marxism was not a form of humanism because, in his view, dialectic materialism had overcome abstract-anthropocentric conceptualizations. It was situated beyond the pale of empirical altruism, for it sought the fundamental laws and constants of development. We can detect here a secret connection between the sophisticated syllogism of the Althusserian school and the conservative imperatives of neo-Stalinist dogmatism: humanism was merely a pellicle, a treacherous surface hiding the real ideological priorities. Therefore humanism was to be always concrete, to serve the interests of the revolution. Havel's answer to such fantasies of revolutionary praxis, and the essential lesson of the 1989 revolutions, is self-empowerment through citizenship. Thus the subtitle of the *Power of the Powerless* is "citizens against the state."

Dissidents and critical intellectuals successfully created a horizon of expectation that had not existed in Eastern Europe since the Prague Spring. It is not surprising that John Paul II played a crucial role in articulating this new grammar of opposition to Communism by defining human solidarity and liberty as non-negotiable values. Significantly (and electrifyingly), one of the pope's most influential encyclicals was titled "The Splendor of Truth." Historian Stephen Kotkin provided a telling quotation for this state of things: the pope's message was "the inviolable right, in God's and man's order of things, for human beings to live in freedom and dignity."[104] Civil society was the territory of retrieved human autonomy that escaped and countered the grip of Communist partocracy (the "uncivil society," as Kotkin puts it). The discourse of truth and rights did indeed have revolutionary power. It struck at the heart of the political system itself, for, as Kołakowski once put it, "the lie is the immortal soul of communism." In challenging it, while simultaneously avoiding conventional ideological dichotomies, the activists of this civil society exploded long-held myths of fatality, futility, impotence, resignation, abandonment, and conformity.

The whole philosophy of dissent was predicated on a strategy of long "penetration" of the existing system, leading to the gradual recovery and restoration of the public sphere (the independent life of society) as an alternative to the all-embracing presence of the ideological party-state. The primacy of the Communist party-states was rejected, for, according to dissident thought, there was "something unconditional that is higher than they are, something that is binding even on them, sacred, inviolable."[105] This was the individual with his and her rights, dignity, and freedom. Accordingly, the successful reconstruction of the life of a nation from the tragedy and destruction caused by a criminal regime depends upon the capability of a society to build upon foundations of trust between *freed* individuals. Both utopian absolutism and postmodern relativism were rejected through each individual's possession of doubt by means of knowledge and moral action. The best deterrent for the treacherousness of history remained the permanent reminder of its murderous embodiments. Or, to evoke Russian dissident Vladimir Bukovsky's lament on Communism's totalitarian temptation: "Ah, our beloved Ilich, how many people he has lured into darkness, how many supplied with justification for their crimes! But to me he brought light." Indeed, for Bukovsky, after reading *The Gulag Archipelago,* learning about and experiencing firsthand the criminality of Soviet regime, Lenin's works transformed into "a living history of the crimes of the Bolsheviks."[106]

Communism was indeed a fantastic scenario of human self-aggrandizement, an exercise in unbounded magic and self-delusion, an attempt to escape from the constraints of alleged bourgeois pettiness and an offer for millions to vicariously live in "another country." If one maintains a number of ethical criteria in interpreting the main traumatic experiences of the last century, it is hard not to agree with Anne Applebaum:

> Now, at the end of the twentieth century, it finally makes sense to look back at the evolution of communism as a single phenomenon. While we have not perhaps reached the end of the end of the history of communism, the story already has a clear beginning and a clear middle: it is now possible to trace the direct lines of influence, ideological and financial, from Lenin to Stalin to Mao to Ho Chih Minh to Pol Pot, from Castro to the MPLA in Angola. It is also possible to trace the links between their remarkably similar systems of repression. . . . Communism now looks bad enough by itself.[107]

Undoubtedly, for long decades Karl Marx's ideas were distorted almost beyond recognition. But it is impossible to completely separate the Bolshevik praxis from these ideas. There is a temptation to present the Soviet experiment as an aberration in the history of the revolutionary, socialist left, and to exempt the basic Marxist schema from any culpability for this experiment. Those so tempted (from French Socialist politician Jacques Attali to influential American historian Geoff Eley) often invoke the role of modern social democratic movements and parties in advancing the causes of both political democracy and social justice. Yet the undeniably profound achievements of social democracy in the West have more to do with the legacies of Ferdinand Lassalle and Eduard Bernstein, Léon Blum and Willy Brandt, Olaf Palme and Michael Harrington—all committed democrats—than with the revolutionary chiliasm and dialectical critique of law and morality that are deeply rooted within Marxism and can be found in the *Communist Manifesto*.

Marxism failed in the twentieth century because it underestimated the existential quandaries of human existence, the needs of many for deep spiritual or cultural sources of meaning, and thus the profound importance of the human right to privacy. It aimed to create a perfect society whose materialization in the Communist experiments, from Moscow to Phnom Penh, came closer to Kafka's penal colony than to the paradisiacal visions of traditional utopians.[108] The myth of a singular world proletarian revolution has long since been dispelled. It was not this myth, however, that made Communism such a poignantly seductive ideology. More important was the promise of universal transformation, the promise that this miserable Vale of Tears will be replaced by an Arcadian world in which all individuals will be happy and free.

From the Eleventh Thesis on Feuerbach to the last line of the *Manifesto*, Marx issued a persistent call to mobilize understanding and harness the forces of modernity, all in the name of a radical transformation of the world, a reconciliation of man with nature and history. Such a totalizing vision no doubt possesses great intellectual and moral appeal. But if we have learned anything from the past century, it is that the domain of morality and politics is a domain of finitude, difference, and limit. The riddles of history have no final solutions worth seeking. Like Germans after Hitler, like Italians after Mussolini, like Chileans after Pinochet, East Europeans have engaged in efforts to reckon with a traumatic past. This necessarily involves analyses of the ideological blueprints that galvanized murderous political passions, catalyzed mass resentment, and organized nihilistic social energies in disastrous forms of social engineering.[109] When living for almost a century in the company of the Devil, one cannot anymore find refuge in angelic reverence. The reconciliation and healing of a nation besmirched by the bloody mire of evil depend on the recognition and non-negotiability of human dignity as a primordial moral truth of the new society.

CHAPTER 6

Malaise and Resentment

Threats to Democracy in Post-Communist Societies

Societies produce stereotypes (which are the height of
artifice), and then consume them as commonplace (which is
the height of naturalness). That is how bad faith can pass for
good conscience.

—Eugen Weber, *My France*

. . . shared hatreds make for strange bedfellowships.

—Albert Hirschman, *The Rhetoric of Reaction*

Turning and turning in the widening gyre
The falcon cannot hear the falconer;
Things fall apart; the centre cannot hold;
Mere anarchy is loosed upon the world,
The blood-dimmed tide is loosed, and everywhere
The ceremony of innocence is drowned;
The best lack all conviction, while the worst
Are full of passionate intensity.

—W. B. Yeats, *The Second Coming*

The over two decades that have passed since the collapse of Communist
regimes in Central and Eastern Europe have proved that more than one
possible future could be reasonably canvassed for the region. Even
when many hastened to predict the worst, the likelihood of nightmarish
scenarios, pace Jan Urban or G. M. Tamás, was somewhat dubious.[1] *Bellum omnium contra omnes,* a state of wild and protracted anarchy, and

the loss of recently acquired civic rights in favor of Stalino-Fascist simulations of cohesion and collective will are not in the offing in most post-Leninist states. The Milosevic-style expansionist chauvinism has not been emulated outside the borders of the former Yugoslavia, although similar outbursts of hatred and intolerance have accompanied the breakdown of the Soviet Union, especially in the Caucasus. Human rights have been trampled in Belarus under the plebiscitary regime headed by Alexander Lukashenko, but this remains rather an exceptional case among European post-Communist states. Pluralism seems to have settled solidly, and democratic procedures are now widely recognized, accepted, and practiced. The general landscape after Communism's demise, however, is one of disenchantment, dispirited political cultures, the rise of new collectivisms, marginalization of former heroes, and the return of the former Communists. Adam Michnik's term for this trend was "the velvet restoration."[2] I proposed the "velvet counterrevolution" to indicate the direction of this phenomenon, especially its strong anti-intellectual and illiberal tendencies.[3] The conservative-populist turn in Hungarian politics under Prime Minister Viktor Orbán after 2009 has resulted in bitter controversies regarding perceived limitations to freedom of the press and ethnocentric approaches to the nature of national identity.

Central and Eastern European societies have evolved from authoritarian, extremely centralized, and bureaucratic Leninist regimes toward democratic forms of political and economic organization.[4] To focus exclusively on their difficulties during the transition period is to miss the drama of social and political experimentation in that region. More than twenty years after 1989, what remains at stake is the validity of the liberal democratic paradigm in traditionally authoritarian societies ("What can they look back to?" historian Tony Judt once asked, correctly). In other words, it is important to identify the building blocks on which open societies can be established in order to function properly. We must assess the trajectory of the great transformations unleashed by the extraordinary events of 1989: Are the newly awakened societies propitious to pluralism, or does the upper hand belong to illiberal, antimodern forces? In 2002, Judt stated that, in the context of the European Union accession, for purposes of European moral reconstruction, "the crucial reference point for Europe now will be the years immediately preceding the events of 1989."[5] As we celebrated the twentieth anniversary of that year's revolutions, we have the possibility of contemplating the first two post-Communist decades' illusions, expectations, and balance sheet and of speculating on the years to come.

ANNUS MIRABILIS 1989

The revolutions of 1989 were, no matter how one judges them, truly world-historical events, in the Hegelian sense: they established a historical cleavage (only to some extent conventional) between the world before and after 1989.[6] The Leninist systems were terminally sick, and the disease affected first and foremost their capacity for self-regeneration. After decades of toying with the idea of intrasystemic reforms, it had become clear that Communism did not have resources for readjustment and that the solution lay not within but outside, even against, the existing order.[7] The demise (implosion) of the Soviet Union, consummated before the incredulous eyes of the world in December 1991, was directly and intimately related to the earlier dissolution of the East European "outer empire," provoked by the revolutions of 1989. It is now obvious that the historical cycle inaugurated by World War I, the Bolshevik seizure of power in Russia in October 1917, and the long European ideological warfare (or rather global civil war) that followed had come to an end.[8]

The road to 1989–91 was prepared by the less visible, often marginal, but in the long run critically significant workings of what we now call civil society (including Solidarity in Poland, Charter 77 in Czechoslovakia, unofficial peace, environmental, and human rights groups in the GDR, Democratic Opposition in Hungary).[9] In examining the wreckage of Leninism, we should thus avoid any one-dimensional, monistic approach. There is no single factor that explains the collapse: economics as much as politics and culture as much as insoluble social tensions converged in making these regimes irretrievably obsolete. But these were not autocracies: they derived their only claim to legitimacy from the Marxist-Leninist "holy writ," and once this ideological aura ceased to function, the whole edifice started to falter.[10] They were, to use sociologist Daniel Chirot's apt term, "tyrannies of certitude," and it was precisely the gradual loss of ideological commitment among the ruling elites, once a truly messianic ardor, that accelerated the inner disintegration of Leninist regimes.[11] By 1989, three central myths of Leninism had collapsed: its infallibility, its invincibility, and its irreversibility.

196 | Democracy in Post-Communist Societies

Under the circumstances, any analysis of the year 1989 should be framed by two crucial theoretical hypotheses. The first, which constitutes the core of Stephen Kotkin's argument in the much discussed volume *The Uncivil Society,* is that by 1980s, the political elites of the Communist states were in disarray, experiencing loss of self-confidence, rampant cynicism, and ideological decay. Eastern Europe was ruled by *uncivil societies* (Communist bureaucratic castes) beset with insecurity, anxiety, despondency, and demoralization. They had lost their self-confidence and were looking for alternative sources of legitimization. However, I would like to point to a second dimension that enabled the watershed of 1989. Communism in the region underwent the exhaustion of the utopian impulse. To use Ken Jowitt's formulation, the charismatic impersonalism of Leninist parties fell into disrepute. In spite of Mikhail Gorbachev's endless injunctions of "revisionist" ideological zeal, late socialism failed to reinvent the heroic mission of its central agent of progress in history: the Communist Party.

To return to Kotkin, I would contend that indeed "the collapse of Communism was a collapse of establishments"[12] Nevertheless, when talking about the establishment one should *also* understand the essential myth of a charismatic party mobilizing a revolutionary movement to radically transform society for the achievement of socialism. By 1989, across East-Central Europe one found a complex picture of waning faith in utopia (though by no means extinct—e.g., Nicolae Ceaușescu died singing the International) combined with routinization engineered by pragmatic elites (think of leaders such as Károly Grósz in Hungary, Mieczysław Rakowski in Poland, Petar Mladenov in Bulgaria, or Hans Modrow in the GDR). All Communist regimes seemed to undergo a process of indefinite corrosion. But once a new type of leadership emerged at the Moscow center, one that gradually grew disenchanted with the radically transformative logic of the Soviet past, systemic collapse accelerated at a formidable pace. Tony Judt cogently pointed out that "Lenin's distinctive contribution to European history had been to kidnap the centrifugal political heritage of European radicalism and channel it into power through an innovative system of monopolized control: unhesitatingly gathered and forcefully retained in one place."[13] When the influence of this heritage in the arithmetic of power within the Soviet bloc waned, erosion gave way to the crumbling of apparently unshakable establishments.

Precisely because they ended an historical cycle and ushered in a new one, the importance of these revolutions cannot be overestimated: they represent the triumph of civic dignity and political morality over ideological monism, bureaucratic cynicism, and policed dictatorship.[14] Rooted in an individualistic concept of freedom, programmatically skeptical of all ideological blueprints for social engineering, these revolutions were, at least in their first stage, liberal and nonutopian.[15] Unlike traditional revolutions, they did not originate in a millenialist vision of the perfect society, and they rejected the role of any self-appointed vanguard in directing the activities of the masses. They spoke a new political vernacular: "the 'rights talk' as a way of thinking about politics."[16] Moreover, no political party directed their spontaneous momentum, and in their early stages they even insisted on the need to create new political forms, different from ideologically defined, traditional party differentiations. At the same time, as one observer of the events between 1989 and 1991 remarked, "Dissidents did not take up their cudgels against former revolutionaries or their organizations like the CPSU—they demanded an end to the state of revolution."[17]

HOPES AND DISAPPOINTMENTS

The fact that the aftermath of these revolutions has been plagued by ethnic rivalries, unsavory political bickering, rampant political and economic corruption, and the rise of illiberal parties and movements, including strong authoritarian, collectivistic trends, does not diminish their generous message and colossal impact. And, it should be noted, it was precisely in the countries where the revolutions did not occur (Yugoslavia) or were derailed (Romania) that the exit from state socialism was particularly problematic. The revolutions of 1989 did indeed create a fundamentally new and dangerous situation in which the absence of norms and predictable rational behavior on the part of the actors created the potential for global chaos. This observation was made not to deplore the end of the pre-1989 arrangements, but simply to point to the fact that this threshold year and the end of Leninism placed all of us in a radically novel situation. Understanding the revolutions of 1989 helps us grasp the meaning of the ongoing debates about liberalism, socialism, nationalism, civic society, and the very notion of human freedom at the end of a most atrocious century.[18]

These facts should be kept in mind especially when writers question the success of these revolutions by referring exclusively to their ambiguous legacies. The "reactionary rhetoric" brilliantly examined by Albert Hirschman uses arguments of futility, jeopardy, and perversity to delegitimize change per se or make it look impossible or undesirable.[19] This line of reasoning, often encountered in the more sophisticated approaches, argues along the following logic: the postrevolutionary environment has unleashed long-dormant ugly features of national political cultures, including chauvinism, racism, residual Fascism, ethno-clerical fundamentalism, and militarism, and it is therefore more dangerous than the *status quo ante;* or, nothing really changed and the power-holders (party-state bureaucrats) have remained the same, simply affixing to themselves new masks; or, no matter what the women and men of the revolutions of 1989 had hoped, the results of their endeavors have been extremely disappointing, allowing political scoundrels, crooks, and demagogues to use the new opportunities to establish their domination. If there is a main moral of the great revolutionary drama that unfolded in Eastern Europe in 1989, it is that history is never a one-way avenue, and that the future is always pregnant with more than one alternative. In other words, there is no ironclad determinism governing mankind's history. Indeed, as Jeffrey Isaac argues, the revolutions of 1989 had not only more than one cause but also more than one meaning, and they proposed a challenging agenda not only for the post-Communist societies but for Western democracies as well.[20] Moreover, we should focus on their pluralist heritage and enduring impact on both Eastern Europe and the world. Isaac warned that the "we" who celebrate the "velvet revolutions" of 1989 ought to do so with circumspection and with a sense of self-limitation because of the complexities behind the "normality" of post-Communist societies.[21]

The meaning of those events, the role of dissidents (critical, unregimented intellectuals) in the resurrection of long-paralyzed civic societies, the overall crisis of those regimes, and the decline of the Communist Parties' hegemony have generated an enormous interpretative literature. The initial temptation was to acclaim the role of dissidents in the breakdown of Soviet-style regimes and the rise of civic initiatives from below.[22] The dissident as a hero turned out to be a political myth in Central and Eastern Europe, but the myth raised these societies to a higher level of moral self-awareness. In my view, it is less relevant how large or numerous a dissident group or movement was. I remember an intervention by the former dissident and human rights activist, the late Mihai Botez, at a roundtable organized by Freedom House in 1988, in which he insisted that the deficit of visibility does not necessarily mean the absence of civil society, even in a country like Romania under Ceausescu. There were many informal networks of communication between Romanian intellectuals. The November 1987 anti-Communist Braşov work-ers' protest movement was also an expression of deep-seated social un-rest. In an insightful review of the historiography of the revolutions of 1989, Barbara Falk insisted that "there is no clear-cut line between resis-tance and dissent—it is more of a continuum or full spectrum." The na-ture, impact, and role of this continuum of resistance in the demise of Communist regimes await more in-depth research and analysis. I con-sider her characterization of this spectrum a telling starting point:

> At the pole of "resistance" lie activities such as absenteeism, alcoholism or drug abuse, and the preference for personal travel and sporting activities rather than trade-union- or workplace-sponsored events. Closer to the middle would be private or family discussions on alternative historiography, listen-ing to a banned radio broadcast, writing an essay "for the drawer," publicly telling jokes, or reading *samizdat*. Closer to the middle on the other side, toward the pole of dissent, would be activities taken in support or in the "gray zone"—agreeing with a petition, participating in a pilgrimage per-haps, or discussing with friends a particular broadcast or spreading news obtained there. Finally, at the "dissent" end of the continuum is the produc-tion and distribution of *samizdat,* public protest, active involvement in inde-pendent groups outside the control of the party-state—all of which risked regime persecution and/or imprisonment. One could also further differen-tiate between individual moral resistance or organized opposition—particularly by the late 1980s or in states such as Poland where the opposi-tion was extremely well organized, expansive, and multidimensional.[23]

We must also not overlook that what mattered were the perceptions of the dissidents' role among the elites (i.e., the so-called *intelligentsia*) and within sectors of the population, in the grey area (bystanders). It was no coincidence that as soon as the Ceauşescu regime fell apart in Romania, the new ruling group, the leaders of the National Salvation Front, made sure to convey the message to the population that its ruling council had incorporated the few dissident intellectuals in the country known to the people via the Radio Free Europe broadcasts. Dissidents could legitimize post-1989 rule; their presence and ideas gave the events significance. It was meaningful not only that Communism collapsed or that the elite imploded, but also how the story unfolded and which ideas and prin-ciples filled in the void after its demise. For example, in the Soviet Union, Ludmila Alexeyeva, a founding member of the Moscow Helsinki Group, declared at the height of perestroika that "we take no offence at Gor-bachev and his associates for not citing us as sources. We are happy that our ideas have acquired a new life." After the failed coup d'état of

August 1991, one of its most ardent supporters, the nationalist writer Aleksandr Prokhanov, bitterly stated that "the conception of Elena Bonner has won."[24]

The revolutions of 1989 were first and foremost revolutions of the mind, and critical intellectuals played the role of "revolutionary subjects." Euphoric accounts of the revolutionary wave, often compared to the 1848 Spring of the Nations, abounded, and Timothy Garton Ash offered some of the most eloquent articles along this line in his gripping contributions to the *New York Review of Books,* later collected in the volume *The Magic Lantern.*[25] Whether the term *revolutions* is the most appropriate to describe these changes is of course an open question. What is beyond dispute is the world-historical impact of the transformations inaugurated by the events of 1989 and the inauguration of a new vision of the political. In the twentieth century, many intellectuals engaged in a frantic search for utopia and frequently participated in the legitimation of ideology-driven despotisms: "It was thus altogether appropriate that it was the disaffection of Europe's intellectuals from the grand narrative of progress that triggered the ensuing avalanche."[26] According to Garton Ash,

> The year 1989 left realities. Yet there was something new; there was a big new idea, and that was the revolution itself—the idea of the non-revolutionary revolution, the evolutionary revolution. The motto of 1989 could come from Lenin's great critic Eduard Bernstein: "The goal is nothing, the movement is everything." . . . So this was a revolution that was not about the *what* but about the *how.* That particular motto of peaceful, sustained, marvelously inventive, massive civil disobedience channeled into an oppositional elite that was itself prepared to negotiate and to compromise with the existing powers, the powers that were (in short, the roundtable)—that was the historical novelty of 1989. Where the guillotine is a symbol of 1789, the roundtable is a symbol of 1989.[27]

One needs to keep in mind that the critical intellectuals of Eastern Europe, the agents of civil society in 1970s and 1980s, did not wish to seize power. The essence of their actions and writings, and implicitly of their influence over the subjects of Communist rule, was their commitment to the restoration of truth, civility, and morality in the public sphere, the rehabilitation of civic virtues, and the end of the totalitarian method of control, intimidation, and coercion. Stephen Kotkin accurately pointed out that the most vulnerable aspect of Communist systems was their endemic lying. In this context, I contend that the dissidents' discourse of an active, self-conscious, empowered social body amounted to a formidable challenge to the party's Big Lie. The rehabilitation of notions such as freedom, dignity, citizenship, sovereignty of the people, and pluralism provided a radical symbolic and practical-political challenge to the totalitarian world. Moreover, for the first time in the history of Communism in the region, there appeared a group of thinkers who by action and word tried "to fill the anomic space between the individual and the state."[28] In other words, a different future for societies under Communism could be glimpsed once intellectuals and sectors of the population were no longer silent. Civil society *did* matter in the context of 1989. Anne Applebaum stessed, in a review of Stephen Kotkin's *Uncivil Society,* that alternative forms of organization "helped form the crowds and then helped the crowds create change (impelling Václav Havel to the presidency of the Czech Republic, for example). Maybe more importantly, they affected the midlevel bureaucrats, the people who had been following orders all along but, with the threat of a Soviet invasion withdrawn, no longer wanted to do so. People like the policeman who spontaneously opened the barrier at the Berlin Wall, just to take one famous example, were moved to switch sides by, yes, the civil society that had been growing around them."[29] Even if the civil society was not as coherent, numerous, influential, or visible as the uncivil one, it provided a mobilization ideal in an environment dominated by coercion, cynicism, and paralysis. I would go as far as to say that the importance of civil society lay not particularly in its political weight, but in the fact that it became almost a self-fulfilling prophecy.

The dominant trend, however, was to regard the revolutions of 1989 as part of the universal democratic wave: a confirmation of the ultimate triumph of liberal democratic values over collectivist-Jacobin attempts to control human minds. It is thus clear that dissent was an expression not only of resistance to the dominant ideology of power, a repudiation of the power of ideology, but also an affirmation of a political community based on dialogue and open-mindedness: "*Samizdat,* and the creation of alternative cultures of resistance and dissent that were made possible by it, can be understood as the result of long-range historical processes and part and parcel of the trans-European project of modernity. After all, free expression made possible the creation and nurturing of the very idea of 'the public' and 'public opinion,' as Jürgen Habermas reminds us in his early masterpiece, *The Structural Transformation of the Public Sphere.*"[30] Earlier, similar interpretations of the 1989 upheaval inspired the reflections on the future of liberal revolution by political philosopher Bruce Ackerman, for whom the dramatic changes in

East and Central Europe were part of a global revival of liberalism. In other words, their success or failure would condition the future of liberalism in the West as well, because we live in a world of political, economic, and cultural-symbolic interconnectedness and interdependence.[31]

After decades of state aggression against the public sphere, these revolutions reinstituted the distinction between what belongs to the government and what is the territory of the individual. Emphasizing the importance of political and civic rights, they created space for the exercise of liberal democratic values. In some countries these values have become the constitutional foundation on which the institutions of an open society can be safely built. In others, the reference to pluralism remained somewhat perfunctory. But even in the less successful cases of democratic transition (Western Balkans), the old order, based on suspicion, fear, and mass hopelessness, is irrevocably defunct. In other words, while the ultimate result of these transitions is not clear, the revolutions have succeeded in their most important task: disbanding the Leninist regimes and permitting the citizens of these countries to fully engage in shaping their own destinies. In the end, "the return to Europe" heralded in 1989 stood for "normalcy and the modern way of life." Echoing Judt, the vital step was made—Communism became the past.[32]

As I mentioned before, the crucial question to be addressed is: Were the events of 1989 genuine revolutions? If the answer is positive, then how do we assess their novelty in contrast to other similar events (the French Revolution of 1789 or the Hungarian one in 1956)? If the answer is negative (as some today like to argue), then it is legitimate to ask ourselves: What were they? Simply mirages, results of obscure intrigues of the beleaguered bureaucracies that mesmerized the world but did not fundamentally change the rules of the game? These last words, *the rules of the game,* are crucial for interpreting what happened in 1989; focusing on them, we can reach a positive assessment of those revolutions and their heritage. In my view, the upheaval in the East, and primarily in the Central European core countries, represented a series of political revolutions that led to the decisive and irreversible transformation of the existing order. Instead of autocratic, one-party systems, the revolutions created emerging pluralist polities. They allowed the citizens of ideologically driven tyrannies (closed societies) to recover their main human and civic rights and to engage in the building of open societies.[33] Historian Konrad Jarausch argues that the emphasis on people power typical of these revolutions substantiated their novelty: their peaceful path toward regime change against all odds.[34] Moreover, instead of centrally planned command economies, after 1989, all these societies have embarked on creating market economies. In these efforts to meet the triple challenge (creating political pluralism, a market economy, and a public sphere, i.e., a civil society) some succeeded better and faster than others. But it cannot be denied that in all the countries that used to be referred to as the Soviet bloc, the once monolithic order was replaced by political and cultural diversity.[35] While we still do not know whether all these societies have become properly functioning liberal democracies, it is nevertheless important to emphasize that in all of them, Leninist systems based on ideological uniformity, political coercion, dictatorship over human needs, and the suppression of civic rights have been dismantled.[36]

POLITICS AND MORALITY

In a way, the revolutions of 1989 were an ironic vindication of Lenin's famous definition of a revolutionary situation: those at the top cannot rule in the old ways, and those at the bottom do not want to accept these ways any more. They were more than simple revolts because they attacked the very foundations of the existing systems and proposed a complete reorganization of society. It is perhaps worth remembering that Communist Parties were not in power as a result of legal rational procedures. No free elections brought them to the ruling positions; rather they derived their spurious legitimacy from the ideological (and teleological) claim that they represented the "vanguard" of the working class, and consequently, they were the carriers of a universal emancipatory mission.[37] Once ideology ceased to be an inspiring force and influential members of the ruling parties, the offspring and beneficiaries of the *no-menklatura* system, lost their emotional commitment to the Marxist radical behest, the Leninist castles were doomed to fall apart. Here enters the what is often called the Gorbachev effect.[38] It was indeed the international climate generated by the shockwaves of the glasnost and perestroika initiated by Mikhail Gorbachev after his election as general secretary of the Communist Party of the Soviet Union in March 1985 that allowed for an incredible amount of open dissent and political mobilization in East and Central Europe. It was Gorbachev's denunciation of the ideological perspective on international politics (de-ideologization) and the abandoning of the "class struggle" perspective that changed the rules of Soviet-East European relations.

Very few analysts insisted on the less visible but nonetheless persistent illiberal and neo-authoritarian components of the anti-Communist upheaval in the East. To quote Ralf Dahrendorf's somber forecast: "The greatest risk is probably of another kind altogether. I hesitate to use the word, but it is hard to banish from one's thoughts: fascism. By that I mean the combination of a nostalgic ideology of community which draws harsh boundaries between those who belong and those who do not, with a new political monopoly of a man or a 'movement' and a strong emphasis on organization and mobilization rather than freedom of choice."[39] Swept away by the exhilarating revolutionary turmoil, most observers preferred to gloss over the heterogeneous nature of the anti-Communist movements: in fact, not all those who rejected Leninism did it because they were dreaming of an open society and liberal values. Among the revolutionaries were quite a few enragés, ill disposed towards the logic of compromise and negotiations. There were also populist fundamentalists, religious dogmatists, nostalgics of the pre-Communist regimes, including those who admired pro-Nazi dictators like Romania's Marshal Ion Antonescu and Hungary's Admiral Miklós Horthy. It was only after the disintegration of Yugoslavia and the velvet divorce that led to the breakup of Czechoslovakia into two countries (the Czech Republic and Slovakia) that scholars and policy makers realized that the liberal promise of these revolutions should not be taken for granted and that the aftermath of Communism is not necessarily liberal democracy. In the early 1990s it became increasingly clear that the post-Communist era was fraught with all sorts of threats, including bloody ethnic conflicts, social unrest, and the infectious rise of old and new sorts of populisms and tribalisms.[40]

Actually, the appeals of the civil society paradigm, as championed and articulated within the dissident subcultures of the post-totalitarian order, were to a great extent idealized during the first postrevolutionary stage. Many intellectuals shared these values, but there were many who found them too abstract and universalistic (among the latter, Václav Klaus, Havel's rival, nemesis, and successor as president of the Czech republic). The majority of the populations in East-Central Europe had not been involved in the antisystemic activities and had not appropriated the values of moral resistance. Years ago, Hungarian philosopher and former dissident G. M. Tamás insisted on the relative marginality of the dissidents as an explanation for their lack of influence after 1989.[41] The case of Solidarity was, of course, different, but even there the normative code of civic opposition failed to generate a positive concept of the "politics of truth." In reality, dissent in most East-Central European societies was an isolated, risky, and not necessarily popular experience. Those belonging to the "gray area" between government and opposition tended to regard dissidents as moral challengers, neurotic outsiders, quixotic characters with little or no understanding of the real game. The appeals of the civil society vision, with its repudiation of hierarchical structures and skepticism of institutional authority, showed their limits in the inchoate, morally fractured, and ideologically fluid post-Communist order. Moreover, as Tony Judt noticed, "One of the reasons for the decline of the intellectuals was that their much remarked-upon emphasis on the *ethics* of anti-Communism, the need to construct a morally aware civil society to fill the anomic space between the individual and the state, had been overtaken by the practical business of constructing a market economy."[42]

The world after Leninism is marred by broken dreams, shattered illusions, and often unfulfilled expectations. This explains the defeat of former Communists in Poland in September 2005: perceived as cynical operators, the former apparatchiks lost to center-right parties that advocated a "moral revolution." In brief, the battle for the soul of man after Communism has not ended. In some countries, discomfiture and dismay have prevailed. In others, individuals seem to enjoy the new conditions, including the opportunity to live without utopian dreams. To quote Alexander Yakovlev, the former Bolshevik ideologue turned apostate: "Social utopias are not harmless. They deform practical life, they push an individual, society, state agencies, and social movements into imposing their approaches and concepts, including the use of extreme methods of force. Social utopias deprive a person of the ability to perceive the reality of actual features. They sharply reduce or sometimes even completely destroy people's ability to withstand effectively the real difficulties, absurdities, and defects of private and public life."[43] In contrast to Leninism's social utopia, in 1989 civil society was a powerful metaphor of the revolt and revival of the independent mind that gained preeminence as party-states became increasingly decrepit and their elites disenchanted. Civil society was the symbol for the possibility of an alternative to decaying regimes plagued with the incurable maladies of clientelism, corruption, and cynicism. Sickness, however, can be an excruciatingly long process, and in the mid-1980s Timothy Garton Ash, an astute interpreter of Central European politics, used the predictive metaphor *Ottomanization*. Later, the philosopher Leszek Kołakowski insisted that while everyone (even the leaders) had known that Communist regimes could not last forever, hardly anyone foresaw when the debacle would occur. With no end in sight, what remained was that, by the 1980s, Eastern Europe had forged a political myth that provided both criticism and opposition to

Communism, as well as a strategic vision for Communism's aftermath. I agree with Stephen Kotkin, who stated that "1989 did not happen *because* of a broad freedom drive or an establishment self-enrichment drive."[44] What Kotkin seems to disregard, however, is the debilitating and corrosive effect of the dissidents' arguments for authenticity ("living within the truth") and for a return to normalcy over a system that had lost its eschatological impetus. Simple but pervasive ideas continuously chipped at the foundation of the party-state monolith. It may not have been a broad drive for freedom, the triumphal march of civil society that was presented in earlier literature, but the role of ideas in the demise of Communism should not be underestimated. A secular religion brought to power and preserved by ideas, Communism perished as a result of ideas. Once Marxism and Leninism were discredited, both domestically and internationally, as Grand Narratives, Communism's realities remained merely what they were: loss, waste, failure, and crime.[45] Only if we add this corrective to Kotkin's interpretation can we understand the passion, idealism, and high expectations of 1989 *together with* the ensuing frustrations, malaise, and disappointments.

The recollection of the oppression under Communist regimes is used to bolster a sense of uniqueness. Suffering is often exploited to justify a strange competition for what I call the most victimized nation status. No less important, because Communism was seen by many as an alien imposition—a dictatorship of "foreigners"—contemporary radical nationalism is also intensely anti-Communist. The memory of trauma and guilt under Leninism, along with the duty of remembrance regarding the Fascist past of some of these countries can provide the historical and moral benchmarks necessary to sustain a constitutional patriotism that can challenge communitarian reductionism. Instead, we are witnessing an ethnicization of memory and an externalization of guilt. The evils of the Communist regimes are assigned to those perceived as *aliens:* the Jews, the national minorities, or other traitors and enemies of an organically defined nation. Or, we encounter the "mismemory of Communism" that creates "two moral vocabularies, two sorts of reasoning, two different pasts": that of things done to "us" and that of things done by "us" to "others." This is what Tony Judt called "voluntary amnesia."[46]

Former Communists did make sometimes spectacular comebacks. This was possible because after 1989 there were no tribunals and no recourses to state-endorsed vengeance. This shows that the refusal to organize collective political justice was after all the correct approach. Let me say that the controversies regarding the treatment of the former party and secret police activists and collaborators were among the most passionate and potentially disruptive in the new democracies. Some argued, together with Poland's first post-Communist and anti-Communist prime minister, Tadeusz Mazowiecki, that one needed to draw a "thick line" with the past and fully engage in a consensual effort for building an open society. Others, for reasons that went from unconditional anti-Communism to cynical manipulation of an explosive issue, argued that without one form or another of "purification" the new democracies would be fundamentally perverted. The truth, in my view, resides somewhere in between: the past cannot and should not be denied, covered with a blanket of shameful oblivion. Confronting the traumatic past, primarily via remembrance and knowledge, results in achieving moral justice.[47] Real crimes did take place in those countries, and the culprits should be identified and brought to justice. But legal procedures and any other form of legal retribution for past misdeeds should always take place on an individual basis, and preserving the presumption of innocence is a fundamental right for any human being, including former Communist apparatchiks. In this respect, with all its shortcomings, the lustration law in the Czech Republic offered a legal framework that prevented mob justice. In Romania, where no such law was passed and access to personal secret police files was systematically denied to citizens (while these files were used and abused by those in power), the political climate continued to be plagued by suspicion, murky intrigues, and dark conspiratorial visions.[48]

Even after NATO's eastward enlargement and the entry of most East European countries into the European Union (with the notable exception of the Western Balkans), there is a striking tension between pluralist-democratic and ethnocratic or radical parties and groups in these societies. Often during post-Communism, it seemed as if there was a yearning for new figures for the future, an expectation of the materialization of what Walter Benjamin called the "Messianic time." The search for new eschatologies was more visible in the East, where all social contrasts are exacerbated by the breakdown of old identities. But the return of myth was part of the universal uneasiness with the cold, calculated, *zweckmassig* rationality of the iron cage: prophets and demagogues (often the same persons) did have audiences in the East as well as in the West. The latter is, however, better protected: institutions function impersonally, procedures are deeply embedded in civic cultures. In the post-Communist world they are still under construction or yet to entirely meet requirements of a fully functioning liberal democracy. Things are of course extremely complex: there is a feeling of exhaustion, of too much rhetoric, a sentiment that politicians are there simply to cheat. On the other hand, it is precisely this exhaustion of traditional worldviews, this postmodern syndrome of repudiating grandiose teleological constructs in favor of minidiscourses that is conducive to ennui and yearning for alternative visions that would not reject boldness and inventiveness. Yes, this is a secularized world, but the profane substitutes for traditional mythologies still have a future.

After the extinct period of "legitimation from the top" (through ideological rituals of simulated participation, mobilization, and regimentation), in most of these countries nascent legal-procedural legitimation was paralleled (or countered) by something that, echoing Eric Hobsbawm's insightful analysis of the new discourses of hatred, could be called *legitimation from the past*.[49] The more inchoate and nebulous this past, the more aggressive, feverish, and intolerant were the proponents of the neoromantic mythologies. The rise of nationalism as a compensation for perceived failure and externally imposed marginality, as flight from the complexities of modernity into the politics of collective salvation, was linked to this ambiguous Leninist legacy of distorted modernity and dictated human needs, and to the pre-Leninist ethnic-oriented cultural forms in the region. In other words, the discomfiture with democratic challenges and the prevailing constitutional pluralist model was linked not only to the transition from Leninism but to the larger problem of legitimation and the existence of competing visions of the common good, as well as the coalescence of movements and parties around different and frequently rival symbols of collective identity. To put it simply, the post-Communist first wave of primordial passions and the appeal of the new exclusionary discourses remind us that neither the premises nor the outcomes of modernity have been universally accepted. This point was correctly raised by S. N. Eisenstadt in a path-breaking analysis of the revolutions of 1989: "These problems, however, do not simply arise out of the breakdown of 'traditional' empires, the transition from some 'premodern' to fully modern, democratic society, or from a distorted modernity to a relatively tranquil stage which may well signal some kind of 'end of history.' The turbulence evident in Eastern Europe today bears witness to some of the problems and tensions inherent in modernity itself, attesting to the potential fragility of the whole project of modernity."[50]

POST-COMMUNIST PARADOXES

I think that in the first ten years of post-Communism we dealt with a resilient, persistent form of barbarism that was situated in the very heart of modernity. Radical nationalism was the absolute exacerbation of difference, its reification, the rejection of the claim to a common humanity, and the proclamation of the ethno-national distinction as the primordial fact of human existence. As Franz Grillparzer wrote many years ago, "From humanity, through nationality, to barbarity"—a maxim dear to the hearts of intellectuals like Hannah Arendt, Walter Benjamin, and Adam Michnik, who rehabilitated the notion of pariah and emphasized the nobility of exclusion in contrast to the humiliation of forced inclusion. Jack Snyder's by now classical thesis still holds valid: the political elites' willingness to be accountable affects the degree of nationalist instrumentalization during the transition to democracy. To avoid surrendering their authority, these elites hijack political discourse, while hampering and taking advantage of the citizens' reduced capacity for political participation.[51]

The main threat in some (if not most) of the countries of Central and Eastern Europe is that of a lapse into "competitive authoritarianism," where "formal democratic institutions are widely viewed as the principal means of obtaining and exercising political authority. Incumbents violate those rules so often and to such an extent, however, that the regime fails to meet conventional minimum standards for democracy." As Levitsky and Way point out, up until the second decade of post-Communism, Croatia, Ukraine, and Serbia were textbook examples for this model, and Russia and Belarus still seemed to fall in this category. It could be argued that better terms for this democratic degeneration are *delegative democracy* and *illiberal democracy*.[52] I chose the first to stress the fundamental danger of a deep-seated, persistent, and widening gap between political and civil societies in the former Soviet bloc. It is not surprising that, in most of these countries, critical intellectuals (many of them former dissidents under the Communist regime) insist on the need for moral clarity. The political class, however, remains narcissistically self-centered and impervious to such injunctions to live truthfully. After all, it was Karl Marx who said that any new society will carry for a long time its birthmarks, in this case the habits, mores, visions, and mentalities *(forma mentis)* associated with the Leninist faith.

Furthermore, as Karen Dawisha has argued, electocracies should not be automatically regarded as liberal democratic communities.[53] Thus, in reality constitutionalism remains marred by its very universalistic formalism (its coldness, and its often decried tediousness) and the subsequent failure to adjust to pressures resulting from collective efforts aimed at reverting, subverting, and obliterating the project of modernity (by which I tentatively understand the substantive construction of politics in an anti-absolutist, individualistic, and contractual way).[54] But the return of the repressed, real and often disturbing, does not exhaust the picture. Indeed, despite all the setbacks, the ongoing debates in Europe (and in Eastern Europe in particular) remain fundamental to the attempt at a *reinvention of politics.* Julia Kristeva is thus right: "The problem of the twentieth century was and remains the rehabilitation of the political. An impossible task? A useless task? Hitler and Stalin perverted the project into a deathly totalitarianism. The collapse of communism in Eastern Europe, which calls into question, beyond socialism, the very basis of the democratic governments that stemmed from the French Revolution, demands that one rethink that basis so that the twenty-first century will not be the reactionary domain of fundamentalism, religious illusions, and ethnic wars."[55]

This clustered experience is best described by what Hanson and Ekiert identified as the key paradox of post-Communism: "The 'Leninist legacy' mattered both *less* and *more* than scholars originally expected." In other words, the impact of the common Communist experience has been mediated by specific "choices made by strategically located actors in various critical moments of the unfolding processes of change."[56] Moreover, similar challenges posed by the past produced varying policies and institutional frameworks. Nevertheless, the ideological extinction of Leninist formations left behind a vacuum to be filled by syncretic constructs drawing from the pre-Communist and Communist heritage (from nationalism, in both its civic and ethnic incarnations, to liberalism, democratic socialism, conservatism, populism, neo-Leninism, or even more or less refurbished Fascism). We see a fluidity of political commitments, allegiances, and affiliations—the breakdown of a political culture (that Leszek Kołakowski and Martin Malia correctly identified as Sovietism) and the painful birth and consolidation of a new one. The moral identity of the individuals has been shattered by the dissolution of all previously cherished—or at least accepted—values and icons. In the immediate aftermath of 1989, individuals seemed eager to abandon their newly acquired sense of autonomy on behalf of different forms of protective, pseudosalvationist groups and movements. This was emphasized by Havel: "In a situation when one system has collapsed and a new one does not yet exist, many people feel empty and frustrated. This condition is fertile ground for radicalism of all kinds, for the hunt for scapegoats, and for the need to hide behind the anonymity of a group, be it socially or ethnically based."[57] Assumed responsibility for personal actions, risk-taking, and questioning of institutions on the base of legitimate claims for improvement are still developing.[58] All established ranks, statuses, traditions, hierarchies, and symbols have collapsed, and new ones are still tottering and quite problematic. Envy, rancor, and resentment have replaced the values of solidarity, civility, and compassion that once drove the East European revolutionaries. As Polish sociologist Jacek Kurczewski noted, "Poverty is accompanied by envy, a feeling that becomes dominant in times of economic change. The feeling expresses itself not so much in a striving for communism, but in a defense of socialist mechanisms of social security under conditions of a capitalist economy and suspicion of everyone who has achieved success in these new conditions."[59] Instead of enjoying promises of emancipation and revolutionary change, many individuals are now sharing a psychology of helplessness, defeat, and dereliction.

There are immense problems in the continuity of both social and personal memory. Without a complete legal, political, and historical reckoning in relation to the totalitarian Communist experience, civic consensus and political trust can hardly mature. Despite the ever-widening rescue operation of and working through fragmented memories (both individual and collective), transparency about a guilty and traumatic past by means of "politics of knowledge" (to use Claus Offe's term) has yet to be achieved. Few years ago, Timothy Garton Ash was struggling to find an explanation for this state of affairs: " Any explanation for the absence of wider truth commissions must be speculative. I would speculate that part of the explanation, at least, lies in this combination of the historically defensible but also comfortable conviction that the dictatorship was ultimately imposed from outside and, on the other hand, the uneasy knowledge that almost everyone had done something to sustain the dictatorial system."[60] The externalization of responsibility (the delocalization of the history of the Communist regimes by blaming them on either the Soviets or alien groups) and the forgetting of "the millions of Lilliputian threads of everyday mendacity, conformity and compromise" (in the words of T. Garton Ash) can sustain only a vague recognition of the need for a shared vision of the public good—a point that has been emphasized by Václav Havel, George Konrád, and Adam Michnik. The willingness to assume responsibility for one's actions, to take risks, and to question institutions on the basis of legitimate claims for improvement is still embryonic.[61] This may explain the political turmoil and antigovernment demonstrations in Hungary in the fall of 2006 or the parliamentary putsch in April 2007 against Romanian president, Traian Băsescu, in full disregard of the Constitutional Court's decision.[62]

It is thus tempting to assume that the major difficulties in the articulation of ideologically differentiated political platforms in Eastern Europe were connected not only to the absence or weakness of clear-cut interest groups and lobbies, but also to increasing atrophy of the Western sources of inspiration ("models") for such endeavors. The famous law of political synchronization (of the East with the West) may this time play against the revival of ideological politics.[63] The difficulty of identifying clear divisions between left and right polarization in post-Communist regimes is linked to the ambiguity and even obsolescence of traditional taxonomies. As Adam Michnik and other former dissidents have often argued, the question after 1989 is not whether one is left or right of center, but whether one is "West of center." Liberal values are sometimes seen as left-oriented simply because they emphasize secularism, tolerance, and individual rights. At the same time, as shown by the new radical-authoritarian trends (often disguised as pro-democratic) in Russia, Ukraine, Bulgaria, Romania, Slovakia, and elsewhere, lingering habits inherited from Leninist and pre-Leninist authoritarianism continue: intolerance, exclusiveness, rejection of all compromises, extreme personalization of political discourse, and the search for charismatic leadership. Karen Dawisha has identified a few of the features of the "surviving past" of what she called "communism as a lived system": the respect for centralized power, a large sphere for private interactions, and horizontal networks of mutual cooperation and informal connections, and finally, fixation on a supposed "separateness" from the West.[64] We deal with the same impotent fury against the failure of the state to behave as a "good father," part of a patrimonial legacy characteristic, to different degrees, of all these societies (less so perhaps in Bohemia). Peter Reddaway correctly labeled this a yearning for the state as a "nanny."[65]

For instance, Romanians felt regret not for Nicolae Ceaușescu but rather for the age of predictability and frozen stability, when the party-state took care of everything. For many, the leap into freedom has turned out to be excruciatingly painful. What disappeared was the certainty about the limits of the permissible, the petrified social ceremonies that defined an individual's life itinerary: former prisoners are now free to choose between alternative futures, and this choice is insufferably difficult for many of them. The Leninist psychological leftovers can be detected at both ends of the political spectrum, and this explains the rise of new alliances between traditionally incompatible formations and movements. In Russia, we see a Stalinist-nationalist coalition, with its own national-Bolshevik traditions. In Romania it took the form of a rapprochement between Romania's allegedly pro-Western Social Democratic Party (whose honorary chairman is a former ideological apparatchik, ex-president Ion Iliescu) and the Greater Romania Party headed by former Ceauşescu court poet, the rabid xenophobic demagogue Corneliu Vadim Tudor. In the Czech Republic, the ideology of the Communist Party of Bohemia and Moravia merged nostalgia for dogmatic Leninism with chauvinistic stances. Simply put, the old Marxist internationalist dream has long since been abandoned.

It would be a serious fallacy to view these trends as marking the rise of neo-Communism. For such a development to take place, ideological zeal and utopian-eschatological motivation are needed. Neither former Polish president Aleksander Kwaśniewski nor former Hungarian prime-minister Ferenc Gyurcsányi, both linked to the post-Communist Left, can be described as ideologically driven. Instead, the successors to the Leninist parties have to cope with widespread sentiments of disaffection from socialist rhetoric. The Serbian socialists, East Germany's Party of Democratic Socialism (now part of *die Linke*), and Romania's Social Democratic Party are emblematic of the ongoing trend toward cooperation between radical nationalist forces and those who yearn for bureaucratic collectivism. Another indication of the weak institutionalization and shallow social insertion of post-Communist parties is the phenomenon of "electoral volatility."[66] The mainstream political parties are still challenged periodically by "unorthodox political formations" (e.g., Bulgaria, Poland, and Romania). The status quo remains fragile because of its unpopularity among sections of the population still attracted by ever-resurgent fantasies of salvation.

This tendency is a result of the ideological chaos created by the collapse of state socialism, which left populism as the most convenient and frequently the most appealing ersatz ideology. It was relatively easy to get rid of the old regime with its spurious claim to cognitive infallibility, but much more daunting to install a pluralist, multiparty order, a civil society, rule of law, and a market economy. Freedom, it turned out, was easier to gain than to guarantee. Uprootedness, loss of status, and uncertainties about identity provide fertile ground for paranoid visions of conspiracy and treason; hence the widespread attraction of nationalist salvationism. Leszek Kołakowski points to a paradoxical attitude toward prophetic stances in contemporary Central and Eastern Europe: the intellectuals' disillusionment with redemptive-apocalyptical teleologies led them to retreat from political matters, which generated an ethical pauperization of politics, as there remain fewer intellectual teachers. The door is wide open to pseudodoctrines and negative political eclectisms.[67] Marching with Stalin's (or Ceauşescu's) portrait is an expression not of Stalinism (or Ceauşescuism) but rather of disaffection with the status quo, perceived as traumatic, anarchic, corrupt, politically decadent, and morally decrepit. Especially in Russia, where this disaffection is linked to the sentiment of imperial loss, cultural despair can lead to dictatorial trends. Exaggerated though they may be, references to "Weimar Russia" capture the psychology of large human groups whose traditional collectivistic values have disappeared and who cannot recognize themselves in the new values of individual action, risk, and intense competition. Recent developments in Russia strengthen the impression that the experiment of open politics in Russia lost out to the push for the reaffirmation of imperial status.[68] Following Martin Krygier, I consider that, twenty years after the demise of Communism, in the former Soviet bloc we are experiencing a new ideosphere, which is by definition comprehensive, inclusive, and provisional. Moreover, the postmodern political condition renders transitory even organicist, syncretic, and redemptive radicalisms (as political movements).[69] For instance, the last Romanian general elections (in 2009) produced encouraging results: the xenophobic, chauvinistic Romania Mare Party did not amass enough votes to get into parliament. However, this hardly means that the ideas that sustained it for so many years have disappeared from the public sphere.

Leninist regimes kept their subjects ignorant of the real functioning of the political system. Tony Judt observed that "by concentrating power, information, initiative and responsibility into the hands of the party-state, Communism had given rise to a society of individuals not merely suspicious of one another and skeptical of any official claims or promises, but with no experience of individual or collective initiative and lacking any basis on which to make informed public choices."[70] Furthermore, the chasm between official rhetoric and everyday reality, the camouflaging of the way decisions were reached, the anti-elective pseudo-elections, and other rituals of conformity neutralized critical faculties and generated a widespread wariness toward the validity of politics as such. Furthermore, anti-Communism tended to be just another supra-individual, nondifferentiated form of identity. The problem now is that the aggregation of social interests needs a clarification of the political choices, including an awareness of the main values that people advocate. As Martin Palouš put it, "The most important and most dynamic factor in post-totalitarian politics has to do with the way people in post-communist societies perceive and conceptualize the social reality and political processes they are a part of."[71] The difficulties and ambiguities of the left-right polarization in post-Communist regimes are linked to the ambiguity and even obsolescence of the traditional taxonomies.

With the private sector and entrepreneurial class still in the making, political liberalism and the civic center associated with it are under siege. Most political parties in the region are coalitions based on personal and group affinities rather than on an awareness of common interests, leading to fragmentation, divisiveness, political convulsions, and instability. One reason for the rise of populist movements is the paternalist temptation, a response to the felt need for protection from the destabilizing effects of the transition to competition and market. Another significant factor is the perception that the civic-romantic stage of the revolution is over and the bureaucracy now is intent upon consolidating its privileges. The campaigns against historic figures of Solidarity (including Adam Michnik, Bronisław Geremek, Tadeusz Mazowiecki, and Lech Wałęsa) as "traitors" and "protectors of the establishment" were an expression of the search for a "second revolution" that would legislate morality. Critical intellectuals seemed to have lost much of their moral aura and were often attacked as champions of futility, architects of disaster, and incorrigible daydreamers. Their status was extremely precarious precisely because they symbolized the principle of difference that neo-authoritarian politics tends to suppress. In the context of widespread disenchantment with political involvement, their moderation remains a crucial element of social equilibrium. It is essential to avoid mass hysteria, to recognize the need for constitutional consensus, and to foster a culture of predictable procedures. If these kinds of attacks gather momentum, they could jeopardize the still precarious pluralist institutions. Ralf Dahrendorf poignantly expressed this imperative: "Where intellectuals are silent, societies have no future." In a deeply fragmented social and public environment, under the constant pressures of globalization, Dahrendorf believed that, despite its diminished appeal, the nexus of ideas and action had in no way lost its revitalizing potential as a force of freedom.[72]

Political reform in all these post-Communist societies has not gone far enough in strengthening the counter-majoritarian institutions (including independent media and the market economy) that would diminish the threat of new authoritarian experiments catering to powerful egalitarian-populist sentiments. The main dangers in this regard are tendencies linked to statism, clericalism, religious fundamentalism, ethnocentrism, and militaristic Fascism. These themes appeared clearly in the discourse of ethnocratic populism, as evinced by Vadim Tudor's Greater Romania Party, but also among supporters of Slovakia's Vladimir Mečiar, Serbia's Radical Party, and the xenophobic groups and movements in Russia generically associated with Vladimir Zhirinovsky's Liberal Democratic Party or Gennady Zyuganov's Communist Party of the Russian Federation. Even Hungarian prime minister Viktor Orbán has resorted to such rhetorical strategies to weaken his liberal and socialist adversaries. Some observers have foreseen a split in the region, with the more advanced countries (Poland, Hungary, the Czech Republic, and the Baltic states) developing a culture of impersonal democratic procedures, while the Southern tier was supposed to be beset by what Ken Jowitt has called "movements of rage." Yet developments in Hungary, Poland, or Latvia in recent years have shown that such regional divisions are not so clear-cut. Marc Howard's insights on the demobilized nature of the civil societies within the countries of the former Soviet bloc offer a persuasive explanation for the absence of a middle path between apathy and violence. The comprehensive penetration of society by the state under Communism produced a "monstrous autonomy of the political,"[73] leading to disengagement, mistrust of voluntary associations, and deep engagement in private rather than public spheres of interaction. Democratic protest and opposition in Central and Eastern Europe have been shaped by a combination of inherited disaggregation and a general disappointment with the reality of nonpaternalistic social life.

The weakness of the region's political parties is primarily determined by the *general crisis of values and authority*. There is an absence of social glue, and the existing formations have failed to foster the consensus needed in order to generate constitutional patriotism. The Leninist *"mis-development"* left the region's societies with the difficult task of reconstituting normal communitarian bounds that allow for overt and unmitigated social interaction. The unmastered past of the totalitarian experience of the twentieth century in Central and Eastern Europe prevents these countries from institutionalizing the logical connection between democracy, memory, and militancy. Joachim Gauck argued that "reconciliation with the traumatic past can only be achieved not simply through grief, but also through discussion and dialogue."[74] In this sense,

Charles Villa-Vicencio, the former director for research of the South African Truth and Reconciliation Commission, defined reconciliation as "the operation whereby individuals and the community create for themselves a space in which they can communicate with one another, in which they can begin the arduous labour of understanding" painful history. Hence justice becomes a process of enabling the nation with the aid of a culture of responsibility.[75] A new identity can be based upon negative contrasts, "on the one hand, with the past that is being repudiated; on the other, with anti-democratic political actors in the present (and/or potentially in the future)."[76] This process of putting into question the "actual intersubjective liabilities of particular collectives" can lead to a redefinition of "anamnestic solidarity." The latter would be based upon an ethical framework circumscribed by both the knowledge of the truth and the official acknowledgement of its history. The destructive power of silence and of unassumed guilt would in this way be preempted. To paraphrase political scientist Gesine Schwan, the fundamental abilities and values of individuals are nourished so as to sustain their well-being, social behavior, and trust in communal life. The moral consensus over a shared experience of reality is preserved, making possible the democratic life of the specific society.[77] Though some have argued along these lines, I don't believe that some sort of collective communicative silence *(kommunikatives Beschweigen)* about the past can enable post-Communist countries to evolve into functioning democracies.[78] I agree with Tony Judt that radical evil can never be satisfactorily remembered, but, as proved by the German experience, a consistent appeal to history can function simultaneously as exorcism and therapy.[79]

The transition from an illegitimate and criminal regime to democracy and a culture of human rights is indeed a process dependent on the specific conditions of each postauthoritarian society. It implies a series of compromises and negotiations, but the act of healing a community must not be confused with moral consensus about a traumatic past. The history of violence must not legitimize transition. There is a need for unfettered transparency and total truth. After 1989, the present and the future must "stand up to the scrutiny of a gaze educated by the moral catastrophe"[80] produced by the totalitarian experience of the twentieth century. Otherwise, the web of lies becomes oppressive and the imperturbable fog extends infinitely into a state of moral perplexity. Political radicalization in the guise of historical retribution ("righting the wrongs of the past") is often used to achieve mass mobilization and delegitimize adversaries. This is not to say that the politics of amnesia, deliberately pursued by former or successor Communists, has resulted in any needed catharsis. On the contrary, as demonstrated by the furious reactions in Romania to President Băsescu's condemnation of the Communist regime as "illegitimate and criminal,"[81] the past does not fade away and often strikes back with a vengeance. There prevails a feeling of having been betrayed by the politicians, as well as a quest for a new purity. This is the rationale both for the "radical revolutionism" of the Kaczyński brothers in Poland and Viktor Orbán in Hungary (at the right end of the spectrum) and for the political resurrection of Communist parties in Lithuania, Romania, and Bulgaria. It also explains the power of Putin's neo-authoritarian politics of "managed democracy" in a memory regime of institutionalized amnesia and historical falsification. As for Putin himself, he has abandoned the Yeltsin era's adamant anti-Leninism and has become, especially since 2006, the proponent of an increasingly aggressive version of neo-Stalinist and neo-imperialist restoration. The high school history textbook (dealing with the period 1945 to 1991) commissioned by the Kremlin and published in 2008 symbolizes the return to some of the most egregious Stalinist falsifications and a radical break with the legacies of glasnost. Putinism is an ideological conglomerate bringing together Great Russian nationalism, imperial authoritarianism, and a drive to restore the lost grandeur of the Stalin era.[82] The narrative about the past offered by the Putin administration is the quintessential formula of "reconciliation without truth."[83] In other words, we are dealing with an apocryphal reconciliation.

The ideological syncretism of Stalino-Fascism capitalizes on delayed political justice. Think of Russia, where much ado about the trial of the old party has not resulted in anything significant. Demagogy, overblown rhetoric, and continual scapegoating undermine the legitimacy of the existing institutions and pave the way for the rise of ethnocentric crackpots. The harmful effects of long-maintained forms of amnesia cannot be overestimated. The lack of serious public discussions and lucid analyses of the past, including an acknowledgment by the highest state authorities of the crimes against humanity perpetrated by the Communist dictatorships, fuels discontent, outrage, and frustration and encourages the rise of demagogues, leading to vindictive references to the need for purification through retribution. Thus we see the creation of new mythologies to explain the current predicament: "Judeo-Masonic conspiracies" that endanger "national interests."[84] Nations are presented almost universally as victims of foreigners, and the Communist regimes are described as engineered by aliens to serve foreign interests. Russian nationalists, including some of the most gifted fiction writers belonging to the Siberian School, have not tired of blaming the Jews for the Bolshevik destruction of traditional values and structures. Some of the most frantic propagandists for such dark visions are former Communists, including a number of former Communist intellectuals. Writing primarily about the tragic events in his native Yugoslavia, American poet Charles Simic touched a depressing and unfortunately accurate note when he observed, "The terrifying thing about modern intellectuals everywhere is that they are always changing idols. At least religious fanatics stick mostly to what they believe in. All the rabid nationalists in Eastern Europe were Marxists yesterday and Stalinists last week."[85]

Several years before the end of Communism in Europe, political scientist and historian Joseph Rothschild argued that "ethno-nationalism, or politicized ethnicity, remains the world's major ideological legitimator and delegitimator of states, regimes, and governments."[86] Since nationalism provides the fuel of identity myths of modernity, more so than Marxist socialism, liberal universalism, or constitutional patriotism, one must see what its main forms are in the post-Communist world. Is nationalism a fundamental threat to the emergence of politically tolerant structures? Is it necessarily a poisonous form of chauvinism, a new totalitarian ideology, a destructive force inimical to liberal values? Are these societies hostages to their past, doomed to eternally reenact old animosities and conflicts? In reality, one needs to distinguish between varieties of nationalism: the inclusive versus the exclusive, the liberal versus the radical, or, as Yael Tamir proposed, the polycentric versus the ethnocentric.[87] Ethnocentrism is a form of nationalism that turns the real distinction between the in-group and the others into an insuperable attribute, a fact of destiny that places one's nation into a position superior to all the others.

Under post-Communism, ethnocentric nationalism, rather than the liberal version, prevailed. Resistant to rational analysis, it appeals to sentiment, affect, and emotion. Truth-content is practically irrelevant in narratives intended to foster dignity and pride. Beliefs, values, and mores are thrust into the straitjacket of a specific "regime of truth" that produces and sustains specific power alignments. The social framing of nationalism crystallizes into "ordered procedures for the production, regulation, distribution, circulation and operation of statements."[88] It therefore functions as universal truth. Idealized interpretations of history turn into identity markers because they provide us with gratification, satisfaction, and perceived magnitude. They create a sense of authenticity. Considering that for Central and Eastern Europe the past is "not just another country, but a positive archipelago of vulnerable historical territories,"[89] the incessant reliance on mismemory rather than on *Vergangenheitsbewältigung* (coming to terms with the past) deepened the already widespread cynicism and the privatization of memory. Such escapism in counterhistories produces divisiveness rather than cohesion and regional antagonism rather than integration. Nostalgia in the former Soviet bloc often took the form of "regret for the lost certainties of Communism, now purged of its darker side."[90] These falsified narratives have the function of remaking and denying the facts. The truth is argued away and the characters of the traumatized and guilty past are deprived of their real identities. Victims and heroes are assigned pejorative counterimages, while perpetrators and bystanders find refuge in the absence of atonement.[91]

Delays in the coalescence of a political class in the region are linked to the weakness of a democratic core elite: political values remain vague, programs tend to overlap, and corruption is rampant. Think of the short life expectancy of some political parties in the region. In fact, parties that were dominant in the first years after the collapse have either lost electoral significance (e.g., the Hungarian Democratic Forum [MDF] or the National Peasant Christian and Democratic Party), or significantly altered their orientations and allegiances (e.g., the Hungarian Civic Union [FIDESZ] or the National Liberal Party in Romania). Other problems are related to delays in the coalescence of a political class. This is particularly dangerous in Russia, where there is a conspicuous absence of political competition between ideologically defined and distinct parties. The public is thus inclined to see privatization as the springboard for the rise of a new class of profiteers (a transfiguration of the old political elite into a new economic one). The political arena is still extremely volatile, and the ideological labels conceal as much as they reveal. The decisive choice is between personalities, parties, and movements that favor individualism, an open society, and risk-taking, and those that promise security within the homogeneous environment of the ethnic community. Strategy is as important as tactic, and the will to reform is as important as the articulation of concrete goals.

MEANINGS, OLD AND NEW

I would like to return now to Ralf Dahrendorf's memorable statement that citizens of Central and Eastern Europe are still trying to make sense of their existence. As mentioned earlier, a constant of the recent history of the region is the recurrence of charismatic politics and of pseudo-party politics. If these societies are to move past these problems, they must overcome two fundamental elements of the legacy of the Communist past: anomy (which led to fragmentation, neotraditionalism, and uncivility, to what Romanian philosopher Andrei Pleşu termed "public obscenity") and lies (which led to dissimulation and the disintegration of consensus, and ostentatiously brought forth a human type characterized by Russia sociologist Yuri Levada as *homo prevaricatus,* the heir of *homo sovieticus*). Since forewarned is forearmed, I believe that it is better to look into the real pitfalls and avoid them rather than play the obsolete pseudo-Hegelian tune of the "ultimate liberal triumph." Indeed, what we see here is not the strength but rather the vulnerability of liberalism in the region—the backwardness, delays, and distortions of modernity, as well as its periodic confrontation with majoritarian, neoplebiscitarian parties and movements.[92] The lesson of the 1989 revolutions is therefore multifarious. It refers to the rebirth of citizenship, a category abolished by both Communism and Fascism,[93] but it also involved re-empowering the truth. What we have learned from 1989 represents an unquestionable argument in favor of the values that we consider essential and exemplary for democracy today.

Let us end by noting the *vital* role played by international factors in the process of the democratization of Eastern and Central Europe. Without NATO's enlargement and accession to European Union, the fate of the region most probably would have been very different. Because of normalization by integration into a democratically validated supragovernmental organization, the political, cultural, economic, and social environments in these countries have received a huge boost in their struggle with mytho-exclusionist fantasies. In this sense, external intervention was as important, if not more important, than domestic dynamics. What seemed in the early 1990s a somber future turned into an extremely favorable present. Ken Jowitt rightly diagnosed that only adoption by a richer sister from the West could save the tormented Eastern sister from a new wave of salvationist authoritarianism. And indeed his doomsday vision of colonels, priests, and despots was proven wrong. This was a surprise, though, for none of us thought that NATO and the European

Union would turn eastward. There were calls for this, but they seemed more like hoping against hope. It is no surprise, then, that Jowitt emphatically stated in 2007 that integration in the EU was the best news that the countries of Central and Eastern Europe had received in five hundred years. One should not forget, however, the part played by the shock of Yugoslavia's secession wars. This tragic and violent example made both the EU and NATO understand where ignorance of the dangers of nationalism, populism, and demagogy in the region can lead. Their push eastward had as great a civilizing role as the exercise of democracy within these societies. The specter that one should be wary of now is, to invoke Jowitt once again, the transformation of the former members of the Warsaw Pact into the ghetto of a united Europe.[94]

Any assessment of the last two decades should raise the question, What is it left of 1989? This turning point was the most powerful shake-up in the twentieth century of the seduction exerted by millenarian ideologies. The teleological utopias of the last century were fundamentally rebuked by the revolutions of 1989, which were their polar opposite. They were anti-ideological, antiteleological, and anti-utopian. They rejected the exclusive logic of Jacobinism and refused to embark on any new chiliastic experiments. In this sense, they can be called nonrevolutionary. Indeed, the Leninist extinction could be explained, following Stephen Kotkin for instance, by appealing to "a narrative of global political economy and a bankrupt political class in a system that was largely bereft of corrective mechanisms."[95] But this would ultimately overlook (or significantly diminish) the equally relevant tale of a slow but unstoppable awakening of society by reinstating the centrality of truth and human rights (especially after the 1975 Helsinki Agreement). The uncivil society was not merely confronted with the erosion of its Leninist worldview. It also imploded in the face of an alternative set of values that inspired independent reflection, autonomous initiatives, and mass protest. In other words, the upheaval of 1989 was not only the result of the agency of the uncivil society. It acted in the presence of a powerful political myth—civil society. Political myths are to be judged not in terms of their truthfulness, but of their potential to become true: speaking about civil society led to the emergence of civil society. In East Central Europe, exhilarating new ideas, such as the return to Europe, destroyed obsolete ideas. People took to the streets in Berlin, Leipzig, Prague, Budapest, and Timisoara, convinced that the hour of the citizen had arrived.

In 1989, public demonstrations did not lead directly to the collapse of the Communist elites in power. Maybe civil society was not the immediate cause of the demise of Erich Honecker, Wojciech Jaruzelski, Todor Zhivkov, Miloš Jakeš, and Gustáv Husák. But the dynamics, the ideas, and most important, the aftermath of the events accompanying the shattering of Communist parties' rule across the region cannot be understood without emphasizing the significance of civil society as a constellation of fundamental ideas, as a political myth, and as a real, historical movement that accompanied the implosion of Eastern European party-states. To take my point even further, the very idea of revolutions in 1989 rests on the impact of civil society, which replaced the existing political, social, and economic system with one founded on the ideals of democratic citizenship and human rights. Yes, there were many masks, travesties, charades, and myths involved in the events that took place in Bucharest, Prague, and Sofia. In most countries, the resilience of the old elites prevented a radical coming to terms with the Communist past. But this obfuscates the fact that the core value restored, cherished and promoted by the revolutions of 1989 was common sense. The revolutionaries believed in civility, decency, and humanity, and they succeeded in rehabilitating these values. This is the most significant lesson of 1989. The illusions of that year ought not to be discarded: they were crucial for the defeat of Leninism. In 1989, people were not afraid anymore; their moral frustration, social numbness, and political impotence disappeared. The individual finally regained a central role on the political stage. The years passed and ultimately those nightmarish scenarios for Central and Eastern Europe have been invalidated. Far from being over, the revolutions of 1989 remain a symbol of contemporary times—an age of diversity, difference, and tolerance.

Conclusions

Totalitarianism was a novel political, social, and cultural construct that first suspended and then abolished traditional distinctions between good and evil. An imperfect concept, to be sure, it was not an empty signifier or a mere Cold War propaganda weapon, as some have suggested in recent years. Those who developed the concept of totalitarianism during the interwar period knew what appalling realities it designated: from the exiled Mensheviks to the emigré scholars from Fascist Italy and Nazi Germany, these intellectuals knew that something unprecedented and quite terrifying had occurred.[1] The concept of totalitarianism offered important and still valid interpretive keys for understanding the unique blending of ideology, organization, and terror in unprecedented attempts to create perfectly homogenized communities through genocidal methods. All these experiments included quasi-religious, unavowed yet palpable mystical components. In fact, they were political religions, with their own rituals, prophets, saints, zealots, inquisitors, traitors, renegades, heretics, apostates, and holy writs. The totalitarian story began with the Bolshevik dream of total revolution and became a global phenomenon in the 1920s and 1930s with the rise to power of totalitarian party-movements in Italy and Germany. For example, the Romanian Iron Guard was a totalitarian movement that combined political radicalism and religious fanaticism. Its short-lived stay in power (September 1940–January 1941) was marked by a frantic attempt to carry out, using murderous violence, what historian Eugen Weber once called the archangelic revolution.[2] Whereas these Fascist dictatorships collapsed as a result of World War II, Soviet Communism lasted for more than seven decades and ended only in December 1991 in the USSR. The catalyst for this final wreckage was the liberal, anti-Leninist revolutionary upheaval of 1989. In transformed incarnations, it is still alive in China and a few other countries.

To paraphrase Hannah Arendt, during the reign of these totalitarian movements, conscience broke down. Furthermore, "the insanity of such systems lies not only in their first premise but in the very logicality with which they are constructed."[3] Communism was a radical economic, moral, social, and cultural doctrine centered upon the accomplishment of radical transformative ends. Fascism appeared as its arch rival, yet it shared with Communism the collectivistic, antiliberal, anticapitalist approach, the neoromantic dream of the total community, and the longing for a completely purified existence.[4] With its universalistic goals, eschatological promises, and totalizing ambitions, it was often described as a political or secular religion (and so was Fascism in its Italian, German, and Romanian incarnations). The ultimate purpose of Communism was to create a new civilization founded upon a New Man. Two factors were fundamental for this doctrine: the privileged role of the party and the revolutionary transformation of human nature. One of the main distinctions between radicalism of the extreme Left and the extreme Right is the emphasis the former placed on the institution of the party as an immanent incarnation of absolute, transcendental historical knowledge. In the words of historian Walter Laqueur,

> The Fascist experience in Italy and Germany has shown the crucial role of the Duce and the Führer. Hitler and Mussolini created their parties in their image, and it is perfectly legitimate to talk about the Hitler and the Mussolini "movement," for theirs were not political parties in traditional sense. . . . But Stalin's role in the Soviet Union was initially less decisive. Communist power was already firmly established. There is every reason to believe that if Stalin had been shot or died of a disease or had never existed, the party would have still remained in power in the 1920s and 1930s.[5]

Communism advanced a new conception of human existence (society, economy, social and individual psychology, art). According to this conception, building the New Man was the supreme goal of political action. Communism's ambition was to transcend traditional morality, yet it suffered from moral relativism. It assigned to the party-state its own morality, granting *only* to it the right to define the meaning and ultimate aim of human existence. The state became the supreme and absolute value within the framework of an eschatological doctrine of revolution. Through the cult of absolute unity on the path to salvation by knowledge of history, Communism produced a new, total social and political project centered on purifying the body of the communities that fell under its ideological spell. Its revolutionary project was total and totalizing. As a potent political myth, Communism promised immanent deliverance, the chance to achieve prosperity, freedom, and equality. In fact, throughout the twentieth century, the Communist Weltanschauung was the foundation for ideologically based totalitarian political experiments with terrible human costs.

As for Fascism—and especially its paroxistic version, National Socialism—it emphasized the lack of equality between biologically defined groups and a predestined mission for the Aryan nations. At the same time, it praised heroism, youth, and valiance and despised bourgeois modernity as much as the Communists did. Placing Fascism at the right end of the political spectrum masks the strong socialist origins of these movements based on ethnic ressentiment.[6]

Marxism's fundamental thesis was the centrality of class struggle (historical violence) in the development of society. For Marx (and later for twentieth-century Marxist philosophers Ernst Bloch, Antonio Gramsci, and Georg Lukács), the revolutionary class symbolized the viewpoint of totality, thereby creating the epistemic premises for grasping historical truth. In the name of proletarian (authentic) democracy, formal liberties could be curtailed, even suppressed. Marx's myth of the proletariat as the messiah class, the heart of Communism, nurtured a revolutionary project imbued with a sense of prophetic mission and charismatic-heroic predestination. This became an immensely appealing mythological matrix embraced by intellectuals worldwide.[7] Marx gave an ultimate apocalyptic verdict: since the bourgeoisie is guilty of the barbarous distortion of human life, it deserves its fate.[8] Marx viewed the social universe primarily (but not only) in terms of social and economic determinism. Freedom meant for Marx and his disciples "understood necessity," that is, efforts to carry out the presumed goals of history. All human reality was subordinated to the dialectical laws of development, and history was projected into a sovereign entity, whose diktat was beyond any human questioning. He declared his social theory the ultimate scientific formula.

The ingredient that allowed the realization of the revolutionary mission was revolutionary class consciousness.[9] Through it, mankind's prehistory would end and its real history could begin. According to the young Marx, the revolutionary intellectuals were those who created the doctrine, but the proletarians were not perceived as an amorphous mass into which a self-appointed group of teachers had the duty of injecting the consciousness of the historical truth. Nevertheless, Karl Marx's *Eleventh Thesis on Feuerbach* best expressed the revolutionary mission of critical thinking: "The philosophers have only *interpreted* the world, in various ways; the point, however, is to *change* it."[10] With the rubble of the past cleared away, the chosen agent of history would point the way to a new society that would bring about the complete fulfillment of the human spirit.

Communism was simultaneously an eschatology (a doctrine of mundane salvation) and an ecclesiology (a ideology of the revolutionary party or movement). Reality as it stood was fatally reified; it was to be superseded, on the one hand, by the emancipation and revolution of the proletariat, and on the other hand, by the utopia of the classless society. Subsequently, Communism's vision of the future society relied upon a "dictatorship over needs" (Agnes Heller, Ferenc Fehér, and György Márkus). It presupposed the dissolution of the autonomous individual within the all-devouring framework of total control, the disastrous politicization of the psyche, the manipulation of the subjective field, the attempted obliteration of the private sphere as an ultimate sanctuary of the ego. It was a total experiment in social engineering. Once it constructed its vision of modernity on the principle of a chosen, socially homogenized community crossing the desert of history from darkness into light, there could be only one solution for those who failed to qualify to their inclusionary criteria: stigmatization, elimination, and eventually, extermination

The Marxist eschatology was a rationalized theodicy: history replaced God, the proletariat was the universal redeemer, and the revolution meant ultimate salvation, the end of human suffering. History had only one direction, as it unfolded from scarcity to abundance, from limited to absolute freedom. Freedom, in turn, was understood as overcoming necessity via revolutionary praxis. Hegel had said that all that was real was rational. For Marx, all that was real was historical, and history was governed by dialectical laws. The kingdom of necessity was the realm where economy could not ensure full equality among human beings, where the political was dependent on partisan interests and the social sphere was painfully atomized. In contrast, in the kingdom of freedom there was an identity between existence and essence, antagonism disappeared, men and women recovered their lost sense of work as joy, as unfettered creativity. In this context, human existence could fully reach its development, and the condition for the freedom of all lay in each individual's liberation. At the basis of Communism, therefore, lay a teleological fundamentalism. Its final station was the City of God on earth, that is, the triumph of the proletariat.

Marxian social theory's cult of totality as the ultimate explanatory archetype set the stage for its degeneration, in Bolshevik (Leninist) terms, into dogma and the ruthless persecution of heretics. Marx's emphasis on human emancipation as the conscious absorption of society by the individual and his equation of social conflict with class antagonism resulted in advocacy of the elimination of "superstructural" intermediaries (laws, institutions, etc.) regulating the relationship between civil society and the state. Marx failed to give instructions on the achievement of social unity. The utopian, eschatological vision of Marx's body of political thought was translated into a revolutionary program of action by Vladimir Ilyich Lenin (born Ulianov). Lenin operated a creative understanding of necessity that led to the Bolshevik version of man's salvation. In Lenin's vision, the monolithic vanguard party became the repository of human hope, a tightly knit fraternity of illuminated militants, and therefore the true vehicle of human freedom. The combination of Marxism with party/power set the Communist body politic on the path to self-purification (permanent purge and revolutionary offensive).

For Lenin, the fate of the Communist revolution predicted by Karl Marx depended on the maturity and political will of the revolutionary party. His vision of the new type of party was formulated in the pamphlet *What Is To Be Done* (1902), which articulated the Leninist concept of revolutionary practice in the twentieth century. Lenin's notion of the party led to the split within Russian social democracy between moderates (Mensheviks) and radicals (Bolsheviks). Leninism consists fundamentally of Lenin's theory of the vanguard revolutionary party, the doctrine of proletarian revolution in the age of imperialism, and the emphasis on the dictatorship of the proletariat as a new type of state emerging from the collapse of the old, bourgeois order. From the outset, the Leninist regime in the Soviet Union was based on abuses, violence, and repression directed against any form of political opposition. Bolshevism was the opposite of a rule-of-law state.[11] These authoritarian features of Leninism were further exacerbated by Stalin, who transformed the Soviet Union into a totalitarian state. Bolshevik humanism was conditioned only by the success of the cause it was engaged in. The individual's existence maintained its weight in the world insofar as it contributed to the construction of social utopia.

Like Marx, Lenin saw the proletarian revolution as a global phenomenon, but he modified some basic tenets of the Marxist theory. Lenin noticed the passivity of the workers in the advanced industrial countries and explained it as a consequence of the ability of the bourgeoisie to co-opt the working class within the system. According to Lenin, the bourgeoisie succeeded in ideologically corrupting the proletarians and their parties. It was therefore important to create a new type of political party that would refuse any form of collusion with the existing dominant forces and would eventually exert exclusive political power. For Lenin, a tightly knit, phalanxlike revolutionary organization, structured almost like a military order, was needed to inject revolutionary consciousness into the proletariat and direct the workers in the revolutionary battles. The party was the embodiment of historical reason and militants were expected to carry out its orders without hesitation or reservation. Discipline, secrecy, and rigid hierarchy were essential for such a party, especially during clandestine activities (like those in Russia). The main role of the party was to awaken proletarian self-consciousness and instill the revolutionary doctrine (faith) into the dormant proletariat. Instead of relying on the spontaneous development of consciousness in the working class, Leninism saw the party as a catalytic agent bringing revolutionary knowledge, will, and organization to the exploited masses. It was with Lenin that the mystique of a new type of party became an indelible feature of radical politics in the twentieth century.

The Fascists absorbed the Bolshevik lesson, internalizing Lenin's cult of the party, but they never developed a mystical partolatry. The main distinction, therefore, was that neither the Fascist Party in Italy nor the National Socialist German Workers Party (NSDAP) became charismatic institutions like the Bolshevik Party. They were the sounding boards for the leaders' harangues, collective entities meant to ensure the perpetuation of the *Führerprinzip*. Alfredo Rocco was Mussolini's minister of justice and a close friend of Il Duce. His views emphasized organicism, romanticism, and statism as key components of the Fascist ideology: "To the existence of this ideal content of Fascism, to the truth of this Fascist logic we ascribe the fact that though we commit many errors of detail, we very seldom go astray on fundamentals, whereas all the parties of the opposition, deprived as they are of an informing, animating principle, of a unique directing concept, do very often wage their war faultlessly in minor tactics, better trained as they are in parliamentary and journalistic maneuvers, but they constantly broke down on the important issues."[12] Benito Mussolini, Italy's Fascist dictator between 1922 and his death in 1945, contributed in 1932 to the *Enciclopedia Italiana* with a famous entry on the doctrine of Fascism:

> Thus Fascism could not be understood in many of its practical manifestations as a party organization, as a system of education, a discipline, if it were not always looked at in the light of its whole way of conceiving life, a spiritualized way. . . . The man of Fascism is an individual who is nation and fatherland, which is a moral law, biding together individuals and the generations into a tradition and a mission, suppressing the instant for a life enclosed within the brief round of pleasure in order to restore within duty the higher life free from the limits of time and space: a life in which the individual, through the denial of himself, through the sacrifice of his own private interests, through death itself, realizes that completely spiritual existence in which his value as a man lies. Fascism is a religious conception in which man is seen in his immanent relationship with a superior law and with an objective Will that transcends the particular individual and raises him to conscious membership in a spiritual society. Whoever has seen in the religious politics of the Fascist regime nothing than mere opportunism has not understood that Fascism besides being a system of government is also, above all, a system of thought.[13]

Ideological absolutism, sanctification of the ultimate goal, suspension of critical faculties, and the cult of the party line as the perfect expression of the general will were imbedded in the original Bolshevik project and definitely imbued Mussolini's political imagination.

I argue that the seeds of Stalin's regime were sowed by Lenin.[14] He carried to an extreme Leninism's intolerant logic and turned the USSR into a police state. The Communist Party was transformed from a revolutionary elite into a bureaucratic caste whose sole aim was to preserve and enhance the leader's power and its privileges. Gradually, the dictatorship of the proletariat became an empty slogan legitimizing Stalin's absolute reign and secret police repression against the population. Invoking Lenin's struggle against factionalism, Stalin completely destroyed any intraparty democracy, viciously persecuted all (real or imaginary) opponents, and imposed a monolithic dictatorship based on permanent purges and mass terror. In the physical absence of the numinous leader incarnating the absolute power of the party, Lenin, the congregation of his disciples had to reinvent itself by means of founding its charisma on the scriptures of its founding fathers. The invented tradition of Marxism-Leninism was then thrust upon the party ranks as a means of stabilizing the normative identity of the party. The "return to Leninism" became an important theme of the anti-Stalin opposition, especially among Trotsky's supporters. Later, after Stalin's death in 1953, Nikita Khrushchev proclaimed the restoration of the Leninist norms of party life and denounced Stalin's "cult of personality" (i.e., the quasi-religious adoration of the supreme leader) as non-Leninist. In the 1980s, Mikhail Gorbachev deepened Khrushchev's critique of Stalinism and sought to instill pluralism within Soviet institutions. In his democratizing efforts, Gorbachev went beyond the logic of Leninism and abandoned both the concept of the dictatorship of the proletariat and the party's claim to monopoly of power.

In 1919 Lenin created the Third (Communist) International—the Comintern, a global institution that the Fascists were never able to establish. Earlier he had lambasted the Second International for its loss of revolutionary fervor and complicity with bourgeois parliaments and governments. The Comintern consecrated Moscow's centrality and hegemonic role within world Communism. For a party to be accepted into the Comintern it had to unconditionally acquiesce to twenty-one conditions, including complete subordination to Soviet dictates. Lenin created the Comintern as an instrument for expanding the revolution and allowing Soviet Russia to escape "imperialist encirclement." Later, Stalin transformed it into a mere instrument of Soviet foreign policy and by implication Russian imperialism. The Comintern was disbanded in 1943, but Communist parties continued to toe the Stalinist line. In the aftermath of World War II, Leninist parties came to power in East-Central Europe, China, North Korea, and North Vietnam (a Soviet-style regime existed in Mongolia since the 1920s). Later, in 1960, Fidel Castro publicly espoused Leninism and proclaimed the Communist nature of the Cuban Revolution. In all these cases, Communism represented the sum of political and ideological techniques (tactics) used by revolutionary parties to seize and consolidate monopolistic dictatorial regimes. Their only claim to legitimacy derived from the organized belief-structure shared by the elites and inculcated into the masses, according to which the party was the sole beneficiary of direct access to historical truth.

Marx proclaimed Communism to be the *genuine* resolution of the conflict between man and nature and between man and man: "Communism is the riddle of history solved, and knows itself to be the solution."[15] The explanation for the consequences of this doctrine is founded upon a few essential factors: the vision of its followers, a superior elite whose utopian goals sanctify the most barbaric methods; the denial of the right to life of those who are defined as "degenerate parasites and predators"; the deliberate dehumanization of state-defined enemies and victims; and the falsification of the idea of good (Alain Besançon). The revolutions of 1989 demonstrated that Communism had exhausted its appeal and led to the breakdown of the Leninist regimes in East-Central Europe. In December 1991, the USSR came to an end. The demise of Communism in Europe allowed space for alternative political mythologies, which left a proliferation of what I called *fantasies of salvation*.

In his monumental volume *Postwar,* Tony Judt argues that the Europe of our days is "bound together by the signs and symbols of its terrible past." The remarkable accomplishment of forging a democratic identity this way "remains forever mortgaged to that past" because the latter "will have to be *taught* afresh with each passing generation."[16] The main lessons of the twentieth century that this book has tried to highlight are that no ideological commitment, no matter how frantically absorbing, should ever prevail over the sanctity of human life and that no party, movement, or leader holds the right to dictate that followers renounce their critical faculties to embrace a pseudo-miraculous, in fact mystically self-centered, delusional vision of mandatory happiness. Anne Applebaum judiciously emphasized that the most important path to understanding the terrible historical experience of the past century is by empathizing with and trying to comprehend the people who lived through it.[17] It is now clear, based on the abysmal experiences of totalitarian states, that contempt for the individual and his/her rights inevitably leads to the destruction of any trace of democracy. The Communist "people's democracies" were actually a mockery of this very term, in fact its antithesis. They shared with the Fascist regimes a hyperdeterministic, quasi-scientific ideological hubris. No less importantly, conspiratorial visions of world history, including the current Islamist fantasies, result in an obsession with infiltrated enemies, a politics of vindictive mythological scapegoating, and state-organized persecution, exclusion, and extermination of those ideologically branded as "perfidious vermin" and "treacherous scum" (Jews, kulaks, etc.).[18] As Hannah Arendt put it in 1946 (and these words should stay with us as an enduring warning),

> One of the most horrible aspects of contemporary terror is that, no matter what its motives and ultimate aims, it invariably appears in the clothes of an inevitable logical conclusion made on the basis of some ideology or theory. To a far lesser degree, this phenomenon was already to be seen in connection with the liquidation of the anti-Stalinists in Russia—which Stalin himself predicted and justified in 1930.... The obvious conclusion was that one

had to deal with these factions as with a hostile class or with traitors. The trouble is, of course, that nobody except Stalin knows what the "true interests of the proletariat" are ... This "scientificality" is indeed the common feature of all totalitarian regimes of our time. But it means nothing more than that purely man-made power—mainly destructive—is dressed in the clothes of some superior, superhuman sanction from which it derives its absolute, not-to-be-questioned, force. The Nazi brand of this kind of power is more thorough and more horrible than the Marxist or pseudo-Marxist, because it assigns to nature the role Marxism assigns to history ... But neither science nor "scientificality," neither scholars nor charlatans supplied the ideas and techniques that operated the death factories. The ideas came from politicians who took power-politics seriously, the techniques came from modern mob-men who were not afraid of consistency.[19]

Tens of millions of dead, the memory of barbed wire and gas chambers, and a sense of unbearable tragedy are the main legacies left by the reckless ideological pledges of the twentieth century to build the City of God here and now.

Notes

PROLOGUE

1. Primo Levi, *If This Is a Man* (London: Abacus, 1987), p. 395.

2. See Virgil Ierunca, *Fenomenul Piteşti* (Bucureşti: Humanitas, 1990). I also recommend the documentary *Demascarea* (The Unmasking), directed by Nicolae Mărgineanu, script by Alin Mureşan, produced by the Institute for the Investigation of the Crimes of Communism and the Memory of the Romanian Exile, Bucharest, 2011. The Piteşti experiment was unleashed by local officers and their agents among the inmates based on orders coming from the highest Securitate echelons. It came to an end suddenly and inexplicably before Stalin's death, and the organizers, charged with conspiracy to compromise the Communist regime, were executed in 1954, carrying to the grave the secrets of the operation. The story, however, continued to circulate in Romanian prisons and reached the West in the 1960s.

3. Timothy Snyder, *Bloodlands: Europe between Hitler and Stalin* (New York: Basic Books, 2010), p. 408.

4. Peter Fritzsche, "On Being the Subjects of History: Nazis as Twentieth-Century Revolutionaries," in *Language and Revolution: Making Modern Political Identities,* ed. Igal Halfin (London: Frank Cass Publishers, 2002), p. 151.

5. See Susan Neiman, *Evil in Modern Thought: An Alternative History of Philosophy* (Princeton, N.J., and Oxford: Princeton University Press, 2002).

6. See Leszek Kołakowski, *Modernity on Endless Trial* (Chicago: University of Chicago Press, 1990), p. 189.

7. According to Snyder, there were three periods in the mass murder perpetrated by the Soviet and Nazi regimes: "In the first (1933–1938), the Soviet Union carried out almost all of the mass killing; in the second, the German-Soviet alliance (1939–1941), the killing was balanced. Between 1941 and 1945 the Germans were responsible for almost all of the political murder." Timothy Snyder, *Bloodlands,* p. 155. For a fascinating account of antifascism, see Michael

Scammell, *Koestler: The Literary and Political Odyssey of a Twentieth-Century Skeptic* (New York: Random House, 2009), pp. 101–51; for the role of the Comintern's Agitprop international network and the crucial participation of Willi Münzenberg and his circle, see Sean McMeekin, *The Red Millionaire: A Political Biography of Willi Münzenberg, Moscow's Secret Propaganda Tsar in the West* (New Haven, Conn., and London: Yale University Press, 2003); and Jonathan Miles, *The Dangerous Otto Katz: The Many Lives of a Soviet Spy* (New York: Bloomsbury, 2010). Espionage on behalf of Stalin, hostility to Hitler, and attraction to a utopian "other world" blended in experiences such as those of Katz or the Cambridge leftist enthusiasts.

8. Throughout the volume I will alternate between the terms *totalitarianism* and *political religion*. I chose to employ this conceptual parallelism because I consider that the two terms have complementary functions. Following Philippe Burrin, I believe that "totalitarianism sheds light on the mechanism of power and forms of domination, while political religion aims at the system of beliefs, rituals and symbols that establish and articulate this domination. Totalitarianism emphasizes the modernity of phenomena, particularly the techniques of power, while political religion draws attention to a long-term perspective and the historical sediment and modern reapplication of fragments of a religious culture for political purposes." See Philippe Burrin, "Political Religion: The Relevance of a Concept," *History and Memory* 9, nos. 1–2 (1997): 346n28.

9. Emilio Gentile, "Political Religion: A Concept and Its Critics—A Critical Survey," *Totalitarian Movements and Political Religions* 6, no. 1 (June 2005): 19–32. Gentile provides the following definition of "the sacralization of politics": "This process takes place when, more or less elaborately and dogmatically, a political movement confers a sacred status on an earthly entity (the nation, the country, the state, humanity, society, race, proletariat, history, liberty, or revolution) and renders it an absolute principle of collective existence, considers it the main source of values for individual and mass behavior, and exalts it as the supreme ethical precept of public life." Emilio Gentile and Robert Mallett, "The Sacralisation of Politics: Definitions, Interpretations and Reflections on the Question of Secular Religion and Totalitarianism," *Totalitarian Movements and Political Religions* 1, no. 1 (2000): 18–55.

10. Halfin, "Introduction," in *Language and Revolution*, pp. 1–20.

11. Ian Kershaw, *Hitler 1936–45: Nemesis* (New York and London: W.W. Norton, 2000), p. 249.

12. Ian Kershaw and Moshe Lewin, "Introduction. The Regimes and their Dictators: Perspectives of Comparison," in *Stalinism and Nazism: Dictatorships in Comparison* (New York: Cambridge University Press, 1997), p. 25.

13. Roger Griffin, *Modernism and Fascism: The Sense of Beginning under Mussolini and Hitler* (London and New York: Palgrave Macmillan, 2007), p. 4.

14. Robert Gellately, *Lenin, Stalin, and Hitler: The Age of Social Catastrophe* (New York: Alfred A. Knopf, 2007), pp. 71–72. See also the impressive documentation in Donald Rayfield, *Stalin and His Hangmen: The Tyrant and Those Who Killed for Him* (New York: Random House, 2004).

15. See Jeffrey Herf, *The Jewish Enemy: Nazi Propaganda during World War II and the Holocaust* (Cambridge, Mass.: Harvard University Press, 2006).

16. Gellately, *Lenin, Stalin, and Hitler,* p. 310.

17. See the pioneering volume edited by Ian Kershaw and Moshe Lewin, *Stalinism and Nazism;* Marc Ferro, ed., *Nazisme et communisme: Deux régimes dans le siècle* (Paris: Hachette, 1999); Henri Rousso, ed., *Stalinisme et nazisme: Histoire et mémoire comparées* (Paris: Editions Complexe, 1999); Shlomo Avineri and Zeev Sternhell, eds., *Europe's Century of Discontent: The Legacies of Fascism, Nazism, and Communism* (Jerusalem: Hebrew University Magnes Press, 2003); Michael Geyer and Sheila Fitzpatrick, eds., *Beyond Totalitarianism: Stalinism and Nazism Compared* (New York: Cambridge University Press, 2009).

18. See Daniel Chirot, *Modern Tyrants: The Power and Prevalence of Evil in Our Age* (New York: Free Press, 1994), pp. 1–24.

19. See Richard Overy, *The Dictators: Hitler's Germany and Stalin's Russia* (London and New York: Penguin Books, 2005), pp. 483–580.

20. Arthur Koestler, *The Trail of the Dinosaur and Other Essays* (New York: Macmillan, 1955), p. 15.

21. See Steven Lukes, "On the Moral Blindness of Communism," in Helmut Dubiel and Gabriel Motzkin, *The Lesser Evil: Moral Approaches to Genocide Practices* (New York and London: Routledge, 2004), pp. 154–65.

22. Richard Overy, *The Dictators,* pp. 303–6.

23. Hans Maier, "Political Religions and Their Images: Soviet Communism, Italian Fascism and German National Socialism," *Totalitarian Movements and Political Religions* 7, no. 3 (September 2006): 273.

24. Richard J. Evans, *The Coming of the Third Reich* (London: Penguin Books, 2003), pp. 239–40.

25. Griffin, *Modernism and Fascism,* p. 30.

26. *Inside Kremlin Politics: Conversations with Felix Chuev,* ed. Albert Resis (Chicago: I.R. Dee, 2007), pp. 262 and 270.

27. It can hardly be considered a coincidence the fact that the term *byvshie liudi* (former people), which became commonplace in Bolshevik speak, implied that those to whom it applied were not quite human. Moreover, according to Bernice Glatzer Rosenthal, the term *lishentsy,* which became a legal category, etymologically "was related to the superfluous man (*lishnii chelovek*) of 19th century Russian literature." Bernice Glatzer Rosenthal, *New Myth, New World—from Nietzsche to Stalinism* (University Park: Pennsylvania State University Press, 2002), p. 204.

28. Orlando Figes, *The Whisperers: Private Life in Stalin's Russia* (New York: Metropolitan Books, 2007), p. 249. Molotov's case is particularly baffling on the matter of loyalty to party-state vs. loyalty to one's family. His wife, old Bolshevik and Central Committee member Polina Zhemchuzhina, was accused of Zionism and cosmopolitanism in 1949. When the Politburo gathered to decide her fate, Molotov dared to abstain from voting. A few days later, he apologized for his conduct, praising the "rightful" punishment decided by the Soviet motherland for his spouse. He subsequently divorced her, opting for unflinching loyalty to Stalin. Upon the dictator's death, Polina came back from deportation. She remarried Molotov, and they lived happily ever after. Zhemchuzhina never criticized her husband and never publicly denounced Stalin's murderous regime. All in all, it could be said that she was the epitome of "the

238 | Notes to Prologue

comrade in life and in struggle," as the Communist magnates' spouses used to be called. Molotov's grandson, Vyacheslav Nikonov, is currently an influential Russian political commentator close to Vladimir Putin.

29. David Priestland, *Stalinism and the Politics of Mobilization: Ideas, Power, and Terror in Inter-War Russia* (Oxford and New York: Oxford University Press, 2007), p. 214. Yaroslavsky's wife, Klavdia Kirsanova (1888–1947), was the rector of the Comintern's Leninist School. See Pierre Broué, *Histoire de l'Internationale Communiste: 1919–1943* (Paris: Fayard, 1997), p. 1025.

30. Roger Griffin, *The Nature of Fascism* (London and New York: Routledge, 1993), p. 235.

31. Pierre Hassner, "Beyond History and Memory," in *Stalinism and Nazism: History and Memory Compared,* ed. Henri Rousso, English language edition edited and introduced by Richard J. Golsan, trans. Lucy B. Golsan, Thomas C. Hilde, and Peter S. Rogers (Lincoln and London: University of Nebraska Press, 2004), pp. 283–85.

32. Eugen Weber, "Revolution? Counterrevolution? What Revolution?" *Journal of Contemporary History* 9, no. 2 (April 1974): 24–25.

33. Michael Geyer (with assistance from Sheila Fitzpatrick), "Introduction: After Totalitarianism—Stalinism and Nazism Compared," in *Beyond Totalitarianism,* ed. Geyer and Fitzpatrick, pp. 1–37.

34. Georgi Dimitrov, *The Diary of Georgi Dimitrov, 1943–1949,* ed. Ivo Banac (New Haven, Conn.: Yale University Press, 2003), p. 65.

35. Kershaw, *Hitler 1936–45,* p. 315.

36. *The Diary of Georgi Dimitrov,* p. 66. For fascinating details regarding the publication of Dimitrov's diary as well as of other essential books in the Yale University Press series Annals of Communism, see Jonathan Brent, *Inside the Stalin Archives: Discovering the New Russia* (New York: Atlas, 2008).

37. Kershaw, *Hitler 1936–45,* p. 321.

38. Snyder, *Bloodlands,* p. 370.

39. See Wendy Z. Goldman, *Terror and Democracy in the Age of Stalin* (New York: Cambridge University Press, 2007).

40. Priestland, *Stalinism and the Politics of Mobilization,* pp. 37–47.

41. Ibid., p. 421.

42. Eugen Weber, *Varieties of Fascism: Doctrines of Revolution in the Twentieth Century* (New York: D. Van Nostrand, 1964), p. 78.

43. Quoted in Gentile and Mallett, "The Sacralization of Politics," pp. 28–29.

44. Overy, *The Dictators,* p. 650.

45. Felix Patrikeeff, "Stalinism, Totalitarian Society and the Politics of 'Perfect Control,'" *Totalitarian Movements and Political Religions* 4, no. 1 (Summer 2003): 40.

46. Overy, *The Dictators,* p. 306.

47. Sheila Fitzpatrick, "Politics as Practice: Thoughts on a New Soviet Political History" in *Kritika: Explorations in Russian and Eurasian History* 5, no. 1 (Winter 2004): 27–54. For S. Kotkin's insight on "speaking Bolshevik," J. Hellbeck's description of "personal Bolshevism," and Volkov's discussion of the identitarian function of *kul'turnost',* see Stephen Kotkin, *The Magnetic Mountain* (Berkeley: University of California Press, 1995); Jochen Hellbeck, "Fashioning the Stalinist

Soul: The Diary of Stepan Podlubnyi, 1931–1938," *Janrbücher für Geschichte Osteuropas,* no. 2 (1997); and Vadim Volkov, "The Concept of *Kul'turnost'*— Notes on the Stalinist Civilizing Process," in *Stalinism—New Directions,* ed. Sheila Fitzpatrick (London and New York: Routledge, 2000), pp. 210–30.

48. Michael Halberstam, "Hannah Arendt on the Totalitarian Sublime and Its Promise of Freedom," in *Hannah Arendt in Jerusalem,* ed. Steven E. Aschheim (Los Angeles: University of California Press, 2001), pp. 105–23.

49. Overy, *The Dictators;* Peter Fritzsche, "Genocide and Global Discourse," *German History* 23, no. 1 (2005): 109; Emilio Gentile, *The Struggle for Modernity: Nationalism, Futurism, and Fascism* (Westport, Conn.: Praeger, 2003), p. 98; Geyer, "Introduction," in *Beyond Totalitarianism,* ed. Geyer and Fitzpatrick, p. 33; Emilio Gentile, *The Sacralization of Politics in Fascist Italy* (Cambridge, Mass.: Harvard University Press, 1996).

50. Griffin, *The Nature of Fascism,* p. 193. For an extensive discussion of the relationship between "sense-making crisis" and Fascism, see Roger Griffin and Matthew Feldman, eds., *Fascism: Critical Concepts in Political Science,* vol. 2, *The Social Dynamics of Fascism* (New York: Routledge, 2004).

51. See Eric Voegelin, "The Political Religions," in *Modernity without Restraint: Collected Works* (Columbia: University of Missouri Press, 2000), 5:19–74.

52. Historian Stephen Kern, quoted in Griffin, *Modernism and Fascism,* p. 161.

53. Hermann Rausching, *Hitler Speaks* (London, 1939), p. 185, quoted in Richard Pipes, *Russia under the Bolshevik Regime* (New York: Knopf, 1993), p. 259. Regarding the last sentence, it is worth quoting here Richard Pipes's comment: "And one may add, what Bolshevism did and what it became."

54. The formulation belongs to Walter Benjamin, who coined it in *On the Concept of History.* See Griffin, *Modernism and Fascism,* p. 223.

55. See Nolte, *La guerre civile européenne.*

56. Zeev Sternhell, *Neither Left nor Right: Fascist Ideology in France* (Princeton, N.J.: Princeton University Press, 1994).

57. Robert C. Tucker, *Stalin in Power: The Revolution from Above, 1928–1941* (New York: Norton, 1990); Alexander N. Yakovlev, A *Century of Violence in Soviet Russia* (New Haven, Conn.: Yale University Press, 2002).

58. Timothy Snyder, "Hitler vs. Stalin: Who Killed More?" *New York Review of Books Blog,* March 10, 2011, p. 2, http://www.nybooks.com/articles/archives/2011/mar/10/hitler-vs-stalin-who-killed-more/.

59. Snyder, *Bloodlands,* p. 391.

60. Joshua Rubenstein and Vladimir P. Naumov, *Stalin's Secret Pogrom: The Postwar Inquisition of the Jewish Anti-Fascist Committee* (New Haven, Conn.: Yale University Press, 2001).

61. Martin Amis, *Koba the Dread: Laughter and the Twenty Million* (New York: Hyperion, 2002), p. 220.

62. Erik van Ree, "Stalin as Marxist: the Western Roots of Stalin's Russification of Marxism," in *Stalin: A New History,* ed. Sarah Davies and James Harris (Cambridge: Cambridge University Press, 2005), pp. 159–80. The model van Ree describes was the blueprint transferred onto Eastern Europe. A comparative

analysis of the various forms of localizing Stalinism in the region with the type of ideology extensively described by Erik van Ree in his *The Political Thought of Joseph Stalin—A Study in Twentieth-Century Patriotism* (London and New York: Routledge Curzon, 2002) could prove illuminating for cases such as Ceaușescu's Romania, Gomułka's Poland, Enver Hoxha's Albania, or Erich Honecker's GDR. For an example, see my notion of "national-Stalinism" in Vladimir Tismaneanu, *Stalinism for All Seasons: A Political History of Romanian Communism* (Berkeley: University of California Press, 2003), pp. 18–36.

63. Nolte, *La guerre civile européenne*, p. 47.

64. Gellately, *Lenin, Stalin, and Hitler*, p. 579.

65. Ibid., p. 581.

66. Nolte, *La guerre civile européenne*, p. 239.

67. I am developing a point made by Denis Hollier and Betsy Wing in their article "Desperanto," in "Legacies of Antifascism," special issue, *New German Critique* 67 (Winter 1996): 19–31. They discuss the cases of dissident anti-Fascists (to varying degrees from one individual to the other), such as Walter Benjamin, Georges Bataille, Ernest Hemingway, and André Malraux, and their reaction to the illogic and senselessness of the late 1930s trials in Moscow, implicitly pointing out their inevitable disenchantment and awakening (especially p. 22 and p. 26).

68. Kershaw, *Hitler 1936–45*, p. 573.

69. Vladislav Zubok, *Zhivago's Children: The Last Russian Intelligentsia* (Cambridge, Mass.: Harvard University Press, 2009), pp. 561–62.

1. UTOPIAN RADICALISM AND DEHUMANIZATION

1. Here I take issue with those interpretations that regard Marxism as an ideological counterpart to different versions of Fascism. Whereas Marxism is doubtless a revolutionary theory, a critique of liberal-bourgeois modernity, its main thrust is related to the democratic heritage of the Enlightenment (a point also made by Shlomo Avineri). Fascism, by contrast, rejected liberal individualism and democracy without any claim to fulfilling these "mediocre" projects. There is therefore no way to invoke a "betrayed" Fascist original doctrine and therefore no possibility to think of "another Nazism" or "dissident, humanist Fascism." For the line of thought I take issue with, see A. James Gregor, *The Faces of Janus: Marxism and Fascism in the Twentieth Century* (New Haven, Conn.: Yale University Press, 2000). In a similar vein, Gorbachev's former chief ideologue, Alexander Yakovlev, found the seeds of totalitarian terror, especially the war against the peasantry, in the *Communist Manifesto*. In my view (and here I follow Hannah Arendt, Claude Lefort, Cornelius Castoriadis, Richard Pipes, and Robert C. Tucker), the continuity between Marx and Lenin was fundamental. Fascism, and especially Nazism, did not find its origin in a distorted interpretation of the democratic search for emancipation.

It is important to acknowledge that Lenin had a less fanatical perspective on this issue, discarding calls for the total destruction of the bourgeoisie and admitting the need to recruit members of the former capitalist class into the construction of the new order. See George Legget, *The Cheka: Lenin's Secret Police* (Oxford: Oxford University Press, 1981), p. 115. Ernst Nolte invoked Zinoviev's exterminist statement, made at the beginning of "Red Terror," as a main argument for his historical precedence, "Schreckbild" theory of Nazism as a "counterfaith" opposed to Bolshevism. See Ernst Nolte, *La guerre civile européenne, 1917–1945: National-socialisme et bolchévisme* (Paris: Editions des Syrtes, 2000), pp. 24 and 90. For the precedence approach, see also Richard Pipes, *The Russian Revolution* (New York: Vintage Books, 1990): "Like the French Jacobin, Lenin sought to build a world inhabited exclusively by 'good citizens.' . . . Lenin habitually described those whom he chose to designate as his regime's 'class enemies' in terms borrowed from the vocabulary of pest control, calling kulaks 'bloodsuckers,' 'spiders,' and leeches.' As early as January 1918 he used inflammatory language to incite the population to carry out pogroms 'over the rich, swindlers, and parasites. Variety here is a guarantee of vitality, of success and the attainment of the single objective: *the cleansing of Russia's soil of all harmful insects, of scoundrel fleas, bedbugs—the rich,* and so on.' Hitler would follow this example in regard to the leaders of German Social democracy, whom he thought of mainly as Jews, calling them in *Mein Kampf* '*Ungeziefer,*' or 'vermin,' fit only for extermination" (Pipes, pp. 790–91). On the issue of radical evil *(das radikal Böse)* and totalitarianism, see Hannah Arendt's discussion in the *Origins,* and also Jorge Semprun, *L'écriture et la vie* (Paris: Gallimard, 1994), pp. 174–75: "A Buchenwald, les S.S., les Kapo, les mouchards, les tortionnaires sadiques, faisaient tout autant partie de l'espèce humaine que les meilleurs, les plus purs d'entre nous, d'entre les victimes. . . . La frontière du Mal n'est pas celle de l'inhumain, c'est tout autre chose. D'où la necessité d'une éthique qui transcende ce fonds originaire où s'enracine autant la liberté du Bien que celle du Mal . . . [At Buchenwald, the SS, the *Kapos,* the informers, the sadistic tortures were as much part of the human species as the best and the purest among us, from the victims. It follows from this premise the necessity of an ethics that transcends this original background in which are rooted both the liberty of Good and the one of Evil]."

2. Zygmunt Bauman, *Life in Fragments: Essays in Postmodern Morality* (Oxford and Cambridge, Mass.: Blackwell, 1995), pp. 192–206. On the concentration camps as the essence of both Communist and Nazi systems in their radical stages, see Tzvetan Todorov, *Voices from the Gulag: Life and Death in Communist Bulgaria* (University Park: Pennsylvania State Univesity Press, 1999), especially Istvan Deak's unequivocal foreword.

3. "Que fascisme et communisme ne souffrent pas d'un discrédit comparable s'explique d'abord par le caractère respectif des deux idéologies, qui s'opposent comme le particulier à l'universel. Annonciateur de la domination des forts, le fasciste vaincu ne donne plus à voir que ses crimes. Prophète de l'émancipation des hommes, le communiste bénéficie jusque dans sa faillite politique et morale de la douceur de ses intentions." See François Furet's letter to Ernst Nolte, in "Sur le fascisme, le communisme et l'histoire du XXe siècle," *Commentaire* 80 (Winter 1997–98): 804.

4. Eugen Weber, "Revolution? Counterrevolution? What Revolution?" *Journal of Contemporary History* 9, no. 2 (April 1974): 24–29. See also Jules Monnerot, *Sociology and Psychology of Communism,* trans. Jane Degras and Richard Rees (Boston: Beacon Press, 1953).

5. For a similar position on the Stalinism-Nazism comparison, see Ian Kershaw and Moshe Lewin, "Introduction. The Regimes and their Dictators: Perspectives of Comparison," in *Stalinism and Nazism: Dictatorships in Comparison* (New York: Cambridge University Press, 1997), p. 5.

6. Timothy Snyder, *Bloodlands: Europe between Hitler and Stalin* (New York: Basic Books, 2010), p. 380.

7. Peter Fritzsche, "Nazi Modern," *Modernism/Modernity* 3.1 (1996): p. 14.

8. George Lichtheim, *The Concept of Ideology and Other Essays* (New York: Random House, 1967), pp. 225–37.

9. Roger Griffin, *The Nature of Fascism* (London and New York: Routledge, 1993), pp. 36 and xi.

10. Richard Pipes, *The Russian Revolution* (New York: Vintage Books, 1991), p. 554–55.

11. Leszek Kołakowski, *Main Currents of Marxism: The Founders, the Golden Age, the Breakdown,* trans. P.S. Falla (New York: W.W. Norton, 2005), p. 422.

12. Nolte elaborated his main theses in a controversial book published in German in 1997 that came out in French translation with a preface by Stéphane Courtois, *La guerre civile européenne, 1917–1945: National-socialisme et bolchevisme* (Paris: Editions des Syrtes, 2000).

13. Roger Griffin, *Modernism and Fascism: The Sense of Beginning under Mussolini and Hitler* (London and New York: Palgrave Macmillan, 2007), pp. 9–10.

14. Karl Dietrich Bracher, *The German Dictatorship: The Origins, Structure, and Effects of National Socialism,* trans. Jean Steinberg with an introduction by Peter Gay (New York and Washington: Praeger, 1970), p. 9.

15. Peter Fritzsche and Jochen Hellbeck, "The New Man in Stalinist Russia and Nazi Germany," in *Beyond Totalitarianism: Stalinism and Nazism Compared,* ed. Michael Geyer and Sheila Fitzpatrick (New York: Cambridge University Press, 2009), p. 341.

16. Katerina Clark and Karl Schlögel, "Mutual Perceptions and Projections: Stalin's Russia in Nazi Germany—Nazi Germany in the Soviet Union," in *Beyond Totalitarianism,* ed. Geyer and Fitzpatrick, p. 412. The two authors discuss this communality and shared experiences of Germany and Russia/USSR, but they insist that "there is no Berlin-Moscow connection without Rome, and no Russia-German discourse without Italian fascism. These were the sites of synchronized historical experience of an entire epoch *[Synchronisierung von Epochenerfahrung]*" (p. 421).

17. Deitrich Beyrau, "Mortal Embrace: Germans and (Soviet) Russians in the First Half of the Twentieth Century," in "Fascination and Enmity: Russia and Germany as Entangled Histories, 1914–1945," special issue, *Kritika: Explorations in Russian and Eurasian History* 10, no. 3 (Summer 2009): 426.

18. Raymond Aron quoted in Pierre Rigoulot and Ilios Yannakakis, *Un pavé dans l'histoire: Le débat francais sur Le Livre Noir du communisme* (Paris: Robert Laffont, 1998), pp. 96–97.

19. On July 24, 1943, the Fascist Grand Council met for the first time since the beginning of the war. Its members voted 19–7 to request the king seek a policy more likely to save Italy from destruction. As Mussolini went to meet

with the king, the Grand Council informed Il Duce that Marshal Badoglio had been nominated prime minster and had the dictator arrested. Mussolini would later be freed by German paratroopers, but the ability of the supreme body of the National Fascist Party to depose Il Duce was in sharp contrast with the Nazi Party's inability to get rid of Hitler, to overcome the Führer principle. See Ian Kershaw, *Hitler 1936–45: Nemesis* (New York and London: W.W. Norton, 2000), pp. 593–99.

20. See the chapter "Losing All the Wars" in R.J.B. Bosworth, *Mussolini's Italy: Life under the Fascist Dictatorship 1915–1945* (London: Penguin Books, 2005).

21. Griffin, *Modernism and Fascism,* p. 181.

22. Ian Kershaw, *Hitler* (London: Penguin Books, 2009), p. xxxvii.

23. Ian Kershaw, *The 'Hitler Myth': Image and Reality in the Third Reich* (Oxford and New York: Oxford University Press, 1987), p. 173

24. Karl Dietrich Bracher, *The German Dictatorship,* p. 350.

25. Kershaw, *The 'Hitler Myth,'* p. 257.

26. Emilio Gentile, *The Sacralization of Politics in Fascist Italy* (Cambridge, Mass.: Harvard University Press, 1996), pp. 132–36.

27. Emilio Gentile, *The Struggle for Modernity: Nationalism, Futurism, and Fascism* (Westport, Conn., and London: Praeger Publishers, 2003), p. 138.

28. Bosworth, *Mussolini's Italy,* p. 421.

29. Igal Halfin, *From Darkness to Light: Class, Consciousness, and Salvation in Revolutionary Russia* (Pittsburgh, Penn.: University of Pittsburgh Press, 2000), pp. 156–57.

30. Erik van Ree, *The Political Thought of Joseph Stalin—a Study in Twentieth-Century Patriotism* (London and New York: Routledge Curzon, 2002), pp. 160–62.

31. Gentile quotes the fascist catechism of 1939: "The DUCE, Benito Mussolini, is the creator of Fascism, the renewer of civil society, the Leader of the Italian people, the founder of the Empire." In Gentile, *The Struggle for Modernity,* pp. 137–38.

32. Yoram Gorlizki and Hans Mommsen, "The Political (Dis)Orders of Stalinism and National Socialism," in *Beyond Totalitarianism,* ed. Geyer and Fitzpatrick, p. 85.

33. Kenneth Jowitt, *New World Disorder: The Leninist Extinction* (Berkeley: University of California Press, 1992), p. 4.

34. Bosworth, *Mussolini's Italy,* p. 506. In the first broadcast after his return to Italy (September 18, 1943), Mussolini announced that the new state would be "Fascist in a way that takes us back to our origins."

35. Quoted in Michael Burleigh, "Political Religion and Social Evil," *Totalitarian Movements and Political Religions* 3, no. 2 (Autumn 2002): 56.

36. Norman Naimark, "Stalin and the Question of Genocide," in *Political Violence: Belief, Behavior, and Legitimation,* ed. Paul Hollander (New York: Palgrave Macmillan, 2008), p. 47; Norman Naimark, *Stalin's Genocides* (Princeton, N.J.: Princeton University Press, 2010).

37. Ben Kiernan, *The Pol Pot Regime: Race, Power, and Genocide in Cambodia under the Khmer Rouge, 1975–1979* (New Haven, Conn., and London: Yale

University Press, 2002); Vladimir Tismaneanu, *Stalinism for All Seasons: A Political History of Romanian Communism* (Berkeley: University of California Press, 2003).

38. François Furet, *The Passing of an Illusion,* pp. 261 and 224.

39. Anson Rabinbach, "*Introduction: Legacies of Antifascism,*" in "Legacies of Antifascism," special issue, *New German Critique* 67 (Winter 1996): 14. Besides the articles from the special issue of the *New German Critique* that I quoted in this section, two others bring forth excellent insight about the anti-Fascism of Weimer Germany and of postwar Italy: Antonia Grunenberg, "Dichotomous Political Thought in Germany before 1933," and Leonardo Paggi, "Antifascism and the Reshaping of Democratic Consensus in Post-1945 Italy," in "Legacies of Antifascism," special issue, *New German Critique* 67 (Winter 1996).

40. Dan Diner and Christian Gundermann, "On the Ideology of Antifascism," in "Legacies of Antifascism," special issue, *New German Critique* 67 (Winter 1996): 123–32.

41. Geoff Eley, "Legacies of Antifascism: Constructing Democracy in Postwar Europe," in "Legacies of Antifascism," special issue, *New German Critique* 67 (Winter 1996): 75 and 81.

42. For an illuminating study on this topic, see Ekaterina Nikova, "Bulgarian Stalinism Revisited," in *Stalinism Revisited: The Establishment of Communist Regimes in East-Central Europe,* ed. Vladimir Tismaneanu (Budapest and New York: CEU Press, 2009).

43. Gale Stokes, ed., *From Stalinism to Pluralism: A Documentary History of Eastern Europe since 1945* (New York and Oxford: Oxford University Press, 1996), pp. 38–42.

44. Kołakowski, *Main Currents,* p. 885. For the latest account of the "philosophy debate" and of the post-1945 ideological offensive against science in the USSR, see Ethan Pollock, *Stalin and the Soviet Science Wars* (Princeton, N.J., and Oxford: Princeton University Press, 2006). For Zhdanovism (its origins, nature, and impact), see Kees Boterbloem, *The Life and Times of Andrei Zhdanov, 1896–1948* (Montreal: McGill-Queen's University Press, 2004). Boterbloem shows how the cultural wars of 1946–48 were "dress rehearsed" as early as 1940 (pp. 210–13). Between 1945 and 1947, there was no attempt by Stalin to liberalize or reform the regime (despite the populace's expectations and signals along these lines within the Politburo). On the contrary, during those years there was continuity with the prewar situation and a noticeable radicalization by means of the reignition of the politics of purge. See Michael Parrish, *The Lesser Terror: Soviet State Security, 1939–1953* (New York: Praeger, 1996); and Yoram Gorlizki and Oleg Khlevniuk, *Cold Peace: Stalin and the Soviet Ruling Circle, 1945–1953* (Oxford: Oxford University Press, 2004).

45. Anne Applebaum, *Gulag: A History* (Anchor Books, 2003), pp. 436–37; and Richard Overy's review of this book, "A World Built on Slavery," *Daily Telegraph,* May 20, 2003.

46. Snyder, *Bloodlands,* p. 328.

47. For a telling account of the paradoxes and pitfalls of the European anti-Fascist Left in the aftermath of the Second World War, see Simone de Beauvoir's novel *The Mandarins* (New York: W.W. Norton, 1991).

48. Quoted in Alexander Bloom, *Prodigal Sons: The New York Intellectuals and Their World* (New York: Oxford University Press, 1986), p. 232.

49. Michael Burleigh called this practice an act of indulging in "vicarious utopianism."

50. Tony Judt, *Past Imperfect: French Intellectuals, 1944–1956* (Berkeley: California University Press, 1992), p. 75.

51. Anson Rabinbach, "Introduction," p. 17. I do agree with Henri Rousso's rebuke of those who consider that anti-Fascism has run its historical course and argue that it is not relevant for the analysis of recent history. The absence of an identifiable adversary does not preclude the danger of totalitarian repeat or seduction. Having anti-Fascism and anti-Communism as inherent facets of European culture is crucial in learning from and avoiding the last century's ideological hubris. Rousso argues that "[to the position] that antifascism continues to prosper despite the fact that its target disappeared more than a half century ago, we could reply that anti-communism finds itself in an identical situation today, for while there is no real adversary, there is nevertheless a temptation to create one out of whole cloth." Henry Rousso, "Introduction: The Legitimacy of an Empirical Comparison," in *Stalinism and Nazism*, p. 5.

52. See Marcel Gauchet, *A l'épreuve des totalitarismes* (Paris: Gallimard, 2010).

53. Martin Malia, "Foreword: The Uses of Atrocity," in Stéphane Courtois, Nicolas Werth, Jean-Louis Panné, Andrzej Paczkowski, Karel Bartošek, and Jean-Louis Margolin, *The Black Book of Communism: Crimes, Terror, Repression,* ed. Mark Kramer, trans. Jonathan Murphy (Cambridge, Mass.: Harvard University Press, 1999), p. xvii. Courtois and several collaborators put together a follow-up to the Livre Noir, *Du passé nous faisons table rase! Histoire et mémoire du communisme en Europe* (Paris: Laffont, 2002).

54. For an insightful approach to ideological despotisms, see Daniel Chirot, *Modern Tyrants: The Power and Prevalence of Evil in Our Age* (New York: Free Press, 1994). I examined the relationship between ideology and terror in Leninist regimes in my book *The Crisis of Marxist Ideology in Eastern Europe: The Poverty of Utopia* (London and New York: Routledge, 1988). Daniel Chirot's review essay on *The Black Book* can be found in *East European Politics and Societies* 14, no. 3 (Fall 2000).

55. V.I. Lenin, *The Proletarian Revolution and the Renegade Kautsky* (Beijing: Foreign Languages Press, 1972), p. 11.

56. Vyshinsky quoted in Stéphane Courtois, in "Crimes, Terror, Repression," his conclusion to *The Black Book of Communism* (Cambridge, Mass.: Harvard University Press, 1999), p. 750.

57. For this argument and Arendt's quote, see Philippe Burrin, "Political Religion: The Relevance of a Concept," *History and Memory* 9, nos. 1–2 (1997): 338.

58. Ian Kershaw, *Hitler, the Germans, and the Final Solution* (New Haven, Conn., and London: Yale University Press, 2008); Jeffrey Herf, *The Jewish Enemy: Nazi Propaganda during World War II and the Holocaust* (Cambridge, Mass.: Harvard University Press, 2006) .

59. Andrei Oisteanu, *Inventing the Jew: Antisemitic Stereotypes in Romanian and Other Central-East European Cultures* (Lincoln: University of Nebraska

Press, 2009); Jan T. Gross, *Fear: Anti-semitism in Poland after Auschwitz* (New York: Random House, 2006).

60. E.A. Rees *Political Thought from Machiavelli to Stalin Revolutionary Machiavellism* (New York: Palgrave MacMillan, 2004), p. 99.

61. Fyodor Dostoyevski, *Demons,* trans. Richard Pevear and Larissa Volokhonsky, intro. Joseph Frank (New York: Knopf, 2000). One of the characters in the novel became the symbol of a mentality often referred to as *shigalyovshchina,* described by noted Dostoyevsky scholar Joseph Frank as "social–political demagogy and posturing with a tendency to propose extreme measures and total solutions" (p. 727). Needless to add, for many critics of Bolshevism, Lenin was an emblematic exponent of this mindset.

62. E.A. Rees, *Political Thought,* p. 132.

63. Emilio Gentile and Robert Mallett, "The Sacralisation of Politics," p. 52.

64. Michael Scammell, "The Price of an Idea," *New Republic,* December 20, 1999, p. 41.

65. I am responding here to some observations made by Hiroaki Kuromiya in his review article "Communism and Terror," *Journal of Contemporary History* 36, no. 1 (January 2001): 191–201. I consider that his conclusion that "the issue of terror will remain important, it will no doubt be studied merely as part (if a central part) of a larger episode in world history" needs one caveat. Communism is indeed part of a larger framework in world history, that of the ascendance of *radical evil,* in our times as man fell victim to statolatry (Luigi Sturzo), when the ends superseded any considerations about the means, when human beings became superfluous. Communism did generate consequences not produced by any other revolution or terror, besides the Fascist one. This is a point consistently overlooked in other reactions to the *Black Book,* such as Ronald Grigor Suny, "Obituary or Autopsy? Historians Look at Russia/USSR in the Short Twentieth Century," *Kritika: Explorations in Russian and Eurasian History* 3, no. 2 (Spring 2002): 303–19; or Ronald Aronson, "Communism's Posthumous Trial," *History and Theory* 42, no. 2 (May 2003): 222–45. One can try and situate in the same category the genocide in Rwanda and that in Ukraine (as Aronson does), just for the sake of a Manichean capitalism versus Communism polarity, but it is hardly knowledge-productive. One can argue about terror as an epiphenomenon of specific historical circumstances (civil war, famine, capitalist offensive, etc., as Suny does), but the criminal nature of the Soviet regime lay bare from its inception (e.g., in the RFSR 1918 Constitution).

66. Tony Judt, "The Longest Road to Hell," *New York Times,* December 22, 1997, A27.

67. See Rigoulot and Yannakakis, *Un pavé dans l'histoire.*

68. Personal conversation with Annette Wieworka, Washington, D.C., November 13, 2010. I also discussed extensively these issues with Stephane Courtois at the Sighet, Romania, Summer School on the "Memory of Communism," June 2009.

69. Snyder, *Bloodlands,* pp. 402 and 406.

70. Kershaw, *Hitler 1936–45,* p. 462.

71. Christopher R. Browning and Lewis H. Siegelbaum, "Frameworks for Social Engineering. Stalinist Schema of Identification and the Nazi *Volksgemeinschaft*," in *Beyond Totalitarianism,* ed. Geyer and Fitzpatrick, p. 262.

72. Igal Halfin, "Intimacy in an Ideological Key: The Communist Case of the 1920s and 1930s," in *Language and Revolution: Making Modern Political Identities,* ed. Igal Halfin (London: Frank Cass Publishers, 2002), p. 175.

73. See Tony Judt, "The Longest Road to Hell." Amir Weiner also makes an excellent point on this issue: "When Stalin's successors opened the gates of the Gulag, they allowed 3 million inmates to return home. When the Allies liberated the Nazi death [concentration] camps, they found thousands of human skeletons barely alive awaiting what they knew to be inevitable execution." See Amir Weiner's review of the *Black Book of Communism* in *Journal of Interdisciplinary History* 32, no. 2 (Winter 2002): 450–52.

74. Ian Kershaw, "Reflections on Genocide and Modernity," in *In God's Name: Genocide and Religion in the Twentieth Century,* ed. Omer Bartov and Phyllis Mack (Oxford: Berghahn, 2001), pp. 381–82.

75. Kershaw, *Hitler 1936–45,* p. 470.

76. Stéphane Courtois, "Introduction: The Crimes of Communism," in *The Black Book,* p. 23.

77. Jeffrey Herf, "Unjustifiable Means," *Washington Post,* January 23, 2000, pp. X09. Herf, however, adds an important caveat to his argument (one stressed by other scholars discussing the *Black Book*): the crimes of Communism were a constant focus of scholarship and of official discourse during the Cold War, while the Holocaust intensively preoccupied academia and the public only starting in the 1970s.

78. Scammell, "The Price of an Idea," p. 41.

79. "Vilnius declaration of the OSCE parliamentary assembly and resolutions adopted at the eighteenth annual session" (Vilnius, June 29 to July 3, 2009), http://www.oscepa.org/images/stories/documents/activities/1.Annual%20Session/2009_Vilnius/Final_Vilnius_Declaration_ENG.pdf. The Prague Declaration and the OSCE Resolution are hardly singular. Other official, pan-European or trans-Atlantic documents have been made to condemn the criminality of Communism and Stalinism following the example of the criminalization of Fascism and Nazism, for example, the EU Parliament resolution on European conscience and totalitarianism or the building of the Victims of Communism Memorial in Washington, D.C. This monument was dedicated by President George W. Bush on Tuesday, June 12, 2007. June 12 was chosen because it was the twentieth anniversary of President Ronald Reagan's famous Brandenburg Gate speech. See http://www.globalmuseumoncommunism.org/voc.

80. Quoted in Carolyn J. Dean, "Recent French Discourses on Stalinism, Nazism and 'Exorbitant' Jewish Memory," *History and Memory* 18, no. 1 (Spring–Summer 2006): 43–85. Though I disagree with Carolyn Dean's conclusions regarding authors such as Furet, Courtois, Besançon, and Todorov, I think her detailed presentation of the French debate on "which is more evil, Communism or Nazism" shows the intrinsic fallacy of such an argumentation: it is a dead end knowledge-wise, for any resolution on the topic will always be partisan.

81. Ibid., p. 73.

82. For recent analysis of the fate of the *Black Book of Nazi Crimes against the Soviet Jews,* see Amir Weiner, *Making Sense of War: The Second World War and the Fate of the Bolshevik Revolution (*Princeton, N.J.: Princeton University Press, 2001); and Jonathan Brent and Vladimir Naumov, *Stalin's Last Crime: The Plot against the Jewish Doctors* (New York: HarperCollins, 2003).

83. Igal Halfin, "Introduction," in *Language and Revolution: Making Modern Political Identities,* ed. Igal Halfin (London: Frank Cass Publishers, 2002), p. 6.

84. Christian Gerlach and Nicolas Werth, "State Violence—Violent Societies," in *Beyond Totalitarianism,* ed. Geyer and Fitzpatrick, p. 213.

85. Eric D. Weitz, "On Certainties and Ambivalences: Reply to My Critics," *Slavic Review* 61, no. 1 (Spring 2002): 63. See the other contributions to the debate stirred by Weitz's initial article: Eric D. Weitz, "Racial Politics without the Concept of Race: Reevaluating Ethnic and National Purges," *Slavic Review* 61, no. 1 (Spring 2002): 1–29. He received replies from Francine Hirsch, "Race without the Practice of Racial Politics," *Slavic Review* 61, no. 1 (Spring 2002): 30–43; Amir Weiner, "Nothing but Certainty," *Slavic Review,* vol. 61, no. 1 (Spring 2002): 44–53; and Alaina Lemon, "Without a 'Concept'? Race as Discursive Practice," *Slavic Review,* vol. 61, no. 1 (Spring 2002): 54–61. Peter Fritzsche offered, later on, interesting responses to Weitz's approach in "Genocide and Global Discourse," *German History* 23, no. 1 (2005): 96–111.

86. Halfin, "Introduction," in *Language and Revolution,* p. 5.

87. Golfo Alexopoulos, "Soviet Citizenship, More or Less Rights, Emotions, and States of Civic Belonging," *Kritika: Explorations in Russian and Eurasian History* 7, no. 3 (Summer 2006): 487–528; and Golfo Alexopoulos, *Stalin's Outcasts: Aliens, Citizens, and the Soviet State, 1926–1936* (Ithaca, N.Y.: Cornell University Press, 2003). Alexopoulos's research leads us to a conclusion similar to Jowitt's: "The practice of giving and taking rights for political purposes produced a highly fragmented society where individuals experienced different and unstable states of civic belonging" (p. 490). Similarly, Jowitt argued that "the critical issue facing Leninist regimes was citizenship. The political individuation of an article potential citizenry treated contemptuously by an inclusive (not democratic), neotraditional (not modernized) Leninist polity was the cause of Leninist breakdown." Ken Jowitt, "Weber, Trotsky and Holmes on the Study of Leninist Regimes," *Journal of International Affairs* (2001): 44.

88. Golfo Alexopoulos, "Soviet Citizenship," p. 521. It should be noted here that Alexopoulos makes this statement in agreement with Weitz's racialization thesis.

89. The UN Convention on the Prevention and Punishment of the Crime of Genocide provides the following definition: "Genocide means any of the following acts committed with intent to destroy, in whole or in part, a national, ethnical, racial or religious group, as such: (a) killing members of the group; (b) causing serious bodily or mental harm to members of the group; (c) deliberately inflicting on the group conditions of life calculated to bring about its physical destruction in whole or in part; (d) imposing measures intended to prevent births within the group; (e) forcibly transferring children of the group to another group."

90. Stephen Kotkin, *The Magnetic Mountain* (Berkeley: University of California Press, 1995), p. 17.

91. Omer Bartov, "Extreme Opinions," *Kritika: Explorations in Russian and Eurasian History* 3, no. 2 (Spring 2002): 281–302.

92. Igal Halfin, "Intimacy in an Ideological Key," p. 175.

93. Both quotations are from David Priestland, *Stalinism and the Politics of Mobilization: Ideas, Power, and Terror in Inter-War Russia* (Oxford and New York: Oxford University Press, 2007), pp. 397–98 and 388.

94. For the role of excision in Soviet population politics, see Amir Weiner, "Nature, Nurture, and Memory in a Socialist Utopia: Delineating the Soviet Socio-Ethnic Body in the Age of Socialism," *American Historical Review* 104, no. 4 (October 1999): 1114–55.

95. Andre Liebich, *From the Other Shore: Russian Social Democracy after 1921* (Cambridge, Mass.: Harvard University Press, 1997).

96. Michael Scammell, "The Price of an Idea," p. 41.

97. Griffin, *Modernism and Fascism,* pp. 332–33. See also Enzo Traverso, *The Origins of Nazi Violence* (London: New Press, 2003), pp. 136 and 144.

98. Nicolas Werth, "Strategies of Violence in the Stalinist USSR," in *Stalinism and Nazism: History and Memory Compared,* ed. Henry Rousso, English language edition edited and introduced by Richard J. Golsan, trans. Lucy B. Golsan, Thomas C. Hilde, and Peter S. Rogers (Lincoln and London: University of Nebraska Press, 2004), p. 90. As pointed out by Werth, Overy, Martin, and Applebaum, legal decisions such as Article 58–10 of the Soviet Penal Code, the State Theft Law of 1947, the 1933 instructions adding to the existent 1924 resolution of the TsIK regarding *sotsvredbye* (socially harmful) elements, NKVD Decrees 00447 and 00485, etc., generated an ever-widening array of criteria for criminalizing larger and larger sections of Soviet society.

99. Both quotes come from Dan Diner, *Cataclysms: A History of the Twentieth Century from Europe's Edge* (Madison: University of Wisconsin Press, 2007), p. 185. For his discussion of the role of forced labor under Soviet Communism, see pp. 191–93.

100. Richard Overy, *The Dictators: Hitler's Germany and Stalin's Russia* (London and New York: Penguin Books, 2005), p. 595.

101. Georgi Dimitrov, *The Diary of Georgi Dimitrov, 1943–1949,* ed. Ivo Banac (New Haven, Conn.: Yale University Press, 2003), p. 65.

102. For discussions about "Soviet subjectivity," see Igal Halfin, "Intimacy in an Ideological Key" and Jochen Hellbeck, "Working, Struggling, Becoming: Stalin-Era Autobiographical Texts," in *Language and Revolution,* ed. Igor Halfin, pp. 114–35. See also Jochen Hellbeck, "Speaking Out: Languages of Affirmation and Dissent in Stalinist Russia," *Kritika: Explorations in Russian and Eurasian History* 1, no. 1 (Winter 2000): 71–96; and Igal Halfin, "Between Instinct and Mind: The Bolshevik View of the Proletarian Self," *Slavic Review* 62, no. 1 (Spring 2003): 34–40. For a critique of this approach, see Aleksandr Ėtkind, "Soviet Subjectivity: Torture for the Sake of Salvation?" *Kritika: Explorations in Russian and Eurasian History* 6, no. 1 (Winter 2005): 171–86.

103. Quoted in David Priestland, *Stalinism and The Politics of Mobilization,* p. 293.

104. Gentile, *The Sacralization of Politics,* p. 94.

105. For this point, see Richard Overy, *The Dictators,* p. 633.

106. Igal Halfin, "Introduction," p. 14.

107. Orlando Figes, *The Whisperers: Private Life in Stalin's Russia* (New York: Metropolitan Books, 2007), p. 116.

108. Dan Diner, *Cataclysms,* pp. 192–93. A side comment to this discussion could be a reminder that in a Communist system the meaning and significance of forced labor should be explained starting from Marxian terminology. According to Marx, labor was "the aggregate of those mental and physical capabilities which a human being exercises whenever he produces." Robert C. Tucker, ed., *The Marx-Engels Reader,* 2d ed. (New York and London: W. W. Norton), p. 309. Therefore, forced labor in the gulag represented a method of exhausting individuals, of absolute takeover of the self. The *zeks* were *spent* human beings. This is maybe one of the crucial lessons offered by authors such as Aleksandr Solzhenitsyn, Nadejda Mandelstam, and Varlam Shalamov. For the liminal nature of gulag experience, what German philosopher Karl Jaspers defined as *Grenzsituationen* (limit-situations), and the impossibility of communicating it, see the chapters "Return" and "Memory," in Figes, *The Whisperers,* pp. 535–656.

109. After 1945, the gulag increasingly merged with the civilian economy, which was being transformed into "a vast industrial empire" (in the words of Figes). It also became more and more unmanageable, and the consequences of "the culture of the champs" deepened its "contamination" potential. Upon Stalin's death, but also before it, the gulag was seriously shaken by large uprisings such as that of Norilsk. For a short history of the latter, see Figes, *The Whisperers,* pp. 529–34.

110. Overy, *The Dictators,* p. 643.

111. Werth, "Stalin's System during the 1930s," in *Stalinism and Nazism,* ed. Henri Rousso, pp. 74–75. In this contribution Werth identifies four interrelated types of violence in Stalin: "The first arose out of the paranoia of a dictator constructing his own cult against 'comrades in arms'; . . . terror directed at Party or economic cadres; . . . virtual criminalization of the daily behavior or 'ordinary' citizens; . . . violence exercised against a number of non-Russian ethic groups." This rule of arbitrariness for the sake of the etatization of Utopia is best summarized by Dan Diner in the following statement: "In the heyday of Stalinism, despotism and fear were the elixir of rule." Diner, *Cataclysms,* p. 191.

112. Timothy Snyder, "Holocaust: The Ignored Reality" *New York Review of Books* 56, no. 12, July 16, 2009, http://www.nybooks.com/articles/22875.

113. Ibid.

114. Snyder, *Bloodlands,* p. 406.

115. Peter Fritzsche, "On Being the Subjects of History: Nazis as Twentieth-Century Revolutionaries," in *Language and Revolution,* ed. Igal Halfin, p. 151.

116. Norman Naimark, "Totalitarian States and the History of Genocide," *Telos* 136, (Fall 2006): 14. In his piece, Naimark underlines the fact that the author of the concept, Raphael Lemkin, "was convinced that the international community should mount a legal initiative against states that attacked peoples, religious groups, racial minorities, and outlier political groups" (p. 15). Moreover, "all of the early drafts of the Genocide Convention, including the initial

U.N. Secretariat draft of May 1947, included political groups in their definition. The Soviets, Poles, and even some non-communist members of the committees and drafting commissions objected" (p. 17).

117. Dan Diner, *Cataclysms*, p. 90.

118. Souvarine (sometimes spelled Suvarin), quoted in *The Black Book*, 296.

119. See his profound book *Le malheur du siècle: Sur le communisme, le nazisme et l'unicité de la Shoah* (Paris: Fayard, 1998).

120. Bartov, "Extreme Opinions," p. 287.

121. I am paraphrasing Bartov. He gives a commendable portrait of the dogmatic mind: "One had to lie blatantly and consistently to oneself and one's society to make Bolshevism palatable." Ibid., p. 286.

122. Dan Diner, "Remembrance and Knowledge: Nationalism and Stalinism in Comparative Discourse," in *The Lesser Evil: Moral Approaches to Genocide Practices,* ed. Helmut Dubiel and Gabriel Motzkin (New York and London: Routledge, 2004), pp. 86–87.

123. For an excellent discussion on the differences between the gulag and the Holocaust and the process by which the latter's memory has been sacralized, see Gabriel Motzkin, "The Memory of Crime and the Formation of Identity," in *The Lesser Evil,* ed. Dubiel and Motzkin.

124. Helmut Dubiel, "The Remembrance of the Holocaust as a Catalyst for a Transnational Ethnic?" in "Taboo, Trauma, Holocaust," special issue, *New German Critique* 90 (Autumn 2003): 59–70.

125. See Krzystof Pomian, "Communisme et nazisme: Les tragédies du siecle," *L'Histoire* (July–August 1998): 100–105. For a similar view, see Michael Scammel's review of *The Black Book*. In his review, Scammell notices that, in the American edition, some chapters lack bibliographies. In fact, at least in the case of the chapter dealing with Central and South-East Europe, authored by Karel Bartosek, the French edition included a list of further readings that was strangely deleted from the American translation. Indeed, one of my own books published in Romanian in 1996 was mentioned in Bartosek's bibliography (*Fantoma lui Gheorghiu-Dej,* Bucharest, 1995).

126. Peter Gay, *Freud, Jews and Other Germans: Masters and Victims in Modernist Culture* (New York: Oxford University Press, 1978). He defines comparative trivialization thus: "At its heart lies the device of acknowledging Nazi atrocities but, as it were, 'humanizing' them by pointing, indignantly, at crimes committed by others—crimes presumably as vicious as those perpetrated in the Third Reich . . . its historical function is to cover the special horror of German barbarity between 1933 and 1945, and to divert attention from studying barbarity in its own—that is to say, its German context" (pp. xi–xiv).

127. Quoted by Stéphane Courtois in his conclusion to *The Black Book,* p. 751.

128. I don't share philosopher Avishai Margalit's view that the ideological premises of Communism, universalistic and humanist at least in the Marxism texts, would make the application of the radical evil concept inaccurate. But Margalit's analysis of the differences between opportunistic and principled compromises remains illuminatingly useful. See his book *On Compromise and Rotten Compromises* (Princeton, N.J.: Princeton University Press, 2010).

129. Alain Besançon, "Mémoire et oubli du communisme," *Commentaire,* no. 80 (Winter 1997–98): 789–93. The essay was translated as "Forgotten Communism" in the American journal *Commentary* 105, no. 1 (January 1998): 24–27.

130. Omer Bartov, "Extreme Opinions," p. 295.

131. Katerina Clark, *Petersburg: Crucible of Cultural Revolution* (Cambridge, Mass.: Harvard University Press, 1995), pp. 2–3.

132. Martin Malia, "Foreword," in *The Black Book,* ed. Stéphane Courtois, p. xx.

133. Ian Kershaw, *The Nazi Dictatorship—Problems and Perspectives of Interpretation,* 4th ed. (London: Arnold Publishers, 2000), pp. 36–38.

134. Lawrence Olivier, *Canadian Journal of Political Science / Revue canadienne de science politique* 33, no. 2 (June 2000): p. 399.

135. Ronald Grigor Suny, "Obituary or Autopsy?" p. 319.

136. Igal Halfin lists the categories defined by Chapter 13 of the Declaration: "(1) The so-called former people (*byvshie liudi*)—primarily religious functionaries and employees of the tsarist police and military; (2) class aliens—landowners, individuals who lived off unearned income, exploiters, private trades; (3) administrative exiles and individuals who had their rights suspended by a court; (4) individuals economically dependent on the previously listed; and (5) the mentally ill." It is not difficult to see how these categories could balloon to the dimensions of an out-out war against society, as discussed above. See Igal Halfin, *From Darkness to Light: Class, Consciousness, and Salvation in Revolutionary Russia* (Pittsburgh, Penn.: University of Pittsburgh Press, 2000). Of course, Suny could argue that this document falls in line with the principle that "some omelets that are worth broken eggs, but, as anyone making breakfast knows, first one should make sure that all the ingredients are available and remember that eggs must be broken delicately, not smashed so that yokes, whites, and shells all get cooked together" ("Obituary," p. 318).

137. Tony Judt, "The Longest Road to Hell," p. A27.

138. Omer Bartov, "Extreme Opinions," p. 295.

139. Emilio Gentile and Robert Mallett "The Sacralisation of Politics: Definitions, Interpretations and Reflections on the Question of Secular Religion and Totalitarianism," *Totalitarian Movements and Political Religions* 1, no. 1 (2000): p. 52.

140. In my view, the best analysis of the intellectual origins and transmogrifications of Communism and Fascism remains Jacob L. Talmon, *Myth of the Nation and Vision of the Revolution: Ideological Polarizations in the Twentieth Century* (New Brunswick, N.J., and London: Transaction, 1991), with a new introduction by Irving Louis Horowitz (originally published by the University of California Press in 1981).

141. Evans, *The Coming,* p. 324.

142. Griffin, *Modernism and Fascism,* pp. 220 and 240.

143. Snyder, *Bloodlands,* p. 65.

144. *The Black Book,* p. 755.

145. See Weber, "Revolution?" p. 43.

2. DIABOLICAL PEDAGOGY AND THE (IL)LOGIC OF STALINISM

1. Slavoj Žižek, *In Defense of Lost Causes* (London and New York: Verso, 2008), pp. 211–63.

2. One could argue, however, that the activities of the People's Court in Nazi Germany in the context of the obvious defeat in the war came very close to Soviet show trials. This institution functioned similarly to Stalin's courts during the Great Terror when trying the group led by Claus Schenk Graf von Stauffenberg , which tried to assassinate Hitler in July 1944 in a failed attempt commonly known as Operation Valkyrie. See Hans Mommsen, *Germans against Hitler: The Stauffenberg Plot and Resistance under the Third Reich* (London: Tauris, 2009).

3. Ian Kershaw, *Hitler, the Germans, and the Final Solution* (New Haven, Conn., and London: Yale University Press, 2008), p. 400.

4. For one of the most thoughtful and still valid interpretations of the dynamics of the Soviet bloc, see Zbigniew Brzezinski, *The Soviet Bloc: Unity and Conflict* (Cambridge, Mass.: Harvard University Press, 1967).

5. For a detailed discussion, see Vladimir Tismaneanu, *The Crisis of Marxist Ideology in Eastern Europe: The Poverty of Utopia* (London and New York: Routledge, 1988).

6. Claude Lefort, *The Political Forms of Modern Society: Bureaucracy, Democracy, Totalitarianism,* ed. John B. Thompson (Cambridge: Polity Press, 1986), p. 299.

7. G. R. Urban, ed., *Stalinism—Its Impact on Russia and the World* (London: Maurice Temple Smith, 1982), pp. 103–4.

8. John V. Fleming, *The Anti-Communist Manifestos: Four Books that Shaped the Cold War* (New York and London: W. W. Norton, 2009), pp. 21–95.

9. J. Arch Getty and Oleg V. Naumov, *The Road to Terror: Stalin and the Self-Destruction of the Bolsheviks, 1932–1939* (New Haven, Conn., and London: Yale University Press, 1999), p. 527.

10. For "Lenin's Testament" (his letters to the Party Congress), see Robert Service, *Lenin: A Biography* (Cambridge: Belknap Press, 2000), pp. 464–80.

11. Robert C. Tucker, *The Soviet Political Mind: Stalinism and Post-Stalin Change,* rev. ed. (New York: W. W. Norton, 1971), p. 81.

12. Getty and Naumov, *The Road to Terror,* pp. 556–60.

13. Stephen F. Cohen, *Bukharin and the Bolshevik Revolution: A Political Biography, 1888–1938* (New York and Wildwood House: Oxford University Press, 1973), p. 378.

14. Tucker, *The Soviet Political Mind,* pp. 83–85.

15. Cohen, *Bukharin,* pp. 370–71.

16. In a conversation with Lev Kamenev (July 11, 1928) later published abroad by the Trotskyites, Bukharin declared, "Stalin knows only vengeance. We must remember his theory of sweet revenge." According to Tucker, "This was a reference to something that Stalin had said one summer night in 1923 to Kamenev and Dzerzhinsky: 'To choose one's victim, to prepare one's plans minutely, to slake an implacable vengeance, and then to go to bed . . . . There is nothing sweeter in the world' " Tucker, *The Soviet Political Mind,* p. 57.

17. See Vladimir Tismaneanu, "Suicides within the Top Communist Nomen-klatura: The Case of Mirel Costea," *Studies and Materials of Contemporary History,* Academia Română, Institutul de Istorie "Nicolae Iorga," n.s., vols. 9–10, pp. 138–153 [in Romanian with an English summary]. Once I obtained the above-mentioned documents, I published on my personal blog a short article about Costea's tragedy. Soon thereafter I was approached by one of his daughters, Dana Silvan, who lives in Israel. She wrote me that neither she nor her sister (now living in the United States) had any idea that their father had left that last message to them. Her interpretation is that, in emphasizing his boundless loyalty to the party, Costea was in fact trying to protect his wife and his daughters. For the meaning of the Pătrășcanu affair, see my book *Stalinism for All Seasons: A Political History of Romanian Communism* (Berkeley: University of California Press, 2003).

18. Ethan Pollock, "Stalin as the Coryphaeus of Science," in *Stalin: A New History,* ed. Sarah Davies and James Harris (Cambridge: Cambridge University Press, 2005), p. 272. He adds prior to the above quote: "Instead of revealing ulterior motives behind Stalin's actions, top secret documents are saturated with the same Marxist-Leninist language, categories, and frames for understanding the world that appeared in the public discourse." In *Times Literary Supplement* (January 28, 2000), Geoffrey Hosking made a similar remark in reference to the all-pervasiveness of Marxist-Leninist dogma: "Even when writing to each other in private they used the same language and articulated the same thoughts as in their public utterances."

19. Stephen Kotkin, *The Magnetic Mountain* (Berkeley: University of California Press, 1995), pp. 225–37; Stephen Kotkin, "1991 and the Russian Revolution: Sources, Conceptual Categories, Analytical Frameworks," *Journal of Modern History* 70, no. 2 (June 1998): 384–425; and "The State—Is It Us? Memoirs, Archives, and Kremlinologists," *Russian Review* 61 (January 2002): 35–51.

20. According to Stalin, unconditional support for and solidarity with the USSR, the homeland of socialism, was the touchstone of proletarian internationalism. This theory was used to justify the persecution and eventual elimination of all those Communists and other left-wingers who expressed the slightest reservation regarding the Soviet general line as codified by the leader and his associates. For the repression with the Third International apparatus in the USSR, see William J. Chase, *Enemies within the Gates? The Comintern and the Stalinist Repression, 1934–1939* (New Haven, Conn., and London: Yale University Press, 2001).

21. Roger Griffin, *Modernism and Fascism: The Sense of Beginning under Mussolini and Hitler* (London and New York: Palgrave Macmillan, 2007), p. 274.

22. For social engineering utopias in the twentieth century, see James C. Scott, *Seeing Like a State: How Certain Schemes to Improve the Human Condition Have Failed* (New Haven, Conn., and London: Yale University Press, 1998).

23. Karen Dawisha, "Communism as a Lived System of Ideas in Contemporary Russia," *East European Politics and Societies* 19, no. 3 (Summer 2005): 463–93.

24. The initial formulation along these lines came from Hugh Seton-Watson, *The East European Revolution* (New York: Praeger, 1951). Kenneth Jowitt added both conceptual and comparative flesh to this idea in his various articles and books throughout the years, first in his published PhD thesis, *Revolutionary Breakthroughs and National Development: The Case of Romania, 1944–1965* (Berkeley: University of California Press, 1971). Of course, for the Soviet Union, Stephen Kotkin and later Amir Weiner, with his *Making Sense of War: The Second World War and the Fate of the Bolshevik Revolution* (Princeton, N.J.: Princeton University Press, 2001), are maybe the most significant advocates of this idea.

25. I am paraphrasing here Mary Fulbrook's theory of the "octopus" state (in counterdistinction to the pyramidal conceptualization of the Soviet-type regimes). See Mary Fulbrook, "Reckoning with the Past: Heroes, Victims, and Villains in the History of the German Democratic Republic," in *Rewriting the German Past—History and Identity in the New Germany,* ed. Reinhard Alter and Peter Monteath (Atlantic Highlands, N.J.: Humanities Press, 1997), pp. 175–96; Mary Fulbrook, *The People's State: East German Society from Hitler to Honecker* (New Haven, Conn., and London: Yale University Press, 2005).

26. Quoted in François Furet, *The Passing of an Illusion: The Idea of Communism in the Twentieth Century,* trans. Deborah Furet (Chicago: University of Chicago Press, 1999), p. 541.

27. E.A. Rees, "The Sovietization of Eastern Europe," in *The Sovietization of Eastern Europe: New Perspectives on the Postwar Period,* ed. Balázs Apor, Péter Apor, and E.A. Rees (Washington, D.C.: New Academia Publishing, 2008), p. 13.

28. Kenneth Jowitt, *New World Disorder: The Leninist Extinction* (Berkeley and Los Angeles: University of California Press, 1992), pp. 1–12.

29. Norman Cohn, *The Pursuit of the Millennium: Revolutionary Messianism in Medieval and Reformation Europe and Its Bearing on Modern Totalitarian Movements* (New York: Harper and Row, 1961); Arthur Koestler, *The Invisible Writing* (London: Macmillan, 1969).

30. Aleksander Wat, *My Century,* foreword by Czesław Miłosz (New York: New York Review of Books, 1988), p. 92.

31. Georg Lukács, *The Destruction of Reason* (Atlantic Highlands, N.J.: Humanities Press International, 1981). On Lukács, see Leszek Kołakowski, *Main Currents of Marxism: The Founders, the Golden Age, the Breakdown,* trans. P.S. Falla (New York: W.W. Norton, 2005), pp. 989–1032. It remains disturbing that Lukács's abdications between 1929 and 1953 have been leniently treated by authors who seem less inclined to forget Heidegger's no less outrageous idyll with National Socialism.

32. Jochen Hellbeck, "Fashioning the Stalinist Soul," in *Stalinism: New Directions,* ed. Sheila Fitzpatrick (London and New York: Routledge, 2000), p. 111. Also see "Working, Struggling, Becoming: Stalin-Era Autobiographical Texts," *Russian Review,* no. 60 (July 2001): 340–59.

33. Jochen Hellbeck, *Revolution on My Mind: Writing a Diary under Stalin* (Cambridge: Harvard University Press, 2006), pp. 13–14. See also Igal Halfin, "Good and Evil in Communism," in *Terror in My Soul: Communist*

Autobiographies on Trial (Cambridge, Mass.: Harvard University Press, 2003). This subjective identification of victims with the system was very different in Nazi Germany, where a diarist like Victor Klemperer maintained a wounded lucidity. See Victor Klemperer, *I Will Bear Witness: A Diary of Nazi Years, 1933–1941* (New York: Random House, 1998); and *I Will Bear Witness: A Diary of the Nazi Years, 1942–1945* (New York: Random House, 1999).

34. Ferenc Fehér and Agnes Heller, *Eastern Left, Western Left: Totalitarianism, Freedom, and Democracy* (Atlantic Highlands, N.J.: Humanities Press International, 1987), pp. 265–66.

35. Alvin W. Gouldner, *Against Fragmentation: The Origins of Marxism and the Sociology of Intellectuals* (New York: Oxford University Press, 1985), pp. 260–61.

36. See the two volumes of Koestler's memoirs: Arthur Koestler, *Arrow in the Blue* (New York and London: Macmillan Collins, 1952); and *The Invisible Writing: The Second Volume of an Autobiography: 1932–40* (New York: Macmillan, 1954).

37. Tucker, *The Soviet Political Mind*, pp. 31 and 36.

38. Cohen, *Bukharin*, p. 268.

39. Ivan Margolius, *Reflections of Prague: Journeys through the Twentieth Century* (London: Wiley, 2006), p. 153.

40. Ibid., p. 193.

41. Ibid., pp. 220–21.

42. Ibid., pp. 226–27. See also Eugen Loebl, *My Mind on Trial* (New York and London: Harcourt Brace Jovanich, 1976).

43. Branko Lazitch in collaboration with Milorad M. Drachkovitch, *Biographical Dictionary of the Comintern* (Stanford, Calif.: Hoover Institution Press, 1986), p. 135.

44. Jorge Semprun, *Communsim in Spain in the Franco Era: The Autobiography of Federico Sánchez* (Brighton: Harvester Press, 1979), pp. 3–22.

45. For reasons of space, I cannot dwell in this chapter as much as I would wish on other similar frame-ups in Eastern Europe. I want to emphasize that there were cases in which the defendants (Communists or non-Communists) resisted psychological and physical torture and refused to endorse the Stalinist scripts through their confessions. Zavis Kálándra, mentioned in one of the epigraphs of this chapter, was a Czech surrealist poet who condemned the Moscow show trials, engaged in anti-Fascist resistance, and spent the war years in concentration camps. In 1950, he was a codefendant, together with democratic politician Milada Horáková, in a spectacular trial. The trial was a failure because most of the defendants challenged the prosecution. In spite of international pressures, including appeals from Albert Einstein, Eleanor Roosevelt, Winston Churchill, and André Breton, Kálándra, Horáková, and the others were sentenced to death and hanged.

46. Cohen, *Bukharin*, p. 227.

47. Max Horkheimer, *Dawn and Decline* (New York: Seabury Press, 1978), p. 239.

48. Hannah Arendt, *The Life of the Mind* (San Diego and New York: Harcourt Brace Jovanovich, 1978), p. 45.

49. Tucker, *The Soviet Political Mind,* pp. 40–41.

50. James G. Williams, ed., *The Girard Reader* (New York: Crossroad Publishing, 1996), p. 97–141. The same type of mechanism can be identified in the process of imagining the categories "saboteur" and *"kulak"* after 1929 in the USSR.

51. For the significance of this question in the Leninist mindset, see Martin Amis, *Koba the Dread: Laughter and the Twenty Million* (New York: Hyperion, 2002); Service, *Lenin.*

52. Cohen, *Bukharin,* p. 92.

53. Ibid., p. 91.

54. Riegel is paraphrasing here Yemelian Yaroslavsky, Bolshevik luminary and one of Stalin's most trusted party historians. See Klaus-Georg Riegel, "Confessions of Sins within Virtuosi Communities," in *Parler de soi sous Staline: La construction identitaire dans le communism des années trente,* ed. Brigitte Studer, Berthold Unfried, and Irène Hermann (Paris: Éditions de la Maison des Sciences de l'Homme, 2002), p. 116.

55. Igal Halfin, *From Darkness to Light; Terror in My Soul: Communist Autobiographies on Trial* (Cambridge, Mass.: Harvard University Press, 2003); *Intimate Enemies: Demonizing the Bolshevik Opposition, 1918–1928* (Pittsburgh, Penn.: University of Pittsburgh Press, 2007). The mechanisms described by Halfin are "local" manifestations of a more general phenomenon that S.N. Eisenstadt defined as "the ideological sacralization of revolutionary terror" in his book *Fundamentalism, Sectarianism, and Revolution: The Jacobin Dimension of Modernity* (Cambridge: Cambridge University Press, 1999).

56. Peter Haidu, "The Dialectics of Unspeakability: Language, Silence, and the Narratives of Desubjectification," in *Probing the Limits of Representation—Nazism and the "Final Solution,"* ed. Saul Friedlander (Cambridge, Mass., and London: Harvard University Press, 1992), p. 261.

57. Tucker, *The Soviet Political Mind,* pp. 68–69.

58. Philip Rahv, *Essays on Literature and Politics, 1932–1972* (Boston: Houghton Mifflin, 1978), p. 288.

59. Zbigniew Brzezinski, "The Pattern of Political Purges," in "The Satellites in Eastern Europe," special issue, *Annals of the American Academy of Political and Social Science* 317 (May 1958): 79–87.

60. See, for instance, Stanislao G. Pugliese, *Bitter Spring: A Life of Ignazio Silone* (New York: Farrar Straus and Giroux, 2009).

61. A.J. Polan, *Lenin and the End of Politics* (Berkeley: University of California, 1984).

62. Archie Brown, *The Rise and Fall of Communism* (London: Bodley Head, 2009), p. 37.

63. See Rees's comment on Russell in *The Sovietization of Eastern Europe,* ed. Apor, Apor, and Rees, pp. 9–10.

64. Jowitt, *New World Disorder,* pp. 250–62.

65. For a detailed description of the position of "party intellectuals" within the general Czechoslovak debates over national identity in the post-1945 period, under circumstances of a widespread perception among the elites of the interwar republic as a compromised state project, see Bradley F. Abrams, *The*

Struggle for the Soul of the Nation: Czech Culture and the Rise of Communism (Lanham, Md.: Rowman & Littlefield, 2004).

66. Catherine Epstein, *The Last Revolutionaries: German Communists and Their Century* (Cambridge, Mass: Harvard University Press, 2003).

67. Ivo Banac, *With Stalin against Tito: Cominformist Splits in Yugoslav Communism* (Ithaca, N.Y.: Cornell University Press, 1988), p. 29.

68. During his trip to Moscow via Bucharest in January 1948, Georgi Dimitrov visited his old friend Petre Pandrea (Pătrăşcanu's brother-in-law) and talked about issues related to the emerging conflict between Tito and Stalin. They knew each other from the early 1930s in Berlin, where Pandrea studied law and Dimitrov was active with the Comintern's Balkan Bureau. See Petre Pandrea, *Memoriile mandarinului valah* (Bucureşti: Albatros, 2000).

69. Brzezinski, *The Soviet Bloc,* p. 65.

70. Erica Wallach, *Light at Midnight* (New York: Doubleday, 1967), quoted in Margolius, *Reflections of Prague,* p. 193. A personal element: my mother and Erica Wallach were friends during the Spanish Civil War, when my mother worked as a nurse under the supervision of Dr. Glaser, Erica's father. Inasmuch as I know, during the 1951–52 investigations at the Party Control Commission in Bucharest, my mother was questioned regarding her Glaser-Slánsky connections. During World War II, both my parents worked for Radio Moscow's Romanian service, which was part of the Balkan Department subordinated to the Central-East European Section headed by Rudolf Slánský. For show trials and the psychology of true believers, see Egon Balas, *Will to Freedom: A Perilous Journey through Fascism and Communism* (Syracuse, N.Y.: Syracuse University Press, 2000), p. 219.

71. Brzezinski, *The Soviet Bloc,* p. 52.

72. George H. Hodos, *Show Trials: Stalinist Purges in Eastern Europe, 1948–1954* (New York: Praeger, 1987), pp. 11–12.

73. William Korey, "The Origins and Development of Soviet Anti-Semitism: An Analysis," *Slavic Review* 31, no. 1 (Mar., 1972): 111–35. A year later, Korey developed his article into a book. William Korey, *The Soviet Cage: Anti-Semitism in Russia* (New York: Viking, 1973).

74. Timothy Snyder, *Bloodlands: Europe between Hitler and Stalin* (New York: Basic Books, 2010), p. 336.

75. Ibid., p. 335.

76. Ibid., p. 345.

77. Sheila Fitzpatrick, *Tear Off the Masks! Identity and Imposture in Twentieth-Century Russia* (Princeton, N.J.: Princeton University Press, 2005), p. 298.

78. Joshua Rubenstein and Vladimir P. Naumov, eds., *Stalin's Secret Pogrom: The Postwar Inquisition of the Jewish Anti-Fascist Committee* (New Haven, Conn., and London: Yale University Press, 2001); Snyder, *Bloodlands,* pp. 339–77.

79. Jonathan Brent and Vladimir Naumov, *Stalin's Last Crime: The Plot against the Jewish Doctors, 1948–1953* (New York: HarperCollins, 2003); and Louis Rapoport, *Stalin's War against the Jews: The Doctor's Plot and the Soviet Solution* (New York: Free Press, 1990).

80. Joshua Rubenstein, *Tangled Loyalties: The Life and Times of Ilya Ehrenburg* (New York: Basic Books, 1996).

81. Elaine Mackinnon, "Writing History for Stalin: Isaak Izrailevich Mints and the *Istoriia grazhdanskoi voiny*," *Kritika: Explorations in Russian and Eurasian History* 6, no. 1 (Winter 2005): 38–39.

82. "Rootless cosmopolitanism" alternated with a hardly veiled anti-Semitic version, that is, "cosmopolitanism of kith and kin." On the phases of state and public anti-Semitism in the Soviet Union and under Stalin, see in particular Zvi Gitelman, *A Century of Ambivalence: The Jews of Russia and the Soviet Union, 1881 to the Present* (New York : Schocken Books, 1988); and Weiner, *Making Sense of War*.

83. See François Furet, *The Passing of an Illusion*, p. 558.

84. Snyder, *Bloodlands*, p. 334–35.

85. Merker himself was not of Jewish origin, but other high-profile people the Stasi (and NKVD) associated with his trial were Lex Ende, Leo Bauer, and Bruno Goldhammer. See Dorothy Miller, "The Death of a 'Former Enemy of the Working Class'—Paul Merker," *Radio Free Europe Research/Communist Area*, GDR/15, May 14, 1969.

86. Paul Merker was in the Mexico City from 1942 until 1945 and through his articles in *Freies Deutschland* was the only member of the KPD's Politburo who insisted on the central role of antisemitism in Nazi Germany and on the special status of the Jews among Hitler's victims. This was in sharp contrast with Walter Ulbricht's writings and public stances on Fascism, Germany's war crimes, and collective responsibility. Moreover, after 1948, Merker sharply diverged from the Soviet policy of refusing special status and retribution to Jews among Hitler's victims. For the definitive work on Paul Merker's case, see Jeffrey Herf, "East German Communists and the Jewish Question: The Case of Paul Merker," *Journal of Contemporary History* 29, no. 4 (Oct. 1994): 627–61; but also Jeffrey Herf, *Divided Memory: The Nazi Past in the Two Germanies* (Cambridge, Mass.: Harvard University Press, 1997); and Jeffrey Herf, "The Emergence and Legacies of Divided Memory: Germany and the Holocaust after 1945," in *Memory and Power in Postwar Europe: Studies in the Presence of the Past*, ed. Jan-Werner Müller (Cambridge: Cambridge University Press, 2002), pp. 184–205.

87. For a detailed explanation of power struggles in the 1930s and 1940s, see "A Messianic Sect: The Underground Romanian Communist Party, 1921–1944," in my *Stalinism for All Seasons: A Political History of Romanian Communism* (Berkeley: University of California Press, 2003).

88. Franz Borkenau, *World Communism: A History of the Communist International* (Ann Arbor: University of Michigan Press 1962), p. 178.

89. For a details on this interpretation of the events, see Robert Levy, *Ana Pauker: The Rise and Fall of a Jewish Communist* (Berkeley: University of California Press, 2001). For a critique, see Pavel Câmpeanu, *Ceaușescu, Anii numărătorii inverse* (București: Polirom, 2002).

90. "Note Regarding the Conversation of I.V. Stalin with Gh. Gheorghiu-Dej and A. Pauker on the Situation within the RCP and the State of Affairs in Romania in Connection with the Peace Treaty," no. 191, February 2, 1947, in *Vostochnaia Evropa v dokumentakh arkhivov, 1944–1953*, ed. Galin P. Muraschko,

Albina F. Noskowa, and Tatiana V. Volokitina (Moscow, 1997), 1:564–65. See also "Stenograma şedintei Biroului Politic al CC al PMR din 29 noiembrie 1961," pp. 14–16.

91. For a detailed presentation of Leonte Răutu's role in the power politics of Romanian communism, see Vladimir Tismaneanu and Cristian Vasile, *Perfectul Acrobat: Leonte Răutu, Măştile Răului* (Bucureşti: Humanitas, 2008).

92. This article was published both in the Central Committee official journal *Lupta de clasa,* no. 4 (October 1949) and as a brochure at the R.W.P. Publishing House in 1949.

93. Tismaneanu and Vasile, *Perfectul Acrobat,* p. 224.

94. Teresa Toránska, *"Them": Stalin's Polish Puppets* (New York: Harper & Row, 1987), p. 354. In her writing, Marci Shore has provided excellent characterizations of Jakub Berman, detailing his career from his role during the murky history of interwar Polish Communism and its relationship with Moscow during the Great Purge and the Second World War to his involvement in Gomułka's purge trial in the early 1950s up until his resignation in 1957 from the Polish United Workers' Party and retirement in 1969. Another issue that requires clarification is whether Berman's prominent role in the Stalinist purges prevented the duplication of a Slánský-type trial in Poland. See Marci Shore, "Children of the Revolution: Communism, Zionism, and the Berman Brothers," *Jewish Social Studies,* n.s., 10, no. 3 (Spring/Summer 2004): 23–86; and Marci Shore, *Caviar and Ashes: A Warsaw Generation's Life and Death in Marxism, 1918–1968* (New Haven, Conn.: Yale University Press, 2006).

95. Fitzpatrick, *Tear Off the Masks,* p. 50.

96. Erik van Ree, "Heroes and Merchants: Stalin's Understanding of National Character," *Kritika: Explorations in Russian and Eurasian History* 8, no. 1 (Winter 2007): 57.

97. Fitzpatrick, *Tear Off the Masks,* p. 293.

98. Snyder, *Bloodlands,* pp. 376 and 371.

99. See Vladimir Tismaneanu: "The Ambiguity of Romanian Communism," *Telos,* no. 60 (Summer 1984): 65–79; and "Ceausescu's Socialism," *Problems of Communism* (January-February 1985): 50–66. Also see Vladimir Tismaneanu, *Fantoma lui Gheorghiu-Dej* (Bucureşti: Humanitas, 2008). The volume contains several studies on the relationship between Communism and nationalism that I published at the end of the 1980s. For a definition of national Stalinism, see Tismaneanu, *Stalinism for All Seasons,* p. 33. For a comparative discussion about applicability of national Stalinism in the cases of Romania, Albania, Poland, Bulgaria, or the GDR, see Vladimir Tismaneanu, "What Was National Stalinism?" in *The Oxford Handbook of Postwar European History,* ed. Dan Stone (Oxford: Oxford University Press, 2012)f.

100. Snyder, *Bloodlands,* p. 376.

101. I examine anti-Semitism as a political mythology in *Fantasies of Salvation: Democracy, Nationalism, and Myth in Post-Communist Europe* (Princeton, N.J.: Princeton University Press, 1998, paperback 2009).

102. Leszek Kołakowski, *Main Currents of Marxism,* vol. 2, *The Golden Age* (Oxford: Oxford University Press, 1978), p. 85.

103. Nicolas Werth, "Strategies of Violence in the Stalinist USSR," in *Stalinism and Nazism: History and Memory Compared,* ed. Henry Rousso (Lincoln and London: University of Nebraska Press, 2004), pp. 73–95.

3. LENIN'S CENTURY

1. Here we may remember the two epigraphs Raymond Aron chose for *L'opium des intellectuels,* his 1955 devastating demystification of Jean-Paul Sartre's existentialist dialectics. He quoted Marx: "Religion is the sigh of the creature overwhelmed by misfortune, the sentiment of a heartless world, and the soul of soulless conditions. It is the opium of the people." Then, as a counterpunctual response, he used a quote from Simone Weil: "Marxism is undoubtedly a religion, in the lowest sense of the word. Like every inferior form of the religious life it has been continually used, to borrow the apt phrase of Marx himself, as an opiate for the people." See Raymond Aron, *The Opium of the Intellectuals,* intro. Harvey C. Mansfield (New Brunswick, N.J.: Transaction, 2001), p. vii. See also Tony Judt, *Past Imperfect: French Intellectuals, 1944–1956* (Berkeley: University of California Press, 1992).

2. Norman Cohn, *The Pursuit of the Millennium: Revolutionary Messianism in Medieval and Reformation Europe and Its Bearing on Modern Totalitarian Movements* (New York: Harper and Row, 1961), p. xv.

3. See David Ingersoll, Richard Mathews, and Andrew Davison, *The Philosophical Roots of Modern Ideology: Liberalism, Conservatism, Marxism, Fascism, Nazism, Islamism* (Cornwall-on-Hudson, N.Y.: Sloan/Prentice Hall, 2010).

4. Richard J. Evans, *The Coming of the Third Reich* (London: Penguin Books, 2003), p. 397.

5. Ibid., p. 455.

6. Stephen F. Cohen, *Bukharin and the Bolshevik Revolution: A Political Biography, 1888–1938* (New York and Wildwood House: Oxford University Press, 1973), p. 46.

7. Ibid., p. 301. Leon Trotsky uttered similar statements during and after the October Revolution. See Leon Trotsky, *Terrorism and Communism, A Reply to Karl Kautsky,* with a foreword by Slavoj Žižek (London: Verso, 2007).

8. Igal Halfin, *From Darkness to Light: Class, Consciousness, and Salvation in Revolutionary Russia* (Pittsburgh, Penn.: University of Pittsburgh Press, 2000), p. 48.

9. See Andrzej Walicki, *Marxism and the Leap to the Kingdom of Freedom: The Rise and Fall of the Communist Utopia* (Stanford, Calif.: Stanford University Press, 1995).

10. See chapter 3 of the *Communist Manifesto,* in *The Marx-Engels Reader,* ed. Robert C. Tucker, 3d ed. (New York: Norton, 1972), pp. 491–99.

11. Friedrich Engels, *Anti-Dühring: Herr Eugen Dühring's Revolution in Science* (Moscow: Foreign Language Publishing House, 1959), pp. 385–86.

12. See Steven Lukes, *Marxism and Morality* (New York: Oxford University Press, 1985); Leszek Kołakowski, *Main Currents of Marxism,* vol. 2, *The Golden Age* (Oxford: Oxford University Press, 1978), pp. 934–62.

13. Eugen Weber, "Revolution? Counterrevolution? What Revolution?" *Journal of Contemporary History* 9, no. 2 (April 1974): 23. Weber applies a memorable formula for this project of modern revolution: "Liberty, Equality, Fraternity, or Death."

14. Raymond Aron, The *Dawn of Universal History: Selected Essays from a Witness to the Twentieth Century,* intro. Tony Judt (New York: Basic Books, 2002), p. 203.

15. For ongoing efforts to return to an alleged pristine Leninism, see Sebastian Budgen, Stathis Kouvelakis, Slavoj Žižek, eds., *Lenin Reloaded: Toward a Politics of Truth* (Durham, N.C., and London: Duke University Press, 2007).

16. Waldemar Gurian, quoted in Michael Burleigh, "Political Religion and Social Evil," *Totalitarian Movements and Political Religions* 3, no. 2 (2002): 3.

17. See Slavoj Žižek, *Did Somebody Say Totalitarianism?* (London: Verso, 2001), p. 116.

18. See, in this respect, Bertram Wolfe, "Leninism," in *Marxism in the Modern World,* ed. Milorad M. Drachkovitch (Stanford, Calif.: Stanford University Press, 1965), pp. 47–89.

19. See Michael Charlton, *Footsteps from the Finland Station: Five Landmarks in the Collapse of Communism* (New Brunswick, N.J., and London: Transaction Publishers, 1992); Martin Malia, *The Soviet Tragedy: A History of Socialism in Russia, 1917–1991* (New York: Free Press, 1994); David Priestland, *The Red Flag: A History of Communism* (New York: Grove Press, 2009).

20. See Walicki, *Marxism,* pp. 269–397.

21. Mikhail Heller and Aleksandr M. Nekrich, *Utopia in Power: The History of the Soviet Union from 1917 to the Present* (New York: Summit Books, 1986).

22. Lefort quoted in Bernard Flynn, *The Philosophy of Claude Lefort: Interpreting the Political* (Evanston, Ill.: Northwestern University Press, 2005), p. 293.

23. See my *Fantasies of Salvation: Nationalism, Democracy, and Myth in Post-Communist Europe* (Princeton, N.J.: Princeton University Press, 1998).

24. Harry Kreisler, "The Individual, Charisma, and the Leninist Extinction," in *A Conversation with Ken Jowitt* (Berkeley: Institute of International Studies, 2000).

25. Kenneth Jowitt, *New World Disorder: The Leninist Extinction* (Berkeley and Los Angeles: University of California Press, 1992), p. 49.

26. See the quotations on Lenin and terror in Kostas Papaioannou's excellent anthology *Marx et les marxistes* (Paris: Gallimard, 2001), 314.

27. See Arthur Koestler, *Darkness at Noon,* 1st ed., trans. Daphne Hardy (New York: Bantam Books, 1968 [1941]); John V. Fleming, *The Anti-Communist Manifestos: Four Books That Shaped the Cold War* (New York: Norton, 2009), pp. 21–96; Michael Scammell, *Koestler: The Literary and Political Odyssey of a Twentieth-Century Skeptic* (New York: Random House, 2009).

28. *Darkness at Noon* came out in French, to huge public success, during the early Cold War years, under the title *Le zero et l'infini.*

29. Sergey Nechaev, *The Revolutionary Catechism,* in *The Roots of Revolution: A History of the Populist and Socialist Movements in Nineteenth Century Russia,* by Franco Venturi, intro. Isaiah Berlin (New York: Knopf, 1960), pp. 365–66. See also James H. Billington, *Fire in the Minds of Men: Origins of the*

Revolutionary Faith (New York: Basic Books, 1980); and Semen (Semyon) Frank, "The Ethic of Nihilism: A Characterization of the Russian Intelligentsia's Moral Outlook," in Nikolai Berdyaev et al., *Vekhi (Lanmdmarks)* (Armonk, N.J.: M. E. Sharpe, 1994), pp. 131–55.

30. Quoted in Michael Burleigh, *Sacred Causes: The Clash of Religion and Politics from the Great War to the War on Terror* (New York: HarperCollins, 2007), p. 82.

31. Piatakov quoted in Walicki, *Marxism,* 461.

32. Steven Lukes, "On the Moral Blindness of Communism," *Human Rights Review* 2, no. 2 (January-March 2001): 120.

33. Ibid., 121.

34. Ibid., 123.

35. Martin Amis, *Koba the Dread: Laughter and the Twenty Million* (New York: Hyperion, 2002), 90.

36. Roger Griffin, *Modernism and Fascism: The Sense of Beginning under Mussolini and Hitler* (London and New York: Palgrave Macmillian, 2007), p. 171.

37. Mikhail Gorbachev and Zdeněk Mlynář, *Conversations with Gorbachev: On Perestroika, the Prague Spring,* ed. George Shriver, foreword by Archie Brown and Mikhail Gorbachev (New York: Columbia University Press, 2002).

38. Jowitt, *New World Disorder,* 10.

39. A. J. Polan, *Lenin and the End of Politics* (Berkeley: University of California Press, 1984), 73.

40. Elena Bonner, "The Remains of Totalitarianism " *New York Review of Books,* March 8, 2001, 4.

41. Ibid., p. 5.

42. Alain Besançon, *The Rise of the Gulag: The Intellectual Origins of Leninism* (New York: Continnum, 1981); Jacob L. Talmon, *Myth of the Nation and Vision of the Revolution: Ideological Polarization in the Twentieth Century* (New Brunswick, N.J.: Transaction, 1991); Ruth Scurr, *Fatal Purity: Robespierre and French Revolution* (New York: Metropolitan Books, 2006).

43. John Maynard Keynes quoted in Emilio Gentile, *The Sacralization of Politics in Fascist Italy* (Cambridge, Mass.: Harvard University Press, 1996), p. 155.

44. Burleigh, *Sacred Causes,* p. 76.

45. Kołakowski, *Main Currents of Marxism: The Founders, the Golden Age, the Breakdown,* trans. P.S. Falla (New York: W.W. Norton, 2005), pp. 343–44 (subsequent references to *Main Currents* refer to this edition).

46. Halfin, *From Darkness to Light,* p. 37.

47. For the whole argument, see Erik van Ree, "Stalin's Organic Theory of the Party," *Russian Review* 52, no. 1 (January 1993): 43–57.

48. Erik van Ree, "Stalin as a Marxist Philosopher," *Studies in East European Thought* 52 (2000): 294.

49. Ibid., p. 271. I am also paraphrasing Isaak Steinberg's description of the atmosphere in the immediate aftermath of the Bolshevik Revolution: "All aspects of existence—social, economic, political, spiritual, moral, familial—were opened to purposeful fashioning by human hands." Steinberg was a left Socialist

264 | Notes to Chapter 3

revolutionary, who for a brief period was the first Soviet commissar for justice but resigned in protest against Bolshevik extremist violence and in 1923 fled to Germany. After the coming to power of the Nazis, he left for London. During the war he was a central figure in the plans for relocation of the Jewish refugees. See Richard Stites, *Revolutionary Dreams: Utopian Vision and Experimental Life in the Russian Revolution* (New York and Oxford: Oxford University Press, 1989), p. 39.

50. For the mindset of Bolshevik-style illuminated militants, see Eric Hoffer, *The True Believer: Thoughts on the Nature of Mass Movements* (New York: Harper & Row, 1966); Arthur Koestler's contribution in Richard H. Crossman, ed., *The God That Failed* (New York: Columbia University Press, 2001), pp. 15–75.

51. Rosa Luxemburg, "The Russian Revolution," in *Rosa Luxemburg Speaks,* ed. Mary-Alice Waters (New York and London: Pathfinder, 1997), p. 370.

52. Ibid., p. 387.

53. Cohen, *Bukharin,* p. 133.

54. Ibid., p. 172.

55. Ibid., p. 269.

56. Tucker, *The Marx-Engels Reader,* p. 491.

57. Ibid., pp. 473–74.

58. Kołakowski, *Main Currents,* pp. 620–39.

59. See "Proletarians and Communists," *The Manifesto,* in *The Marx-Engels Reader,* ed. Tucker, pp. 483–91.

60. See Karl R. Popper, *The Open Society and Its Enemies,* vol. 2, *The High Tide of Prophecy: Hegel, Marx, and the Aftermath* (Princeton, N.J.: Princeton University Press, 1966), p. 211.

61. François Furet, *The Passing of an Illusion: The Idea of Communism in the Twentieth Century,* trans. Deborah Furet (Chicago: University of Chicago Press, 1999), p. 143.

62. Paul Berman, *Terror and Liberalism* (New York: Norton, 2003).

63. Konrad Jarausch and Michael Geyer, *Shattered Past: Reconstructing German Histories* (Princeton, N.J., and Oxford: Princeton University Press, 2003), p. 165.

64. Isaiah Berlin, *The Crooked Timber of Humanity: Chapters in the History of Ideas* (New York: Knopf, 1991), pp. 91–174.

65. George Mosse, *The Fascist Revolution: Toward a General Theory of Fascism* (New York: H. Fertig, 1999).

66. Roger Griffin, *The Nature of Fascism* (London and New York: Routledge, 1993), p. 235.

67. R.J.B. Bosworth, *Mussolini's Italy: Life under the Fascist Dictatorship 1915–1945* (London: Penguin Books, 2005), p. 130.

68. Emilio Gentile and Robert Mallett, "The Sacralisation of Politics: Definitions, Interpretations and Reflections on the Question of Secular Religion and Totalitarianism," *Totalitarian Movements and Political Religions* 1, no. 1 (2000): 36.

69. Alberto Toscano, *Fanaticism: On the Uses of an Idea* (London and New York: Verso, 2010). I am extending here Priestland's analysis of what he coins

as "revivalist Bolshevism." See David Priestland, *Stalinism and the Politics of Mobilization: Ideas, Power, and Terror in Inter-War Russia* (Oxford and New York: Oxford University Press, 2007), p. 39.

70. Gentile, *The Sacralization of Politics,* p. 55.

71. Evans, *The Coming of the Third Reich,* p. 460.

72. E.A. Rees, *Political Thought from Machiavelli to Stalin: Revolutionary Machiavellism* (New York: Palgrave MacMillan, 2004), pp. 74 and 235–36.

73. T.H. Rigby, "Introduction: Political Legitimacy, Weber and Communist Mono-organisational Systems," in *Political Legitimation in Communist States,* ed. T.H. Rigby and F. Feher (London: Palgrave Macmillan, 1982), p. 5.

74. Gentile and Mallett, "The Sacralisation of Politics," p. 46.

75. Mann takes his point further by identifying two subtypes within this political category: "One driven by revolutionary class ideology, exemplified by the Stalinist regime" and "the other driven by what I shall call a revolutionary 'nation-statist' ideology, exemplified by Nazism." Michael Mann, "Contradictions of Continuous Revolution," in *Stalinism and Nazism: Dictatorships in Comparison,* ed. Ian Kershaw and Moshe Lewin (New York: Cambridge University Press, 1997), p. 136. See his *Fascists* (Cambridge and New York: Cambridge University Press, 2004).

76. David D. Roberts, *The Totalitarian Experiment in Twentieth-Century Europe: Understanding the Poverty of Great Politics* (New York and London: Routledge, 2006), p. 270.

77. See Boris Souvarine, *Staline: Aperçu historique de bolshévisme* (Paris: Éditions Champ Libre, 1977); Ian Kershaw, *Hitler 1936–45: Nemesis* (New York: Norton, 2000); Robert Service, *Stalin: A Biography* (Cambridge: Belknap Press, 2004); and Yuri Felschtinsky, *Lenin and His Comrades* (New York: Enigma Books, 2010).

78. Leszek Kołakowski, *Main Currents of Marxism,* vol. 3, *The Breakdown* (Oxford: Oxford University Press, 1978), p. 90.

79. Berman, *Terror and Liberalism,* p. 50.

80. Peter Ehlen, "Communist Faith and World-Explanatory Doctrine: A Philosophical analysis," in *Totalitarianism and Political Religions,* vol. 2, *Concepts for the Comparison of Dictatorships,* ed. Hans Maier and Michael Schäfer (New York: Routledge, 2007), p. 134.

81. Hans Maier, "Political Religions and Their Images: Soviet Communism, Italian Fascism and German National Socialism," *Totalitarian Movements and Political Religions* 7, no. 3 (September 2006): 269.

82. Graeme Gill, *The Origins of the Stalinist Political System* (Cambridge and New York: Cambridge University Press, 2002), p. 242.

83. Ana Krylova, "Beyond the Spontaneity-Consciousness Paradigm: 'Class Instinct' as a Promising Category of Historical Analysis," *Slavic Review* 62, no. 1 (Spring 2003): 18–19. David Priestland makes a similar point as he identifies two versions of understanding "class" by the Bolsheviks: a neotraditionalist one, "as class origin," which allows for the entrenchment of the bureaucracy produced by mass *vydvizhenie;* and a revivalist one, "as class mentality and culture," which emphasizes the notion of *vospetanie,* which can be turned against the "new class." See Priestland, *Stalinism and the Politics of Mobilization,* p. 415.

84. Quoted by David McLellan, *Marxism after Marx*, 4th ed. (New York: Palgrave Macmillan, 2007), p. 98.

85. Jowitt, *New World Disorder*, pp. 25–27.

86. Rees, *Political Thought from Machiavelli to Stalin*, p. 115.

87. Rees lists N.A. Speshnev, N.P. Ogarev, P.G. Zaichnevskii, M. Bakunin, P.N. Tkachev, and S.G. Nechaev as the founding fathers of "revolutionary Machiavellism." On the relationship between the Russian tradition of radical political thought and Lenin, see also Tibor Szamuely, *The Russian Tradition*, ed. Robert Conquest (London: Fontana, 1974); and Adam Ulam, *In the Name of the People: Prophets and Conspirators in Prerevolutionary Russia* (New York: Viking Press, 1977).

88. Robert Mayer, "Lenin and the Jacobin Identity in Russia," *Studies in East European Thought* 51 (1999): 127–54. Also see Mayer, "Lenin, the Proletariat, and the Legitimation of Dictatorship," *Journal of Political Ideologies* 2 (February 1997): 99–115; and "Plekhanov, Lenin and Working-Class Consciousness," *Studies in East European Thought* 49 (September 1997): 159–85.

89. See Maximilien Robespierre, *Virtue and Terror*, ed. Slavoj Žižek (New York: Verso, 2007).

90. On Lenin's concept of the dictatorship of the proletariat, see Kołakowski, *Main Currents*, pp. 744–49.

91. Luxemburg, "The Russian Revolution," p. 391.

92. Hannah Arendt, "Nightmare and Flight," in *Essays in Understanding, 1930–1954*, ed. Jerome Kern (New York: Harcourt, Brace and Jovanovich), p. 134.

93. Daniel Chirot, "What Was Communism All About?" (review essay on *The Black Book of Communism*), *East European Politics and Societies* 14, no. 3 (Fall 2000): 665–75.

94. Polan, *Lenin and the End of Politics*.

95. Peter Holquist, "'Information is the Alpha and Omega of Our Work': Bolshevik Surveillance in its Pan-European Perspective," *Journal of Modern History* 69, no. 3 (1997): 415–50.

96. I am paraphrasing Roberts, *The Totalitarian Experiment*, p. 415.

97. Klaus-Georg Riegel, "Marxism-Leninism as a Political Religion" in *Totalitarian Movements and Political Religions* 6, no. 1 (June 2005): 98.

98. Martin Malia, *The Soviet Tragedy* (New York: Free Press, 1994); Richard Pipes, *The Russian Revolution* (New York: Vintage, 1990).

99. Quoted by John Patrick Diggins, *Max Weber: Politics and the Spirit of Tragedy* (New York: Basic Books, 1996), p. 239.

100. Ibid., p. 230.

101. Slavoj Žižek, "Introduction between the Two Revolutions," in *Revolution at the Gates: Selected Writings of Lenin from 1917* (London: Verso, 2002), 6.

102. Alexander Yakovlev, *A Century of Violence in Soviet Russia* (New Haven, Conn.: Yale University Press, 2002); see also my review of Yakovlev's book, "Apostate Apparatchik," *Times Literary Supplement*, February 21, 2003, p. 26; and Paul Hollander, *The End of Commitment: Intellectuals, Revolutionaries, and Political Morality* (Chicago: Ivan R. Dee, 2006).

103. Isaac Deutscher, "Marxism and Primitive Magic," in *The Stalinist Legacy: Its Impact on Twentieth Century World Politics,* ed. Tariq Ali (Harmondsworth: Penguin Books, 1984), 11–14.

104. See Robert C. Tucker's interview with George Urban in G.R. Urban, ed., *Stalinism—Its Impact on Russia and the World* (London: Maurice Temple Smith, 1982), pp. 151 and 170.

105. Terry Martin, *The Affirmative Action Empire: Nations and Nationalism in the Soviet Union, 1923–1939* (Ithaca, N.Y.: Cornell University Press, 2001), p. 341.

106. Sheila Fitzpatrick, "Ascribing Class: The Construction of Social Identity in Soviet Russia," in *Stalinism—New Directions,* ed. Sheila Fitzpatrick (London and New York: Routledge, 2000), pp. 20–47.

107. Priestland, *Stalinism and the Politics of Mobilization,* p. 249.

108. Erik van Ree, "Stalin as Marxist: The Western Roots of Stalin's Russification of Marxism," in *Stalin: A New History,* ed. Sarah Davies and James Harris (Cambridge: Cambridge University Press, 2005), p. 172.

109. Roberts, *The Totalitarian Experiment,* p. 231.

110. In Mussolini's Italy, *Carta de Lavoro,* the 1927 charter that encoded the regime's program of modernization, used a strikingly similar characterization of the community on the path to constructing the revolutionary state: "The Italian nation is an organism having a purpose, life and means of action superior to those of any individual or groups who are part of it. It is a moral, political and economic unit which integrally achieves the Fascist State." This charter was designed mainly by Italo Balbo. See Bosworth, *Mussolini's Italy,* p. 227.

111. David Brandenberger, "Stalin as Symbol: A Case Study of the Personality Cult and Its Construction," in *Stalin,* ed. Davies and Harris, p. 250. For his discussion of National Bolshevism, see David Brandenberger, *National Bolshevism: Stalinist Mass Culture and the Formation of Modern Russian National Identity, 1931–1956* (Cambridge, Mass., and London: Harvard University Press, 2002).

112. Gill, *The Origins,* pp. 242–45.

113. Both quotations from Stalin are from Ethan Pollock, "Stalin as the Coryphaeus of Science: Ideology and Knowledge in the Post-War Years," in *Stalin,* ed. Davies and Harris, pp. 283 and 280.

114. Georg Lukács, *History and Class Consciousness* (London: Merlin Press, 1971), p. 51.

115. *Lenin and the Twentieth Century: A Bertram D. Wolfe Retrospective,* compiled and with an introduction by Lennard D. Gerson, foreword by Alain Besançon (Stanford, Calif.: Hoover Institution Press, 1984), p. 86.

116. Dick Howard, *The Specter of Democracy* (New York: Columbia University Press, 2002), p. 19.

117. See Leszek Kołakowski interview in Urban, ed., *Stalinism,* p. 250.

118. Roger Griffin, "Introduction: God's Counterfeiters? Investigating the Triad of Fascism, Totalitarianism and (Political) Religion," *Totalitarian Movements and Political Religions* 5, no. 3 (Winter 2004): 291–325.

119. Kołakowski, *Main Currents,* pp. 989–1032, 1124–1147; Gorbachev's former chief ideologue, Alexander Yakovlev, writes about this in his somewhat vehement contribution to Stéphane Courtois et al., eds., *Du passé nous faisons*

table rase! Histoire et mémoire du communisme en Europe (Paris: Robert Laffont, 2002), pp. 173–210.

120. Katerina Clark, *Petersburg: Crucible of Cultural Revolution* (Cambridge, Mass.: Harvard University Press, 1995), p. 2.

121. Tucker argues that "the Russian revolutionary mentality found no difficulty in adjusting itself to Marxism, or Marxism to itself. Part of the explanation is that this mentality was, even in pre-Marxist days, hostile to capitalism . . . . But the chief facilitating circumstance was . . . that the war between class and class had to be decided in the final analysis by overthrowing the existing *state*. Further, his doctrine appealed to the anarchist streak in the Russian revolutionary mentality, for it visualized the withering away of government after the proletarian revolution. Hence it was entirely possible for a Russian revolutionary whose mind was obsessed with the image of a dual Russia to become a Marxist and continue in that capacity the indigenous revolutionary tradition of warfare against official Russia. . . . He could talk as a Marxist while thinking and feeling as a Russian revolutionary." Robert C. Tucker, *The Soviet Political Mind: Stalinism and Post-Stalin Change,* rev. ed. (New York: W.W. Norton, 1971), p. 130–31.

122. Griffin, *Modernism and Fascism*, p. 172.

123. Steven G. Marks, *How Russia Shaped the Modern World: From Art to Anti-Semitism, Ballet to Bolshevism* (Princeton, N.J.: Princeton University Press, 2003).

124. Alexander Solzhenitsyn et al., *From Under the Rubble,* intro. Max Hayward (Washington D.C.: Regnery Gateway, 1981).

125. Lars T. Lih, "How a Founding Document Was Found, or One Hundred Years of Lenin's *What Is to Be Done?*" *Kriitika: Explorations in Russian and Eurasian History* 4, no. 1 (Winter 2003): 5–49.

126. Halfin, *From Darkness to Light,* p. 14.

127. Klaus-Georg Riegel, "Communities of *Virtuosi:* An Interpretation of the Stalinist Criticism and Self-Criticism in the Perspective of Max Weber's Sociology of Religion," *Totalitarian Movements and Political Religions* 1, no. 3 (Winter 2000): 16–42.

128. Halfin, *From Darkness to Light,* pp. 156–57.

129. Ibid., p. 84.

130. Earnest Tuveson quoted in ibid., p. 47.

131. Ibid., p. 115.

132. There was a crucial distinction between Marx and Lenin on this issue. For Marx, the liberation of the proletariat had to be "the work of the proletarians themselves." Two lines of thought collided on this issue, leading to some of the fiercest debates in twentieth-century left-wing radical parties and movements.

133. Maykovsky wrote these verses in his poem "Vlaadimir Ilyich Lenin" in Vladimir Mayakovsky, *Moia revolutsia* (Moscow: Sovremennik Publishers, 1974).

134. Bolshevism and National Socialism shared the fascination with an anthropological revolution. Mussolini was also committed to creating a new Fascist Man, and so was the Captain of Romania's Iron Guard, Corneliu Zelea Codreanu.

135. Astrid Hadin, "Stalinism as a Civilization: New Perspectives on Communist Regimes," *Political Studies Review* 2 (2004): 166–84.

136. For a discussion of myth versus ideology in relation to Marxism-Leninism, see Carol Barner-Barry and Cynthia Hody, "Soviet Marxism-Leninism as Mythology," *Political Psychology* 15, no. 4 (December 1994): 609–30.

137. Ehlen, "Communist Faith and World-Explanatory Doctrine," in *Totalitarianism*, ed. Maier and Schäfer, p. 129.

138. See A. James Gregor's discussion of the nationalist, mystical writings of Serghei Kurginian and Alexandr Prohanov and their influence over Zyuganov, particularly manifested in the "Declaration to the People," the manifesto of Russian Stalino-Fascism. See A. James Gregor, *The Faces of Janus: Marxism and Fascism in the Twentieth Century* (New Haven, Conn.: Yale University Press, 2000), pp. 144–55; and *Marxism, Fascism, and Totalitarianism: Chapters in the Intellectual History of Radicalism* (Stanford, Calif.: Stanford University Press, 2009).

139. Nikolai Chernyshevsky, *What Is to Be Done?* (Ithaca, N.Y., and London: Cornell University Press, 1989).

140. In addition to Jowitt's contributions, see Tucker, *The Soviet Political Mind;* and Robert Conquest, *Reflections on a Ravaged Century* (New York: Norton, 2000).

141. Luxemburg, "The Russian Revolution," p. 375.

142. Beryl Williams, *Lenin* (Harlow: Logman Publishing Group, 1999), p. 73.

143. Karl Dietrich Bracher, *The German Dictatorship: The Origins, Structure, and Effects of National Socialism,* trans. Jean Steinberg with an introduction by Peter Gay (New York and Washington: Praeger Publishers, 1970), p. 152.

144. Gabriel Almond, *The Appeals of Communism* (Princeton, N.J.: Princeton University Press, 1954); Burleigh, *Sacred Causes,* esp. "The Totalitarian Political Religions," pp. 38–122.

145. Bert Hoppe, "Iron Revolutionaries and Salon Socialists: Bolsheviks and German Communists in the 1920s and 1930s," in "Fascination and Enmity: Russia and Germany as Entangled Histories, 1914–1945," special issue, *Kritika: Explorations in Russian and Eurasian History* 10, no. 3 (Summer 2009): 509.

146. Hoffer, *The True Believer.*

147. Michael Walzer, *The Revolution of the Saints: A Study in the Origins of Radical Politics* (New York: Atheneum, 1976), p. 315.

148. For an excellent analysis of Lefort's writings, see Howard, *The Specter,* 71–82.

149. Claude Lefort, *La complication: Retour sur le communisme* (Paris: Fayard, 1999).

150. Claude Lefort, *The Political Forms of Modern Society: Bureaucracy, Democracy, Totalitarianism,* ed. John B. Thompson (Cambridge, Mass.: MIT Press, 1986), p. 285–86.

151. Lefort, *La complication,* p. 47.

152. Robert C. Tucker, "Lenin's Bolshevism as a Culture in the Making," in *Bolshevik Culture: Experiment and Order in the Bolshevik Revolution,* ed.

Abbott Gleason, Peter Kenez, and Richard Stites (Bloomington: Indiana University Press, 1985), pp. 26–27.

153. One can point to a whole intellectual tradition, and I am thinking here of authors such as Cornelius Castoriadis and, much earlier, Georgi Plekhanov, Yuli Martov, Pavel Akselrod, Emma Goldman, Rosa Luxemburg, Karl Kautsky, Anton Pannekoek, Ruth Fischer, Boris Souvarine, Milovan Djilas, Agnes Heller, and Leszek Kołakowski.

154. Lefort, *The Political Forms,* p. 297.

155. Hitler quoted in Bracher, *The German Dictatorship,* p. 250.

156. Maier, "Political Religions and their Images," p. 274.

157. Peter Holquist, "New Terrains and New Chronologies: The Interwar Period through the Lens of Population Politics," *Kirtika: Explorations in Russian and Eurasian History* 4, no. 1 (Winter 2003): 171–72.

158. Sigrid Meuschel, "The Institutional Frame: Totalitarianism, Extermination and the State," in *The Lesser Evil: Moral Approaches to Genocide Practices,* ed. Helmut Dubiel and Gabriel Motzkin (Portland, Or.: Frank Cass, 2003), pp. 115–16.

159. Bosworth, *Mussolini,* p. 235.

160. Gorlizki and Mommsen, "The Political (Dis)Orders of Stalinism and National Socialism," in *Beyond Totalitarianism,* ed. Geyer and Fitzpatrick, p. 86.

161. Michael Burleigh, "Political Religion and Social Evil," *Totalitarian Movements and Political Religions* 3, no. 2 (Autumn 2002): 1–2.

4. DIALECTICS OF DISENCHANTMENT

1. Kenneth Jowitt, *New World Disorder: The Leninist Extinction* (Berkeley and Los Angeles: University of California Press, 1992), p. 10n17.

2. See Benito Mussolini, "The Doctrine of Fascism," in *Communism, Fascism, and Democracy,* ed. Carl Cohen, 3d ed. (New York: Random House, 1972), pp. 328–39.

3. See Ian Kershaw, *Hitler 1936–1945: Nemesis* (New York and London: Norton, 2000), esp. "Luck of the Devil," pp. 655–84. It is worth quoting here Kershaw's remark about Hitler's extraordinary luck in surviving the attempt on his life organized by Count Stauffenberg and his co-conspirators: "In fact, as so often in his life, it had not been Providence that had saved him, but luck: *the luck of the devil*" (p. 584, italics mine).

4. For Zubok, "Zhivago's children" referred to a generation of intellectuals tested by the years of war, violence, and misery: "The educated cadres trained for Stalinist service turned out to be a vibrant and diverse tribe, with intellectual curiosity, artistic yearnings, and a passion for high culture. They identified not only with the Soviet collectivity, but also with humanist individualism." Vladislav Zubok, *Zhivago's Children: The Last Russian Intelligentsia* (Cambridge, Mass.: Harvard University Press, 2009), pp. 356, 361, and 21.

5. Agnes Heller and Ferenc Fehér, *The Grandeur and Twilight of Radical Universalism* (New Brunswick, N.J., and London: Transaction, 1991), p. 113.

6. See Vladimir Tismaneanu, "Critical Marxism and Eastern Europe," *Praxis International* 3, no. 3 (October 1983): 235–47; *The Crisis of Marxist Ideology*

in Eastern Europe: The Poverty of Utopia (London and New York: Routledge, 1988); "The Neo-Leninist Temptation: Gorbachevism and the Party Intelligentsia," in *Perestroika at the Crossroads,* ed. Alfred J. Rieber and Alvin Z. Rubinstein (Armonk, N.Y.: M.E. Sharpe, 1991), pp. 31–51; "From Arrogance to Irrelevance: Avatars of Marxism in Romania," in *The Road to Disillusion: From Critical Marxism to Postcommunism in Eastern Europe,* ed. Raymond Taras (Armonk, N.Y.: M.E. Sharpe, 1992), pp. 135–50.

7. Frederick C. Corney, "What Is to Be Done with Soviet Russia? The Politics of Proscription and Possibility" in *Journal of Policy History* 21, no 3 (2009): 271.

8. Philosopher Yuri Karyakin quoted in Zubok, *Zhivago's Children,* p. 358.

9. Robert C. Tucker, *The Soviet Political Mind: Stalinism and Post-Stalin Change,* rev. ed. (New York: W.W. Norton, 1971), pp. 148–49.

10. Klaus-Georg Riegel, "Marxism-Leninism as a Political Religion," *Totalitarian Movements and Political Religions* 6, no. 1 (June 2005): 97–126.

11. V.I. Lenin, *What Is to be Done: Burning Questions of Our Movement* (New York: International Publishers, 1969 [1902]), p. 5.

12. J.V. Stalin, *Leninism* (Moscow: International Publishers, 1928), p. 171.

13. For a most disturbing account of this nihilistic moment in the history of world Communism, see especially the last letters of Bukharin and Yezhov to Stalin in Arch Getty and Oleg Naumov, *The Self-Destruction of the Bolshevik Old Guard* (New Haven, Conn.: Yale University Press, 1999). See discussion in chapter 2.

14. Czesław Miłosz, *The Captive Mind* (New York: Vintage Books, 1981), p. 75.

15. Stephen F. Cohen, *Bukharin and the Bolshevik Revolution: A Political Biography 1888–1938* (New York: Vintage Books, 1973), pp. 84. For Soviet intellectuals under Stalin, see Isaiah Berlin, *The Soviet Mind: Russian Culture under Communism* (Washington, D.C.: Brookings Institution Press, 2011); Cristina Vatulescu, *Police Aesthetics: Literature, Film, and the Secret Police in Soviet Times* (Stanford, Calif.: Stanford University Press, 2010); Frank Westerman, *Engineers of the Soul: The Grandiose Propaganda of Stalin's Russia* (New York: Overlook Press, 2011).

16. Robert Horvath, "'The Solzhenitsyn Effect': East European Dissidents and the Demise of the Revolutionary Privilege," *Human Rights Quarterly* 29, no. 4 (November 2007): 885.

17. Bradley F. Abrams, *The Struggle for the Soul of the Nation: Czech Culture and the Rise of Communism* (Lanham, Md.: Rowman & Littlefield, 2004), p. 93.

18. See Carol S. Lilly, *Power and Persuasion: Ideology and Rhetoric in Communist Yugoslavia, 1944–1953* (Boulder, Colo.: Westview Press, 2001); Gareth Pritchard, *The Making of the GDR, 1945–53: From Antifascism to Stalinism* (Manchester: Manchester University Press, 2000); or Krystyna Kersten, *The Establishment of Communist Rule in Poland, 1943–1948,* trans. John Micgiel and Michael H. Bernhard, foreword by Jan T. Gross (Berkeley: University of California Press, 1991).

19. Riegel, "Marxism-Leninism as a Political Religion," pp. 97–126.

20. Horvath, "'The Solzhenitsyn Effect,'" p. 894.

21. Leszek Kołakowski, *Main Currents of Marxism: The Founders, the Golden Age, the Breakdown,* trans. P.S. Falla (New York: W.W. Norton, 2005), p. 863.

22. On the features of the historical-ideological profile of the *Short Course* and the revision of its main tenets within the Soviet historical field in the 1960s and 1970s, see Roger D. Markwick, *Rewriting History in Soviet Russia—the Politics of Revisionist Historiography, 1954–1974,* foreword by Donald J. Raleigh (New York: Palgrave Macmillan, 2001). Kenneth Jowitt employs the formulation by Max Weber in *New World Disorder,* p. 135.

23. Bernice Glatzer Rosenthal, *New Myth, New World—from Nietzsche to Stalinism* (University Park: Pennsylvania State University Press, 2002), p. 238.

24. Stephen F. Cohen, "Bolshevism and Stalinism," in *Stalinism: Essays in Historical Interpretation,* ed. Robert C. Tucker (New York: W.W. Norton, 1977), pp. 12–13.

25. Tucker, *The Soviet Political Mind,* p. xi.

26. E.A. Rees, "Introduction," in *The Sovietization of Eastern Europe: New Perspectives on the Postwar Period,* ed. Balázs Apor, Péter Apor, and E.A. Rees (Washington, D.C.: New Academia Publishing, 2008), p. 21.

27. Hans Maier, "Political Religions and Their Images: Soviet Communism, Italian Fascism and German National Socialism," *Totalitarian Movements and Political Religions* 7, no. 3 (Sept. 2006): 267–81.

28. Corney, "What Is to Be Done," p. 273.

29. Polly Jones, "Introduction: The Dilemmas of De-Stalinization," in *The Dilemmas of De-Stalinization: Negotiating Cultural and Social Change in the Khrushchev Era* (London: Routledge, 2006), p. 12.

30. Miriam Dobson, "'Show the Bandit-Enemies No Mercy!': Amnesty, Criminality and Public Response in 1953," in *The Dilemmas of De-Stalinization,* ed. Jones, p. 22.

31. Jones, *The Dilemmas of De-Stalinization,* p. 13.

32. Zubok, *Zhivago's Children,* pp. 71 and 58.

33. For Khrushchev, the definitive biography is William Taubman, *Khrushchev: The Man and His Era* (New York: W.W. Norton, 2002).

34. Polly Jones, "From the Secret Speech to the Burial of Stalin: Real and Ideal Responses to De-Stalinization," in *The Dilemmas of De-Stalinization,* p. 41.

35. Robert D. English, *Russia and the Idea of the West: Gorbachev, Intellectuals, and the End of the Cold War* (New York: Columbia University Press, 2000), p. 109.

36. One of the best books on this topic remains Wolfgang Leonhard, *Three Faces of Marxism: The Political Concepts of Soviet Marxism, Maoism, and Humanist Marxism* (New York: Paragon Books, 1979), especially the part dealing with the challenge of humanist Marxism, pp. 258–352. For a comprehensive approach to the role of Marxist revisionism, see Kołakowski, *Main Currents;* and Andrzej Walicki, *Marxism and the Leap to the Kingdom of Freedom: The Rise and Fall of the Communist Utopia* (Stanford, Calif.: Stanford University Press, 1995).

37. Kołakowski quoted in Stanley Pierson, *Leaving Marxism: Studies in the Dissolution of an Ideology* (Stanford, Calif.: Stanford University Press, 2001), pp. 134–35.

38. Stanislav Rassadin, the creator of the concept *shestidesiatniki,* quoted in Zubok, *Zhivago's Children,* p. 162.

39. Two classics on Marxist revisionism in Eastern Europe are Leopold Labedz, ed., *Revisionism: Essays on the History of Marxist Ideas* (New York: Praeger 1962); and Leonhard, *Three Faces of Marxism.*

40. Jan Weilgohs and Detlef Pollack, "Comparative Perspectives on Dissent and Opposition to Communist Rule," in *Dissent and Opposition in Communist Eastern Europe: Origins of Civil Society and Democratic Transition* (Burlington, Vt.: Ashgate, 2004), pp. 231–64.

41. Jacek Kuroń and Karol Modzelewski were arrested for their involvement in the distribution of this document. See Barbara Falk, *The Dilemmas of Dissidence in East-Central Europe: Citizen Intellectuals and Philosopher Kings* (Budapest: Central European University, 2003), p. 17; Jacek Kuroń, *La foi et la faute: A la rencontre et hors du communisme* (Paris: Fayard, 1991).

42. Mikhail Gorbachev and Zdeněk Mlynář, *Conversations with Gorbachev: On Perestroika, the Prague Spring,* foreword by Archie Brown and Mikhail Gorbachev (New York: Columbia University Press, 2002), pp. 56–58.

43. See Adam Michnik, *Letters from Prison and Other Essays* (Berkeley: University of California Press, 1985), p. 135.

44. Jones, "Introduction," in *The Dilemmas of De-Stalinization,* p. 5.

45. Jones, "From the Secret Speech," in ibid., p. 41.

46. Jones, "Introduction," in ibid. For example, during the first years after Stalin's death, there was in Moscow a proliferation of "*kompany*—circles of friends, informal groups consisting mostly of educated people in their twenties and thirties. . . . The large groups of friends became a substitute for 'publishing houses, salons, billboards, confession booths, concert halls, libraries, museums, counseling groups, sewing circles, knitting clubs, chambers of commerce, bars, clubs, restaurants, coffeehouses, dating agencies, and seminars in literature, history, philosophy, linguistics, economics, genetics, physics, music, and the arts.' " These informal groups represented one source of the rebirth of civil society in the Soviet Union. See Zubok, *Zhivago's Children,* pp. 47–48.

47. See Stanley Pierson's chapter on Leszek Kołakowski's intellectual journey from revisionism to dissent in *Leaving Marxism,* pp. 128–74; Robert A. Gorman, *Biographical Dictionary of Neo-Marxism* (Westport, Conn.: Greenwood Press, 1985), pp. 232–34.

48. Zubok, *Zhivago's Children,* pp. 214–15.

49. Karl Korsch, *Marxisme et philosophie* (Paris: Editions de Minuit, 1964), p. 39. For what concerns Korsch's philosophical-political outlook and the contemporary meaning of the Hegelian-Marxist radicalism, see: Karl Korsch, *Marxisme et contre-révolution* (Paris: Seuil, 1975); Karl Korsch, *L'anti-Kautsky (La conception matérialiste de l'histoire)* (Paris: Champ Libre, 1973); Paul Breines, "Korsch's Road to Marx," *Telos,* no. 26; and Furio Cerutti, "Lukács ad Korsch: On the Emancipatory Significance of the Dialectics in Critical Marxism," *Telos,* no. 26, originally published in Oskar Negt, ed., *Aktualität und Folgen der Philosophie Hegels* (Frankfurt: Suhrkamp, 1970). Generally, regarding critical Marxism, see Perry Andreson, *Sur le marxisme occidental* (Paris: Maspero, 1977); Predrag Vranicki, *Storia del marxismo,* vols. 1–2 (Roma: Editori Riuniti, 1972);

M Löwy, *Pour une sociologie des intellectuals révolutionnaires—L'évolution politique de Lukács, 1909–1929* (Paris: Maspero, 1976); Neil McInnes, *The Western Marxists* (Newport, N.Y.: Free Press, 1972). We have to mention here the relevant contributions of such authors as Andrew Arato, Dick Howard, Jean-Michel Palmier, Paul Piccone, Jean-Marie Vincent, Pierre V. Zima, Richard J. Bernstein, Aldo Zanardo, Albercht Wellmer, N. Tertulian, and Agnes Heller. I published in Romania several studies on Western Marxism in the *Journal of Philosophy* and a book on *The New Left and the Frankfurt School* (Bucharest: Editura Politică, 1976).

50. For the ideological foundations of the East German Communist regime, see Leslie Holmes, "The Significance of Marxist Dissent to the Emergence of Postcommunism in the GDR," in *The Road to Disillusion: From Critical Marxism to Post-communism in Eastern Europe,* ed. Raymond Taras (Armonk, N.Y.: M.E. Sharpe, 1992), pp. 57–80; and Mary Fulbrook, *The People's State: East German Society from Hitler to Honecker* (New Haven, Conn.: Yale University Press, 2005).

51. Leszek Kołakowski, *Main Currents of Marxism,* vol. 3: *The Breakdown* (Oxford: Oxford University Press, 1978).

52. English, *Russia and the Idea of the West,* p. 122.

53. Georgy Arbatov quoted in ibid., p. 50.

54. Alexandre Zinovyev, *Nous et l'Occident* (Lausanne: L'Age d'Homme, 1981), p. 13.

55. Dick Howard, *The Specter of Democracy* (New York: Columbia University Press, 2002), pp. vii–xvii.

56. Zubok, *Zhivago's Children,* p. 192.

57. Ferenc Fehér, "The Language of Resistance: 'Critical Marxism' versus 'Marxism-Leninism' in Hungary," in *The Road to Disillusion,* ed. Taras, pp. 41–56.

58. Oskar Gruenwald, *The Yugoslav Search for Man: Marxism Humanism in Contemporary Yugoslavia* (South Hadley, Mass.: J.F. Bergin, 1983). One moment when critical thought in the West united with the revisionist spirit in the East to advocate humanist Marxism was the volume edited by Erich Fromm in 1965 and entitled *Socialist Humanism* (London: Allen Lane and Penguin Press, 1967). It included thirty-five contributions by Marxist and non-Marxist thinkers, which indicated the animus of the sixties to offer a humanist interpretation of Marx liberated from the hegemonic Soviet grip.

59. Kołakowski, *Main Currents,* vol. 3; Tismaneanu, *The Crisis of Marxist Ideology in Eastern Europe.*

60. Horvath, "'The Solzhenitsyn Effect,' " pp. 895–96. See Vladimir Tismaneanu, ed., *The Promises of 1968: Crisis, Illusion, Utopia* (Budapest and New York: Central European University Press, 2010).

61. Arthur Marwick, *The Sixties: Cultural Revolution in Britain, France, Italy, and the United States, c. 1958–c. 1974* (Oxford and New York: Oxford University Press, 1998), p. 10. Marwick defined this concept as "the belief that the society we inhabit is the bad bourgeois society, but that, fortunately, this society is in a state of crisis, so that the good society which lies just around the

corner can be easily attained if only we work systematically to destroy the language, values, the culture, the ideology of bourgeois society."

62. Tony Judt, *Postwar: A History of Europe since 1945* (New York: Penguin Press, 2005), p. 401.

63. Agnes Heller, "The Year 1968 and Its Results: An East European Perspective," in *Promises of 1968,* ed. Tismaneanu, pp. 155–63.

64. V. Zubok's account about the generation of "Zhivago's children" shows how, by the end of the sixties, Russian intelligentsia began losing any hope of reforming Soviet-style Communism. The Sinyavski-Deniel trial and publication of Natalia Gorbanevskaya's *Chronicle of Current Events* (which Peter Reddaway called "the journal of an embryonic civil liberties union") signaled the shift to searching for an alternative discourse about democracy among Soviet intellectuals. Another side effect of 1968 was the "the reinvention of Russia" (Y. Brudny). See Zubok, *Zhivago's Children;* Yitzhak M. Brudny, *Reinventing Russia: Russian Nationalism and the Soviet State, 1953–1991* (Cambridge, Mass., and London: Harvard University Press, 1998); and Peter Reddaway, ed., *Uncensored Russia: The Human Rights Movement in the Soviet Union,* with a foreword by Julius Telesin (London : J. Cape, 1972).

65. Zubok, *Zhivago's Children,* p. 296.

66. V. Cerniayev quoted in Victor Zaslavsky, "The Prague Spring: Resistance and Surrender of the PCI," in *Promises of 1968,* ed. Tismaneanu, p. 406.

67. Judt, *Postwar,* p. 447.

68. Paul Auster, "The Accidental Rebel," *New York Times,* April 23, 2008; Jeffrey Herf, "1968 and the Terrorist Aftermath in West Germany," in *Promises of 1968,* ed. Tismaneanu, p. 363.

69. Judt, *Postwar,* p. 449. Wallerstein offered a different reading of 1968. Rather than seeing it as the beginning of the end of revolutionary or radical mass politics, Wallerstein understood it as the starting point of the globalization and generalization of antisystemic movements: the "rainbow coalition" applied to "trans-zonal cooperation"—the only way in which a "desirable transformation of the capitalist world-economy is possible." However, his conviction that these movements were situated *outside* rather *within* (as in Judt's and other authors' analysis) was the real source of his frustration: "a fully coherent alternative strategy" did not appear. Wallerstein was correct in stating that "the real importance of the Revolution of 1968 is less its critique of the past than the questions it raised about the future." But, as the upheavals of 1989 (the publication year of his article) demonstrated, the sixties affected the re-creation of the center rather than the re-enforcement and reinvention of the extremes. See Immanuel Wallerstein and Sharon Zukin, "1968, Revolution in the World-System: Theses and Queries," *Theory and Society* 18, no. 4 (July 1989): 442–48. To paraphrase Marwick, the social movement that developed in the aftermath of the sixties did not confront their societies but rather permeated and transformed them.

70. Edgar Morin, Claude Lefort, and Cornelius Castoriadis, *La brèche: Premières réflexions sur les évènements* (Paris: Fayard, 1968).

71. Charles Maier, "Conclusion: 1968—Did It Matter?" in *Promises of 1968,* ed. Tismaneanu, p. 423.

72. See Paul Berman's introduction in *A Tale of Two Utopias: The Political Journey of the Generation of 1968* (New York: W.W. Norton, 1996).

73. See Vladimir Tismaneanu, *Reinventing Politics; Eastern Europe from Stalin to Havel* (New York: Free Press, 1992; paperback with new afterword, 1993).

74. English, *Russia and the Idea of the West,* p. 100.

75. Ibid., pp. 108–9.

76. Ibid., p. 114.

77. I am rephrasing Alain Besançon's evaluation of Gorbachev's project of reform from his article "Breaking the Spell," in *Can the Soviet System Survive Reform? Seven Colloquies about the State of Soviet Socialism Seventy Years after the Bolshevik Revolution,* ed. George R. Urban (London: Pinter, 1989). The journal *Slavic Review* reignited this discussion through the publication, in Autumn 2004, of Stephen F. Cohen's piece "Was the Soviet System Reformable?" along with replies from Archie Brown, Mark Kramer, Stephen Hanson, Karen Dawisha, and Georgi Derluguian.

78. Quoted in Silvio Pons, "Western Communists, Gorbachev, and the 1989 Revolutions," *Journal of European History* 18 (2009): 366.

79. Vladimir Kontorovich, "The Economic Fallacy," in *National Interest* 31 (Spring 1993): 35–45.

80. Stephen E. Hanson, "Gorbachev: The Last True Leninist Believer?" in *The Crisis of Leninism and the Decline of the Left: The Revolutions of 1989,* ed. Daniel Chirot (Seattle: University of Washington Press, 1991), p. 54. See also Stephen E. Hanson, *Post-Imperial Democracies: Ideology and Party Formation in Third Republic France, Weimar Germany, and Post-Soviet Russia* (Cambridge: Cambridge University Press, 2010).

81. Zubok, *Zhivago's Children,* p. 335.

82. Stephen Kotkin, *Armageddon Averted: The Soviet Collapse, 1970–2000* (Oxford: Oxford University Press, 2001), p. 27. Mark Kramer, who develops Kotkin's point of view, strengthens his argument on Gorbachev's refusal to continue muddling through of the stagnation years by quoting a telling statement made by Islam Karimov during a Politburo meeting in January 1991: "Back in 1985, Mikhail Sergeevich, if I may say so, you didn't have to launch perestroika. . . . Everything would have continued as it was, and you would have thrived, and we would have thrived. And no catastrophes of any sort would have occurred." Mark Kramer, "The Reform of the Soviet System and the Demise of the Soviet State," *Slavic Review* 63, no. 3 (Autumn 2004): 505–12.

83. Archie Brown, *The Rise and Fall of Communism* (London: Bodley Head, 2009), p. 598.

84. For a synthetic analysis of the various trends of thinking that were born in post-Stalinist USSR and which resulted by the end of 1980s in the collapse of Marxism-Leninism as state ideology, see Archie Brown, ed., *The Demise of Marxism-Leninism in Russia* (London: Palgrave Macmillan, 2004).

85. Robert English, "The Sociology of New Thinking: Elites, Identity Change, and the End of the Cold War," *Journal of Cold War Studies* 7, no. 2 (Spring 2005): 43–80.

86. Archie Brown, *Seven Years That Changed the World: Perestroika in Perspective* (London: Oxford University Press, 2007). See also his previous re-

search on Gorbachev and the aftermath of perestroika: Archie Brown, *The Gorbachev Factor* (Oxford: Oxford University Press, 1996); and Archie Brown and Lilia Shevtsova, eds., *Gorbachev, Yeltsin, Putin: Political Leadership in Russia's Transition* (Washington, D.C.: Carnegie Endowment for International Peace, 2001).

87. Zubok, *Zhivago's Children*, p. 120.

88. For an analysis of the transformations within the Soviet leadership and higher ranks of the CPSU in the last decades of the USSR, see Jerry F. Hough, *Democratization and Revolution in the USSR, 1985–1991* (Washington, D.C.: Brookings Institution Press, 1997); and *Soviet Leadership in Transition* (Washington, D.C.: Brookings Institution Press, 1980).

89. See Georgii Arbatov, *The System: An Insider's Life in Soviet Politics* (New York: Times Books, 1992); and Aleksandr Yakovlev, *The Fate of Marxism in Russia* (New Haven, Conn.: Yale University Press, 1993).

90. English, "The Sociology of New Thinking," p. 76. R. English's article is part of a thematic issue of the *Journal of Cold War Studies* 2 (Spring 2005) on the role of ideas in the end of the Cold War and the collapse of the Soviet Union. See also Nina Tannenwald and William C. Wohlforth, "Introduction: The Role of Ideas and the End of the Cold War," 3–12; Nina Tannenwald, "Ideas and Explanation: Advancing the Theoretical Agenda," 13–42; Andrew Bennett, "The Guns That Didn't Smoke: Ideas and the Soviet Non-use of Force in 1989," 81–109; Daniel C. Thomas, "Human Rights Ideas, the Demise of Communism, and the End of the Cold War," 110–41; and William C. Wohlforth, "The End of the Cold War as a Hard Case for Ideas," 165–73.

91. For an intellectual history of the ascendance of this group and of their ideas, see English, *Russia and the Idea of the West*.

92. Robert C. Tucker, *Political Culture and Leadership in Soviet Russia: From Lenin to Gorbachev* (New York and London: W.W. Norton, 1987), p. 132.

93. *Pravda*, February 6, 1990.

94. See Gorbachev and Mlynář, *Conversations with Gorbachev*, pp. 56–58.

95. See comments along these lines in Stephen F. Cohen, "Was the Soviet System Reformable?" *Slavic Review* 63, no. 3 (Autumn 2004): 459–88; Archie Brown, "The Soviet Union: Reform of the System or Systemic Transformation?" *Slavic Review* 63, no. 3 (Autumn 2004): 489–504; and Mark Kramer, "The Reform of the Soviet System," p. 506.

96. Anatoly S. Chernyaev, *My Six Years with Gorbachev,* trans. and ed. Robert D. English and Elizabeth Tucker (University Park: Pennsylvania State University Press, 2000), p. 105.

97. Daniel C. Thomas, "Human Rights Ideas, the Demise of Communism, and the End of the Cold War," *Journal of Cold War Studies* 7, no. 2 (Spring 2005): 129.

98. Brown, *Seven Years*, p. 157.

99. X.I. Ding, "Institutional Amphibiousness and the Transition from Communism: The Case of China," *British Journal of Political Science* 24 (July 1994): 293–318.

100. I am employing Frederick Corney's terminology. See Corney, "What Is to Be Done," p. 267.

101. Quoted in Jacques Levesque, *The Enigma of 1989: The USSR and the Liberation of Eastern Europe* (Los Angeles and London: University of California Press, 1997). See Aleksander Yakovlev, *Ce que nous voulons faire de l'Union Sovietique: Entretiens avec Lilly Marcou* (Paris: Le Seuil, 1991), p. 104.

102. See *Labor Focus on Eastern Europe* 9, no. 3 (November 1987–February 1988): 5–6.

103. Stephen Cohen, "Was the Soviet System Reformable?" pp. 487–88.

104. Brown, "The Soviet Union," pp. 494–95.

105. Karen Dawisha, "The Question of Questions: Was the Soviet Union Worth Saving?" *Slavic Review* 63, no. 3 (Autumn 2004): 513–26; and Stephen Hanson, "Reform and Revolution in the Late Soviet Context," *Slavic Review* 63, no. 3 (Autumn 2004): 527–34.

106. Hanson, "Reform and Revolution," p. 533. It is no surprise that Stephen Cohen, who throughout his scholarly work has sought to find the ever elusive solution from above (Bukharin, Gorbachev) to counter Stalin's Great Break, dismisses arguments in favor of an anti-Soviet revolution from below. For descriptions of the development of alternative politics from below before and during Gorbachev's reign, see Steven M. Fish, *Democracy from Scratch: Opposition and Regime in the New Russian Revolution* (Princeton, N.J.: Princeton University Press, 1995); Mark R. Beissinger, *Nationalist Mobilization and the Collapse of the Soviet State* (Cambridge and New York: Cambridge University Press, 2002); Edward W. Walker, *Dissolution: Sovereignty and the Breakup of the Soviet Union* (Lanham: Rowman & Littlefield, 2003); also Walter D. Connor, "Soviet Society, Public Attitudes, and the Perils of Gorbachev's Reforms: The Social Context of the End of the USSR," *Journal of Cold War Studies* 5, no. 4 (Fall 2003): 43–80; Astrid S. Tuminez, "Nationalism, Ethnic Pressures, and the Break-up of the Soviet Union," *Journal of Cold War Studies* 5, no. 4 (Fall 2003): 81–136; and Mark Kramer, "The Collapse of East European Communism and the Repercussions within the Soviet Union: Part 1," *Journal of Cold War Studies* 5, no. 4 (Fall 2003): 178–256; Kramer, "The Collapse of East European Communism and the Repercussions within the Soviet Union: Part 2," *Journal of Cold War Studies* 6, no. 4 (Fall 2004): 3–64; Kramer, "The Collapse of East European Communism and the Repercussions within the Soviet Union: Part 3," *Journal of Cold War Studies* 7, no. 1 (Winter 2005): 3–96.

107. Kramer, "The Collapse: Part 1," p. 214.

108. Gorbachev and Mlynář, *Conversations,* pp. 110–21.

109. Levesque, *The Enigma of 1989,* pp. 3–5 and 252–58.

110. Brown, "The Soviet Union," p. 489.

111. Václav Havel et al., *The Power of the Powerless: Citizens against the State in Central-Eastern Europe* (Armonk, N.Y.: M.E. Sharpe, 1985), pp. 33–34.

112. Ibid., p. 35.

113. Kramer, "The Collapse: Part 3," pp. 69 and 94. For his discussion of the "demonstration effects" for the Soviet Union, see "The Collapse: Part 2."

114. In making this statement, the historian invokes the authority of the founding fathers of the Soviet human rights movement, Raisa Orlova and Lev Kopelev. See Zubok, *Zhivago's Children,* p. 265.

115. George Konrád, *Antipolitics* (San Diego, Calif.: Harcourt Brace Jovanovich, 1984), p. 123.

116. Falk, *The Dilemmas of Dissidence,* p. 313.

117. Horvath, "'The Solzhenitsyn Effect,'" p. 907. Also see Jan Plamper, "Foucault's Gulag," *Kritika: Explorations in Russian and Eurasian History,* n.s., 3, no. 2 (Spring 2002): 255–80.

118. I am developing Neil Robinson's argument in "What Was Soviet Ideology? A Comment on Joseph Schull and an Alternative," *Political Studies* 43 (1995): 325–32. See also Neil Robinson, *Ideology and the Collapse of the Soviet System: A Critical History of Soviet Ideological Discourse* (Aldershot and Hants: E. Elgar, 1995).

119. "There's More to Politics than Human Rights," an interview with G.M. Tamás, *Uncaptive Minds* 1, no. 1 (April–May 1988): 12.

120. Miklós Haraszti, *The Velvet Prison: Artists under State Socialism* (New York: Basic Books, 1987).

121. Jan Josef Lipski, *KOR: A History of the Workers' Defense Committee 1976–1981* (Berkeley: University of California Press, 1985).

122. Ferenc Fehér, Agnes Heller, and György Márkus, *Dictatorship over Needs* (London: Basil Blackwell, 1983), p. 137.

123. Brown, *Rise and Fall,* p. 588.

124. Johann P. Arnason, "Communism and Modernity," in *Multiple Modernities,* special issue, *Daedalus* 129, no. 1 (Winter 2000): 61–90.

5. IDEOLOGY, UTOPIA, AND TRUTH

1. Goerge Lichtheim, *Thoughts among the Ruins: Collected Essays on Europe and Beyond* (New Brunswick, N.J.: Transaction Books, 1973); Vladimir Tismaneanu, *The Crisis of Marxist Ideology in Eastern Europe: The Poverty of Utopia* (London and New York: Routledge, 1988); Agnes Heller and Ferenc Fehér, *The Grandeur and Twilight of Radical Universalism* (New Brunswick, N.J.: Transaction Books, 1991); Melvin J. Lasky, *Utopia and Revolution* (Chicago: University of Chicago Press, 1976).

2. See the discussion of Jan Patočka's concept of supercivilization in Edward F. Findlay, *Caring for the Soul in a Postmodern Age: Politics and Phenomenology in the Thought of Jan Patočka* (Albany: State University of New York Press, 2002), pp. 126–27.

3. Shlomo Avineri and Zeev Sternhell, *Europe's Century of Discontent: The Legacies of Fascism, Nazism, and Communism* (Jerusalem: Hebrew University Magnes Press, 2003); Tony Judt, *Postwar: A History of Europe since 1945* (New York: Penguin Press, 2005); Bernard Wasserstein, *Barbarism and Civilization: A History of Europe in Our Time* (Oxford: Oxford University Press, 2007).

4. Bernice Glatzer Rosenthal, "Introduction," in *Nietzsche and Soviet Culture: Ally and Adversary* (Cambridge: Cambridge University Press, 1994), p. 17. See also Rosenthal, *New Myth, New World—from Nietzsche to Stalinism* (University Park: Pennsylvania State University Press, 2002).

5. See the discussion on totalitarian experiments and secular religions in Raymond Aron, The *Dawn of Universal History: Selected Essays from a Witness to*

the Twentieth Century, intro. Tony Judt (New York: Basic Books, 2002); Robert Conquest, *Reflections on a Ravaged Century* (New York: Norton, 2000), pp. 57–84; Abbott Gleason, *Totalitarianism: The Inner History of the Cold War* (New York: Oxford University Press, 1995).

6. See Hannah Arendt, *The Origins of Totalitarianism* (San Diego, Calif.: Harcourt Brace Jovanovich, 1973), pp. 458 and 459.

7. Michael Geyer, "Introduction," in *Beyond Totalitarianism: Stalinism and Nazism Compared,* ed. Michael Geyer and Sheila Fitzpatrick (New York: Cambridge University Press, 2009), p. 28.

8. Jacob L. Talmon, *Myth of the Nation and Vision of Revolution: Ideological Polarizations in the Twentieth Century* (New Brunswick, N.J.: Transaction Publishers, 1991); and George Lichtheim, *The Concept of Ideology and Other Essays* (New York: Random House, 1967).

9. Leszek Kołakowski, *Main Currents of Marxism: The Founders, the Golden Age, the Breakdown,* trans. P.S. Falla (New York: W.W. Norton, 2005), p. 1214.

10. Bernard Yack, *The Longing for Total Revolution: Philosophic Sources of Social Discontent from Rousseau to Marx and Nietzsche* (Princeton, N.J.: Princeton University Press, 1986).

11. Findlay, *Caring for the Soul,* p. 157.

12. Ferenc Fehér, "Marxism as Politics: An Obituary," *Problems of Communism* 41, nos. 1–2 (January–April 1992): 11–17.

13. Robert C. Tucker, *Philosophy and Myth in Karl Marx* (Cambridge and New York: Cambridge University Press, 1972).

14. Lucien Goldmann, *Marxisme et sciences humaines* (Paris: Gallimard, 1970).

15. Robert C. Tucker, ed., *The Marx-Engels Reader,* 2d ed. (New York and London: W.W. Norton), p. 488.

16. Ibid., p. 500. It is noteworthy that all Communist newspapers in the USSR, China, and other Soviet-style regimes, as well as Communist dailies in non-Marxist countries, carried the exhortatory last sentence of the *Manifesto* at the top of the front page, above their title. It is also significant that when Václav Havel described the "emptyfication" of ideological rituals in Leninist regimes, he resorted to the parable of a greengrocer who would discover his liberty and reinvent himself as a citizen by refusing to place in the window, on May 1, the party-provided poster with the by now meaningless words "Workers of all countries unite!"

17. Ibid., pp. 482–83.

18. Ibid., pp. 483–84.

19. Rosa Luxemburg quoted in Lars T. Lih, *Lenin Rediscovered: "What Is to Be Done?" in Context* (Chicago: Haymarket Books, 2008), p. 527.

20. Kołakowski, *Main Currents,* p. 770.

21. Anne Applebaum, "Dead Souls: Tallying the Victims of Communism," *Weekly Standard,* December 13, 1999, http://www.anneapplebaum.com/, accessed on October 1, 2011.

22. See Slavoj Žižek, ed., *Revolution at the Gates: Selected Writings of Lenin from 1917* (London: Verso, 2002), p. 113 (Lenin's italics).

23. Robert Horvath, *The Legacy of Soviet Dissent: Dissidents, Democratisation and Radical Nationalism in Russia* (London: Routledge, 2005), p. 20.

24. For a perceptive approach to the main themes of Marxism and an evaluation of what is dead and alive in that doctrine, see Jon Elster, *An Introduction to Karl Marx* (Cambridge and New York: Cambridge University Press, 1988), pp. 186–200; Jeffrey C. Isaac, *Power and Marxist Theory: A Realist View* (Ithaca, N.Y., and London: Cornell University Press, 1987). Shlomo Avineri's masterful book, *The Social and Political Thought of Karl Marx* (Cambridge and New York: Cambridge University Press, 1968), which came out on the 150th anniversary of Marx's birth (a year full of revolutionary pathos, illusions, and resurrected utopias), remains a most useful discussion of Marx's concept of revolution. Avineri's conclusion on the relationship between Marxism and Bolshevism is worth quoting: "One must concede that, with all the differences between Marx and Soviet, Leninist Communism, Leninism would have been inconceivable without Marxism" (p. 258).

25. See Richard H. Crossman, ed., *The God That Failed,* with a foreword by David C. Engerman (New York: Columbia University Press, 2001). For an insightful approach to the literature of antitotalitarian disenchantment, see John V. Fleming, *The Anti-Communist Manifestos: Four Books That Shaped the Cold War* (New York: Norton, 2009). An outstanding contribution to the topic is Michael Scammell, *Koestler: The Literary and Political Odyssey of a Twentieth-Century Skeptic* (New York: Random House, 2009).

26. See Stanislao Pugliese's superb biography, *Bitter Spring: A Life of Ignazio Silone* (New York: Farrar Straus and Giroux, 2009), p. 105. Unlike many fellow ex-Communists, Silone remained attached to the ideals of a democratic Left, defining himself as "a Christian without a Church, a socialist without a party" (p. 244).

27. See Ferenc Fehér and Agnes Heller, *Eastern Left, Western Left: Totalitarianism, Freedom, and Democracy* (Atlantic Highlands, N.J.: Humanities Press International, 1987), especially "An Imaginary Preface to the 1984 Edition of Hannah Arendt's *The Origins of Totalitarianism*" and "In the Bestiarium: A Contribution to the Cultural Anthropology of 'Real Socialism,'" pp. 243–78.

28. Václav Havel, "The Power of the Powerless," in *Open Letters: Selected Writings, 1965–1990* (New York: Vintage Books, 1992), p. 136.

29. James C. Scott, *Seeing Like a State: How Certain Schemes to Improve the Human Condition Have Failed* (New Haven, Conn.: Yale University Press, 1998).

30. Aviezer Tucker, *Philosophy and Politics of Czech Dissidence from Patočka to Havel* (Pittsburgh, Penn.: University of Pittsburgh Press, 2000), p. 191.

31. Ivars Ijabs, "'Politics of Authenticity' and/or Civil Society," in *In Marx's Shadow: Knowledge, Power, and Intellectuals in Eastern Europe and Russia,* ed. Costica Bradatan and Serguei Alex. Oushakine (Lanham: Lexington Books, 2010), p. 246.

32. Findlay, *Caring for the Soul,* p. 150.

33. Costica Bradatan, "Philosophy and Martyrdom: The Case of Jan Patocka," in *In Marx's Shadow,* ed. Bradatan and Oushakine, p. 120.

34. Ibid.

35. Ijabs, "'Politics of Authenticity' and/or Civil Society," p. 255.

36. Vàclav Havel, "The Post-Communist Nightmare, " *New York Review of Books* 27 (May 1993): 8.

37. George Konrád, *The Melancholy of Rebirth: Essays from Post-Communist Central Europe, 1989–1994* (San Diego: Harcourt Brace, 1995), p. 101.

38. Findlay, *Caring for the Soul,* pp. 141–42.

39. Tucker, *Philosophy and Politics,* p. 136.

40. Eric D. Weitz, *A Century of Genocide: Utopias of Race and Nation* (Princeton, N.J., and Oxford: Princeton University Press, 2003), pp. 54–55.

41. Kołakowski, *Main Currents of Marxism,* p. 1212.

42. Andrzej Walicki, *Marxism and the Leap to the Kingdom of Freedom: The Rise and Fall of the Communist Utopia* (Stanford, Calif.: Stanford University Press, 1995), pp. 5–13. For an interesting comparison of Walicki's approach to other seminal attempts to evaluate the degree of influence of Marxism-Leninism in Soviet politics and systemic dynamics, see David Priestland, "Marx and the Kremlin: Writing on Marxism-Leninism and Soviet Politics after the Fall of Communism," *Journal of Political Ideologies* 5, no. 3 (2000): 337–90. For example, Priestland stresses that Walicki noticed a tension between Marx's concern that man be free from subordination to others and his demand that man be free from dependence on nature. He then inscribes this observation, by comparison to other authors (including N. Robinson, S. Hanson, M. Malia, and M. Sandle), into a larger picture of the multiple dichotomies that characterized Bolshevism: "The conflict between participation and technocracy . . . the conflict between voluntarism and evolutionary determinism . . . the tension between a position which one might call 'populist radical' . . . and an 'elitist radicalism.' " Antonio Gramsci wrote about the tension between fatalism and voluntarism as a permanent feature of revolutionary theory.

43. Claude Lefort, *Complications: Communism and the Dilemmas of Democracy* (New York: Columbia University Press, 2007).

44. Neil Robinson, "What Was Soviet Ideology? A Comment on Joseph Schull and an Alternative," *Political Studies* 43 (1995): 325–32. For a detailed application of his approach (the telos of radical democratization and Communism vs. the vanguard party), see Neil Robinson, *Ideology and the Collapse of the Soviet System* (Aldershot: E. Elgar, 1995).

45. Rachel Walker, "Thinking about Ideology and Method: A Comment on Schull," *Political Studies* 43 (1995): 333–42; and "Marxism-Leninism as Discourse: The Politics of the Empty Signifier and the Double Bind," *British Journal of Political Science* 19 (1989): 161–89.

46. In the fifth chapter ("Melancholy, Utopia and Reconciliation") of *Another Country,* Jan-Werner Müller provides an excellent example of the point I am making. The writer Jurek Becker (a former émigré from the GDR) stated that "somehow, across all experiences and beyond all insight, existed the hope that the socialist countries could find another path. That's over now." In justifying his vote against reunification, he stated: "The most important thing about the socialist countries is nothing visible, but a possibility. There not everything has been decided like here." Or Uwe Timm: "One has to remember that socialism in the GDR was an alternative to the FRG, admittedly an ugly, bureaucratically bloated alternative, but still an alternative, and that this 'real socialism,'

despite all ossification, *would have been capable of self-transformation is not a mere assertion*. That is demonstrated by the grassroots democratic movements" (my emphasis). Jan-Werner Müller, *Another Country: German Intellectuals, Unification, and National Identity* (New Haven, Conn., and London: Yale University Press, 2000), p. 125; also see pp. 124–29.

47. Raymond Aron, *Memoirs: Fifty Years of Political Reflection* (New York: Holmes and Meier, 1990), p. 414; Vladimir Tismaneanu, *Despre communism: Destinul unei religii politice* (Nucjhares: Humanias, 2011).

48. Kołakowski, *Main Currents,* p. vi.

49. See Marx and Engels, *Manifestul Partidului Comunist,* ed. Cristian Preda (Bucureti: Ed. Nemira, 1998), p. 150. The volume includes the *Manifesto* as well as a number of post-1989 reactions to it.

50. For the Tamás-Pleşu exchange, see http://www.eurozine.com/articles/2009–06–16-tamas-ro.html. In my own exchange with G.M. Tamás, I argued that his espousal of Alain Badiou's extolment of the "communist hypothesis" amounted to a frivolous ignorance of historical realities and an implicit rejection of bourgeois-liberal modernity. See Vladimir Tismaneanu, "Marxism histrionic (G.M. Tamás & co.)," *Revista 22,* July 20, 2010, http://www.revista22.ro/articol-8603.html (accessed on February 27, 2010).

51. See Tismaneanu, "Marxism histrionic"; and G.M. Tamás, "Un delict de opinie," in *Revista 22* (Bucharest), July 2–26, 2010, pp. 5–9.

52. Review of *The Structural Crisis of Capital* by István Meszáros, *Monthly Review Press,* Feb. 7, 2012, http://www.monthlyreview.org/books/structuralcrisisofcapital.php, accessed August 24, 2010.

53. For the famous slogan "Gray is beautiful," see Adam Michnik, *Letters from Freedom: Post-Cold War Realities and Perspectives* (Berkeley: University of California Press, 1998), pp. 317–27. On the relationship between radical ideas and totalitarian experiments, see H.-R. Patapievici, *Politice* (Bucharest: Humanitas, 1996).

54. I examine these trends in my *Fantasies of Salvation: Democracy, Nationalism, and Myth in Post-Communist Europe* (Princeton, N.J.: Princeton University Press, 1998; paperback edition, 2009).

55. Olivier Mongin, *Face au scepticisme: Les mutations du paysage intellectuel ou l'invention de l'intellectuel démocratique* (Paris: Éditions La Découverte, 1994); in the same vein, Jorge Castaneda emphasized the postutopian transfiguration of radical politics in Latin America.

56. For example, the Budapest School (from old Lukács to Agnes Heller, Ferenc Fehér, György Márkus, Mihaly Vajda, János Kis, György Bence), the experiences of Jacek Kuroń, Krzysztof Pomian, Leszek Kołakowski, and Zygmunt Bauman, Ernst Bloch's impact on East Germany's revisionists, and so on.

57. For example, Carlo Roselli, Norberto Bobbio, Cornelius Castoriadis, Claude Lefort, Edgar Morin, and Jean-François Lyotard.

58. See Tony Judt, *Reappraisals: Reflections on the Forgotten Twentieth Century* (New York: Penguin Books, 2008), p. 133.

59. Raymond Taras, ed., *The Road to Disillusion* (Armonk, N.Y.: M.E. Sharpe, 1992).

60. Milovan Djilas, *Of Prisons and Ideas* (San Diego, Calif., and New York: Harcourt Brace Jovanovich, 1984).

61. Walicki advocates a similar approach when he argues that because of the dilution, domestication and of emptying Marxism of its utopian revolutionary aspect, one is bound to aim at, nowadays, a "defamiliarization" of Marxism "by paying proper attention to its millenarian features." Andrzej Walicki, *Marxism and the Leap to the Kingdom of Freedom: The Rise and Fall of the Communist Utopia* (Stanford, Calif.: Stanford University Press, 1995), p. 2.

62. Findlay, *Caring for the Soul,* p. 132.

63. Václav Havel, "The Power of the Powerless," in *The Power of the Powerless,* ed. Václav Havel et al. (Armonk, N.Y.: M.E. Sharpe, 1990), pp. 36–37.

64. Agnes Heller, "Toward Post-Totalitarianism," in *Debates on the Future of Communism,* ed. Vladimir Tismaneanu and Judith Shapiro (London: Macmillan, 1991), pp. 50–55; see Agnes Heller, "Legitimation Deficit and Legitimation Crisis in East European Societies," in *Stalinism Revisited: The Establishment of Communist Regimes in East-Central Europe,* ed. Vladimir Tismaneanu (Budapest and New York: CEU Press, 2009), pp. 143–60.

65. Leszek Kołakowski, "Totalitarianism and Lie," *Commentary* (May 1983), p. 37.

66. In my *Fantasies of Salvation: Democracy, Nationalism, and Myth in Post-Communist Europe* (Princeton, N.J.: Princeton University Press, 1998), I defined, with reference to Eric Hoffer's analysis of political fanaticism, *ideological hubris* as "the firm belief that there is one and only one answer to the social questions, and that the ideologue is the one who holds it" (p. 28). Also see Eric Hofer, *The True Believer: Thoughts on the Nature of Mass Movements* (New York: Time, 1963); Elie Halevy, a French thinker who, in the 1930s, wrote about the age of tyranny dominated by the "etatisation of thought" and the "organization of enthusiasm." See Alberto Toscano, *Fanaticism: On the Uses of an Idea* (London: Verso, 2010), p. 206. Political religions were also instruments for the organization of social resentment, envy, and hatred. See Gabriel Liiceanu, *Despre ură* (Bucharest: Humanitas, 2007).

67. Richard Shorten, "François Furet and Totalitarianism: A Recent Intervention in the Misuse of a Notion," *Totalitarian Movements and Political Religions* 3, no. 1 (Summer 2002): 10–11. For an extensive presentation of Lefort's analysis of ideology, see Claude Lefort, *The Political Forms of Modern Society* (Oxford: Polity Press, 1986).

68. I am paraphrasing Ken Jowitt's conclusions on the neotraditionalism of the Soviet-type system. See Ken Jowitt, *New World Disorder: The Leninist Extinction* (Berkeley and Los Angeles: University of California Press, 1992), pp. 121–58. See also Ken Jowitt, "Stalinist Revolutionary Breakthroughs in Eastern Europe," in *Stalinism Revisited,* ed. Tismaneanu, pp. 17–24.

69. Roger Griffin, "Ideology and Culture," *Journal of Political Ideologies* 11, no. 1 (Feb. 2006): 77–99.

70. See for instance Stephen Kinzer, "In 'East Germany,' Bad Ol' Days Now Look Good," *New York Times,* August 27, 1994. This restorative theme was the gist of Russian leader Gennady Zyuganov's 1996 presidential campaign. He

challenged Boris Yeltsin in the name of an idealized vision of the historical past, heroic value, ethnic solidarity, and opposition to corruptive Western influences. E.g., David Remnick, "Hammer, Sickle, and Book," *New York Review of Books* 23 (May 1996): 44–51.

71. I am putting together here two of the essential statements Ken Jowitt made in his analysis of Leninism and its legacy. The first: "The political individuation of an articulated potential citizenry treated contemptuously by an inclusive (not democratic), neotraditional (not modernized) Leninist polity was the cause of Leninist breakdown" (Ken Jowitt, "Weber, Trotsky and Holmes on the Study of Leninist Regimes," *Journal of International Affairs* [2001]: 31–49). The second: "It should be equally clear that today [1992] the *dominant and shared* Eastern European reality is severe and multiple fragmentation" (Ken Jowitt, *New World Disorder*, pp. 299–300).

72. Findlay, *Caring for the Soul*, p. 133.

73. Leszek Kołakowski, *Main Currents of Marxism: Its Origins, Growth and Dissolution*, vol. 3, *The Breakdown* (New York: Oxford University Press, 1978), pp. 526–30.

74. Robert D. English, *Russia and the Idea of the West: Gorbachev, Intellectuals, and the End of the Cold War* (New York: Columbia University Press, 2000), p. 109.

75. George Konrád, *The Melancholy of Rebirth*, p. 23.

76. Literary critic Vladimir Potapov quoted in Horvath, *The Legacy*, p. 1. Horvath tellingly describes the nature of the experience associated with reading the *Gulag Archipelago*. He quotes Natalya Eksler's recollections about the peregrinations of a copy of volume 2 that Andrei Amalrik gave her in 1976: "It was borrowed by friends, then returned, then borrowed for the friends of friends, and the book left home for longer and longer intervals before reappearing. Then it somehow vanished for an extended period. And since some friends wanted their children, who had come of age, to read it, we tried to call it back. After a while we were told: 'Wait a little, please. It's in the Urals: let it circulate, since it might be the only copy there.' We waited. After a year, we tried again, and were informed: 'The book is in the Baltics, there is an enormous queue, which they call the queue for The Book.' We waited another few years, and learned that it was now in the Ukraine" (p. 25).

77. For example, the coming of age of the dissident was celebrated at the Theatre Récamier in June 1977, when André Glucksmann and Michel Foucault organized a reception for French intellectuals and East European dissident exiles to protest Brezhnev's visit to Paris. In an interview, Foucault explained that "we thought that on the evening when Mr. Brezhnev is received with grand pomp by Mr. Giscard d'Estaing, other French people could receive other Russians who are their friends." This hospitality marked a vast reversal in attitudes since Brezhnev's arrival in 1971, when hardly a murmur of criticism had been elicited by the decision of the French authorities to welcome the Soviet leader with a police round-up of prominent East European émigré intellectuals, who were banished to a Corsican hotel for the duration of the visit." See Horvath, "'The Solzhenitsyn Effect,'" p. 902.

78. Horvath, *The Legacy,* p. 22.

79. Ibid., p. 24.

80. Vadim Medvedev, Central Committee secretary for ideology, quoted in Horvath, *The Legacy,* p. 6.

81. Tucker, *Philosophy and Politics,* p. 117.

82. Bo Strath, "Ideology and History," *Journal of Political Ideologies* 11, no. 1 (February 2006): 23–42.

83. For the exact quotation, see V. Havel, "Šifra socialismus [Cipher Socialism] " (June 1988), DRS, pp. 202–4; Martin J. Matustik, "Havel and Habermas on Identity and Revolutions," *Praxis International* 10, nos. 3–4 (October 1990–January 1991): 261–77.

84. Václav Havel, *Letters to Olga* (New York: Knopf, 1988), p. 145.

85. Matustik, "Havel and Habermas," p. 269.

86. Václav Havel, "The Post-Communist Nightmare, " p. 48.

87. This statement belongs to L. Kołakowski and appears in his interview with G. Urban, in G. R. Urban, ed., *Stalinism—Its Impact on Russia and the World* (London: Maurice Temple Smith, 1982), p. 277.

88. Steven Lukes, "On the Moral Blindness of Communism," *Human Rights Review* 2, no. 2 (January–March 2001): 113–24.

89. Václav Havel, "New Year Address," *East European Reporter* 4, no.1 (Winter 1989–1990): 56–58.

90. I chose a counterpart to Umberto Eco's category for the extreme Right based on the noticeable communality of features between what he brands ur-Fascism and what I regard as ur-Leninism. If one took each characteristic of ur-Fascism pointed out by Eco, one could find a corresponding characteristic of ur-Leninism: the cult of tradition based on syncretism and the rejection of capitalist modernity (one can easily point to late 1930s and early 1950s Stalinism, to Ceauşescu's national Stalinism, to Honecker's Prussianism, etc.); the cult of action for action's sake (Leninism is fundamentally a mobilization-centered ideology abhorrent of intellectualism and what it considers to be petit-bourgeois culture); monolithic unity ("the party of a new type"); hatred of difference (homogenization of the social, i.e., "the society of non-antagonistic classes" or anticosmopolitanism); reliance on the middle class (Leninism as a social system was sustained through both the creation of a New Class and the transformation of social categories via cultural revolution); "obsession with a plot" (suffice to mention here the "21 Conditions" for the Third International and the ban on factions); antipacifism and the mentality of permanent warfare (read "the deepening of class struggle" and "the continuous revolution"); "contempt for the weak" (the project of the New Man); "selective populism" (one has only to think of, among many other possible examples, Gomułka's anti-Semitic campaign in Poland in March 1968); newspeak (read *langue de bois*). See Umberto Eco, "Ur-Fascism," *New York Review of Books,* June 22, 1995; and Umberto Eco, *Five Moral Pieces,* trans. Alastair McEwen (New York: Harcourt, 2002).

91. Bradatan, "Philosophy and Martyrdom," in *Marx's Shadow,* ed. Bradatan and Oushakine, p. 120.

92. Ulrich Klaus Preuss and Ferran Requejo Coll, eds., *European Citizenship, Multiculturalism, and the State* (Baden Baden: Nomos, 1998), p. 127.

93. Quoted in Paul Lawrence, *Nationalism: History and Theory* (New York: Pearson Education, 2005), p. 170.

94. See Ghia Nodia, "Rethinking Nationalism and Democracy in the Light of the Post-Communist Experience," in *National Identity as an Issue of Knowledge and Morality: Georgian Philosophical Studies,* ed. N.V. Chavchavadze, Ghia Nodia, and Paul Peachey (Washington, D.C.: Paideia Press and the Council for Research in Values and Philosophy, 1994), p. 54.

95. For a discussion of Bourdieu's concept of habitus in the context of the analysis of nationalism, see Paul Warren James, *Globalism, Nationalism, Tribalism: Bringing Theory Back* (London: Sage, 2006), pp. 55–57.

96. Anthony D. Smith, *Nationalism and Modernism: A Critical Survey of Recent Theories of the Nation* (London: Routledge, 1998).

97. Roger Griffin, "Introduction: God's Counterfeiters? Investigating the Triad of Fascism, Totalitarianism and (Political) Religion," *Totalitarian Movements and Political Religions* 5, no. 3 (Winter 2004): 305.

98. See Norman Manea, "Intellectuals and Social Change in Central and Eastern Europe," *Partisan Review*, no. 4 (Fall 1992): 573–74.

99. For the politics of intolerance in Tudjman's Croatia, see Goran Vezic, "A Croatian Reichstag Trial: The Case of Dalmatian Action," *Uncaptive Minds* 7, no. 3 (Fall–Winter 1994): 17–24.

100. Furio Cerutti, "Can There Be a Supranational Identity?" *Philosophy and Social Criticism* 18, no. 2 (1992): 147–62.

101. See Jan-Werner Müller, *Constitutional Patriotism* (Princeton, N.J.: Princeton University Press, 2007).

102. See S. Frederick Starr, ed., *The Legacy of History in Russia and the New States of Eurasia* (Armonk, N.Y.: M.E. Sharpe, 1994); Roman Szporluk, ed., *National Identity and Ethnicity in Russia and the New States of Eurasia* (Armonk, N.Y.: M.E. Sharpe, 1994).

103. Václav Havel, *To the Castle and Back* (New York: Knopf, 2007), p. 328.

104. Stephen Kotkin with a contribution by Jan T. Gross, *Uncivil Society: 1989 and the Implosion of the Communist Establishment* (New York: Modern Library, 2009), p. 116.

105. Jan Patočka quoted in Findlay, *Caring for the Soul,* p. 152.

106. Horvath, *The Legacy,* p. 19.

107. Applebaum, "Dead Souls."

108. For an informative approach to contemporary efforts to resurrect Marxism, including the disconcerting "theological turn" inspired by the writing of Jacob Taubes on Paulinian eschatology, see Göran Therborn, *From Marxism to Post-Marxism* (London: Verso, 2008).

109. Norman Naimark, *Stalin's Genocides* (Princeton, N.J.: Princeton University Press, 2010); Vladimir Tismaneanu, "Democracy and Memory: Romania Confronts Its Commmunist Past," in "The Politics of History in Comparative Perspective," ed. Martin O. Heisler, special issue, *Annals of the American Academy of Political Science* 617 (May 2008): 166–80.

288 | Notes to Chapter 6

6. MALAISE AND RESENTMENT

1. See Jan Urban, "Europe's Darkest Scenario," *Washington Post,* Outlook Section, October 11, 1992, pp. 1–2. See G.M. Tamás, "Post-Fascism," in *East European Constitutional Review* (Summer 2000): 48–56.

2. Adam Michnik, "The Velvet Restoration," in *Revolutions of 1989,* ed. Vladimir Tismaneanu (London: Routledge, 1999), pp. 244–51.

3. See Vladimir Tismaneanu, *Fantasies of Salvation: Democracy, Nationalism and Myth in Post-Communist Europe* (Princeton, N.J.: Princeton University Press, 1998, paperback 2009).

4. For further interpretations of the implications of Jowitt's pioneering approach, see Vladimir Tismaneanu, Marc Howard, and Rudra Sil, eds., *World Order after Leninism* (Seattle: University of Washington Press, 2006).

5. For a thorough analysis of the uses of the past in post-Communist Europe, see Tony Judt, *Postwar: A History of Europe since 1945* (New York: Penguin Press, 2005), esp. "After the Fall: 1989–2005," pp. 637–776; and Tony Judt, "The Past Is Another Country: Myth and Memory in Post-War Europe," in *Memory and Power in Post-War Europe: Studies in the Presence of the Past,* ed. Jan-Werner Müller (Cambridge: Cambridge University Press, 2002), p. 180.

6. See William Outhwaite and Larry Ray, *Social Theory and Postcommunism* (Oxford: Blackwell, 2005); Krishan Kumar, *1989: Revolutionary Ideas and Ideals* (Minneapolis: University of Minnesota Press, 2001).

7. In this chapter I elaborate upon and revisit the main ideas I put forward in my introduction to Vladimir Tismaneanu, ed., *The Revolutions of 1989* (London: Routledge, 1999); as well as *Reinventing Politics: Eastern Europe from Stalin to Havel* (New York: Free Press, 1992; revised and expanded paperback, with new afterword, Free Press, 1993). A previous version of this chapter appeared in *Contemporary European History* 18, no. 3 (2009): 271–88. I developed these ideas in a volume published in Romanian, *Despre 1989* (Bucureşti: Humanitas, 2009). See also Vladimir Tismaneanu, "The Demise of Leninism and the Future of Liberal Values," in *Marx's Shadow: Knowledge, Power, and Intellectuals in Eastern Europe and Russia,* ed. Costica Bradatan and Serguei Alex. Oushakine (Lanham, Md.: Lexington Books, 2010), pp. 221–42; and Vladimir Tismaneanu and Bogdan Iacob, eds., *The End and the Beginning: The Revolutions of 1989 and the Resurgence of History* (New York and Budapest: CEU Press, 2012).

8. Eric Hobsbawn, *The Age of Extremes: A History of the World, 1914–91* (New York: Pantheon Books, 1994), pp. 461–99; see also George Lichtheim, "The European Civil War," in *The Concept of Ideology and Other Essays* (New York: Random House, 1967), pp. 225–37; Bernard Wasserstein, *Barbarism and Civilization: A History of Europe in Our Time* (Oxford: Oxford University Press, 2007), pp. 666–704.

9. See John Keane, *Civil Society: Old Images, New Visions* (Stanford, Calif.: Stanford University Press, 1998).

10. Ernest Gellner, *Conditions of Liberty: Civil Society and Its Rivals* (New York: Allen Lane and Penguin Press, 1994).

11. Daniel Chirot, "What Happened in Eastern Europe in 1989," in *The Revolutions of 1989,* ed. Tismaneanu, pp. 19–50; see also Raymond Taras, ed., *The Road to Disillusion* (Armonk, N.Y.: M.E. Sharpe, 1992).

12. Stephen Kotkin with a contribution by Jan T. Gross, *Uncivil Society: 1989 and the Implosion of the Communist Establishment* (New York: Modern Library, 2009), p. 143.

13. Judt, *Postwar,* p. 584.

14. See Václav Havel's reflections on post-1989 politics in *Summer Meditations* (New York: Vintage Books, 1992) and *To the Castle and Back* (New York: Knopf, 2007).

15. For the exhaustion of ideological-style secular religions, see Agnes Heller and Ferenc Fehér, *The Grandeur and Twilight of Radical Universalism* (New Brunswick, N.J.: Transaction Books, 1991); and S.N. Eisenstadt, "The Breakdown of Communist Regimes," in *The Revolutions of 1989,* ed. Tismaneanu, pp. 89–107.

16. Judt, *Postwar,* p. 564.

17. Russian political scientist Gleb Pavlovsky quoted by Robert Horvath, *The Legacy of Soviet Dissent: Dissidents, Democratisation and Radical Nationalism in Russia* (London: Routledge, 2005), p. 41.

18. Krishan Kumar, *1989: Revolutionary Ideas and Ideals* (Minneapolis and London: University of Minnesota Press, 2001).

19. Albert Hirschman, *The Rhetoric of Reaction: Perversity, Futility, Jeopardy* (Cambridge, Mass.: Belknap Press of Harvard University Press, 1991).

20. Jeffrey Isaac, *Democracy in Dark Times* (Ithaca, N.Y.: Cornell University Press, 1997). Also by the same author, "Rethinking the Legacy of Central European Dissidence," *Common Knowledge* 10, no. 1 (Winter 2004): 119–30.

21. Jeffrey Isaac, "Shades of Gray: Revisiting the Meanings of 1989," in *The Beginning and the End,* ed. Tismaneanu and Iacob, pp. 555–74.

22. William Echikcson, *Lighting the Night* (New York: William Morrow, 1990); Vladimir Tismaneanu, *Reinventing Politics;* Andrew Nagorski, *The Birth of Freedom: Shaping Lives and Societies in the New Eastern Europe* (New York: Simon & Schuster, 1993); Ivo Banac, ed. *Eastern Europe in Revolution* (Ithaca, N.Y.: Cornell University Press, 1992).

23. Barbara J. Falk, "Resistance and Dissent in Central and Eastern Europe: An Emerging Historiography," *East European Politics and Societies* 25, no. 2 (May 2011): 321–22.

24. Horvath, *The Legacy,* pp. 1–2. Elena Bonner was a major human rights activist, widow of the celebrated dissident and physicist Andrei Sakharov.

25. Timothy Garton Ash, *The Magic Lantern: The Revolutions of '89 Witnessed in Warsaw, Budapest, Berlin, and Prague* (New York: Vintage Books, 1993).

26. Judt, *Postwar,* p. 563.

27. Timothy Garton Ash, "Conclusions," in *Between Past and Future: The Revolutions of 1989 and Their Aftermath,* ed. Sorin Antohi and Vladimir Tismaneanu (New York and Budapest: Central European University Press, 2000), p. 398.

28. Tony Judt, *Postwar,* p. 695.

29. Anne Applebaum, "1989 and All That," *Slate,* November 9, 2009, http://www.anneapplebaum.com/, accessed August 6, 2011.

30. Falk, "Resistance and Dissent," p. 349.

31. Bruce Ackerman, *The Future of Liberal Revolution* (New Haven, Conn.: Yale University Press, 1992).

32. Judt, *Postwar,* p. 630.

33. Ivo Banac, ed., *Eastern Europe in Revolution.*

34. Jarausch further stated that "in contrast to all the earlier failures, the success of 1989 might be interpreted as a result of mounting civil resistance which initially sought to democratize socialism but ultimately dared to abolish it altogether." See Konrad Jarausch, "People Power? Towards a Historical Explanation of 1989," in *The End and the Beginning,* ed. Tismaneanu and Iacob, p. 123.

35. See Claus Offe, *Varieties of Transition: The East European and East German Experience* (Cambridge, Mass.: MIT Press, 1997), esp. pp. 29–105.

36. See Ferenc Fehér, Agnes Heller, and György Markus, *Dictatorship over Needs* (New York: St. Martin's Press, 1983).

37. Giuseppe di Palma, "Legitimation from the Top to Civil Society: Politico-Cultural Change in Eastern Europe," *World Politics* 44, no. 1 (October 1991): 49–80. In the same issue, see Timur Kuran, "Now Out of Never: The Element of Surprise in the East European of 1989," pp. 7–48. Kuran identifies Václav Havel and this author as among the very few commentators who "came close to predicting a major change" (p. 12).

38. Karen Dawisha, *Eastern Europe, Gorbachev, and Reform: The Great Challenge* (Cambridge and New York: Cambridge University Press, 1990); and Archie Brown, *The Gorbachev Factor* (Oxford: Oxford University Press, 1996).

39. Ralf Dahrendorf, *Reflections on the Revolution in Europe* (New York: Times Books, 1990), p. 111.

40. Vladimir Tismaneanu, *Fantasies of Salvation.* For post-Communist politics, see Padraic Kenney, *The Burdens of Freedom: Eastern Europe since 1989* (London: Zed Books, 2006).

41. G.M. Tamás, "The Legacy of Dissent," in Tismaneanu, *The Revolutions of 1989,* pp. 181–97.

42. Judt, *Postwar,* p. 695.

43. Alexander Yakovlev, *The Fate of Marxism in Russia* (New Haven, Conn.: Yale University Press, 1993), p. 165.

44. Kotkin, *Uncivil Society,* p. xvii.

45. Judt, *Postwar,* p. 563.

46. Tony Judt, "The Past Is Another Country," pp. 163–66.

47. See A. James McAdams, *Judging the Past in Unified Germany* (Cambridge and New York: Cambridge University Press, 2001).

48. For the turbulent experiences with decommunization, see Tina Rosenberg, *The Haunted Land: Facing Europe's Ghost after Communism* (New York: Random House, 1995); Noel Calhoun, *Dilemmas of Justice in Eastern Europe's Democratic Transitions* (New York: Palgrave, 2004); Brian Grodsky,

The Costs of Justice: How New Leaders Respond to Previous Rights Abuses (Notre Dame, Ind.: Notre Dame University, 2010).

49. See Palma, "Legitimation from the Top to Civil Society," 49–80; Eric Hobsbawm, "The New Threat to History," *New York Review of Books,* December 16, 1993, pp. 62–64.

50. S.N. Eisenstadt, "The Breakdown of Communist Regimes," *Daedalus* 121, no. 2 (Spring 1992): 35, included in Vladimir Tismaneanu, ed., *The Revolutions of 1999.*

51. Jack Snyder, *From Voting to Violence: Democratization and Nationalist Conflict* (New York: Norton, 2000).

52. Steven Levitsky and Lucan Way, "The Rise of Competitive Authoritarianism," *Journal of Democracy* 13, no. 2 (April 2002): 51–65. For the other two terms mentioned, see Guillermo O'Donnell, "Delegative Democracy," *Journal of Democracy* 5 (January 1994): 55–69; and Fareed Zakaria, "The Rise of Illiberal Democracy," *Foreign Affairs* 76 (November–December 1997): 22–41. Milada Anna Vachudova discusses the relevance of the three concepts for the process of democratization in Central and Eastern Europe in *Democracy, Leverage, and Integration after Communism* (Oxford: Oxford University Press, 2005).

53. Karen Dawisha, "Electocracies and the Hobbesian Fishbowl of Postcommunist Politics," in *Between Past and Future*, ed. Antohi and Tismaneanu, pp. 291–305. Also see the special issue of *East European Politics and Societies* 13, no. 2 (Spring 1999), especially pieces by Valerie Bunce, Daniel Chirot, Grzegorz Ekiert, Gail Kligman, and Katherine Verdery.

54. See Agnes Heller and Ferenc Fehér, *The Postmodern Political Condition* (New York: Columbia University Press, 1989), and *The Grandeur and Twilight of Radical Universalism;* Kołakowski's *Modernity on Endless Trial* (Chicago: University of Chicago Press, 1990). These philosophers have long since noticed the dissolution of the "redemptive paradigms" and the rise of the alternative, parallel discourses, although they did not anticipate the ongoing rise of the narratives of hatred and revenge.

55. See Julia Kristeva, *Nations without Nationalism* (New York: Columbia University Press, 1993), pp. 68–69.

56. Grzegorz Ekiert and Stephen E. Hanson, *Capitalism and Democracy in Central and Eastern Europe: Assessing the Legacy of Communist Rule* (Cambridge: Cambridge University Press, 2003). Recent contributions on the legacy approach focusing upon role of the burden of the past in post-Communist development: Grzegorz Ekiert and Jan Kubik, *Rebellious Civil Society* (Ann Arbor: University of Michigan Press, 1999); Anna Grzymała-Busse, *Redeeming the Communist Past: The Regeneration of Communist Successor Parties in East Central Europe* (Cambridge: Cambridge University Press, 2002); Marc Morjé Howard, *The Weakness of Civil Society in Postcommunist Europe* (Cambridge: Cambridge University Press, 2003).

57. See Václav Havel, "Post-Communist Nightmare," *New York Review of Books,* May 27, 1993, p. 8.

58. See John Rawls' discussion of criteria for assessing civic freedom and the idea of a well-ordered society in *Political Liberalism* (New York: Columbia University Press, 1993), pp. 30–40.

59. Quoted in Michal Cichy, "Requiem for the Moderate Revolutionist," *East European Politics and Societies* 10, no. 1 (Winter 1996): 145.

60. Timothy Garton Ash, "Trials, Purges and History Lessons: Treating a Difficult Past in Post-Communist Europe," in *Memory and Power in Post-War Europe,* ed. Müller, p. 277. The activity of a Truth Commission represents "nonjudicial truth-seeking as a transitional justice tool" (Priscilla Hayner). It can therefore set the stage for future prospects for justice. See Priscilla B. Hayner, *Unspeakable Truths: Facing the Challenge of Truth Commissions* (New York: Routledge, 2002).

61. For seminal contributions to this discussion, see Jerzy Szacki, *Liberalism after Communism* (Budapest: Central European University Press, 1995); Ronald Dworkin et al., *From Liberal Values to Democratic Transition: Essays in Honor of János Kis* (Budapest: Central European University Press, 2004); János Kis, *Politics as a Moral Problem* (New York and Budapest: Central European University Press, 2008).

62. See the commentary by Vladimir Tismaneanu and Paul-Dragoş Aligică, "Romania's Parliamentary Putsch," *Wall Street Journal (Europe),* April 20, 2007. On May 19, 2007, Băsescu overwhelmingly won in a national referendum (74.5 percent voted against his impeachment).

63. This "synchronization" was the thrust of interwar Romanian liberal theorist Eugen Lovinescu's approach to the country's modernization.

64. Karen Dawisha, "Communism as a Lived System of Ideas in Contemporary Russia," *East European Politics and Societies* 19, no. 3 (2005): 463–93. Directly related to Dawisha's insight is the problem of nostalgia for the Communist past. For example, Alexei Yurchak details the mechanisms of socialization in the late years of the Soviet Union, emphasizing the depth of integration in the socialist milieu despite the latter's outwardly seemingly incremental nature. See Alexei Yurchak, *Everything Was Forever, until It Was No More: The Last Soviet Generation* (Princeton, N.J.: Princeton University Press, 2006).

65. See Michael McFaul, Nikolai Petrov, and Andrei Ryabov, *Between Dictatorship and Democracy: Russian Post-Communist Reform* (Washington, D.C.: Carnegie Endowment for International Peace, 2004); Peter Reddaway, "Russia on the Brink," *New York Review of Books,* January 28, 1993, pp. 30–35. Reddaway notices a multilayered feeling of moral and spiritual injury related to loss of empire and damaged identity: "Emotional wounds as deep as these tend to breed anger, hatred, self-disgust and aggressiveness. Such emotions can only improve the political prospects for the nationalists and neo-communists, at any rate for a time." Recently Reddaway has become even more pessimistic: Peter Reddaway and Dmitri Glinski, *The Tragedy of Russia's Reforms: Market Bolshevism against Democracy* (Washington, D.C.: U.S. Institute of Peace Press, 2001).

66. Grigore Pop-Eleches, "Transition to What? Legacies and Reform Trajectories after Communism," in *World Order after Leninism,* ed. Tismaneanu, Howard, and Sil.

67. Kołakowski, *Modernity on Endless Trial*, p. 41. A few years ago I discussed the role of eclectism in the ideological milieu of Central and Eastern Europe: Vladimir Tismaneanu, "In Praise of Eclectism," *The Good Society* 11, no. 1 (2002).

68. Stephen E. Hanson and Jeffrey S. Kopstein, "The Weimar/Russia Comparison," *Post-Soviet Affairs* 13, no. 3 (July–September 1997): 252–81. On the failed democratization process in Russia, see M. Steven Fish, *Democracy Derailed in Russia: The Failure of Open Politics* (Cambridge: Cambridge University Press, 2005).

69. See Martin Krygier, "Conservative-Liberal-Socialism Revisited" *The Good Society*, 11, no. 1 (2002): 6–15.

70. Judt, *Postwar*, p. 692.

71. Martin Palouš, "Post-Totalitarian Politics and European Philosophy," *Public Affairs Quarterly* 7, no. 2 (April 1993): 162–63.

72. Ralf Dahrendorf, *After 1989: Morals, Revolution, and Civil Society* (New York: St. Martin's Press, 1997). For an update on Dahrendorf's predictions and evaluation about Europe after the revolution, see his new introduction and postscript in the second edition of his *Reflections on the Revolution in Europe* (New York: Transaction Books, 2005).

73. Claude Lefort, *The Political Forms of Modern Society* (Oxford: Polity Press, 1986), p. 84.

74. Joachim Gauck, "Dealing with the STASI Past," in "Germany in Transition," special issue, *Daedalus* (Winter 1994): 277–284.

75. Charles Villa-Vicencio and Erik Doxtader, eds., *Pieces of the Puzzle: Keywords on Reconciliation and Transitional Justice* (Cape Town: Institute for Justice and Reconciliation, 2005), pp. 34–38.

76. Jan-Werner Müller, *Constitutional Patrotism* (Princeton, N.J., and Oxford: Princeton University Press, 2007), pp. 97–119.

77. Gesine Schwan, *Politics and Guilt: The Destructive Power of Silence,* trans. Thomas Dunlap (Lincoln and London: University of Nebraska Press, 2001), pp. 54–134.

78. Herman Lübbe argued in 1983 that this communicative silence has allowed federal Germany to make a successful transition to democracy after 1945. See Hermann Lübbe, "Der Nationalsozialismus im politischen Bewusstsein der Gegenwart," in *Deutschlands Weg in die Diktatur: Internationale Konferenz zur nationalsozialistischen Machtübernahme im Reichstagsgebäude zu Berlin: Referate und Diskussionen. Ein Protokoll,* ed. Martin Broszat et al. (Berlin: Siedler, 1983), p. 329–49.

79. Judt, *Postwar*, p. 830.

80. Jürgen Habermas, *The New Conservatism: Cultural Criticism and the Historians' Debate* (Cambridge, Mass.: MIT Press, 1991), p. 234.

81. The full English version of the speech by Romania's president Traian Băsescu before the joint session of the Romanian parliament on December 18, 2006, can be found on www.presidency.ro (section "Presidential Commission for the Analysis of the Communist Dictatorship in Romania"—CPADCR). The most vocal critics of this condemnation have been Vadim Tudor's Greater Romania Party (and its viciously anti-Semitic and anti-Western weekly) and the Social

Democratic Party chaired by Mircea Geoană, former ambassador to Washington and foreign minister (2001–2004). Iliescu is the honorary chairman of this party.

82. Leon Aron analyzed the manner in which the Putin administration is sponsoring and imposing the creation of a "new Russian history" that relativizes or altogether ignores the exterminist experience of Sovietism. See Leon Aron, "The Problematic Pages: To Understand Putin, We Must Understand His View of Russian History," *New Republic,* September 24, 2008. Also see Orlando Figes, "Putin vs. the Truth," *New York Review of Books* 56, no. 7 (April, 30, 2009); and Masha Lipman, "Russia, Again Evading History," *Washington Post,* June 20, 2009. Also see David Brandenberger, "A New *Short Course?* A.V. Filippov and the Russian State's Search for a 'Usable Past,' " *Kritika: Explorations in Russian and Eurasian History* 10, no. 4 (2009): 825–33. See also the responses to this essay in the same journal: Vladimir Solonari, "Normalizing Russia, Legitimizing Putin," pp. 835–46; Boris N. Mironov, "The Fruits of a Bourgeois Education," pp. 847–60; and Elena Zubkova, "The Filippov Syndrome," pp. 861–68.

83. Frederick C. Corney, "What Is to Be Done with Soviet Russia? The Politics of Proscription and Possibility," *Journal of Policy History* 21, no. 3 (2009): 276.

84. Dominick LaCapra called this phenomenon "fetishized anti-Semitism, that is, anti-Semitism in the absence of minimal presence of Jews." See Dominick LaCapra, "Revisiting the Historians' Debate—Mourning and Genocide," *History and Memory* 9, nos. 1–2 (Spring–Winter 1997): 80–112.

85. Charles Simic, "The Spider's Web," *New Republic,* October 25, 1993, p. 19.

86. Joseph Rothschild, *Ethnopolitics: A Conceptual Framework* (New York: Columbia University Press, 1981), p. 14.

87. Yael Tamir, *The Enigma of Nationalism: Essays in the Psychological* (Princeton, N.J.: Princeton University Press, 2008), p. 430.

88. Michel Foucault, *Power/Knowledge: Selected Interviews and Other Writings 1972–1977,* ed. Colin Gordon, trans. Colin Gordon et al. (New York: Pantheon, 1980), p. 133.

89. Tony Judt, "The Past Is Another Country: Myth and Memory in Postwar Europe," in *Memory and Power,* ed. Müller, p. 172.

90. Judt, *Postwar,* p. 768

91. Amos Funkenstein, "History, Counterhistory and Narrative," in *Probing the Limits of Representation—Nazism and the "Final Solution,"* ed. Saul Friedlander (Cambridge, Mass., and London: Harvard University Press, 1992), pp. 66–81.

92. I refer here to Georges Mink's distinction among "partis consensuelists, tribunitiens et querelleurs" in "Les partis politiques de l'Europe centrale postcommuniste: Etat des lieux et essai de typologie," *L'Europe Centrale et Orientale en 1992,* Documentation française, pp. 21–23.

93. In his seminal *Postwar,* Tony Judt assessed that "seventy years of energetic claims to the contrary notwithstanding—that there was indeed no Communist society as such: only a wilting state and its anxious citizens" (p. 658).

94. For Jowitt's first statement, see *New World Disorder.* The last were made during his keynote address, "Stalinist Revolutionary Breakthroughs in Eastern Europe," at the conference "Stalinism Revisited: The Establishment of Commu-

nist Regimes in East-Central Europe and the Dynamics of the Soviet Bloc" (November 29–30, 2007, Washington, D.C.), included in *Stalinism Revisited,* ed. Vladimir Tismaneanu.

95. Kotkin, *Uncivil Society*, p. xvii.

CONCLUSIONS

1. Sigmund Neumann, *Permanent Revolution: Totalitarianism in the Age of International Civil War* (New York: Praeger, 1965 [1942]); Franz Neumann, *The Democratic and the Authoritarian State: Essays in Political and Legal Theory,* edited and with a preface by Herbert Marcuse (London: Free Press, 1957); André Liebich, *From the Other Shore: Russian Social Democracy after 1921* (Cambridge, Mass.: Harvard University Press, 1997).

2. See Eugen Weber, *Varieties of Fascism: Doctrines of Revolution in the Twentieth Century* (Malabar, Fl.: Robert E. Krieger, 1982).

3. Hannah Arendt, *The Origins of Totalitarianism,* 1st ed. (New York: Harcourt Brace, 1951), pp. 431–32.

4. See Carl Cohen, ed., *Communism, Fascism, and Democracy: The Theoretical Foundations* (New York: Random House, 1972).

5. See Walter Laqueur, *Stalin: The Glasnost Revelations* (New York: Scribner's, 1990), p. 135.

6. Zeev Sternhell with Mario Sznajder and Maya Asheri, *The Birth of Fascist Ideology: From Cultural Rebellion to Political Revolution* (Princeton, N.J.: Princeton University Press, 1994); Roger Griffin, ed., *International Fascism: Theories, Causes, and the New Consensus* (London: Arnold, 1998); Aristotle Kallis, ed., *The Fascism Reader* (London: Routledge, 2003); Michael Mann, *Fascists* (Cambridge: Cambridge University Press, 2004); Constantin Iordachi, ed., *Comparative Fascist Studies* (London: Routledge, 2010).

7. Raymond Aron, *The Opium of the Intellectuals,* intro. Harvey C. Mansfield (New Brunswick, N.J.: Transaction, 2001).

8. Milorad M. Drachkovitch, ed., *Marxism in the Modern World* (Stanford, Calif.: Stanford University Press, 1965), especially the contributions of Raymond Aron, Bertram Wolfe, and Boris Souvarine; Melvin J. Lasky, *Utopia and Revolution* (Chicago: University of Chicago Press, 1976); Isaac Deutscher, *Marxism, Wars and Revolutions: Essays from Four Decades* (London: Verso, 1984).

9. Georg Lukács, *History and Class Consciousness* (London: Merlin Press, 1971); Georg Lukács, *A Defense of "History and Class Consciousness": Tailism and the Dialectic,* with a introduction by John Rees and a postface by Slavoj Žižek (London: Verso, 2000).

10. Robert C. Tucker, ed.) *The Marx-Engels Reader,* 2d ed. (New York and London: W.W. Norton), p. 145.

11. See "Reflections on the Changing Role of the Party in the Totalitarian Polity," the epilogue to Leonard Shapiro, *The Communist Party of the Soviet Union,* 2d ed., revised and enlarged (New York: Vintage Books, 1971). It is worth mentioning that Shapiro chose as a motto for his masterpiece Alexis de Tocqueville's words: "He who seeks in liberty anything other than Liberty itself is destined for servitude."

12. Cohen, ed., *Communism, Fascism, and Democracy,* p. 317.

13. Benito Mussolini, "The Doctrine of Fascism," in ibid., pp. 328–39.

14. Robert Gellately, *Lenin, Stalin, and Hitler: The Age of Social Catastrophe* (New York: Alfred A. Knopf, 2007); Alexander N. Yakovlev, A *Century of Violence in Soviet Russia* (New Haven, Conn.: Yale University Press, 2000); Richard Pipes, *Communism: A History* (New York: Modern Library, 2003).

15. Tucker, *Marx-Engels Reader,* p. 84.

16. Tony Judt, *Postwar: A History of Europe since 1945* (New York: Penguin Press, 2005), p. 831.

17. Anne Applebaum, "The Worst of the Madness," *New York Review of Books,* October 28, 2010.

18. Robert C. Tucker, "Stalin, Bukharin, and History as Conspiracy," in *The Soviet Political Mind: Stalinism and Post-Stalin Change,* rev. ed. (New York: W. W. Norton, 1971), pp. 49–86.

19. Hannah Arendt, *Essays in Understanding, 1930–1954,* ed. Jerome Kern (New York: Harcourt, Brace and Jovanovich), pp. 203–5.

Index

authoritarianism *(continued)*
Stalinist, 177, 228–29; Western
post-Marxism vs., 177. *See also*
totalitarianism
Azerbaijan, 152

Bacilek, Karol, 65
Badiou, Alain, 176
Bahro, Rudolf, 140
Bakunin, Mikhail, 52
Balbo, Italo, 102
Balkans: Stalinist agenda, 72; Western, 202,
207. *See also* Albania; Croatia; Serbia
Baltic states: Gorbachev and use of force in,
152; impersonal democratic procedures,
216; Nazi and Soviet mass killings, 44;
Soviet/Russian occupation, 188. *See also*
Latvia; Lithuania
Banac, Ivo, 72
Bartov, Omer, 36
Băsescu, Traian, 212, 218
Bauman, Zygmunt, 19
Baumler, Alfred, 12
Bayer, Wilhem-Raymund, 137
Belarus: "competitive authoritarianism,"
209; Holocaust impacts, 75; human
rights, 194
Belgrade, April student protests, 142
Beniuc, Mihai, 82
Benjamin, Walter, 207, 209
Berdyaev, Nikolai, 4, 113
Bergelson, David, 76
Berlin, Isaiah, 101, 170
Berlin Wall, fall of, 79, 143, 175, 201
Berman, Jakub, 78, 83
Berman, Paul, 103–4, 144
Bernstein, Eduard, 149, 191, 200
Bernstein, Leonard, 186
Besançon, Alain, 46, 49, 123, 168–69,
232
Big Lie: Communist, 51, 70, 168, 169, 172,
179, 182, 190, 200–201, 221;
post-Soviet, 218. *See also* amnesia;
falsification; truth
bin Laden, Osama, Al Qaeda, 101
biological distinctions: Nazi, 8, 41, 226.
See also ethnocentricity
The Black Book of Communism, 30–38,
46–49, 51, 53, 168
Blanquism, 96
Bloch, Ernst, 141, 226
Blomberg-Frisch affair, 54
Blum, Léon, 191
Bogdanov, Aleksandr, 162

Bohemia: Communist Party, 213; and
patrimonial legacy, 212
Bolshevism, 32, 83, 90–122, 150, 191;
Communist Manifesto and, 165;
conversion of; converting into an
emerging version of Communist-
Fascism, 64; critics, 4, 21, 48–49; cult of
the party, 229–30; cult of totality, 228;
de-Bolshevization, 131; Declaration of
the Rights of Toiling and Exploited
People (1918), 50; vs. democracy, 4, 5,
20–23, 49, 96–97, 99, 112–13, 119–21,
150–51; dream of total revolution, 224;
Fascism vs., 3, 20, 21; Gorbachev and,
145–46, 153; humanism, 94, 228–29;
ideology, 13, 14–15, 70, 118; Judeo-
Bolsheviks, 3, 13, 31, 219; justice
subordinated to party interests, 30;
"language of magic," 110; Menshevik
split with, 91, 120, 228; messianism, 10,
23, 87, 93, 113, 115–22; mission, 5, 52,
89, 105; "modern agenda of subjectivization," 42–43; and morality, 63,
69–70, 95; New Faith, 112, 127–28;
norms of culture of, 77; October
Revolution (1917), 32, 71, 92, 106,
116–18, 153, 195; Old, 8, 55, 76, 85,
93, 94, 104; party charisma, 8–9, 54–57,
92–98, 104–5, 114–16, 229–31;
political "sins," 8; post-Soviet Russia,
114; revolutionary passion, 4–5, 70–71,
88–90, 93–94, 98–99; Stalinist-
nationalist traditions of, 213; "substitu-
tionism," 91, 112; takeover of power,
88–89, 105, 108, 118; terror, 10, 14, 27,
38–40, 42–43, 67–69, 100, 106–7,
121–22, 168–69; victory in the civil war,
99. *See also* Communist Party;
Communist utopia; Leninism; Stalinism;
vanguard party
Bonapartism, 25, 125
Bonner, Elena, 96, 200
Borkenau, Franz, 80
Bormann, Martin, 8–9
Bosworth, R.J.B., 26
Botez, Mihai, 198–99
Bourdieu, Pierre, 187
bourgeoisie, 5; both Communism and
Fascism vs., 13, 20, 45, 92, 102, 176,
226; Communism vs., 5, 13, 14, 15, 20,
30, 45, 61, 71, 74, 78, 81, 89–90, 92,
99–113, 128, 164–70, 176, 226, 228,
229, 231; Fascism vs., 13, 20, 21, 45, 92,
102, 121, 176, 226; Jewish, 14, 74, 78

and, 156, 160, 182; Romanian bureaucracies, 71, 81–82; terror and, 45, 47, 49, 59, 66–67, 70; utopia and, 162–77, 189–90. *See also* millennialism; mythologies; revisionism

Iliescu, Ion, 213

imperialism: Chinese propaganda of, 27; Communism vs., 27, 46, 72–73, 74; ideological, 155; "imperialist encircle-ment," 231; "martyrological imperial-ism," 34; proletarian revolution in the age of, 228; Russian, 218, 231; of Sovietization, 60; of Soviet oligarchy, 178; Stalinist, 231; World War II aftermath against Communism, 73; Zionist link with Western, 64. *See also* hegemony

individual: contempt for, 20, 113, 154, 232; dissidents and, 183–84, 190–91; dissolution of, 6, 10–12, 42, 44, 52, 61, 93; reinvention of politics and, 183–84; revolutions (1989–91) and, 197, 202. *See also* citizenship; dehumanization of the enemy; human rights

intellectuals, 224; "conspiracy of academi-cians," 148; dissidents, 190, 198–201, 204–5, 209; Marxist revolutionary, 227; one of three layers in Communist societies, 139–40, 146–48; post-Communism, 198–201, 204–5, 209, 214, 215. *See also* dissidents

intentionality: ideology and, 12–17; Nazi evil, 41; Soviet criminality, 27

International (organization): Second, 231; Third (Comintern), 3, 8, 20, 66, 80, 231

International (song), sung by Ceaușescu while dying, 196

international factors: in democratization of Eastern and Central Europe, 221–22. *See also* European Union; international-ism, Communist; NATO; West

internationalism, Communist, 59, 71, 80, 165; Gorbachev and, 203; Marxist, 213; proletarian class, 59, 165. *See also* International (organization)

internationalism, Communist Stalinist definition, 59

Isaac, Jeffrey, 198

Islamist fantasies, 232

Israel, Stalin supporting State of, 76

Istrati, Panait, 70

Italy: *The Black Book of Communism*, 30; Fascist, 23–26, 43, 52, 54, 102, 121–22,

176, 224, 229–30; paralysis of universities, 143; Salo Republic, 23, 26. *See also* Mussolini, Benito

Jacobinism, 157, 201; Communist, 62–63, 96, 106, 168, 222

Jakeš, Miloš, 223

Jarausch, Konrad, 202

Jaruzelski, Wojciech, 223

Jaurès, Jean, 128

Jew: *The Black Book of Communism* and, 37; Communism as victim of, 206, 219; conspiracy theories about, 76, 78–79, 188, 218; cosmopolitanism (accused), 65–66, 71, 77, 79; Eastern Europeans vs., 75, 85; "education through labor," 85; Judeo-Bolsheviks, 3, 13, 31, 219; "Judeo-Masonic conspiracies," 218; Judeo-plutocracy, 3, 31; pogroms, 13, 14, 77, 113; Stalin vs., 9, 13, 14, 31, 37–38, 64–66, 74–80, 85. *See also* Nazism vs. Jews

Jewish Anti-Fascist Committee, Soviet, 76

Jewish Democratic Committee, 80

Jewish Telegraphic Agency, 75

Jowitt, Kenneth: charismatic impersonal-ism, 95; Eastern Europe, 216, 221–22; Leninism, 10, 14–15, 22, 71, 92–93, 105, 114, 123–24, 181, 196; "movements of rage," 216; post-Cold War order, 22; Stalinism, 14–15, 26, 60

Judt, Tony: amnesia about oppression, 35, 36, 206, 217; Communism and Nazism morally indistinguishable, 33; Communist utopia, 50–51; French absence of consensus about justice, 29; Leninism, 196, 214; post-Communism, 194, 202, 205; *Postwar*, 232; sixty-eighters, 142, 144

"June nights," 82

Kaczynski brothers, 218

Kádár, János, 46, 140

Kafka, Franz, 192

Kaganovich, Lazar, 52, 66, 89

Kalandra, Zášvis, 53

Kamenev, Lev, 57, 75

Kant, Immanuel, "Concerning the Indwelling of the Evil Principle with the Good, or, on the Radical Evil in Human Nature," 18

Katz, Otto, 78–79

Kautsky, Karl, 30, 96–97, 116

Tucker, Robert C.: Bolshevism's deradicalization, 93; Bukharin, 55, 57, 58; Leninism, 112, 113, 119; philosophy and myth, 164; pre-Gorbachev Soviet Union, 148–49; reversion, 110; show trials, 63; Stalin, 13, 55, 64, 126–27
Tudjman, Franjo, 188–89
Tudor, Corneliu Vadim, 213, 216
Tudoran, Dorin, 26
Țugui, Pavel, 82
tyrannies of certitude, 5
tyrannies of corruption, 5

Übermensch, 129, 162
Ukraine: "competitive authoritarianism," 209; Holocaust impacts, 75; radical-authoritarian trends, 212
l'univers concentrationnaire, 1
Urban, George, 54–55; *Communist Reformation*, 123; *Stalinism*, 161
Urban, Jan, 193
ur-Fascism, 185
ur-Leninism, 185
Urválek, Josef, 64
USSR. *See* Soviet Union
utopia, 18–52, 161–92, 233; anti-anti-utopianism, 50; *Communist Manifesto* and, 166–67; enduring magnetism of, 162–71; Fascist, 19, 43, 52, 102, 121–22, 162; ideology and, 162–77, 189–90; intellectuals in frantic search for, 200; West and, 143, 157–58, 174–75. *See also* Communist utopia; eschatology; redemptive mythologies; salvationism

Vajda, Mihaly, 170
vanguard party, 203; Gorbachev and, 149; Lenin and, 5, 83, 92, 97, 109, 114, 118, 167, 169, 228; Mlynář and, 134. *See also* Bolshevism; Communist Party
van Ree, Erik, 14, 84, 98
Velikhov, Evgeny, 148
"velvet counterrevolution," 194
"velvet revolutions" (1989), 198. *See also* revolutions (1989–91), Eastern and Central Europe
Vietnam: North, 231; War, 143
Villa-Vicencio, Charles, 217
violence: Communist, 3, 24, 27, 30, 38–52, 64, 66, 67, 86, 88–90, 97, 99, 102, 121–22, 168–69; Fascist, 41, 88–90, 102; sanctified by Communism and Fascism, 3, 44, 52, 102, 162, 168–69;

World War I, 12. *See also* class struggle; murder; terror
Voegelin, Eric, 12
voluntarism: Leninist, 15; Marxist, 96
Voronov, Ivan, 148
Voznesensky, Andrei, 136
Vranicki, Predrag, 141
Vyshinsky, Andrei, 30–31, 57

Wałęsa, Lech, 215
Walicki, Andrzej, 174
Walker, Rachel, 174
Wallach, Erica Glaser, 73
Warsaw Pact, 222
Wat, Aleksander, 61
Way, Lucan, 209
Weber, Eugen: archangelic revolution, 224–25; comparing totalitarianisms, 8, 103; Fascism, 10, 19, 20, 224–25; *My France*, 193
Weber, Max, 90–91, 108–9, 129
Weil, Nicolas, 37
Weitz, Eric, 38, 173
Werth, Nicolas, 33, 38, 41, 86
West: anti-Fascism, 27–30; Communist parties, 142; Communist "separateness" from, 212; crisis of self-confidence, 185; democracy, 5, 123, 143, 150, 191–92; and democratization of Eastern and Central Europe, 221–22; dissident movement, 17; humanism, 2, 61, 62; law of political synchronization, 212; Marxism, 98, 132, 138, 142–43, 177; New Left, 141, 143; post-Marxism, 177; sixty-eighters, 142, 143–44; social democracy, 150, 191–92; and utopia, 143, 157–58, 174–75
who-whom principle (*kto-kogo*), 67, 162
Wielgohs, Jan, 134
Wieworka, Annette, 33
Wing, Betsy, 16
World Marxist Review, 148
World War I, 101, 109, 195; aftermath, 4, 11–12, 102, 195; nationalism during, 165
World War II, 225; aftermath, 9, 28, 29, 61, 72–73, 75, 85, 142, 231; Merker, 78–79; Nazi defeat, 15–16; Romanian party's Moscow émigré center, 79; Russianization of Stalinism, 60

Xoxe, Koçi, 74

CPSIA information can be obtained
at www.ICGtesting.com
Printed in the USA
BVHW031331281221
624881BV00024B/429/J